Recalibrating Retirement Spending and Saving

Recalibrating Retirement Spending and Saving

EDITED BY

John Ameriks and Olivia S. Mitchell

*This book has been printed digitally and produced in a standard specification
in order to ensure its continuing availability*

OXFORD
UNIVERSITY PRESS

Great Clarendon Street, Oxford OX2 6DP

Oxford University Press is a department of the University of Oxford.
It furthers the University's objective of excellence in research, scholarship,
and education by publishing worldwide in

Oxford New York

Auckland Cape Town Dar es Salaam Hong Kong Karachi
Kuala Lumpur Madrid Melbourne Mexico City Nairobi
New Delhi Shanghai Taipei Toronto
With offices in
Argentina Austria Brazil Chile Czech Republic France Greece
Guatemala Hungary Italy Japan South Korea Poland Portugal
Singapore Switzerland Thailand Turkey Ukraine Vietnam

Oxford is a registered trade mark of Oxford University Press
in the UK and in certain other countries

Published in the United States
by Oxford University Press Inc., New York

© Pension Research Council, The Wharton School, University of Pennsylvania, 2008

The moral rights of the author have been asserted

Database right Oxford University Press (maker)

Reprinted 2009

ISBN 978-0-19-954910-8

Preface

People often avoid thinking about retirement because it is a daunting, and even frightening, prospect. Insofar as many individuals will end up spending decades out of the labor market, this life phase will likely demand numerous overhauls of retirement plans, periodic recalibrations of spending and saving needs, sporadic reassessments of work and leisure opportunities, and perhaps unwillingly, frequent reevaluations of how, and with whom, people seek to age gracefully. This book offers guidance for this process, as we draw on the best thinking from an energetic set of academics, financial experts, regulators, and plan sponsors who explore how to help retirees better manage their saving and spending during their golden years.

Previous research studies directed at the Pension Research Council and the Boettner Center of the Wharton School of the University of Pennsylvania have focused on public and private pensions as well as retirement adequacy in the USA and around the world. Here, by contrast, we take a forward-looking perspective for retirement in the twenty-first century.

Specifically, our focus is to evaluate what new challenges retirees face during the 'decumulation' phase of the life cycle. We show how both the definition and the structure of work in the labor market and at home play a key role, as do Individual Retirement Accounts, Social Security, company-sponsored pensions, and annuity programs. Health care, housing needs, and long-term care concerns also represent critical aspects that must be taken into account, when thinking of how to pace the disbursement of retirement savings. Also treated are practical considerations such as tax and estate planning aspects of the decumulation process, along with a discussion of possible roles for retirement payout regulation so as to ensure solvency and credibility.

As with all of the research volumes issued by the Pension Research Council, we owe much to our contributors and coeditors. In this instance, John Ameriks from the Vanguard group served ably in both roles, and we owe him and his colleagues a debt of gratitude. The Wharton School helped support the conference where initial research findings were reported. Additional financial support was received from the Pension Research Council, the Boettner Center for Pensions and Retirement Research, and the Ralph H. Blanchard Memorial Endowment at the Wharton School of the University of Pennsylvania. The manuscript was expertly prepared and carefully edited by Hilary Farrell with help from Andrew Gallagher.

On behalf of these institutions and individuals, we thank all of our fine collaborators and supporters for their help in recalibrating the meaning of retirement.

The Pension Research Council

The Pension Research Council of the Wharton School at the University of Pennsylvania is an organization committed to generating debate on key policy issues affecting pensions and other employee benefits. The Council sponsors interdisciplinary research on the entire range of private and social retirement security and related benefit plans in the USA and around the world. It seeks to broaden understanding of these complex arrangements through basic research into their economic, social, legal, actuarial, and financial foundations. Members of the Advisory Board of the Council, appointed by the Dean of the Wharton School, are leaders in the employee benefits field, and they recognize the essential role of social security and other public sector income maintenance programs while sharing a desire to strengthen private sector approaches to economic security. More information about the Pension Research Council is available on the Internet at http://www.pensionresearchcouncil.org or send an email to prc@wharton.upenn.edu.

Contents

List of Figures

List of Tables

Notes on Contributors

John Ameriks is a Senior Investment Analyst in Vanguard's Investment Counseling and Research Group. He previously held the position of Senior Research Fellow at the TIAA-CREF Institute. Dr. Ameriks has published research related to individual and household financial decisions regarding saving, portfolio allocation, and retirement income strategies. He received his AB from Stanford University and Ph.D. in Economics from Columbia University.

Phyllis C. Borzi is Research Professor in Health Policy at the School of Public Health and Health Services, The George Washington University. She is also Of Counsel with O'Donoghue & O'Donoghue LLP, a Washington, DC law firm. Previously she was Pension and Employee Benefit Counsel for the Subcommittee on Labor-Management Relations, at the U.S. House of Representatives Committee on Education and Labor. Professor Borzi has written and spoken extensively on ERISA issues for decades and is a Charter Fellow and the immediate past president of the American College of Employee Benefits Counsel. She received her JD from Catholic University Law School, MA from Syracuse University, and BA from Ladycliff.

David Brazell is a member of the Business Taxation Division of the Office of Tax Analysis in the U.S. Department of the Treasury. His interests include the formulation of tax policy and tax administrative rulings, primarily in the areas of depreciation policy, tax accounting, health tax policy, the taxation of insurance products, and the taxation of life- and property-casualty insurance companies. He has worked in the administrations of six different presidents, worked as a consultant to the Republic of South Africa on insurance tax issues, and served as an analyst with the Institute of Political Economy. He earned his MS degree in Economics from the University of Wisconsin–Madison, and his BA degree in Economics and International Affairs from the University of Colorado, Boulder.

Jason Brown is an economist in the Office of Economic Policy at the U.S. Treasury Department. His research interests include long-term care and long-run health spending growth. He currently specializes in health economics and health policy. He received his Ph.D. in Economics from Stanford University.

Andrew Caplin is a Professor of Economics and the Co-Director of the Center for Experimental Social Science of New York University. He received his BA from Cambridge University and his Ph.D. from Yale University.

Peter C. Carlson is the Pricing Actuary for Prudential's Retirement Income Strategies unit, where he is responsible for product development and pricing of new retirement solutions for Prudential's 401(k) & 403(b) participants. Peter is a codeveloper of the Income Bridge Approach to retirement income planning, and he currently has three retirement business methods pending in the US patent office. Peter received his BS in Economics from the Wharton School, and he recently completed the examination requirements for his FSA and CFA designations.

Sewin Chan is an Associate Professor of Public Policy in the Robert F. Wagner Graduate School of Public Service at New York University. Dr. Chan's recent research focuses on the economics of aging and retirement. Her work includes study of the economic impact of job loss on older workers, individual responsiveness to financial retirement incentives, and the well-being of caregiving grandparents. Dr. Chan received her BA from Cambridge University and Ph.D. in Economics from Columbia University.

G. Victor Hallman is a Lecturer in the Insurance and Risk Management Department at the Wharton School, University of Pennsylvania. His writing and research interests include estate planning, private wealth management, insurance planning, and tax policy. He received a BS in Economics, MA, and Ph.D. degrees from the University of Pennsylvania and a JD from the Rutgers School of Law.

Sarah Holden is Senior Director of Retirement and Investor Research at the Investment Company Institute (ICI). At the Institute, Dr. Holden conducts and oversees research on the US retirement market, retirement and tax policy, investor demographics and behavior, and international issues. She is responsible for analysis of 401(k) plan participant activity using data collected in a collaborative effort with the Employee Benefit Research Institute (EBRI), known as the EBRI/ICI Participant-Directed Retirement Plan Data Collection Project. In addition, she analyzes the role of mutual funds in the retirement marketplace including defined contribution plan and IRA markets. She is also responsible for managing investor research on a range of topics relevant to the fund industry and policy formation. Prior to joining the Institute, Dr. Holden worked as a staff economist in the Flow of Funds Section of the Research Division at the Federal Reserve Board. Dr. Holden is a graduate of Smith College and holds both Master's and Ph.D. degrees in Economics from the University of Michigan.

Erik Hurst is a Professor of Economics at the University of Chicago's Graduate School of Business. His work centers on household financial behavior with a particular emphasis on consumption and savings. Dr. Hurst received both Master's and Ph.D. degrees in Economics from the University of Michigan.

Vladyslav Kyrychenko is a Ph.D. candidate at the Schulich School of Business at York University. His research interests include investments, asset allocation, insurance, and retirement income. He received his MA in Economics from the Central European University.

Steven Laufer is a second-year graduate student in Economics at New York University, where he previously worked as a Junior Research Scientist. His research interests are macroeconomics and applied microeconomics, with a focus on housing. His BS degree is from Harvard and his MS degree is from the University of Chicago, both in Physics.

James I. Mahaney is a Vice President with the Retirement Income Strategies division of Prudential Retirement. Mr. Mahaney is the creator of the Income Bridge Approach to retirement income planning, which seeks to help individuals use a portion of their retirement savings to maximize Social Security benefits. He earned an undergraduate degree from Denison University, and an MS in Financial Services and in Management from The American College.

Moshe A. Milevsky is an Associate Professor of Finance at York University in Canada, and the Executive Director of the Individual Finance and Insurance Decision Centre. His interests are pension economics, finance, and retirement income. He earned his BA in Mathematics and Physics from Yeshiva University, MA in Mathematics and Statistics from York University, and Ph.D. in Business Finance from York University.

Olivia S. Mitchell is the International Foundation of Employee Benefit Plans Professor of Insurance and Risk Management, the Executive Director of the Pension Research Council, and the Director of the Boettner Center on Pensions and Retirement Research at the Wharton School. Concurrently Dr. Mitchell is a Research Associate at the National Bureau of Economic Research and a coinvestigator for the AHEAD/Health and Retirement Studies at the University of Michigan. Her areas of research and teaching are private and public insurance, risk management, public finance and labor markets, and compensation and pensions, with a US and an international focus. She received her BA in Economics from Harvard University and MA and Ph.D. degrees in Economics from the University of Wisconsin–Madison.

Martha Priddy Patterson is the Director of Human Capital Total Rewards in the Washington, DC, office of Deloitte Consulting LLP. Her interests include employee benefits with a focus on retirement, health and welfare benefits law, and regulation. She holds a JD from the University of Texas School of Law and a BA from Vanderbilt University. She is a fellow of the

American College of Employee Benefits Counsels as well as a member of the bar of the District of Columbia, U.S. Court of Appeals for the D.C. Circuit, and the U.S. Supreme Court.

Brian Reid is the Chief Economist at the Investment Company Institute. His research focuses on a variety of mutual fund topics, including fees and expenses, trends in the mutual fund market, and shareholder behavior. Previously, Dr. Reid was a staff economist at the Federal Reserve Board, where he researched monetary policy issues. He received a BS in Economics from the University of Wisconsin–Madison and Ph.D. in Economics from the University of Michigan.

Jason S. Scott directs the research and development group at Financial Engines, where he focuses on creating robust models for analyzing mutual funds and individual securities. Previously, Scott was a litigation consultant with Cornerstone Research, where he focused primarily on securities and valuation cases. His pension interests include valuing the 401(k) tax benefit, examining the determinants of defined contribution employee participation, and analyzing the impact of pension plan lump-sum distribution options on retirement income. He received his Ph.D. in Economics from Stanford University.

William F. Sharpe is the cofounder of Financial Engines, Inc., and is the STANCO 25 Professor of Finance, emeritus, at Stanford University's Graduate School of Business. Dr. Sharpe received the Nobel Prize in Economic Sciences for his work in developing models to aid investment decisions, and he is known internationally for having developed the Sharpe Ratio for investment performance analysis, the binomial method for the valuation of options, the gradient method for asset allocation optimization, the returns-based style analysis for evaluating the style and performance of investment funds, and the Capital Asset Pricing Model. Previously, he taught at the University of Washington and the University of California at Irvine. Dr. Sharpe received his Ph.D., MA, and BA in Economics from the University of California at Los Angeles.

Todd Sinai is an Associate Professor of Real Estate at the Wharton School; he is also Faculty Research Fellow at the NBER and a Visiting Scholar at the Federal Reserve Bank of Philadelphia. His research interests include the economics of housing markets, taxation of real estate and capital gains, commercial real estate and real estate investment trusts, and public economics. He received his Ph.D. from the Massachusetts Institute of Technology and a BA from Yale University.

Nicholas Souleles is an Associate Professor of Finance at the Wharton School. He is a Faculty Research Fellow at the NBER and a Visiting Scholar at the Federal Reserve Bank of Philadelphia. His research areas include applied econometrics, finance, macroeconomics, household consumption, saving, and investments. He received his Ph.D. from the Massachusetts Institute of Technology, BA from the University of Oxford, and BSE from Princeton University.

Ann Huff Stevens is an Associate Professor of Economics at the University of California, Davis. Her recent work includes analysis of parental resources and children's well-being, trends in and effects of job displacement and turnover, and the role of information and pensions on individual retirement decisions. She received her Ph.D. in Economics from the University of Michigan, specializing in labor economics and public finance.

Cassio M. Turra is an Associate Professor of Demography in the Department of Demography/Cedeplar at Universidade Federal de Minas Gerais, Brazil, where he teaches graduate and undergraduate courses on demographic methods, population issues, and economic demography. After earning his Ph.D. in Demography from the University of Pennsylvania in 2004, Turra spent two years as a postdoctoral fellow at the Office of Population Research and the Center for Health and Wellbeing at Princeton University. Turra's research encompasses many aspects of aging, including the relationships between life challenges, social economic environment, and health and mortality in older populations.

Stijn Van Nieuwerburgh is an Assistant Professor of Finance at New York University's Leonard N. Stern School of Business. He is also a Charles Schaefer Family Fellow and a Faculty Research Fellow at the NBER. His research areas include household finance, asset pricing, macroeconomics, real estate, information theory, and human capital. He received a BA in Economics at the University of Gent, an MA in Economics at Stanford University, an MSc in Financial Mathematics at Stanford University, and a Ph.D. in Economics at Stanford University.

Mark Warshawsky is the Director of Retirement Research at Watson Wyatt Worldwide. Prior to joining Watson Wyatt, he was Assistant Secretary for Economic Policy in the U.S. Treasury Department, Director of Research at TIAA-CREF, and senior economist at the IRS and Federal Reserve Board. His areas of expertise include pensions, insurance, health economics, macroeconomics, public finance, securities markets, and corporate finance. He received his Ph.D. in Economics from Harvard University and BA from Northwestern University.

John G. Watson is a Fellow at Financial Engines where he works at the Retirement Research Center. He was a member of the team that designed and implemented the company's forecasting and optimization engines. Dr. Watson received his Ph.D. in Mathematics from Rensselaer Polytechnic Institute, NY. He is a member of the Society for Industrial and Applied Mathematics and Sigma Xi, the scientific research society.

List of Abbreviations

ADL	activities of daily living
AEW	annuity equivalent wealth
AGI	adjusted gross income
AHEAD	Aging and Health Dynamics
BHP	British Household Panel
BIC	bank investment contract
CAMS	Consumption and Activities Mail Survey
CEX	Consumer Expenditure Survey
CFA	Consumer Federation of America
COLA	Cost of Living Adjustment
CPI	consumer price index
CRAT	Charitable Remainder Annuity Trust
CRRA	constant relative risk aversion
CRT	Charitable Remainder Trusts
CRUT	Charitable Remainder Unitrust
CSFII	continuing survey of food intake of individuals
DB	defined benefit
DC	defined contribution
DRC	delayed retirement credit
EBRI	Employee Benefit Research Institute
EGTRRA	Economic Growth Tax Relief Reconciliation Act
EGTRRA	Economic Growth and Tax Relief Reconciliation Act
ELM	Expect to Live More
ERISA	Employee Retirement Income Security Act
ERTA	Economic Recovery Tax Act
ESA	education savings accounts
FAB	Financial Attitudes and Behavior
FDIC	Federal Deposit Insurance Corporation
FES	Family Expenditure Survey
FINPL	Financial Planners
FRA	Full Retirement Age
GAR	Group Annuity Rates
GIC	guaranteed investment contract
GLB	guaranteed living benefit
GMAB	guaranteed minimum accumulation benefit
GMIB	guaranteed minimum income benefit
GMWB	guaranteed minimum withdrawal benefit

HIPAA	Health Insurance Portability and Accountability Act
HMR	high and medium risk
HRS	Health and Retirement Study
HSA	health savings account
IAA	Investment Advisers Act
ICI	Investment Company Institute
IRA	individual retirement accounts
IRC	Internal Revenue Code
IRD	income in respect of a decedent
IRS	Internal Revenue Service
ISFB	Italian Survey of Family Budgets
LCA	Life Care Annuity
LIMRA	Life Insurance Marketing Research Association
LOGACC	log of the investor's account
LR	low risk
LTC	long-term care
LTCI	long-term care insurance
LTV	loan-to-house value
MRD	minimum required distributions
NAIC	National Association of Insurance Commissioners
NASAA	North American Securities Administrators Association
NOLHIGA	National Organization of Life and Health Insurance Guaranty Association
NSMIA	National Securities Markets Improvement Act
NUA	net unrealized appreciation
OCC	Office of the Comptroller of the Currency
OECD	Organization for Economic Cooperation and Development
PBGC	Pension Benefit Guaranty Corporation
PPA	Pension Protection Act
PPC	price-per-chance
PSID	panel study of income dynamics
Q-TIP	Qualified Terminable Interest Property
RBD	required beginning date
REA	Retirement Equity Act
RHS	Retirement History Survey
RMD	required minimum distribution
SCF	Survey of Consumer Finances
SEC	United States Securities and Exchange Commission
SEP	Simplified Employee Pension
SEPP	substantially equal periodic payment
SHIW	Survey on Household Income and Wealth
SIC	standard industrial classification
SIPA	Securities Investor Protection Act

SIPC	Securities Investor Protection Corporation
SPF	Survey of Participant Finances
SRO	self-regulatory organizations
STBR	stockbroker
TIAA-CREF	Teachers Insurance and Annuity Association, College Retirement Equities Fund
TIPS	Treasury Inflation Protected Securities
TRA	Tax Reform Act
VA	Variable annuities

Part I
Financial and Nonfinancial Retirement Circumstances

Chapter 1

Managing Retirement Payouts: Positioning, Investing, and Spending Assets

John Ameriks and Olivia S. Mitchell

> Money is of no value; it cannot spend itself.
> All depends on the skill of the spender.[1]

Around the world, population aging is on the policy agenda. The tsunami of Baby Boomers, born between the mid-1940s and the 1960s, is relentlessly moving toward and crossing the symbolic threshold of age 60, a larger age wave than ever experienced before. At the same time, of course, people are expecting to live longer in retirement than has been true for any prior generation. In rich and poor countries alike, people are slowly becoming aware that their old age is going to last a very long time indeed.

This volume explores how the new retirees will and should manage financial and other aspects of their new life-cycle phase. Many of those in this older cohort, albeit not all of them, have built up over their lifetimes a quantity of assets by dint of planning, saving, and investing (Madrian, Mitchell, and Soldo 2007). So for them the question now becomes, how will they manage to position, invest, and spend what they have, so as not to run out too soon? This volume is an exploration of how to deploy one's accumulated assets in the near and long term, so as to best meet the myriad spending, investment, and other objectives of retirement.

The complexity of this topic should not be underestimated, and the concerns are many. For instance, how do, and how should, retirees think about spending and managing their retirement portfolios? Will they begin drawing down their assets right away after an abrupt transition from work to retirement, or will they defer retirement and then gradually transition into nonwork after that? Will they use private annuities to replace extinct defined benefit pensions? What will become of the substantial wealth they hold in the form of home equity? What are the economic and other objectives driving these financial decisions, and will they run out before they die?

To address these difficult questions, we have invited a number of pre-eminent economists, finance experts, tax authorities, regulatory analysts, and experts on human behavior to outline their views on how retirees and their advisers might successfully solve their most salient concerns. The book addresses these and related differences in a systematic and comprehensive manner. In our first section, we focus on Boomers' financial and non-financial circumstances as they cross the retirement threshold. Next, we take up the question of retirement plan distributions, touching on topics like inheritance, estate taxes, and payout strategies from individual retirement assets. As we show below, the question is whether people can, on their own, figure out sensible investment and payout plans, or whether additional regulatory and market developments are needed to ease the path beset by pitfalls. Finally, we focus on new financial products for retirement risk management. Throughout, our intention is to cast new light on these thorny problems to find not only optimal but reasonable and prudent solutions as well.

Financial and Nonfinancial Retirement Circumstances

To understand how people will and should position and spend their financial resources in retirement, it is worth noting that nonfinancial factors will also play an important role in retirement. Perhaps the most significant of these is the decision of whether and how much to work at older ages. A conventional view of the economic life cycle assumed that young people went to school, building skills during the first quarter of their lives; middle-aged folk worked in the labor market during the next half of their lives; and then people left work to consume their saving during the last quarter of their life cycle. That pattern remains a sensible simplification of many peoples' paths, but it leaves open very important questions around how and when important transitions occur, and the implications of change and deviations from this basic pattern.

Accordingly, it is of interest to ask whether work and retirement patterns are changing over time. The chapter by Sewin Chan and Ann Huff Stevens (2008) argues that they are, with many older individuals continuing to work even after they officially leave their main jobs. Using US data from the Health and Retirement Study (HRS), the analysis shows that one-third to half of all workers who partially or fully retire make at least one transition back into the workforce thereafter.

This unretirement pattern has important implications for how we might best think about the adequacy of retirement savings. In particular, human capital is a critically important asset for many people with perhaps more than residual value well beyond age 60. Extended capacity and willingness to work also has potential implications for how one should think about this generation's attitude toward financial risk in retirement. If recent retirees feel they have an option to return to work, in contrast to earlier generations, today's retirees may be more willing to bear more and different financial risk than in the past. In addition, Chan and Huff Stevens note that one must also take into account the attitudes and perspectives of those who move in and out of retirement. Motivations for work in retirement also go beyond economics, as many of those who return to work after retiring state that dissatisfaction with retirement was an important factor. To the extent that some of the world's most rapidly aging countries, such as China, also have very low levels of work among those in their 60s, there is likely to be a multidimensional payoff to deferred retirement.

A related aspect of retirement decision-making that is often ignored has to do with the role of housing wealth in later life. This is particularly critical in view of recent volatility and declines in housing prices around the world. The chapter by Todd Sinai and Nicholas Souleles (2008) shows that more than 60 percent of individuals' net worth is typically tied up in housing, in the US Federal Reserve Survey of Consumer Finances. Similar high concentrations of retirement wealth in housing are characteristic of many other countries as well, ranging from Australia to Singapore to Japan (Mitchell et al., 2006).

The economic significance of housing as an asset also changes substantially over the lifetime, so a key question is how much housing wealth can be utilized to provide nonhousing consumption in retirement. To examine this point, the authors begin by noting that retirees who sell their homes must still live somewhere. In their data, the median 65-year-old household is found to have accessible only 34 percent of its housing equity, or about $36,000, while 15 percent of older households have no housing equity available. By age 90, the amount of home equity available for consumption rises to 84 percent, or about $94,000. If a reverse mortgage program were available, and given current expenses associated with these, they argue that the median 90-year-old household could spend up to 75 percent of housing equity (before accounting for fees). In other words, managing the housing asset is a critical component of the retirement decumulation process. It is therefore of interest that Japan, New Zealand, and France, just to name a few, are currently working on mechanisms to allow 'house-rich but cash-poor' older individuals to access some of their home equity.

In addition to a focus on work and homeownership, attention must be devoted to how people spend their time in retirement. Many financial planners assert that retirees must maintain a constant expenditure level, or at least an income close to preretirement levels, if they are to sustain retirement well-being. Yet the chapter by Erik Hurst (2008) challenges this notion, underscoring the key difference between welfare-enhancing 'consumption' and expenditure. As in studies with UK data, he finds that

US household spending levels do fall 10–20 percent following retirement. Yet the author does not interpret this as indicating that individuals are financially underprepared for retirement. Rather, he explores differences in the constituents components of 'consumption' between retirees and pre-retirees, and with this he largely resolves the puzzle. Comparing nonretired 61–65-year-olds to retired 66–70-year-olds, the author finds that the value of food consumed at home drops 8 percent while spending on food away from home falls 16 percent. Nevertheless, total out-of-pocket expenditures decline much less, only by 3 percent, and overall consumption by only 1 percent. Furthermore, much of the fall in retiree spending can be attributed to work-related expenses, primarily transportation, clothing, and food consumption. Indeed, when he looks closely at food consumption patterns, he finds that retirees shift spending on food consumed outside the home to the production of food at home. As a result, retirees are not eating less but instead are simply preparing food more economically at home. He also notes that entertainment expenditures actually increase slightly.

These results are important, inasmuch as they challenge the orthodox view that most people arrive at retirement's doorstep unprepared. And it also challenges the financial advisers' goal of a 75 percent income replacement rate for retiree targeting purposes. It should be noted, in addition, that perhaps as many as one-quarter of the retirees Hurst examines will struggle to maintain spending levels after leaving the workforce. Again relying on food expenditure data, those in the bottom quartile of preretirement wealth reported expenditure declines of 31 percent, which he worries may indicate that these retirees are actually living with less food. Hurst also raises concerns about the impact of unexpected retirements, perhaps due to health problems or other shocks, on retirement expenditures. In other words, some important percentage of retirees will be forced to draw in their belts during their golden years. Similar studies of expenditure and consumption would be well worth conducting in other countries seeking to compare how cohort well-being changes after retirement.

Retirement Payouts: Balancing the Objectives

Adverse events and risk have an important influence on financial decisions before and after retirement, particularly the risk of health shocks, the risk of living longer than expected, and the risk that prices might rise too quickly to be managed. These concerns contribute to the overall worry that many older persons confront, namely, the risk of 'running out of money.' One topic we examine is what tools retirees can use to manage these risks in retirement, including health and long-term care insurance (LTCI) as well as immediate life annuities. Yet the question remains as to whether retirees avail themselves of these tools sensibly and efficiently.

A case in point has to do with the drawdown process from Individual Retirement Accounts (IRAs), an increasingly popular means of accumulating tax-protected retirement funds in the USA. Similar schemes are, of course, available in the UK and Canada. The work by Sarah Holden and Brian Reid (2008) is of interest in that it takes a careful look at ownership, value, allocations, and withdrawals for IRAs. Not surprisingly, the authors find that that older taxpayers hold the largest share of IRA assets which peak for persons aged 70–74 averaging over $124,000; taxpayers over age 60 account for only 30 percent of total taxpayers but account for 56 percent of IRA assets. To date, IRA withdrawals have been small: for instance, withdrawals accounted for only 4 percent of IRA assets (in 2004). Tax rules impose a 10 percent penalty for withdrawing IRA funds before the age of $59^1/_2$, so most people wait; indeed, 45 percent wait to tap them after retirement. Additional exemptions are added for first-time homeowners, medical expenses, higher education expenses, reservists, and taxpayers affected by recent natural disasters. Generally IRA withdrawals must begin by age $70^1/_2$. In their chapters, the authors develop a model to estimate the probability of IRA withdrawals using a variety of data-sets. Their projections show that current IRA withdrawal trends will continue, with higher withdrawals when the head of the household is older, nonwhite or Hispanic, or less educated. Withdrawals are also more likely in households with a mortgage compared to those that rent their homes or own them outright.

In many countries, retirement payouts are shaped by tax and inheritance regulation, a topic taken up in Victor Hallman's chapter (2008). As the USA has had high estate taxes in the past, retirees often seek income-tax-favored savings plans to pass along wealth to succeeding generations or to charity. Hallman considers Roth IRAs to be particularly useful assets, since funds held in this form grow tax-free and minimum distribution rules do not apply to the original owners. The author also discusses possible changes in tax policy that might require tax-subsidized retirement accounts to be used mainly for the support of participants in their old age. For instance, these could include eliminating the exclusion for net unrealized appreciation, life expectancy payouts for individual nonspouse beneficiaries with payouts longer than 10 years, and 'inherited IRA' payouts.

A related topic of practical interest to virtually all retirees is when they should begin collecting their Social Security benefits. Of course the age at which one may collect one's retirement benefit varies substantially across nations [Organization for Economic Cooperation and Development (OECD) 2005], and in the USA, it is being raised from age 65 to 67 for most Baby Boomers. In their chapter, James Mahaney and Peter Carlson (2008) take a hard look at recent changes in the US Social Security eligibility rules against the backdrop of a national transition from defined benefit to defined contribution pensions, tax considerations, and low interest rates. The authors point out that workers nearing retirement should integrate their decision to claim Social Security benefits in their overall strategy for retirement decumulation. Most important is the fact that Social Security rules have recently boosted the age for full retirement and they also now provide an 8 percent increase in Delayed Retirement Credits for those who defer claiming Social Security payments until age 70. Furthermore, and not widely appreciated, there is a recently passed rule allowing married couples to file for and then suspend receipt of Social Security benefits on attaining full retirement age. Delaying taking the primary earner's benefit early increases the monthly benefit, the longer the couple waits. There is also a so-called 'tax torpedo,' which hits retirees when taxes finally come due on tax-deferred saving, triggering higher income taxes and taxes on Social Security benefits. As the authors note, it may no longer be sensible to take Social Security early. It would be of great interest to replicate this analysis in other countries, to see whether the interaction of spouse, survivor, and other dependent benefits also generates difficult-to-understand retirement incentives.

A theme running through many chapters in this volume is how to protect retirees' nest eggs against a wide range of threats. Financial literacy is a key problem in this regard, inasmuch as a wide range of international studies have shown that older individuals are not well versed in key financial concepts pertinent to wise deployment of retirement assets (Lusardi and Mitchell 2007a, 2007b). The chapter by Phyllis Borzi and Martha Priddy Patterson (2008) expresses concern that Baby Boomers approaching retirement must increasingly administer their own retirement portfolios, but for many this will be the largest sum of money they have ever been asked to manage. The authors believe those who seek to relieve retirees of their 401(k) 'burdens' require greater protection to ensure the funds last throughout the retirement period. Accordingly, this chapter lays out the legal and regulatory frameworks governing insurance products that embody a form of guarantee, and securities which are regulated but not guaranteed. Inasmuch as most efforts to date have been geared toward disclosure, consumers remain ill-informed; therefore, the discussion emphasizes the role of better financial education for retirees.

Financial Products for Retirement Risk Management

Recent years have seen a proliferation of simple 'rules of thumb' devised by financial planners who seek to guide the asset decumulation process in retirement. A challenge to these approaches is provided in the chapter by William Sharpe, Jason Scott, and John Watson (2008). They particularly target the '4 percent rule' which has retirees spend a constant, inflation-adjusted amount equal to 4 percent of their initial wealth every year; that tactic requires funds to be invested with a constant percentage in equities ranging from 50 to 75 percent. The authors argue that this formula and others proposed by planners are inefficient, volatile, and may lead to bankruptcy or large surpluses. In their place, the authors suggest the concept of investment 'lockboxes,' which involves a spending strategy producing more efficient retiree drawdowns. In their approach, fractions of initial wealth are allocated to virtual accounts or so-called lockboxes; money in each lockbox is independently invested, and each year the retiree can spend only the contents of that lockbox designated for that year. This concept, in the authors' view, protects against age-related problems in savings and retirement spending.

Many older workers and retirees worry about health problems in later life, and these concerns naturally influence retirement spend-down patterns. The chapter by Cassio Turra and Olivia Mitchell (2008) shows how anticipated poor health would influence the decision to purchase a life annuity. Using a dynamic discrete choice economic model of behavior, they incorporate the effect of health shocks on people's valuation of lifetime income flows. One approach incorporates the effect of health via differences in survival over the life cycle, while a second posits that retirees consider both the effects of uncertain out-of-pocket medical expenses and uncertain survival when deciding whether and how much to annuitize. The authors show that differences across people in health status and anticipated health-care costs help explain why many people do not fully annuitize at retirement. For someone with health problems, a life annuity priced using annuitant mortality rates implies expected payouts that are well below the population expected value; poor health can lower annuity equivalent wealth values by almost 20 percent when retirees expect to be in poor health. When both adverse selection and uncertain medical expenses are accounted for, annuity equivalent wealth values prove to be quite low for people in poor health and about 25 percent higher for people in good health. This, the authors suggest, may be a partial explanation for why payout annuities are not more common in the retiree portfolio.

Related work by John Ameriks et al. (2008), Andrew Caplin, Steven Laufer, and Stijn Van Nieuwerburgh focuses on the demand for payout products, while taking into account both bequest motives and a potential desire to avoid the government means-tested health care provided to the poor, Medicaid. The model explicitly allows for the possibility that retirees may wish to use some assets to provide a bequest at death, while at the same time hoping to maintain high enough wealth levels to avoid bankruptcy (and reliance on Medicaid) in circumstances where they need long-term care. This model is then used to analyze the demand for standard annuities along with newer insurance product designs including 'longevity insurance,' reversible annuities, and long-term care (LTC). They show that standard annuities are an unattractive proposition given typical costs/loads, but hybrid products could be more appealing, including longevity insurance and credible combinations of long-term policies with annuities. This implies that the inclusion of an LTC component in Social Security might encourage families to become more involved in planning for older relatives' needs.

Important developments in the variable annuity market are taken up by Moshe Milevsky and Vladyslav Kyrychenko (2008), particularly products which include a Guaranteed Minimum Income Benefit (GMIB). These riders allow plan holders to annuitize an account at a guaranteed rate for lifetime income. Their evidence suggests that people who purchase the variable annuity tend to boost their risk exposure by 20–25 percentage points when they have a GMIB, which leads some insurers to restrict purchasers' portfolio choices. The study also finds a strong distribution channel effect, with high-risk allocations of around 80 percent when sales are made by career insurance agents, financial planners, wirehouses, and banks.

The idea of creating annuities with a tier of coverage for LTC is also examined by David Brazell, Jason Brown, and Mark Warshawsky (2008), who contend that the life annuity and LTCI markets naturally attract opposing risk groups. That is, life annuities appeal to those with higher than average life expectancies, leading to problems with adverse selection in the market. Those who believe they have a greater chance of needing LTC are more inclined to seek coverage, but underwriting can prevent coverage for this population. The chapter argues that it might be effective to combine life annuities with LTCI, including a combined Life Care Annuity (LCA) product. Of course, the tax treatment of such products is critical, and unresolved issues remain with regard to the requirements and tax treatment of an LCA in a qualified retirement plan.

Conclusions

The cutting-edge research in this volume offers important insights for employees, retirees, employers, and policymakers all over the world, who seek insights for the retirement path ahead. To avoid running out of money, some older individuals will have to continue working; and, as we show, this is for some a very sensible and invigorating way to stretch retirement assets farther. Efforts to raise retirement ages around the world are clearly a response consistent with rising longevity and the feasible extension of the worklife. In addition, there will be the need to adjust consumption, where possible substituting home-produced goods and spending less on market-purchased items.

For most people reaching retirement age in the twenty-first century, however, well-being at older ages will depend to a large degree on how wisely people use their accumulated assets to finance their retirements. A key issue that this volume reveals and emphasizes is the multiplicity of retiree needs and desires. In particular, an expressed 'need to replace income' represents many and quite diverse—even contradictory—objectives. They range from the desire to sustain one's own living standard via expenditures of time and money, to the desire for financial protection in exigent situations, and, for at least some, the attractiveness of being able to leave resources behind to loved ones and worthy causes. As the analysis here suggests, helping retirees calibrate and manage their retirement assets is a complicated challenge. To get to an optimal solution, retirees and their advisers require an understanding of investment issues, insurance matters, tax rules, regulations, features of public programs, and of course a clear understanding of financial priorities and how they must be ranked and compared. Much more attention to these issues is vital for better understanding and better decision-making.

Despite several concerns raised by this volume, there is clearly room for optimism. The fact that retirement decumulation seems so complex is, in part, attributable to the fact that so little research has been undertaken on the topic to date. We can only imagine how complex and incomprehensible the dashboard of an early automobile would seem to someone whose prior driving experience was limited to the 'control panel' on a horse! In time, society will grow more comfortable in understanding the challenges and solutions confronting retirees, and relatively simple (even if not perfectly optimal) solutions will be found. New and better financial and risk management services and products will emerge, which meet the market tests of ease of use and effectiveness. And eventually, after vigorous debate and consensus-building, sensible policy reforms will emerge.

Solving the challenges of spending and investing in retirement requires attention to new concerns never even imagined by our parents and grandparents. The important work of the scholars and practitioners gathered in this volume represents an important step toward this end.

Note

[1] Ralph Waldo Emerson (1849).

References

Ameriks, John, Andrew Caplin, Steven Laufer, and Stijn Van Nieuwerburgh (2008). 'Annuity Valuation, Long-term Care, and Bequest Motives,' Chapter 11, this volume.

Borzi, Phyllis C. and Martha Priddy Patterson (2008). 'Regulating Retirement Payouts: Solvency, Supervision, and Credibility,' Chapter 8, this volume.

Brazell, David, Jason Brown, and Mark Warshawsky (2008). 'Tax Issues and Life Care Annuities,' Chapter 13, this volume.

Chan, Sewin and Ann Huff Stevens (2008). 'Is Retirement Being Remade? Developments in Labor Market Patterns at Older Ages,' Chapter 2, this volume.

Emerson, Ralph Waldo (1849). 'The Young American,' *Nature; Addresses, and Lectures.* Speech presented February 7, 1844, to the Mercantile Library Association, Boston, Massachusetts. Boston, MA: James Munroe and Company, pp. 349–383.

Hallman, G. Victor (2008). 'Retirement Distributions and the Bequest Motive,' Chapter 6, this volume.

Holden, Sarah and Brian Reid (2008). 'Managing the IRA in Retirement,' Chapter 5, this volume.

Hurst, Erik (2008). 'Understanding Consumption in Retirement: Recent Developments,' Chapter 3, this volume.

Lusardi, Annamaria and Olivia S. Mitchell (2007*a*). 'Baby Boomer Retirement Security: The Roles of Planning, Financial Literacy, and Housing Wealth,' *Journal of Monetary Economics,* 54(1): 205–24.

—— —— (2007*b*) 'How Much Do People Know about Economics and Finance? Review of the Evidence and Implications for Financial Education Programs,' *Business Economics,* January: 35–45.

Mahaney, James I. and Peter C. Carlson (2008). 'New Approaches to Retirement Income Phasing,' Chapter 7, this volume.

Madrian, Brigitte, Olivia S. Mitchell, and Beth Soldo (eds). (2007). *Redefining Retirement: How Will Boomers Fare?* Oxford: Oxford University Press.

Milevsky, Moshe A. and Vladyslav Kyrychenko (2008). 'Asset Allocation within Variable Annuities: The Impact of Guarantees,' Chapter 12, this volume.

Mitchell, Olivia S., John Piggott, Michael Sherris, and Shaun Yow (2006). 'Financial Innovations for an Aging World,' in C. Kent, A. Park, and D. Rees (eds.), *Demography and Financial Markets.* Reserve Bank of Australia/Australian Treasury. Report of the G-20 Meetings. Pegasus Press, pp. 299–336.

Organization for Economic Cooperation and Development (OECD). (2005). *Pensions at a Glance—Public Policies across OECD Countries.* 2005 Edition. Paris: OECD.

Sharpe, William F., Jason S. Scott, and John G. Watson (2008). 'Efficient Retirement Financial Strategies,' Chapter 9, this volume.

Sinai, Todd and Nicholas Souleles (2008). 'Net Worth and Housing Equity in Retirement,' Chapter 4, this volume.

Turra, Cassio and Olivia S. Mitchell (2008). 'The Impact of Health Status and Out-of-Pocket Medical Expenditures on Annuity Valuation,' Chapter 10, this volume.

Chapter 2

Is Retirement Being Remade? Developments in Labor Market Patterns at Older Ages

Sewin Chan and Ann Huff Stevens

'Retirement' is often thought of informally as a discrete and permanent exit from the labor force at older ages, usually following a long-term job. Nevertheless, recent research has suggested that this method of retiring is far from universal. This chapter shows that retirement behavior is even more complex than had been previously thought, with many individuals returning to the labor force from retirement, as well as moving toward retirement in stages.

For many years, writers have noted that some older people have moved gradually rather than suddenly to retirement, with workers transitioning from nonretirement to 'partial retirement' before completely retiring. Some authors, using data from 1990s, argued that between one-third to half of all retirees took on so-called *bridge jobs* before completely withdrawing from the labor force, depending on exact definitions of such bridge jobs. These typically include fewer hours of work, less responsibility, and lower wages than the worker's preretirement job. More recent evidence suggests that perhaps a majority of retiring workers today use partial retirement as a stepping stone to full retirement. Another interesting pattern has been called *retirement reversals*, whereby individuals resume or increase work activity following a period of complete or partial retirement. As described below, we find widespread evidence of this as we follow older individuals for up to a dozen years.

Understanding the complex nature of the retirement process is important for many aspects of the economics of older individuals. Much of the existing work on modeling retirement decisions has focused on a discrete one-time choice to retire, despite the fact that this behavior correctly characterizes only a minority of workers. The actual decision-making process is more complex because individuals have, and use, other options on the way to retirement. Furthermore, the possibility of a return to the labor force is important for understanding savings and investment allocation decisions for older individuals. For example, an individual may be willing to allocate a greater share of portfolio wealth to risky assets in early retirement if she knows that she may be able to return to the workforce for some period of time. It may also be the case that some retirement reversals are the result of errors in saving decisions. Some individuals may return to work because they have either misestimated the level of resources that they would have in retirement or underestimated the level of expenses that they would incur in retirement.

With the Baby Boomer generation heading toward the latter phase of its working careers, it is especially important to understand better the complexities of retirements that, for many, will not look like the standard stereotype of one-shot retirement. The complexities of retirement behavior may have an important influence on the relative merits of different public policies regarding retirement. In what follows, we first review the existing research on bridge jobs and partial retirement. We then investigate retirement reversals using data from the Health and Retirement Study (HRS), a representative longitudinal survey of older individuals that was launched in 1992 and continues to interview many of the same individuals over time.

Previous Research on Retirement Patterns

The use of bridge jobs and partial retirement before a worker becomes fully and permanently retired has long been of interest to economists. A *bridge job* is usually defined as employment which follows the worker's long-term career job. This need not be part-time work, and bridge job workers need not consider themselves partially retired. On the other hand, partial retirement often implies part-time work, or at least work that involves less effort than the worker was accustomed to. Partial retirement need not involve a bridge job if a worker can reduce hours on one's main career job. Accordingly, gradual retirement could involve any combination of bridge jobs and partial retirement.

The popularity of a gradual rather than discrete approach to retirement first became evident to researchers from studies using the Retirement History Survey (RHS)—a nationally representative sample of older men and unmarried women aged 58–63 in 1969, who were then interviewed every two years between 1969 and 1979.[1] Ruhm (1990) used that survey to define the worker's 'career job' as the longest spell of employment with a single firm, up to and including the position held at the start of the RHS, and a 'bridge job' as any job held subsequent to that. He found that most workers retired from bridge jobs, rather than directly from their career jobs, and that the period of postcareer job employment was often lengthy (five years or more) for a substantial portion of workers, especially those who left their career job at relatively younger ages. In terms of job characteristics, the bridge job was usually in a different industry or occupation or both [less than one-quarter of workers had the same one-digit Standard Industrial Classification (SIC) industry and occupation code in their first bridge job]. As expected, drops in earnings between the career and bridge jobs were smaller for those who did remain in the same industry and occupation.

Another main pathway to gradual retirement is partial retirement. Using a self-reported measure of partial retirement (workers could identify themselves as 'not retired', 'partially retired', or 'retired'), Ruhm found that almost half reported being partially retired at some point over the 10-year survey period, and that while the typical duration of partial retirement was relatively short (40 percent were under two years), there was a considerable right tail (more than 20 percent lasted for over eight years). Only a small proportion of partial retirees (less than one in seven) remained with their career employer.

New opportunities for researchers to investigate bridge jobs and partial retirement have become available with the development of the HRS, a large nationally representative longitudinal survey of older individuals beginning in 1992 and continuing every two years to date; new cohorts were introduced in 1998 and again in 2004. Cahill, Giandrea, and Quinn (2005) used the first six waves of this data, and they conclude that bridge jobs have continued to be important for more recent groups of workers.[2] They define a bridge job as any job after a 10-year job (differing slightly from Ruhm's definition), and they find that half to two-thirds of workers with full-time career jobs now take on bridge jobs before exiting the labor force. They also find that bridge jobs are most common among younger workers in the 50+ age range, workers without defined benefit plans, and those at the lower- and upper-end of the wage distribution.

Retirement reversals are also a topic of interest to labor market analysts. Ruhm (1990) documented the extent of retirement reversals in the older RHS, and he found it relatively widespread. Focusing on household heads who first reported being fully retired in 1971, about one-quarter re-entered the labor force within eight years; more than two-thirds of them moved into partial retirement. Similarly, about a quarter of those in partial retirement reversed their status to not retired. In both cases, he concluded that over three-quarters of the reversals were within four years of the retirement or partial retirement date. More recently, Maestas (2005, 2007) uses 1990s data from the HRS and again finds that about a quarter of retirees who are followed for at least five years 'unretire'. Her definitions of complete retirement and especially partial retirement differ from Ruhm's, though her findings on the incidence of reversals are in a similar range as ours.

Evidence on Retirement Patterns in the HRS

To understand retirement patterns among an older population, we draw on several waves of the HRS to track labor force status of individuals over time. Before presenting results, it is worth noting that defining a retirement reversal is complicated by the existence of at least three distinct retirement states, namely, being *not retired, partly retired,* and *fully retired.* Yet there are multiple ways of classifying people into these categories, as indicated by Gustman and Steinmeier (2000). For instance, one could use self-reports, which rely on respondent views of what might constitute full, partial, or nonretirement. Thus, two people working at the same job could legitimately report different retirement states, depending on their work history and experiences. For example, people working at a 40-hour per week job may consider themselves partly retired if their preretirement job involved 60 hours per week.

An alternative approach would define people's retirement status based on their time devoted to work (hours per week or per year). Under this measure, partial retirement would correspond to part-time work, and full retirement would correspond to little or no work. One problem is that this would be misleading for anyone who worked part-time his entire life. Also, the concept does not capture important aspects of partial retirement such as having less responsibility and expending less effort.[3] A variant of this would define retirement as a *reduction* in labor market activity (hours, wages, or earnings). While this measure captures the dynamic process of leaving the labor market, it is also true that changes in hours, wages, or earnings might also be involuntary, perhaps because of a job loss.[4]

Finally, retirement status can use the bridge job concept, defining partial retirement as work after leaving a long-term job (defined as lasting more than, say, 10 years, or the longest spell of employment). In practice, it may be difficult to empirically implement, unless information is available on work activity for individuals' entire working lives. For example, if a 52-year-old woman leaves a 10-year job (her longest to date), does this mean she is moving into a bridge job, or will this new job eventually become her longest career job? That issue aside, the bridge job concept is unworkable for defining retirement reversals because by definition one could never reverse into nonretirement, only into partial retirement.

In what follows, the measure we elect as most appropriate and interesting for analysis is the question based on self-reported retirement status. This is because we are primarily interested in self-perceptions of retirement, although we do show that self-reports are importantly correlated with more objectively measured labor market outcomes. Specifically, we start with the HRS question: 'At this time, do you consider yourself to be completely retired, partly retired, or not retired at all?'. A disadvantage of this question is that one of the permitted responses was 'irrelevant', thought to be an

TABLE 2-1 Distribution of Self-Reported Retirement Status

	Number of Observations	%		
		Not Retired	Partly Retired	Fully Retired
Wave				
1	9,991	79.9	13.3	6.8
2	9,589	70.5	19.4	10.1
3	9,091	59.9	27.6	12.5
4	10,669	63.3	26.2	10.6
5	10,279	57.0	31.4	11.6
6	10,157	48.3	38.6	13.2
7	10,159	44.4	41.4	14.2
All person-waves	69,935	58.1	30.3	11.6

Source: Authors' calculations from Health and Retirement Study (1992–2004).

Notes: The sample includes HRS men and women aged 50+ who report ever working over the period indicated above. Retirement status based on self-reports; those with missing values for retirement status are excluded.

answer, for instance, if the individual never held paid employment. This option generated a large number of missing values, and the application of this code appears to have been somewhat inconsistent across or even within waves.[5] On the other hand, a key reason to use this particular question is that it is the only place in the HRS where a respondent can self-identify himself as 'partly retired'.

To handle the missing values, we make use of another HRS question: 'Are you working now, temporarily laid off, unemployed and looking for work, disabled and unable to work, retired, a homemaker, or what?' Multiple responses were allowed for this employment status question, and we used an algorithm to impute missing values of the retirement status measures.[6] Among those whose reported employment status included 'retired,' we classified retirement status as 'partly retired' if they also reported 'working now,' 'unemployed and looking for work', or 'temporarily laid off, on sick or other leave'; otherwise, we classified retirement status as 'fully retired'. Among those whose reported employment status did *not* include 'retired', we classified retirement status as 'not retired' if they also reported 'working now,' 'unemployed and looking for work', or 'temporarily laid off, on sick or other leave'; otherwise, we left retirement status missing. This fills in about 45 percent of the missing values for self-reported retirement status.

Table 2-1 shows the distribution of our retirement status measure across seven waves of the HRS survey (we exclude any remaining missing values). Our sample includes all men and women aged 50+ who report ever working, which yields us 69,935 person-wave observations. Of these, just over

TABLE 2-2 Labor Market Activity, by Retirement Status

	Not Retired	Partly Retired	Fully Retired
Hours of work per week			
Average	40.6	18.2	0.7
Median	40	16	0
Weeks of work per year			
Average	46.4	31.2	1.5
Median	52	40	0
Number of observations	38,086	8,412	23,437

Source: See Table 2-1. Individual-level sampling weights are used. Retirement status based on self-reports.

half are not retired, 12 percent are partly retired, and about one-third are fully retired. Because average age rises across the waves, there is a corresponding increase in the fraction retired across waves. The sample is approximately evenly split between men and women, although the women are slightly less likely to be fully or partly retired. All the analyses below use individual-level sampling weights.

As is clear, the measure of retirement status is highly correlated with labor market outcomes. Table 2-2 further shows that there are important differences in hours of work per week and weeks of work per year, according to reported retirement status. These differences coincide with intuitive notions of retirement status. The patterns are as expected with hours and weeks being greatest for the not retired, followed by the partly retired, and then the fully retired. Average and median hours of work among the partly retired are slightly lower for women compared with men, but all are within ranges that we would normally consider to be part-time work (15–20 hours per week).

Using all seven waves of data available from the HRS, we are able to generate up to six wave-to-wave retirement status transitions for each individual. Table 2-3 shows the distribution of the resulting 53,233 transitions with nonmissing retirement status, representing 14,033 different individuals. The table gives the fraction of transitions across survey waves that involve retirement, reversals in retirement, and no change in retirement status. Each row in the table sums to 100 percent of the observed transitions. About 5 percent of the observations are transitions from more retired to less retired states, 15 percent are transitions toward being more retired, and the remaining 80 percent of the observations show no change in retirement status. These proportions are essentially the same for both men and women. Thus, movements away from retirement are about one-third as common as movements toward retirement.

TABLE 2-3 Distribution of Retirement Transitions Across Adjacent Waves

Percent Transitioning	Reverse Retirements			Retirements			No Change in Retirement Status		
From Wave t	Fully Retired	Fully Retired	Partly Retired	Not Retired	Not Retired	Partly Retired	Not Retired	Partly Retired	Fully Retired
To Wave t + 1	Not Retired	Partly Retired	Not Retired	Fully Retired	Partly Retired	Fully Retired	Not Retired	Partly Retired	Fully Retired
	1	2	3	4	5	6	7	8	9
Adjacent waves t and t + 1									
1–2	0.5	1.3	1.7	6.4	5.3	1.8	69.5	3.2	10.2
2–3	0.7	1.7	2.3	7.9	6.6	3.1	57.4	4.5	15.9
3–4	0.7	2.1	2.3	7.1	4.9	3.9	47.7	6.4	24.8
4–5	0.6	1.8	2.2	5.3	4.5	3.0	55.3	5.5	21.9
5–6	0.8	2.3	2.1	6.4	4.9	3.7	46.6	6.2	27.0
6–7	1.0	2.6	1.7	5.2	5.2	4.1	42.9	6.6	30.7
All person-waves	0.7	2.1	2.0	6.2	5.1	3.4	51.7	5.6	23.2

Source: See Table 2-1.

Note: Sample includes only those who report ever working; 53,233 person-wave transitions are included and 8,367 person-wave transitions with missing values for retirement status are excluded.

TABLE 2-4 Incidence of Retirement Reversals

By Person-Wave	Fully Retired in Wave t % Reversing to			Partly Retired in Wave t % Reversing to	Fully or Partly Retired in Wave t % Reversing to
	Not Retired	Partly Retired	Not or Partly Retired	Not Retired	Less Retired
Adjacent waves t and t + 1					
1–2	4.2	11.0	15.2	25.0	18.7
2–3	3.6	9.4	13.0	23.2	16.6
3–4	2.4	7.8	10.2	18.3	12.7
4–5	2.4	7.3	9.7	20.6	13.0
5–6	2.6	7.7	10.3	17.8	12.4
6–7	2.9	7.5	10.4	13.8	11.3
All person-waves	2.8	7.9	10.7	18.5	13.0

By Individual	Fully Retired in Any Wave % Who Reversed to			Partly Retired in Any Wave % Who Reversed to	Partly or Fully Retired in Any Wave % Who Reversed to
	Not Retired	Partly Retired	Not or Partly Retired	Not Retired	Less Retired
	7.1	18.8	25.6	30.7	31.8

Sources: See Tables 2-1 and 2-3.

Incidence of Retirement Reversals

Next, we define a retirement reversal as a transition from a more to a less retired state, that is, from completely to partly or not retired, or from partly to not retired. Table 2-4 illustrates the incidence of reverse retirements among those fully or partly retired. Just over 10 percent of those fully retired reverse their retirement in the next wave, with three-quarters of them moving to partial retirement rather than becoming not retired. Among the partly retired, transitions to not retired are more prevalent, at over 18 percent. Taken together, about one in eight full or part retirees reverses his or her retirement status over the two-year period between survey waves.

The second panel of Table 2-4 presents similar statistics by individual instead of by person-wave. The evidence suggests that the lifetime prevalence of retirement reversals is high. Just over one-quarter of HRS respondents who ever fully retired are, at some later point, observed making a transition to a less retired state, with the majority of those transiting to partly retired status. Furthermore, more than 30 percent of those individuals ever reporting partly retired status at some point transit to being not retired. These figures likely understate the lifetime prevalence of retirement reversals, since we observe individuals in the sample for less than their entire lifetimes.

Our measure of retirement reversal is based on a self-assessment of being retired or not. As discussed above, this definition of retirement reversal need not imply that individuals are increasing their hours of work or earnings when they reverse retirement. As such, it is interesting to observe the changing patterns in work activity that correspond to changes in self-reported retirement status. Table 2-5 shows changes in hours and weeks worked by retirement transition. Again, the patterns are as expected. Those reversing retirements on average increase their work hours, with those transiting from full retirement to not retired seeing the biggest increases: over one-third of this group increase their work hours by more than 30 hours per week. Those making less dramatic reversals from full to partly retired, or partly to not retired, increase their hours of work by 8–10 hours on average. An analogous pattern can be seen for those who are in the process of retirement. The greatest decrease in hours is among those making a transition from not retired to fully retired, on average a 35-hour reduction per week. Those who are partly retiring or moving from part to full retirement experience a smaller average decrease in hours. Those who do not change retirement status experience little change on average. These tabulations confirm that transitions between retirement states, based on self-reported status, do capture substantive changes in the extent of paid work activity.

Characteristics Associated with Retirement Reversals

Respondent characteristics by retirement status are presented in Table 2-6. Not surprisingly, the fully retired are most likely to have a spouse who is also fully retired, followed by the partly retired.[7] Retirement status also increases with age: the average age of the not-retired group is 57, versus 64 for the fully retired group. Marital status, race, and ethnicity do not vary substantially by retirement status. The fully retired are less likely to have more than a high-school education, while self-reported health status follows an expected pattern with those who are more retired reporting worse health. The measure of respondents' financial assets is net of debt and includes the value of stocks and mutual funds, checking and savings accounts, and CDs and bonds. It does not take account of pension assets (including IRAs), the value of housing, other properties, vehicles, or businesses. Those who are not retired have lower financial assets on average than the partly or

TABLE 2-5 Changes in Labor Market Activity Across Adjacent Waves, by Retirement Transition

Transition	Reverse Retirements				Retirements			
From Wave t	Fully Retired	Fully Retired	Partly Retired	More Retired	Not Retired	Not Retired	Partly Retired	No change in
To Wave t+1	Not Retired	Partly Retired	Not Retired	Less Retired	Fully Retired	Partly Retired	Fully Retired	Retirement Status:
Average change in hours per week	+18.7	+9.6	+8.8	+10.6	−34.7	−16.7	−10.7	−0.8
% Increasing work per week by								
> 10 hours	54	40	38	41				10
> 20 hours	49	27	27	30				5
> 30 hours	36	13	18	18				3
% Decreasing work per week by								
> 10 hours					85	58	42	13
> 20 hours					82	44	30	6
> 30 hours					76	31	16	4
Average change in weeks per year	+23.4	+17.3	+7.0	+13.9	−41.5	−12.2	−19.2	−0.3
Number of observations	414	1,197	1,116	2,727	3,495	2,732	1,926	42,353

Sources: See Tables 2-1 and 2-3. Individual-level sampling weights are used. Retirement status based on self-reports.

TABLE 2-6 Sample Characteristics by Retirement Status

	Not Retired	Partly Retired	Fully Retired
% Female	48.8	43.0	46.4
% Married	75.6	76.5	74.0
% With fully retired spouse	8.6	19.0	33.6
Average age	57.4	62.0	64.2
% High school graduate	35.7	36.1	39.2
% More than high school	49.3	48.5	38.3
% White	87.0	87.5	86.8
% Hispanic	6.9	4.0	4.9
Self-reported health			
% Excellent	21.6	17.4	11.1
% Very good	35.2	34.1	26.9
% Good	29.6	31.1	29.7
% Fair	11.3	13.5	20.4
% Poor	2.3	3.8	11.8
Financial assets ($)			
Average	89,528	125,365	129,464
Median	11,600	20,500	19,200
% Reporting retirement better than before			35.7
Average no. of jobs reported			
Lasting less than 5 years	0.5	0.9	0.4
Lasting 5 years or more	1.8	1.9	1.6
Number of observations	38,086	8,412	23,437

Source: See Table 2-1.

fully retired.[8] The HRS also asked fully retired respondents (based on self-report) the following question: 'Thinking about your retirement years compared to the years just before you retired, would you say the retirement years have been better, about the same, or not as good?' Over a third report that their retirement is better than before.

Finally, the HRS tracks the number of jobs lasting more than five years that a respondent has ever had. Jobs of fewer than five years' duration are recorded if that job is in progress at or after the respondent's first HRS interview, or if it was the most recent job that ended for a respondent who was not working at the first HRS interview. Those who are partly retired on average have slightly more jobs of both durations than either the not retired or the fully retired. While not shown in the table, women on average report more short-duration jobs, and fewer long-duration jobs, across all retirement categories.

The same set of sample characteristics is displayed in Table 2-7, but now we array the results by whether individuals are observed reversing their

TABLE 2-7 Characteristics of the Fully and Partly Retired, by Retirement Reversal

	Reversed Retirement	Did not Reverse Retirement
% Female	45.2	42.5
% Married	74.4	75.3
% With fully retired spouse	19.1	34.6
Average age in wave $t + 1$	62.5	65.3
% High school graduate	35.8	38.3
% More than high school	44.6	41.9
% White	84.6	88.5
% Hispanic	5.2	4.0
Self-reported health in wave t		
% Excellent	19.3	13.8
% Very good	30.7	30.6
% Good	30.4	30.3
% Fair	14.5	17.4
% Poor	5.0	7.9
Financial assets in wave t ($)		
Average	97,491	124,367
Median	15,000	23,000
% Reporting retirement better in wave t than before	23.3	33.1
Average no. of jobs reported by wave t		
Lasting less than 5 years	1.0	0.5
Lasting 5 years or more	1.8	1.7
Number of observations	2,727	18,688

Sources: See Table 2-1 and 2-4.

retirement status. The sample for Table 2-7 includes only those who are fully or partially retired, and at risk of reversing their retirement. It is interesting that those who undergo a retirement reversal are less likely to have a retired spouse, and more likely to be younger, nonwhite, Hispanic, and in somewhat better health. The reversers also have lower levels of financial assets than nonreversers, raising the possibility that some reversals may reflect greater financial needs. Those reversing a retirement are less likely to report that their retirement years have been better than before, and they tend to have had more short-term jobs than those who did not reverse their retirement.

In Table 2-8, we analyze the contribution of these characteristics in a multivariate context by using a simple linear probability model to examine the correlates of retirement reversal behavior. Again only transitions starting from full or partial retirement are considered. We display estimates for a model with men and women together, because separate models do not

TABLE 2-8 Explaining Retirement Reversals

Dependent Variable Transitioned from More Retired in Wave t to Less Retired in Wave t + 1	Estimated Coefficient	Standard Error
Female	0.004	(0.007)
Married	0.029	(0.008)
Has fully retired spouse	−0.059	(0.006)
Age in wave t + 1 (left out: 50–54)		
55–59	−0.042	(0.027)
60	−0.052	(0.030)
61	−0.109	(0.029)
62	−0.132	(0.028)
63	−0.142	(0.028)
64	−0.150	(0.028)
65	−0.150	(0.028)
66	−0.156	(0.028)
67	−0.155	(0.028)
68	−0.173	(0.028)
69	−0.177	(0.028)
70 and above	−0.178	(0.027)
Education (left out: less than high school)		
High school graduate	−0.015	(0.008)
More than high school	−0.006	(0.010)
White	−0.033	(0.009)
Hispanic	0.026	(0.013)
Self-reported health in wave t (left out: excellent)		
Very good	−0.020	(0.010)
Good	−0.028	(0.010)
Fair	−0.058	(0.011)
Poor	−0.105	(0.013)
Financial assets in wave t (left out: highest quartile)		
Lowest quartile	0.024	(0.011)
2nd quartile	0.002	(0.008)
3rd quartile	−0.016	(0.007)
Reports retirement is better in wave *t* than before	−0.010	(0.006)
No. of jobs reported by wave t		
Lasting less than 5 years	0.081	(0.004)
Lasting 5 years or more	0.013	(0.003)
Constant	0.252	(0.051)
Number of observations	20,250	
R^2	0.095	

Source: Authors' computations using sample in Table 2-7.

Notes: Linear probability model with robust standard errors in parentheses. Explanatory variables are binary indicators except for the number of jobs reported by wave *t*; also included are industry/occupation indicators, indicators for longest job ever held, and an indicator for being partly retired in wave *t*.

yield substantially different results. Indeed, we can see that the coefficient on female term in the displayed pooled regression is small and statistically insignificant. Being married significantly increases the likelihood of a reversal, but if that spouse is fully retired, the chance of a reversal is significantly lower overall. Age has the expected pattern, with older individuals being significantly less likely to reverse their retirement. Relative to those aged 50–54, a 65-year-old woman is 15 percentage points less likely to reverse her retirement. Those with more education tend to be less likely to reverse, but these coefficients are both small and statistically insignificant. As suggested by Table 2-7, whites are significantly less likely to reverse than nonwhites while Hispanics are more likely to reverse. The worse the self-reported health is, the less likely a retirement reversal. Compared to those who self-report excellent health, someone self-reporting poor health is 10 percentage points less likely to reverse. All of the health coefficients are statistically significant. Those in the lowest quartile of the financial wealth distribution are significantly more likely to reverse their retirement, while those reporting that their retirement years have been better than before are less likely to reverse. For both of these variables, the magnitudes of the coefficients are quite small. Reporting a large number of jobs significantly increases the likelihood of a reversal, particularly if those jobs lasted for fewer than five years. The regression also includes industry and occupation indicators for the longest job that the respondent ever held; these coefficients are jointly statistically significant (but not reported here in detail).

It is also interesting that while many characteristics of those who reverse are statistically significant, some 90 percent of the variation in the data remains unaccounted for by the variables we are able to include. One possibility is that expectations may make a difference; indeed Maestas (2005) finds that people who were questioned before retirement, and said they expected to work after retirement, do in fact reverse retire more often. Of course, this simply raises the anterior question of why some people plan such a complex labor supply pattern late in their working lives.

Conclusions

This chapter has highlighted the importance of nontraditional retirement paths, mentioned in previous work and confirmed in the most recent data from the HRS. We show that many individuals have retirement paths that involve neither discrete transitions from full-time work to leisure, nor permanent departures from employment. Focusing on reverse retirements, we show that approximately one-third of older individuals reverse their retirement status over the period studied, a finding consistent with earlier research. We also find that individuals who reverse or partly reverse their retirements tend to be married, younger, nonwhite, and healthier. Those in the lowest quartile of nonretirement net financial assets are also more likely to reverse.

This analysis is descriptive and cannot be interpreted causally, so the next challenge is to integrate these complexities into policies toward and strategies for current and future retirees. For example, saving and investment patterns should differ to the extent that people plan to and do continue work after retirement. Of course, some individuals may face health or financial difficulties that limit the flexibility with which they can approach retirement. Consequently, integrating more complex retirement paths into policy design requires a better understanding of the underlying determinants of these paths into and out of retirement at older ages.

Notes

[1] Other studies of partial retirement using the RHS data include Gustman and Steinmeier (1984) and Honig and Hanoch (1985), among others.

[2] An additional wave of data is used in Giandrea, Cahill, and Quinn (2007) to show the continuing trend for gradual retirement. Other studies of bridge job behavior using the HRS include Quinn and Kozy (1996).

[3] Maestas (2005, 2007) uses a definition that is a composite of (a) and (b) whereby retirement is self-reported (by stating either complete or partial retirement), but the designation of complete or partial is based solely on hours or weeks of work. Under her definition, someone who self-reports complete retirement but works a few hours a week would be reclassified as partially retired. Below we follow Ruhm (1990) in giving the self-reports precedence.

[4] In Chan and Stevens (2001), we show that older workers experience substantial and persistent reductions in earnings following a job loss.

[5] 'Irrelevant' is defined as 'doesn't work for pay or is homemaker; hasn't worked for 10 or more years' for those who are self-employed or unemployed in waves one and two. For wave two employees, and for all respondents in waves three and four, it is defined as 'doesn't work for pay or is homemaker; hasn't worked for one or more years'. From wave five onward, it is defined as 'doesn't work for pay or is homemaker'. Gustman and Steinmeier (2000) report that respondents who satisfied these criteria may be placed in the 'irrelevant' category by the respondent or the interviewer, but this was not required.

[6] Note that 'partly retired' is not one of the options for this employment status question, and so we could not use it as our main retirement status measure.

[7] Note that 'not having a fully retired spouse' could imply either that the spouse was still working, had never worked, or that the individual did not have a spouse.

[8] Dollar figures are not adjusted for inflation.

References

Cahill, Kevin E., Michael D. Giandrea, and Joseph F. Quinn (2005). 'Are Traditional Retirements a Thing of the Past? New Evidence on Retirement Patterns and Bridge Jobs,' Bureau of Labor Statistics Working Paper no. 384. Washington, DC: BLS.

Chan, Sewin and Ann Huff Stevens (2001). 'The Effects of Job Loss on Older Workers: Employment, Earnings and Wealth,' in P. P. Budetti, R. V. Burkhauser, J. M. Gregory, and H. A. Hunt (eds.), *Ensuring Health and Income Security for an Aging Workforce.* Kalamazoo: W. E. Upjohn Institute for Employment Research, pp. 189–212.

Giandrea, Michael D., Kevin E. Cahill, and Joseph F. Quinn (2007). 'An Update on Bridge Jobs: The HRS War Babies,' Bureau of Labor Statistics Working Paper no. 407. Washington, DC: BLS.

Gustman, Alan and Thomas Steinmeier (1984). 'Partial Retirement and the Analysis of Retirement Behavior,' *Industrial and Labor Relations Review,* 37(3): 403–15.

—— (2000). 'Retirement Outcomes in the Health and Retirement Study,' *Social Security Bulletin,* 63(4): 57–71.

Honig, Marjorie and Giora Hanoch (1985). 'Partial Retirement as a Separate Mode of Retirement Behavior,' *Journal of Human Resources,* 20(1): 21–46.

Maestas, Nicole (2005). 'Back to Work: Expectations and Realizations of Work after Retirement,' Rand Working Paper no. WR-196-1.

—— (2007). 'Cohort Differences in Retirement Expectations and Realizations,' in B. Madrian, O. S. Mitchell, and B. J. Soldo (eds.), *Redefining Retirement: How Will Boomers Fare?* Oxford: Oxford University Press, pp. 13–35.

Quinn, Joseph F. and Michael Kozy (1996). 'The Role of Bridge Jobs in the Retirement Transition: Gender, Race and Ethnicity,' *The Gerontologist,* 36(3): 363–72.

Ruhm, Christopher J. (1990). 'Bridge Jobs and Partial Retirement,' *Journal of Labor Economics,* 8(4): 482–501.

Chapter 3

Understanding Consumption in Retirement: Recent Developments

Erik Hurst

According to the standard life-cycle model of consumption, forward-looking agents will smooth their marginal utility of consumption across predictable income changes such as retirement.[1] But a large empirical literature shows that household expenditure falls precipitously upon retirement—a phenomenon now known as 'the retirement consumption puzzle' (Attanasio 1999). Indeed Bernheim, Skinner, and Weinberg (2001: 854) go so far as to state that 'contrary to the central tenets of life-cycle theory, there is little evidence that households use savings to smooth effects on consumption of predictable income discontinuities' such as retirement.

This chapter reviews recent research on expenditure patterns as people transition into retirement. In doing so, we highlight several stylized facts that have emerged with respect to the behavior of consumption around retirement. We conclude that the preponderance of evidence suggests that pessimistic views regarding households' ability to smooth predictable changes in retirement income may be prematurely negative. Observed declines in expenditures, aside from work-related expenses, primarily occur in food and the declines are largest for those who involuntarily retired. This is not to discount the possibility that some households are myopic with respect to their consumption decisions (or have time inconsistent preferences); rather, it is just that these households are only a relatively small fraction of the total population. As a result, one must conclude that standard models of life-cycle consumption, augmented with home production and uncertain health shocks, do well in explaining the consumption patterns of most households as they transition into retirement.

We recognize that, just because households smooth their consumption as they transition into retirement, this need not imply that they have saved adequately for retirement. It is possible that households who planned insufficiently would not learn about their saving shortfall until well after they have retired (perhaps when they receive a future health shock). In this chapter, we show that most households have the ability to sustain their consumption in retirement.

The remainder of the chapter is organized around summarizing the existing literature to provide support for the stylized facts to be developed. First, we review recent literature on the retirement consumption puzzle and show that almost all of the declines in spending at the time of retirement are in the consumption categories of food- and work-related expenses. Second, we discuss the work that shows that food consumption is constant in retirement (despite declining food expenditures) and that households allocate much more time to food production in retirement. Next we discuss the ample work on the heterogeneity in consumption declines upon retirement within the population. The fourth section addresses how involuntary retirement (often via health shocks) can explain a portion of the heterogeneity in consumption declines upon retirement. The last section concludes and offers some perspective by drawing on the literature about whether households save adequately for retirement.

Documenting Stylized Facts about Changing Expenditures at Retirement

A large volume of research has emerged during the last decade examining household expenditures at the time of retirement which we review in this section.[2] In doing so, we draw particular attention to a fact that emerges when aggregating results across papers: the extent to which expenditures decline in retirement varies with the measure of consumption examined. In particular, essentially all of the declines in expenditures at the time of retirement documented within the literature occur in two consumption categories: work-related expenses (clothing and transportation costs) and food (meals at home and meals away from home).

The fact that work-related expenses decline in retirement is not at all surprising. Any model that has some expenditures which are strong complements with working (such as business attire) will predict those expenditures will fall as households exit the labor force. However, to the extent that food is a large share of households' budgets and is often considered a necessity with a relatively low income elasticity, food-spending declines in retirement could be seen as a puzzle. As is detailed below, what the literature has documented as a 'retirement consumption puzzle' is actually a misnomer. In actuality, the literature has primarily documented a 'retirement food consumption puzzle.' Moreover, the true puzzle is why food expenditures fall sharply *despite* the fact that the remaining portion of the households' non-work-related/nonfood expenditures remain roughly constant.

A recent study focused on the differential life-cycle spending patterns for different consumption categories (Aguiar and Hurst 2007*b*); that analysis uses the Consumer Expenditure Survey (CEX) as opposed to other US micro data-sets, such as the Panel Study of Income Dynamics (PSID), the Retirement History Survey (RHS), or the Health and Retirement Study (HRS). The CEX differs from these other surveys in two key ways. First, it has broader measures of consumption than the other surveys. Second, the CEX is a cross-sectional survey with only a short (4 quarter) panel component. The PSID, HRS, and RHS follow the same individual over much longer periods. To get around this potential drawback, Aguiar and Hurst use multiple cross sections from the CEX to create a synthetic panel by following a given cohort over time. In doing so, they compare the spending patterns of all households of a given cohort between the ages of 60 and 62 to the spending patterns of all households of the same cohort between the ages of 66 and 68 (six years later). Of particular interest is the life-cycle profile of spending in 11 categories of nondurable consumption, including total food, alcohol and tobacco, nondurable transportation, clothing and personal care, domestic services, entertainment services, utilities, charitable giving, net gambling receipts, all other nondurable expenditures (including business services), and housing services. The authors exclude education and health expenditures from their measure of nondurable expenditures. They also compute the service flow of housing for homeowners by using the self-reported answer to the question of what the homeowners would charge (net of utilities) to someone who wished to rent their housing structure today. For renters, the service flow of housing is their monthly out-of-pocket expenditures on rent.

Aguiar and Hurst's (2007*b*) main finding was to demonstrate that spending on total food, clothing, and nondurable transportation falls for people between their early and late 60s, by 10, 22, and 20 percent respectively. Conversely, spending on housing services, utilities, charitable giving, net gambling receipts, and entertainment remains constant or rises during the retirement years. For example, between the early and the late 60s, entertainment spending increases by 9 percent and charitable giving increases by 40 percent. These results are hard to reconcile with households being ill-prepared for retirement. Why is it that households would forgo food (a necessity) while simultaneously increasing their spending on entertainment (going to the movies, golf games, and vacations) and charitable giving? The authors conclude that the Becker model of consumption commodities handily explains the observed life-cycle patterns of different consumption categories (Becker 1965). Specifically, spending on goods that are complementary to time (like entertainment) will increase in retirement, while spending on goods that are substitutes to time (like food production) will fall during retirement.

This general conclusion is consistent with those provided by Fisher et al. (2006) who also use CEX data from a similar time period but who employ a different empirical strategy. This study compares the spending patterns of *nonretired* households between the ages of 60 and 64 with spending patterns of *retired* households between the ages of 65 and 69 five years later. In so doing, the analysis must assume that retirement status prior to and after the age of 65 is completely exogenous to factors that determine household consumption. This assumption is likely not valid given that households will also optimize over their choice of retirement age. Moreover, that study only looks at total spending (with and without housing services) and food spending. Subject to these caveats, those authors find that most of the action of the decline in total expenditures at the time of retirement occurs within the food categories (food at home and food away from home). Specifically, for their third cohort, food at home and food away from home fell upon retirement by roughly 8.3 and 15.9 percent, respectively.[3] The corresponding changes over these age ranges for their broad measure of consumption excluding housing services and their broad measure of consumption including housing services were −3.1 and −1.2 percent. Again, the declines in food spending, associated with retirement for CEX households, were much larger than the declines in total spending.[4]

In other words, the declining expenditures at the time of retirement in the USA appears to be mainly a result of less food spending and fewer work-related expenditures. Changes in other categories are either close to zero or close to positive, as households transition to retirement. In particular, spending on luxury goods, like entertainment services, actually increases as households transition into retirement.

There is research offering a different view of the spending patterns of retirees, including that of Laitner and Silverman (2005) who use CEX data and a different methodology. That paper reports that total expenditures drop by 16 percent upon retirement. Although they do not disaggregate the consumption decline into separate categories, their decline in total spending is much larger than the declines reported above using nearly identical data-sets. The technical explanation for this difference is that their structural model estimates the change in spending at retirement using both an age effect and a retirement effect. This permits a large offsetting positive age effect for households during their 60s, which offsets the negative retirement effect. In other words, a household's desired consumption level would appear to be increasing during their 60s, but almost all households retire during their 60s, so consumption becomes suppressed. The reason we believe they estimate such a strong age effect is that households with higher permanent incomes tend to retire later than households with lower permanent incomes, yet they assume retirement timing is exogenous to factors that determine consumption levels.

International data have also been developed on changes in consumption at the time of retirement. Banks, Blundell, and Tanner (1998) use data from Britain's Family Expenditure Survey (FES), and they draw conclusions similar to those of Aguiar and Hurst (2007*b*) and Fisher et al. (2006). Moreover, they document that the declines in food expenditures and the declines in work-related expenditures (including canteen and restaurant meals, transport, and adult clothing) are much larger than total nondurable expenditures. Miniaci, Monfardini, and Weber (2003) use the Italian Survey of Family Budgets (ISFB) to analyze consumption declines by consumption category for older Italian households. Not only are their results for Italy consistent with the results for the USA and the UK, but they also analyze a much broader set of consumption categories. The only decline in expenditures found for retired Italian households occurred in either work-related categories (clothing and transportation) or food (food at home and food away from home). All other components of nondurable consumption either remained constant or actually increased through retirement years (households in their 60s). These remaining categories include health expenditures, fuel expenditures, and other housing expenditures. Again, their results show that to the extent that nondurable consumption falls in retirement, it is mostly (if not completely) driven by work-related expenditures and food expenditures. Battistin et al. (2006) also studied Italians using the Bank of Italy Survey on Household Income and Wealth (SHIW); they use a regression discontinuity approach to instrument for retirement status. This approach provides identification since different Italians are eligible for the state-provided pension at different ages (and as a result, the incentive to retire at a given age differs among the different groups). They conclude that nondurable consumption falls by roughly 9 percent as households transition to retirement, with the greatest declines in spending in meals away from home, clothing, and transportation.

The measured decline in work-related expenses can be reconciled with the standard life-cycle model of consumption with work-specific expenditures (such as formal dress and work-related transportation). Yet the observed decline in food expenditures is harder to explain. Given that food is a necessity and therefore has a small income elasticity, some argue that analyzing food expenditures provides a strong test of consumption smoothing during retirement. The prevailing view has been that, if retired households do not smooth food expenditures, this implies it is unlikely they will smooth spending on other components of their consumption bundle. For this reason, much of the literature on the US retirement consumption puzzle has mainly focused on food expenditures. For example, Bernheim, Skinner, and Weinberg (2001) use the PSID to examine changes in household spending at the time of retirement. Their measure of consumption includes food expenditures at home, food expenditures away from home, and the imputed or actual rental value of one's residence. They show results for their composite measure of consumption and separately for food at home and food away from home. Results for a measure of consumption that only includes the imputed or actual rental value of one's residence at the time of retirement are not shown. They find that, on average, their composite expenditure measure falls by 14 percent.

A variety of other studies confirm that food expenditures drop sharply upon retirement. Hurst (2006) uses a different methodology and a different time period from the PSID and finds similar results with respect to food spending. If one follows a specific household through retirement, food spending declines by 12 percent at the median on average. Likewise, Haider and Stephens (2007) use panel data from the RHS and find that households that retire when expected experience a 10 percent decline in food expenditures, on average. However, the latter authors also analyze data from the HRS and find no decline in food spending among the recently retired. This latter result is interesting in the sense that it is the only study reporting that food expenditures do not decline sharply with the incidence of retirement. Fisher et al. (2006) suggest that either period effects or cohort effects from the late 1990s may explain the lack of findings in the HRS data analyzed Haider and Stephens (2007).[5]

Hurd and Rohwedder (2003, 2006) take a different approach to analyzing changes in spending at the time of retirement by using retroactive survey data. Instead of using the data-sets described previously, where households are asked about their spending patterns during the last month or during the last quarter, these studies rely on household retrospective assessments of how much their expenditures fell upon retirement. For example, someone in their survey currently 69 years old but who retired when he was 63 would be asked to recount his change in spending from six years earlier. This recall is provided by a supplemental survey called the Consumption and Activities Mail Survey (CAMS), matched to the HRS. The CAMS survey asked current retirees to report how their total spending changed with retirement in two steps. First, they report the direction of the change in spending at the time of retirement (increase, decrease, or stay the same). Second, the household is asked to report the percentage change in spending, if they report that their spending increased or decreased. Using a very different methodology than the earlier surveys, these analyses show, on average, that total spending falls by roughly 14 percent at the time of retirement. The median decline in spending, however, is zero. This corresponds almost exactly to the median results on total spending changes discussed above.

Ameriks, Caplin, and Leahy (2007) use data from two separate surveys of Teachers Insurance and Annuity Association-College Retirement Equities Fund (TIAA-CREF) participants: the Survey of Participant Finances (SPF) and the Survey of Financial Attitudes and Behavior (FAB). Similar to the

CAMS data, households are asked to assess the direction of their change in spending at the time of retirement and the amount of the change. The TIAA-CREF samples differ from the CAMS, in the sense that TIAA-CREF respondents are much more educated and much wealthier than the households in CAMS. These surveys again report that, at the median, there is no decline in total spending at the time of retirement.

One thing that distinguishes the last studies by Hurd and Rohwedder (2003, 2006) and Ameriks, Caplin, and Leahy (2007) from the other work on the retirement consumption puzzle is that these surveys also ask households before retirement about their *expected* declines in spending at retirement. In other words, this work speaks to the question of whether preretired households expect their expenditures to fall upon retirement. Interestingly, nearly 70 percent of preretired respondents in CAMS expected their expenditures to fall in retirement, while almost 60 percent of preretired TIAA-CREF households expected to decrease their expenditures upon retirement. This research sheds light on the fact that for most households declines in spending are forecastable well in advance of the actual date of retirement.

What does this synthesis of all of the above research allow one to conclude about the retirement consumption puzzle? Evidence from many countries does show that household expenditures drop at retirement. But these studies also show that most of the declines are found in work-related expenditures and in food expenditures. Broader measures of consumption always show less of a decline than the narrow categories of food or work-related expenses. Moreover, although it is rarely directly documented, it appears that total expenditures excluding food and work-related items remain relatively constant as households transition to retirement. Furthermore, these spending declines at retirement are predictable by households, before actual retirement.

Explaining the 'Retirement Food Consumption Puzzle'

From the life-cycle perspective, it makes sense that expenditures that are complements with working (i.e., professional clothing) should fall when households exit the labor force. But without augmentation, the model still has a difficult time explaining why food expenditures would fall while the rest of the consumption bundle remains relatively constant. If that were truly the case, the retirement consumption puzzle should be more appropriately named the 'retirement food consumption' puzzle. A possible explanation for this phenomenon is offered by Aguiar and Hurst (2005) who argue that consumption is the output of 'home production,' which uses as inputs both market expenditures and time. People will tend to substitute away from market expenditures toward time spent in home production, including more intensive searching for bargains, as the relative price of time falls. Naturally, retirees have a lower opportunity cost of time relative to their preretired counterparts and, as a result, should be able to engage in nonmarket production to reduce the cost of their consumption bundle while keeping their actual consumption intake relatively constant. This could explain the behavior of food expenditures during retirement given that food is amenable to home production.

Testing this hypothesis requires data on how food consumption changes in retirement. Aguiar and Hurst (2005) rely on the Continuing Survey of Food Intake of Individuals (CSFII), conducted by the U.S. Department of Agriculture, which tracks the dollar value, the quantity, and the quality of food consumed by US households. Using a variety of statistical tests, they find no actual deterioration in a household's diet as they transition into retirement.[6] Actual food consumption does not decline despite the declining expenditure. This just pushes the question back a step: how do retirees maintain their food consumption despite their declining food expenditures? Using detailed time diaries from National Human Activity Pattern Survey and from the American Time Use Survey, the authors show that retirees dramatically increase their time spent on food production relative to otherwise similar nonretired households. The fact that retirees allocate more time to nonmarket production than their nonretired counterparts was also shown by Hurd and Rohwedder (2003, 2006) using the CAMS supplement to the HRS and by Schwerdt (2005) using data from the German Socio-Economic Panel.

In separate work, Aguiar and Hurst (2007a) examine the mechanism by which retirees reduce their spending on food. Is it that retirees are shopping more frequently and, as a result, are paying less for their exact same food consumption bundle? Or, are they actually switching their consumption bundle from relative expensive premade groceries (like using the grocery store's salad bar to purchase a premade salad) to relatively cheaper raw ingredients which they can combine themselves into a meal (like buying all the vegetables separately and chopping them up themselves to make the salad). Household data provided by the ACNielsen company tracks the purchases of the household at the universal product code (UPC) level and links those purchases to detailed information about the purchaser. This permits the authors to show that, holding constant the exact good (as measured by UPC code), retirees pay lower prices for their grocery bundle than slightly younger nonretired households. In all, about 20 percent of the declining expenditures on food for older households can be attributed to increased shopping intensity resulting in lower prices paid for the same good. The remaining 80 percent, they find, is due to increased amounts of home production.

Broadly, their results suggest that retired households should experience a slight decline in nonfood items simply resulting from the increased shopping intensity of retired households. This is consistent with the facts in Aguiar and Hurst (2005) which show retired households spend 60 percent more time shopping for nonfood goods then their nonretired counterpoints.

The Heterogeneity of Expenditure Declines Across Individuals

A decade of research on the retirement expenditure puzzle has taught us three things: (a) declines in expenditure, on average, are anticipated at retirement; (b) the bulk of the decline in expenditures at retirement is concentrated among work-related expenditures and food; and (c) the decline in food expenditures can be explained by an increase in home production of food by retirees in the sense that the time allocated to food production goes up dramatically in retirement and actual food intake does not change in any meaningful way as households retire. Yet the literature has also demonstrated one additional fact about changes in expenditure among retirees: there is a tremendous amount of heterogeneity in expenditure changes experienced by retirees.

This point was first made by Bernheim, Skinner, and Weinberg (2001) who use panel data from the PSID which permit the authors to follow a given household as it transitions through retirement. An innovative element of their research is that they examined food consumption declines for individuals with differing amount of retirement resources,[7] characterized along two dimensions: (a) accumulated total assets prior to retirement relative to preretirement nonasset income; and (b) postretirement nonasset income relative to preretirement nonasset income. Their hypothesis was that households with higher accumulated assets prior to retirement or higher income replacement rates postretirement should be better able to maintain consumption during retirement. The authors' empirical results are striking. First, they show that that essentially all households, independent of preretirement wealth and postretirement income replacement rates, experienced a decline in (primarily food) expenditure during retirement. Second, the declines in expenditure are largest for households with the lowest retirement resources. For example, households in the lowest preretirement wealth quartile (irrespective of postretirement income replacement quartile) experienced a 31 percent decline in expenditures up to four years after retirement. Expenditure declines for households in the second, third, and top preretirement wealth quartiles (irrespective of postretirement income replacement quartile) are 14, 14, and 9 percent, respectively.[8] In other words, the declines in expenditures for the wealthiest households (top preretirement wealth quartile) are similar to the declines in expenditures for households in the second and third preretirement wealth quartiles. Those households in the bottom preretirement wealth quartile, however, experienced a much larger decline in expenditures at retirement.

While the declines in food expenditures for the households in the top three wealth quartiles can be explained by changing home production and shopping activities, such a modification to the life-cycle model has a hard time matching the magnitudes of the decline in expenditures for households in the bottom quartile of the wealth distribution. To this end, Aguiar and Hurst (2005) show that some households— those with very little accumulated wealth (less than $1,000 of nonpension assets)—do experience some decline in the quantity and quality of food intake associated with retirement. Other researchers have confirmed the existence of important heterogeneity in expenditure decline around the time of retirement. For example, Hurst (2006) uses PSID data and relates preretirement wealth on a full vector of income and demographic variables. Next, he splits households into a sample with low preretirement wealth residuals (bottom 20 percent) and all other households. He shows that the food expenditure declines associated with retirement are twice as large for those households with low preretirement wealth residuals compared to other households (20 percent declines vs 10 percent declines).

A related point is that the CAMS HRS supplement shows substantial heterogeneity in expenditure changes at the time of retirement. Specifically, Hurd and Rohwedder (2003) report that only slightly over half (53 percent) of households currently retired report experiencing a decline in total expenditure at the time of retirement. Of the remaining households, 12 percent reported experiencing an *increase* in total expenditures at the time of retirement, while 36 percent reported that retirement was associated with no change in total expenditures. And actual drops in expenditure at retirement grew as net worth declined: households in the lowest wealth quartile experienced a 22 percent decline in actual expenditure while households in the second, third, and top wealth quartile experienced 17, 13, and 7 percent declines, respectively.[9]

Given these results, the focus of changes in expenditures in retirement should be limited to the minority of households who enter retirement with very low wealth and, as a result, experience very dramatic declines in expenditures at the time of retirement relative to other households with higher amounts of wealth.

The Role of Unanticipated Retirement in Explaining Observed Heterogeneity

One concern that motivates the identification of the 'retirement consumption puzzle' is that retirement is often endogenous to life events which change household consumption trajectories. Among the most commonly cited causes of involuntary retirement are health shocks. For instance, McClellan (1998) finds that workers who have worse health are more likely to have subsequent negative health shocks and are more likely to retire early. Hurd and Rohwedder (2005) find that 29 percent of the CAMS sample report that adverse health was 'very important' or 'moderately important' for their decision to enter retirement.

A health shock can affect the optimal consumption decision in multiple ways. First, households who are forced to retire earlier than expected will likely experience a sharp permanent decline in their lifetime resources. According to standard life-cycle theories, such a shock should cause a household to optimally lower their level of consumption, all else equal. As a result, one should expect to see declining consumption growth as households transition into their retirement.[10] Also, health shocks should cause a reallocation of the consumption bundle, all else equal, toward health expenditures away from other consumption categories. If the measure of consumption excludes health expenditures, one may observe declining expenditures in retirement. Third, health shocks often affect consumption needs. For example, someone stricken with a severe illness that affects ability to work may also have decreased appetite causing one to spend less on food during a given period. Lastly, the health shock could alter the household's expected length of life. Again, according to standard consumption theories, an abrupt change in the planning horizon will alter the household's consumption path.

A relevant question is whether health shocks (or unexpected retirement, more generally) can explain observed heterogeneity in expenditure declines at the time of retirement, particularly among those with low pre-retirement wealth.[11] Haider and Stephens (2007) tackle the question of unexpected retirements directly using RHS data. They instrument for the time of a household's retirement with that household's own expectation of their retirement date some years prior to their actual retirement, and then the authors compare the overall change in food spending for all households as they transition to retirement with the overall change in food spending for only those households where the date of retirement was predicted well in advance. Their estimate of the decline in food expenditures at the time of retirement, when age is used as an instrumental variable for retirement status, is roughly -15 percent. Using retirement expectations as an instrument instead reduces the estimated decline in food expenditures at retirement to −10 percent. In other words, the decline in food expenditures for households where the date of retirement is not forecastable is much larger than the decline in food expenditures for households where the date of retirement is known in advance.

The importance of involuntary early retirement is underscored by Smith (2006) who examines the British Household Panel (BHP). She divides her sample retirees into households who retire 'voluntarily' and those who retire 'involuntarily'; involuntary retirees are those who transition into retirement from a nonwork employment state (usually unemployment or long-term disability). She links this to total spending on food consumed at home (meals away from the home are not included). Although her sample sizes are small (226 voluntary retirees and 57 involuntary retirees), she still is able to conclude that those who retire involuntarily experience much larger consumption declines than those who retire voluntarily; she cannot, however, reject that those who retire voluntarily experience any expenditure declines upon retirement. However, those who retire involuntarily experience expenditure declines of over 10 percent.

Taken together, these results indicate that some of the observed heterogeneity in the spending declines associated with retirement is due to involuntary retirement. Specifically, those who are forced to retire involuntarily experience much larger expenditure declines than households who retire when planned. Some of this may be due to health shocks. For instance Hurd and Rohwedder (2005) examine expenditure changes for CAMS households who self-report that poor health was a very important reason for their retirement, and compare these to those households who self-report that poor health was not important at all for their decision to retire. They show that those who experienced a poor health shock forcing them to retire were more likely to report expenditure declines at the time of retirement (68 vs 48 percent) and experienced larger expenditure declines at the time of retirement (25 vs 11 percent). Accordingly, it does seem that adverse health shocks account for some of the large heterogeneity in expenditure declines as households transition to retirement.

Conclusions and Discussion

Until recently, many analysts felt that consumption patterns around the retirement date were poorly captured by life-cycle models. This claim relied on the fact that even though retirement is fairly predictable for most households, consumption expenditures declined precipitously for everyone at that point. Such a phenomenon had been referred to as the 'retirement consumption puzzle.'

Our chapter has confirmed that certain types of expenditures do fall sharply as households enter into retirement—not only in the USA but elsewhere as well. We also show that the expenditure drops are mostly limited to two consumption categories: work-related items (such as clothing and transportation expenditures) and food (both at home and away from home). When broader measures of consumption are analyzed or when expenditure categories that exclude food and work-related expenses are analyzed, the measured declines in spending upon retirement are either close to zero or are increasing. As a result, the retirement consumption puzzle is a bit of a misnomer. The fact that work-related expenses fall upon retirement is in no sense puzzling when viewed through the lens of standard consumption models. What is potentially puzzling is why food expenditures decline sharply at the time of retirement while the rest of the household's consumption bundle remains relatively constant.

Another stylized fact highlighted is that actual food intake (as measured by the quantity and quality of one's diet) remains constant through retirement despite the fact that food expenditures fall sharply. This is partly due to the fact that retirees spend much more time on food production (preparing meals and shopping for groceries) than their nonretired counterparts. We also document substantial heterogeneity across individuals in the population with respect to changing expenditures in retirement. Specifically, expenditures drops are mostly marked for households that have little accumulated wealth prior to retirement.

Last, we conclude that households which experience real consumption declines at retirement often experience involuntary retirement, some due to health shocks. There are other potential explanations as well. Hurst (2006) suggests that households with low preretirement wealth entering retirement may be myopic with respect to their consumption decisions and, as a result, plan insufficiently for retirement. Scholz, Seshadri, and Khitatrakun (2006) run individual earnings, demographic and health trajectories (for an actual household) through a calibrated life-cycle consumption model (with idiosyncratic income and health shocks). They then compare the predicted household wealth on the eve of retirement from such a model to the household's actual preretirement wealth and find that roughly 20 percent of households are ill-prepared to sustain consumption during retirement. The remaining 80 percent of households have accumulated enough wealth to maintain their marginal utility of consumption through retirement.

The bottom line is that, for most households, there is no retirement consumption puzzle. In other words, most households are maintaining their marginal utility of consumption as they transition into retirement across all consumption categories. These results also provide sharp conclusions about the nonseparability of actual consumption and leisure in household utility.[12] Future work can learn more about the households who may, in fact, be ill-prepared to maintain their consumption levels postretirement. Moreover, the data seems to suggest that there may potentially be room for an improved insurance market that would allow households to maintain consumption in the event that they receive a health shock. Studying the consumption needs of such households after a health shock, therefore, would also be a fruitful area for future research. Another fruitful venue for future work is to focus on consumption patterns beyond retirement. As households live longer, the question will shift toward whether households can maintain their consumption well into their periods of retirement. That is, households may be able to smooth their consumption as they transition into retirement but may be unable to sustain that consumption level over their remaining lifetimes.

Acknowledgments

The author thanks Mark Aguiar, Jonathan Fisher, John Laitner, Olivia S. Mitchell, Karl Scholz, Dan Silverman, Jon Skinner, Tim Smeeding, and Mel Stephens for comments on this chapter. He is grateful to Barry Cynamon for his excellent research assistance.

Notes

[1] The classic references include Modigliani and Brumberg (1954) and Friedman (1957). The standard life-cycle model usually assumes that household utility is separable in consumption and leisure; Heckman (1974) proposes a life-cycle model with utility being nonseparable between consumption and leisure.

[2] This survey focuses on recent innovations in retirement spending, although evidence about the existence of a retirement consumption puzzle extends back over two decades. The classic reference is Hamermesh (1984); that paper uses data from the 1973 and 1975 RHS to show that expenditures of retirees fall sharply in the first few years after retirement.

[3] Fisher et al. (2006) create three separate five-year birth year cohorts within the CEX data. We report the results for the third cohort, which in terms of magnitude was in the middle of the first and second cohorts. The first cohort (the cohort that retired during the mid-1990s) looked different than the second and third cohorts. While the second and third cohorts experienced substantial declines in food spending upon retirement, their first cohort experienced little change in food spending upon retirement.

[4] Fisher et al. (2006) only broke out food as a separate consumption category. They did not separately analyze other categories such as work-related expenses or entertainment.

[5] Lundberg, Startz, and Stillman (2003) document declines in food expenditures within the PSID for married households.

[6] Actually, Aguiar and Hurst (2005) find that measured food consumption increases slightly as households transition into retirement. This would be consistent with a modest substitution effect resulting from the fact that the price of 'producing' a unit of food has declined after retirement.

[7] As discussed above, Bernheim, Skinner, and Weinberg (2001) use a composite consumption measure, which is based on food consumed at home, food consumed away from home, and the implicit or actual rental cost of housing.

[8] These statistics come from using Table 2a and Appendix Table A1 of Bernheim, Skinner, and Weinberg (2001).

[9] Ameriks, Caplin, and Leahy (2007), using their survey of TIAA-CREF participants, find results similar to those reported by Hurd and Rohwedder. Specifically, 47 percent of retired households reported experiencing a decline in total expenditures at the time of retirement while 22 percent experienced an increase in expenditures at the time of retirement. As in the other studies, the decline in expenditure was largest for those with low wealth; this is interesting in view of the fact that the TIAA-CREF sample is better educated and much more likely to be high income than the nationally representative sample of CAMS participants. Using the German Socio-Economic Panel, Schwerdt (2005) also finds similar evidence: he shows that households with low retirement income replacement rates experienced much larger expenditure declines than households with high retirement income replacement rates.

[10] This is the view expressed by Banks, Blundell, and Tanner (1998: 769) who state: 'We argue that the only way to reconcile fully the fall in consumption [at retirement] with the life-cycle hypothesis is with the systematic arrival of unexpected adverse information.'

[11] There is a well-established relationship between household wealth and household health. Hurd and Rohwedder (2005) show that those who cite adverse health shocks as a reason for retirement in the CAMS and HRS had significantly worse reported health prior to retirement.

[12] Despite the suggestions of Heckman (1974) and Laitner and Silverman (2005), there is no evidence that consumption and leisure, on average, are substitutes in utility.

References

Aguiar, Mark and Erik Hurst (2005). 'Consumption vs. Expenditure,' *Journal of Political Economy*, 113(5): 919–48.

—— —— (2007*a*). 'Lifecycle Prices and Lifecycle Production,' *American Economic Review*, 97(5): 1533–59.

—— —— (2007*b*). 'Re-examining Lifecycle Consumption.' Department of Economics Working Paper. University of Chicago.

Ameriks, John, Andrew Caplin, and John Leahy (2007). 'Retirement Consumption: Insights from a Survey,' *Review of Economics and Statistics*, MIT Press, 89(2): 265–74.

Attanasio, Orazio (1999). 'Consumption,' in J. B. Taylor and M. Woodford (eds.), *Handbook of Macroeconomics*. Amsterdam, North Holland: Elsevier Science, pp. 731–803.

Banks, James, Richard Blundell, and Sarah Tanner (1998). 'Is There a Retirement Savings Puzzle?' *American Economic Review*, 88(4): 769–88.

Battistin, Erich, Agar Brugiavini, Enrico Rettore, and Guglielmo Weber (2006). 'How Large is the Retirement Consumption Drop in Italy?' Paper presented at the RTN meeting on the Economics of Aging, Venice, October.

Becker, Gary (1965). 'A Theory of the Allocation of Time,' *The Economic Journal*, 75(September): 493–517.

Bernheim, Douglas, Jonathan Skinner, and Steven Weinberg (2001). 'What Accounts for the Variation in Retirement Wealth Among U.S. Households?' *American Economic Review*, 91(4): 832–57.

Fisher, Jonathan, David Johnson, Joseph Marchand, Timothy Smeeding, and Barbara Boyle Torrey (2006). 'The Retirement Consumption Conundrum: Evidence from a Consumption Survey,' Center for Retirement Research Working Paper no. 109.

Friedman, Milton (1957). *A Theory of the Consumption Function*. Princeton, NJ: Princeton University Press.

Haider, Steven and Melvin Stephens (2007). 'Is There a Retirement Consumption Puzzle? Evidence Using Subjective Retirement Expectations,' *Review of Economics and Statistics*, MIT Press, 89(2): 244–64.

Hamermesh, Daniel (1984). 'Consumption During Retirement: The Missing Link in the Life Cycle,' *Review of Economics and Statistics*, 66(1): 1–7.

Heckman, James (1974). 'Life Cycle Consumption and Labor Supply: An Explanation of the Relationship Between Income and Consumption Over the Life Cycle,' *American Economic Review*, 64(1): 188–94.

Hurd, Michael and Susann Rohwedder (2003). 'The Retirement Consumption Puzzle: Anticipated and Actual Declines in Retirement Spending,' NBER working paper no. 9586. Cambridge, MA: National Bureau of Economic Research.

—— —— (2005). 'Changes in Consumption and Activities in Retirement,' DNB working paper no. 39. Amsterdam: De Nederlansche Bank.

—— —— (2006). 'Some Answers to the Retirement Consumption Puzzle,' NBER Working Paper no. 12057. Cambridge, MA: National Bureau of Economic Research.

Hurst, Erik (2006). 'Grasshoppers, Ants and Pre-Retirement Wealth: A Test of Permanent Income Consumers,' NBER Working Paper no. 10098. Cambridge, MA: National Bureau of Economic Research.

Laitner, John and Dan Silverman (2005). 'Estimating Life-Cycle Parameters from Consumption Behavior at Retirement,' NBER Working Paper no. 11163. Cambridge, MA: National Bureau of Economic Research.

Lundberg, Shelly, Richard Startz, and Steven Stillman (2003). 'The Retirement Consumption Puzzle: A Marital Bargaining Approach,' *Journal of Public Economics*, 87(5–6): 1199–218.

McClellan, Mark (1998). 'Health Events, Health Insurance and Labor Supply: Evidence from Health and Retirement Survey,' in D. Wise (ed.), *Frontiers in the Economics of Aging*. Chicago, IL: University of Chicago Press, pp. 301–46.

Miniaci, Raffaele, Chiara Monfardini, and Guglielmo Weber (2003). 'Is There a Retirement Consumption Puzzle in Italy?' Institute for Fiscal Studies Working Paper no. WP03/14.

Modigliani, Franco and Richard Brumberg (1954). 'Utility Analysis and the Consumption Function: An Interpretation of the Cross Section Data,' in K. Kurihara (ed.), *Post-Keynesian Economics*. New Brunswick, NJ: Rutgers University Press, pp. 388–436.

Scholz, John Karl, Ananth Seshadri, and Surachai Khitatrakun (2006). 'Are Americans Saving 'Optimally' for Retirement?' *Journal of Political Economy*, 114(4): 607–43.

Schwerdt, Guido (2005). 'Why Does Consumption Fall at Retirement? Evidence from Germany,' *Economics Letters*, (89): 300–5.

Smith, Sarah (2006). 'The Retirement Consumption Puzzle and Involuntary Early Retirement: Evidence from the British Household Panel Survey,' *The Economic Journal*, 116(510): C130–48.

Chapter 4

Net Worth and Housing Equity in Retirement

Todd Sinai and Nicholas Souleles

Real house prices grew by about 40 percent on average and by as much as 100 percent in some metropolitan areas between 2000 and 2005 in the USA. This rapid growth has renewed interest in identifying the role that housing equity plays in the net worth of retirees, and how much of their housing equity retirees can tap to fund nonhousing consumption. This chapter documents how the evolution of house prices since 1983 has affected life-cycle profiles of net worth. We also estimate how much of the growth of housing equity is actually available for nonhousing consumption for households nearing retirement age and older.

In what follows, we use the Survey of Consumer Finances (SCF) to show that the net worth of retirement-age households rose significantly in the early part of this decade, tracking trends in house prices. Although housing equity also rose, it did not grow as much as net worth, in this part because nonhousing assets appreciated at the same time as housing. In addition, it appears that younger elderly increased their housing debt to offset some of the rise in house values and invested some of the proceeds from the debt in other assets. We then consider how much of households' housing equity is available for nonhousing consumption without moving. Many elderly are reluctant to move, and even if they do move they might not want to downsize.[1] Nevertheless, the elderly can borrow against their house value, essentially transferring wealth from their heirs (after death) to current consumption. We use a convenient measure of the equity available to be extracted from a house: the amount that can be borrowed via a reverse mortgage. In theory, a reverse mortgage is an ideal way to consume home equity without incurring the transactions costs from moving.[2] It provides homeowners a lump-sum loan that accrues interest and is settled against the sale of the house when the homeowner dies or moves out. We consider two forms of reverse mortgages: first, a theoretical 'upper-bound' reverse mortgage product that provides the maximum possible liquidity; and, second, the actual reverse mortgage products available in 2007, which appear to still suffer the drawbacks of having a small market.

Our results show that older homeowners have considerable housing equity that they can borrow against, but nowhere near as much as standard measures of housing equity would imply. These results motivate calculating a modified measure of net worth, 'consumable net worth', that accounts for the fact that, absent moving, not all housing wealth is available for nonhousing consumption. Even among households aged 62–69 who have consumable housing equity, the median consumable net worth in the upper-bound case is only three-quarters of the standard measure of net worth. At age 90, the median household could consume only 91 percent of standard net worth.

Compared to prior research, our chapter makes two contributions. First, we provide updated cohort and over-time analyses of how net worth and housing equity have evolved, including during the recent housing boom, building on Poterba and Samwick (2001) and Coronado, Maki, and Weitzer (2007), among others. The former study uses the SCF to provide a cohort analysis through 1992 that includes housing wealth and housing debt. Coronado, Maki, and Weitzer (2007) analyze home equity and net worth using two waves of the Health and Retirement Study (HRS). Our work uses the SCF, which enables us to examine many more cohorts and much older households (up through age 94, compared to age 61 in the original HRS cohort). Second, we provide new estimates of how consumable housing equity and consumable net worth evolve with age, cohort, and time.[3]

In what follows, we first describe the data used for our calculations. Next, we show how net worth, housing equity, and housing debt evolve over the life cycle, over time, and by birth cohort. Then we turn to calculating the amount of housing equity available for nonhousing consumption and the modified measure of consumable net worth. Finally, we briefly conclude.

Before proceeding, it is worth emphasizing that housing is different than most other assets on household balance sheets because of its dual nature as both an asset and a consumption good. Since people must live somewhere, they have an implicit liability for housing services that is not recorded in standard measures of net housing equity and net worth (Sinai and Souleles 2005). Buying a home provides those housing services, but only the housing asset (net of housing debt) appears on the balance sheet, not the bundled liability.[4] Thus unlike, for instance, a stock portfolio, the housing portfolio cannot be completely liquidated because there would be no provision for the housing service liability. Instead, a household must find another way to extract equity. Complicating the interpretation of the results, changes in house prices do not necessarily lead to increases in real wealth, even if housing equity can be reallocated to nonhousing consumption. Because the price of housing reflects the present value of the entire stream of future housing services, for young households who are most 'short' housing services, increases in house prices can be largely offset by increases in their housing services liability, leaving their real wealth largely unchanged. But for older homeowners who have a smaller remaining implicit housing liability, increases in house prices can translate into larger increases in real wealth, and thus potentially into higher nonhousing consumption.[5] However, this increase in consumption comes at the expense of the next generation, which no longer stands to inherit the increased housing equity, but still inherits the commensurately higher housing liability.

Empirical Evidence

The data used for our analysis of housing trends were obtained from the Federal Reserve Board's SCF. The SCF is conducted every three years, and we use the seven cross-sectional survey waves gathered from 1983 to 2004 (excluding the 1986 Survey). The SCF oversamples high-wealth families, yielding a large number of observations on holders of various assets and liabilities.[6] To make the estimates more representative of the overall population of the USA, we apply the SCF's replicate weights. We exclude households where the head was under the age of 25, age 95+, or born before 1900; and households whose primary residence was a ranch or farm, or a mobile home.[7] This yields almost 113,000 observations across the seven surveys.[8] With population weights, the data are representative of 71 million households in 1983 and 97 million in 2004. All dollar values are inflated to 2004 dollars using the consumer price index (CPI) research series for all urban consumers (CPI-U-RS).

We categorize the SCF households variously by age, birth cohort, survey year, and remaining life expectancy. We define the age of a household by the age of the household head, which, by the SCF convention, is defined as the male spouse of a married couple, the older spouse of a same-sex couple, or the adult in a single-headed household. The birth cohort is the decade in which that household head was born, such as 1910–19 for a head aged 89 in 2004.[9] Remaining life expectancy was obtained from actuarial tables created by the Social Security Administration.[10] These tables report expected remaining lifetime and the distribution of the probability of dying in each future year separately for men and women by age and year. We merge this to SCF respondents by sex, age, and year. In the case of married couples, we assume the expected remaining lifetime for the household is the maximum of the expected remaining lifetimes over both spouses.

Life-Cycle Analysis of Housing Equity and Net Worth

We begin by examining the accumulation and decumulation of assets and liabilities over the life cycle, focusing on the contribution of housing equity to both phases. Since the SCF data are cross-sectional, we do not actually follow the same households over time; instead we must make an assumption to infer what their life-cycle profiles look like. We can assume either that households of different ages observed in the same year are comparable, despite being born in different years, or that households of different ages but from the same birth cohort are comparable, despite being observed in different years. We analyze the results under both assumptions.

The first panel of Figure 4-1 provides a cohort-based life-cycle analysis for household net worth.[11] The household's age, categorized by five-year groupings, is on the horizontal axis; net worth, given in thousands of 2004 dollars, is on the vertical axis. Each line segment corresponds to the median net worth for households born in a particular decade. Most segments span multiple age bins because we have 21 years of surveys. For example, someone born in 1960 will be in the 25–29 bin as of the 1989 survey, the 30–34 bin in the 1992 survey, the 35–39 bin in the 1995 and 1998 surveys, and the 40–44 bin in the 2001 and 2004 surveys. The dots correspond to the median net worth across all households in that age bin, regardless of birth cohort. (Cohort × age groups that have fewer than 11 observations are omitted from the segment drawings, but not from the calculations for the dots.)

The dots illustrate the usual age profile for net worth, with a steady accumulation between age 25 and 64, and generally a decumulation thereafter. Net worth peaks at retirement age at around a median of $250,000 (in 2004 dollars). There are two other notable results in this figure. First, median net worth declines until age 80 (falling to just under $200,000), but then, for the 1900–09 and 1910–19 cohorts, begins to rise again. Second, while the cohort line segments are tightly overlapping for households between the ages of 25 and 54, they diverge after that. That is, for the most recent periods (the most recent age bins), the segments lie above the prior cohorts' segment. This is especially true for the 1930–39 and 1940–49 birth cohorts.

Potential explanations for these patterns can be found in Panel B of Figure 4-1, which calculates the age profile of median net worth by the year of the SCF survey. For clarity, only a subset of the SCF years is displayed. The dots, being sample medians by age computed using all the SCF years, are the same across both panels. In Panel B, the different SCFs' age profiles generally peak between age 55 and 64 and, with the exception of the 2004 SCF, decline with age or are level through age 94. Analogous to the first panel, there is relatively little difference in median net worth across SCFs

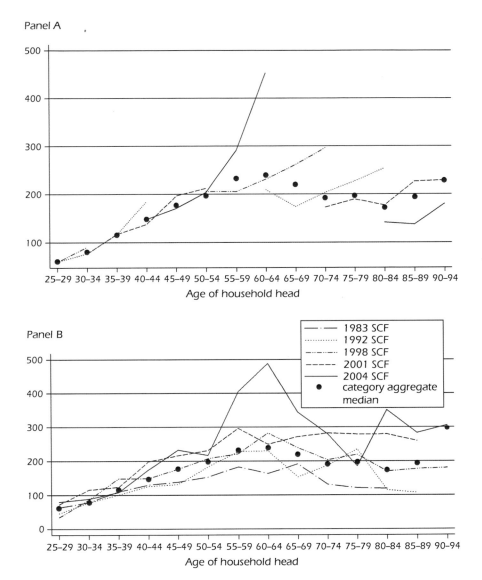

Figure 4-1. Median net worth in the Survey of Consumer Finances (SCF). Panel A: Net worth by age and birth cohort. Panel B: Net worth by age and SCF year. *Source*: Authors' computations from Survey of Consumer Finances 1983–2004. *Note*: Sample limited to homeowners with positive net worth. We exclude age × cohort or age × SCF year cells with fewer than 11 observations. Values are in thousands of 2004 dollars.

for households under age 55. But for older households, net worth grows from 1983 to 1998, and then from 1998 through 2004.[12] These results suggest that the 2001 and 2004 increases in net worth for households approaching retirement age and older are responsible for the earlier patterns in the cohort analysis in the first panel. That is, the upward slant of the cohort lines is due to net worth growing over time for everyone, rather than age-based accumulation. For example, the 1930–39 and 1940–49 cohort lines in the top panel have the steepest increase in their last two age bins because they have the most concentrated exposure to 2001 and 2004 in those bins. Likewise, the upturn in net worth in the top panel between age 85 and 94 could be due to the run-up in the 2000s overwhelming the usual life-cycle drawdown of net worth.

One key factor behind the rise in net worth between 1998 and 2004 is the growth in housing values. As displayed in Figure 4-2, during the seven years between 1998 and 2004, the index of real national average house prices rose by about 25 percent, more than the growth over the 16 years between 1983 and 1998.[13] The index measures house price appreciation from repeat sales of the same houses, thus controlling for changes in the quality or size

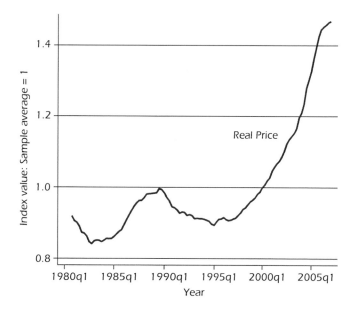

Figure 4-2. Time patterns in real house prices (1980:1–2007:1). *Source*: OFHEO Conventional Mortgage House Price Index; BLS CPI-All Urban Consumers. *Note*: The index is normalized so that the average over the sample period equals one.

of houses. This raises the question: How much of the recent growth in net worth among households of retirement age was due to growth in housing values?

It appears that at least some of the growth in net worth was due to growth in housing values, but not all. Both the cohort and SCF-year graphs of median home equity by age in Figure 4-3 mimic the patterns for net worth in Figure 4-1, indicating that growth in home equity played a role. However, while housing clearly accounts for a large portion of the recent increase in net worth for seniors, the dollar amounts in Figures 4-3A and 4-3B are smaller than for net worth (both on average and for the changes over time). For example, while median home equity for 65- to 69-year olds rose from about $100,000 to $140,000 between 1998 and 2004, median net worth rose from about $220,000 to $320,000. In addition, the rise in the value of home equity between 1983 and 2001 occurred almost exclusively for households aged 65 and over while the increase in net worth was spread across all ages.[14] Indeed, Figure 4-4 shows that while net worth *excluding* housing equity still shows a substantial increase between 1983 and 2004, nonhousing net worth grew over this time period for all ages, not just for those over age 65. These differences suggest that housing equity growth alone cannot fully explain net worth.

Another way to see that net worth rose by more than housing equity is shown in Figure 4-5. Conditional on home-owning, the ratio of housing equity to net worth is relatively constant at about 40–60 percent over the life cycle and over time. (The ratio starts to increase at retirement, rising from 40 percent to about 70 percent for the oldest seniors, consistent with households drawing down their liquid assets first.) This persistence over time can happen only when net worth experiences the same percentage growth as home equity which, given the higher initial level of net worth, implies that net worth increases more in absolute terms than housing equity. In addition, the time pattern of the equity-to-net-worth ratio does not match the growth of house prices. In 1983, equity to net worth was unusually high and for the 1998 through 2004 SCFs the ratio is generally *lower* (for any given age).

While the growth in housing equity may not fully explain the rise in net worth, the growth in house values may do better. That is, if homeowners increased their housing debt to offset rising house values and used the proceeds to invest in other assets, that could explain a pattern of net worth rising faster than housing equity.[15] One fact consistent with this hypothesis is that the growth in net worth was concentrated in the population of homeowners. If one re-graphs Panel A of Figure 4-1 while restricting the sample to homeowners, the results for their net worth look very similar to the original results for the overall population's net worth. By contrast, the corresponding graph for renters looks much different: renters' net worth

Panel A

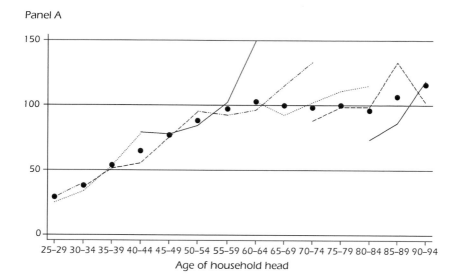

Age of household head

Panel B

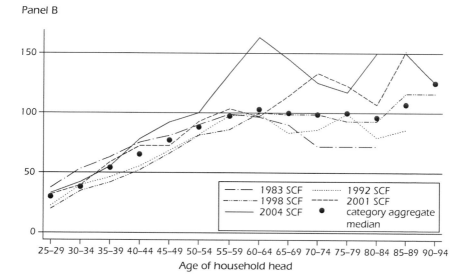

Age of household head

Figure 4-3. Median home equity in the Survey of Consumer Finances (SCF). Panel A: Home equity by age and birth cohort; Panel B: Home equity by age and SCF year. *Source*: See Figure 4-1. *Notes*: Sample limited to homeowners with positive home equity and positive net worth. Values are in thousands of 2004 dollars.

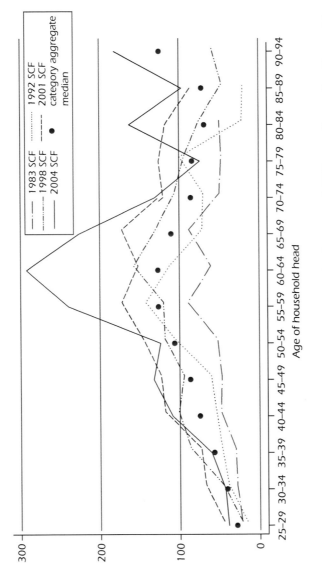

Figure 4-4. Median net worth exclusive of home equity, by age and SCF year. *Source:* See Figure 4-1. *Notes:* Sample is limited to homeowners with positive net worth and home equity, and with $0 <$ home equity/net worth < 1. Values are in thousands of 2004 dollars.

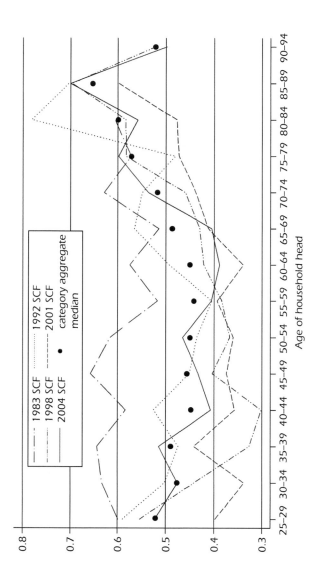

Figure 4-5. Median ratio of home equity to total net worth, by age and SCF year. *Source*: See Figure 4-1. *Notes*: Sample limited to homeowners with positive net worth and home equity, and with zero < home equity/net worth < one. Values are in thousands of 2004 dollars.

does not rise with age and does not increase with house values. (However, the data are somewhat noisy at older ages, since few elderly rent).

Of course, one cannot automatically conclude from these last results that the rise in house values was solely responsible for the growth in net worth for home-owning seniors. First, the population of renters is potentially very different from the population of owners. For example, renters are generally poorer and less likely to own assets that can significantly appreciate. Their median net worth is quite low, under $10,000 for most of the life cycle. Second, the fraction of seniors that rents is small. As shown in Figure 4-6, by age 35, the majority of households own their homes; by retirement age, some 80 percent of households are owners. The homeownership rate does not begin to decline much until age 80, reaching 60 percent only by age 90–94. Thus, the vast majority of elderly do not sell their homes and become renters. In general, there is no clear time pattern across SCFs in the homeownership rate. While the data are somewhat noisy, there is some indication that the homeownership rate among the elderly rose between 1983 and 2004, from 60–70 percent to 70–80 percent, depending on the household's age.

As house values rose more than housing equity, this suggests that home-owners may have reallocated their housing equity into other assets. Yet this appears to be less so the case for the elderly than for households aged 60–64 or younger. Figure 4-7 reports the *gross* value (not subtracting debt) of a household's primary residence. The figure clearly shows the rise in house values in recent years, as the age profiles from more recent SCFs lie above those from earlier SCFs, sometimes by as much as 30 percent. Comparing Figure 4-7 to Figure 4-3, Panel B (home equity), one can see that the dollar increase in house values often exceeds the increase in home equity. In Figure 4-7, there is a steady rise over time in house values, which appears at all ages and is especially pronounced for households aged 65 and over. By contrast, in Figure 4-3B, home equity does not grow much between 1983 and 2001 for those under age 65. For example, the median home equity rose by about $60,000 between 1983 and 2004 for households aged 60–64. House values for the same age group increased by about $100,000 over that same time period. After age 65, however, housing equity tracks house values more closely. The increase in home equity between 1983 and 2004 is much closer to the growth in house values for the 65–69 age group and, by age 70–74, is almost exactly the same.

One possible explanation is that younger households' housing debt, including first and second mortgages as well as home equity loans and lines of credit, rose along with house values. For seniors, this explanation is limited by the fact that few seniors have any housing debt. In the top panel of Figure 4-8, only about 60 percent of home-owning households

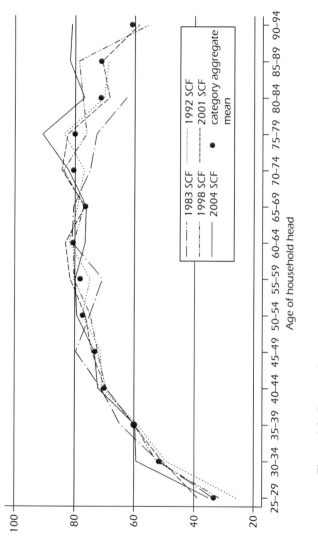

Figure 4-6. Percent homeowners by age and SCF year. *Source.* See Figure 4-1.

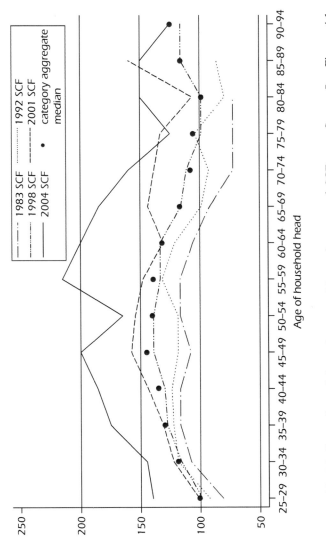

Figure 4-7. Median value of the primary residence by age and SCF year. *Source*: See Figure 4-1. *Notes*: Sample limited to homeowners. Values are in thousands of 2004 dollars.

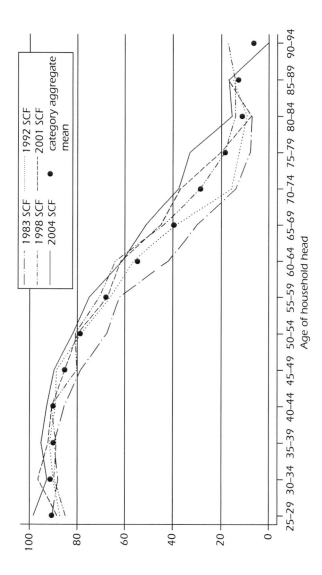

Figure 4-8. Percent of households with any housing debt by age and SCF year. *Source:* See Figure 4-1. *Notes:* Sample is limited to homeowners.

aged 60–64 have any housing debt whatsoever, and this ratio steadily declines with age until it levels out at about 10 percent of households aged 80 and above. While this age profile is relatively stable over time, a smaller fraction of households of almost any age had housing debt in 1983 and a larger fraction held housing debt in 2004. Especially for households aged 65 through 80, borrowing against the house appears to have become steadily more prevalent over the 1983 through 2004 time period, rising by as much as 20 percentage points.

Conditional on having any housing debt, the *amount* of debt rose substantially. In Figure 4-9, the pattern of the dots indicates that median debt amounts decline with age. However, the households surveyed in more recent SCF years have higher debt levels at almost every age through 70–74. Unlike the frequency of having housing debt, the rise in the amount of debt is largely a younger-household phenomenon. (One important caveat: since so few of the very elderly have debt, it is difficult to draw inferences for that age group.)[16]

One reason that the amount of housing debt rose with house values might be that households tend to keep their leverage ratio constant. Figure 4-10 reports median loan-to-house value (LTV) ratios by age for homeowners who have housing debt. Indeed, except from 1983 to 1992, the age profiles of LTV have not changed much over time. Thus the (*percent*) growth in debt has generally kept up with the (percent) growth in house values, keeping the ratio of debt to value roughly constant. This implies that while the *dollar* amount of home equity rose with the increase in house prices, it did not rise as much in absolute terms as house values. And given how few elderly have housing debt, even the apparent increases in leverage between 1992/1998 and 2001/2004 for homeowners aged 75 and older have only a small effect on aggregate leverage.

In the absence of panel data, it is difficult to directly show whether households actually used the proceeds from higher housing debt to invest in other assets. Nonetheless, in the two panels of Figure 4-11 we attempt to shed some light on the matter. Panel A reports the median value of nonhousing assets, measured as total assets minus the value of the primary residence. Panel B reports the median value of nonhousing assets minus housing debt, measured as total assets minus both the value of the primary residence *and* the debt on that house. If housing debt is reallocated, at least in part, to investments in nonhousing assets rather than being wholly spent on current consumption, we would expect the life-cycle profiles in the top panel to increase over time more than the ones in the bottom panel. To elaborate on the comparison: *ceteris paribus*, changes in house values without a change in housing debt should affect neither the top nor the bottom panels since only nonhousing assets are measured.

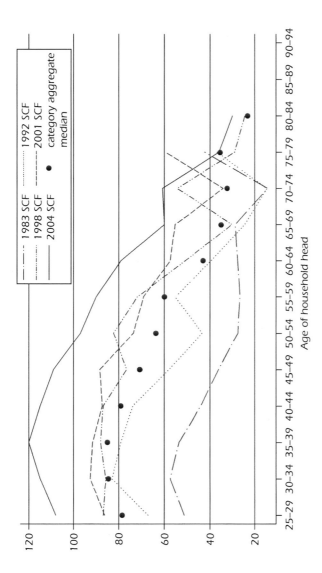

Figure 4-9. Total housing debt for households with any housing debt by age and SCF year. *Source*: See Figure 4-1. *Notes*: Sample is limited to homeowners with any housing debt. Values are in thousands of 2004 dollars.

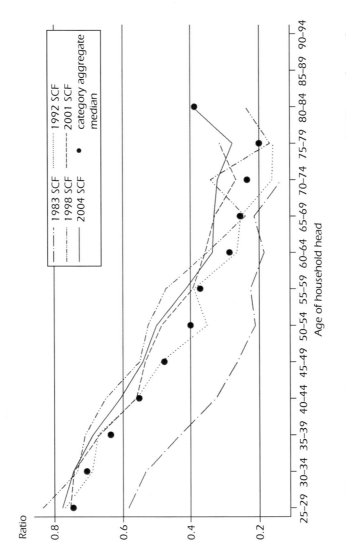

Figure 4-10. Median ratio of home secured loans to home value by age and SCF year. *Source*: See Figure 4-1. *Notes*: Sample is limited to homeowners with positive primary residence debt.

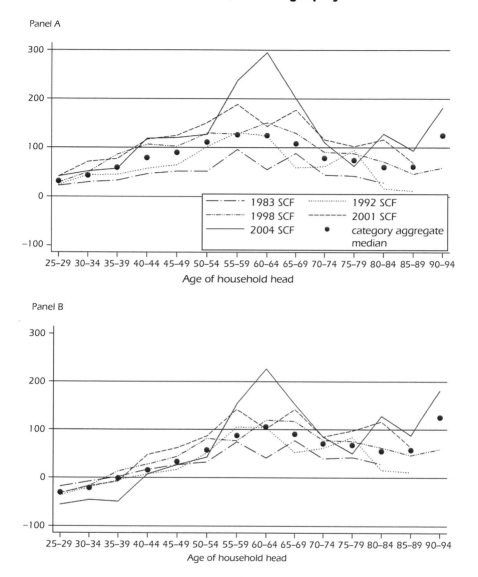

Figure 4-11. Median value of assets minus primary residence value in the Survey of Consumer Finances (SCF). Panel A: Value of assets minus primary residence value by age and SCF year. Panel B: Value of assets minus primary residence value by age and SCF year. *Source*: See Figure 4-1. *Notes*: Sample limited to homeowners. Values are in thousands of 2004 dollars.

Changes in the value of nonhousing assets should have the same effect on both the top and the bottom panels. However, an increase in housing debt that is used to invest in nonhousing assets should raise the life-cycle profile in the top panel (since assets go up but housing debt is not netted out) but *not* in the bottom panel (where housing debt is netted out). Conversely, an increase in housing debt that is spent would have no effect on the top panel but would lower the life-cycle profile in the bottom panel.

For younger households, below age 65, the top panel shows a rising life-cycle profile between 1983 and 2004. By contrast, the bottom panel exhibits no such pattern and, in fact, the 2004 profile lies below most of the other profiles through age 54. This pattern suggests that while nonhousing assets rose faster than house values for the median household in this age range, the difference could be explained by growth in housing debt. For households aged 65 and over, nonhousing assets were also growing steadily between 1983 and 2004. But unlike for younger households, there is less difference between the top and bottom panels for the 65-and-up households and almost no difference by age 75. Again, that is because so few of the very elderly hold housing debt, so at the median there can be little reallocation from housing equity to net worth.

Last, we consider the fact that trends in house values might reflect not just changes in house prices, but also moves to different houses and other changes in the quantity or quality of housing. The SCF does not report a household's entire housing history. But, in addition to (self-reported) current house value, the survey asks for the price that homeowners paid for their current house when they purchased it and how much they spent on remodeling and additions in the interim. This allows us to roughly estimate how much of households' housing equity is due to the capital gain on their current house. Figure 4-12 reports median real housing capital gains expressed as a percentage of house equity. We construct this variable by taking the difference between the self-reported house value (in 2004 dollars) and the self-reported purchase price (in 2004 dollars), subtracting out spending on remodeling and additions, and then dividing by current housing equity.[17] Given the limitations of the data, the resulting measure will likely provide a lower bound on the actual fraction of housing equity due to capital gains.[18]

Even so, in 2001 and 2004 the fraction of housing equity due to capital gains rose substantially, to more than 30 percent of housing equity for the most senior elderly. In earlier years, by contrast, housing capital gains appear to have contributed relatively little to housing equity. In any case, in recent years housing capital gains were clearly a large source of wealth for households in retirement.

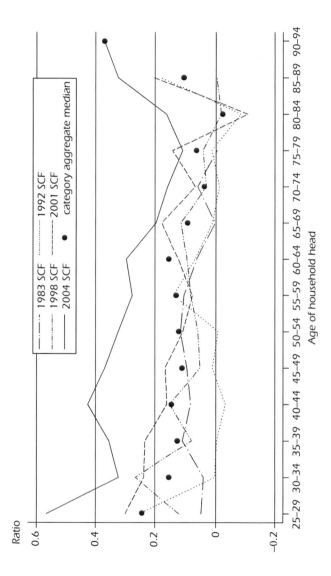

Figure 4-12. Median ratio of capital gains and losses on homes to total home equity, by age and SCF Year. *Source:* See Figure 4-1. *Note:* Sample limited to homeowners who acquired homes after 1966 and have positive home equity.

Consumable Housing Equity and Net Worth

Given the recent increase in housing equity documented above, we next assess how much of that equity the elderly can tap, both in theory and in practice.

Methodology

To implement this, we compute the amount of housing equity consumable by a household without moving, using two variants of a reverse mortgage. First, we calculate the theoretical upper-bound amount that a homeowner could borrow against his house from a risk-neutral lender. Second, as a lower bound, we identify how much a homeowner could borrow using the actual reverse mortgage programs in place in the first quarter of 2007. After computing the resulting amounts of consumable housing equity, we calculate the corresponding modified measures of consumable net worth, which includes only consumable housing equity rather than all housing equity.

We follow Venti and Wise (1991) in computing the maximum fraction of a house's value that could be borrowed using a reverse mortgage from a risk-neutral lender. Suppose a household borrows a lump-sum amount L today, lets it cumulatively compound, and pays off the resulting total liability at death using the proceeds from the sale of the house. This is basically how current reverse mortgages work. Since the bank is risk neutral, it will set the initial loan amount such that in expectation the sale value of the house will exactly equal the mortgage balance at the time of the homeowner's death. In this case, the initial loan amount L is determined by:

$$L = \sum_{t=a}^{A} \left[(1+g)^{t-a} H \right] d(t|a)(1+m)^{-(t-a)} d \qquad (4\text{-}1)$$

where a is the current age of the homeowner, H is the current house value, and $d(t|a)$ is the probability of dying in year t conditional on being age a currently. (In the case of married couples, we use the age of the youngest spouse, which determines the conditional survival probability as used by reverse mortgage lenders.) The nominal mortgage interest rate is m and g is the nominal growth rate of house prices, for simplicity both assumed to be constant and $m > g$. In our calculations, for m we use the average nominal 30-year mortgage interest rate in the year the household reports having taken out the loan. For g, we will use the long-run average national real growth rate in house prices, 1 percent per year, plus the expected 10-year average annual inflation rate from the Livingston Survey in the year of the SCF survey.

TABLE 4-1 'Upper-Bound' Housing Equity Available for Consumption, by Age

Age Category	'Consumable' Housing Equity		Median Ratio 'Consumable' Housing Equity to House Equity	Median Net Worth Using 'Consumable' Housing Equity	Median Ratio 'Consumable' Net Worth to Standard Net Worth
	% > 0	Median Value if > 0			
25–61	34.7	25,690	0.26	117,991	0.59
62–69	88.5	50,499	0.49	173,534	0.74
70–79	95.8	66,728	0.64	160,743	0.80
80–89	99.1	76,752	0.78	164,036	0.86
90–94	100.0	103,093	0.89	217,212	0.91
Median if age ≥ 62	93.6	62,673	0.60	166,116	0.80

Source: Authors' computations.

Notes: 'Consumable' housing equity is defined as the amount of capital that could be extracted from a house by a risk-neutral mortgage lender (given the owners' ages and genders and prevailing 30-year fixed mortgage rates), less the existing debt secured by the primary residence. Net worth using 'consumable' housing equity replaces housing equity in the net worth calculation with 'consumable' housing equity. Sample includes homeowners with houses with values less than $1 million, 1989–2004 SCF.

From L, we net out existing housing debt D to obtain our measure of consumable housing equity, CHE $\equiv L - D$. While L must be nonnegative, CHE can be negative if existing debt exceeds the amount of potential reverse mortgage. (In this case, the household can be thought of as having a net housing liability, in that it will need to pay for a portion of its housing consumption out of income or nonhousing wealth.)

The potential loan amount L is primarily a function of the expected remaining lifetime of the household. If a household is expected to live a long time, any amount it borrows has a long time to compound before it is settled against the proceeds of the house sale. Thus the lender, who in expectation needs to have the sale value of the house equal the accumulated debt in order to break even, will lend a smaller initial amount to a young household, *ceteris paribus*. An older household could borrow a greater fraction of the house value since it will repay the loan sooner.[19]

Results

The results of applying Equation (4-1) are tabulated by age in Table 4-1. The first column reports the fraction of households who have positive consumable housing equity. Very few young households have positive consumable equity (first row of the first column), and for those that do, the median amount of equity is small (first row of the second column). This is because young households have high debt loads relative to house value and long life expectancies. By comparison, older households are more likely to have positive consumable home equity and greater amounts of equity. Given the topic of this chapter, we will focus on the households aged 62 and older.

It is clear from Table 4-1 that older households have the potential for significant consumable housing equity. For those aged 62–69, for example, among the 88.5 percent with positive consumable equity, the median amount is almost $50,500. By age 90, all home-owning households have consumable housing equity, in part because housing debt is almost nonexistent and also because remaining life expectancy is short. The median amount of consumable equity for that age group is about $103,000.

While consumable home equity can be substantial in dollar terms, it can nonetheless be a relatively small fraction of housing equity as measured in the standard way. For example, households aged 62–69 can consume only 49 percent of their standard housing equity.[20] By age 70–79, only about two-thirds of housing equity is consumable, and even by age 90, less than 90 percent is consumable.

Using consumable housing equity also makes a big difference to net worth. The fifth column of Table 4-1 calculates consumable net worth using our measure of consumable housing equity rather than the standard measure of housing equity, and the sixth column compares the result to the standard definition of net worth. For younger households, consumable net worth is only a small fraction of reported net worth, again because they have relatively larger debt and longer life expectancies. (One can think of one's housing asset as being largely dedicated to paying for one's large future housing liability, and so effectively unavailable for nonhousing consumption.) By age 62–69, less than three-quarters of the standard measure of net worth is consumable. Even by age 90, only 91 percent of net worth is consumable.

While Table 4-1 provides a useful theoretical benchmark, in practice reverse mortgage markets do not generally allow one to borrow as much as assumed using Equation (4-1). First, legal and marketing considerations require that lenders collect the lesser of their debt position or the house value. Thus, they reduce the initial loan amounts to be relatively confident that the house value will exceed the debt position at the time of death. Second, problems of adverse selection (long-lived borrowers) and moral hazard (borrowers do not maintain their houses) also reduce the amount that lenders are willing to lend. Finally, current reverse mortgage markets might also suffer from other early-stage problems of a new financial product, such as thinness or lack of familiarity.

To bound the differences between the theoretical and current reverse mortgages, we recalculate consumable housing equity using the actual amount a household could borrow through a current reverse mortgage, using the program parameters in place in the first quarter of 2007. We used the on-line reverse mortgage calculator (www.financialfreedom.com/calculator) to calculate how much a borrower in zip code 60614 (Cook County, Chicago) could obtain from the three primary reverse mortgage programs: Federal Housing Administration/Department of Housing and Urban Development's (FHA/HUD) 'Home Equity Conversion Mortgage (HECM) Advantage', Fannie Mae's 'Homekeeper', and Financial Freedom's 'Cash Account Advantage.' These programs currently lend only to those aged 62 or older, so we computed the potential loan amount for each aged between 62 and 94, and for house values in $25,000 increments between $0 and $1 million. For each age × house value cell, we used the maximum loan amount from the three programs. That loan amount was imputed to households in the SCF using the age of the youngest spouse and their self-reported house value. When the SCF house value lay between the $25,000 bins, we linearly interpolated the loan amount. From this potential reverse mortgage amount we netted out existing housing debt, since that is what a reverse mortgage lender would do.

The amount one can borrow through the reverse mortgage market has been increasing steadily over time and is expected to continue to do so. Thus we view this exercise as providing a lower bound on future access to home equity. However, we did not net out fees, which are sizable in the current reverse mortgage market—they can be upward of 15 percent of the loan amount. Thus, our calculations still overstate currently available consumable equity.

Results appear in Table 4-2, which mimics Table 4-1 but uses the new computation of consumable housing equity. Since households younger than 62 are not eligible for reverse mortgages, their consumable housing equity is no greater than zero. Overall, the actual reverse mortgage programs generally provide positive consumable housing equity to fewer households than does the upper-bound theoretical program, especially at younger ages. For example, only 60 percent of 62–69-year-olds have positive consumable housing equity under the actual reverse mortgage programs versus 88.5 percent under the theoretical upper bound. And for the households with positive equity, the actual programs generally provide a smaller amount of housing equity. In this dimension, the gap increases with age: for households aged 62 and over, median consumable housing equity (conditional on being positive) ranges from $51,000 to $94,000, or about 49 to 76 percent of total housing equity. The ratio of consumable net worth to the standard measure of net worth reflects

TABLE 4-2 Actual Housing Equity Available for Consumption, by Age

Age Category	'Consumable' Housing Equity		Median Ratio 'Consumable' Housing Equity to House Equity	Median Net Worth Using 'Consumable' Housing Equity	Median Ratio 'Consumable' Net Worth to Standard Net Worth
	% > 0	Median Value if > 0			
25–61	0.0	0	0.00	0	0.00
62–69	60.0	50,981	0.49	150,423	0.71
70–79	90.9	62,131	0.58	156,242	0.75
80–89	97.0	68,648	0.65	154,510	0.79
90–94	99.3	93,776	0.76	202,874	0.82
Median if age ≥ 62	80.1	60,429	0.56	154,205	0.75

Source: Authors' computations.

Notes: 'Consumable' housing equity is defined as the maximum amount of capital that could be extracted from a house by a reverse mortgage using the programs available in 2007, netting out the existing debt secured by the primary residence. These programs lend only to those aged 62 and older. Net worth using 'consumable' housing equity replaces housing equity in the net worth calculation with 'consumable' housing equity. Sample includes homeowners with houses with values less than $1 million, 1989–2004 SCF.

these patterns. It ranges from 71 percent for young seniors to 82 percent for the oldest seniors and is always lower than under the theoretical program.

Comparisons between Tables 4-1 and 4-2 are complicated by the fact that in Table 4-1 we used the mortgage interest and expected inflation rates at the time of the SCF survey year, but in Table 4-2, by applying the 2007 reverse mortgage program, we implicitly use 2007 rates. Table 4-3 attempts to provide a better comparison by using just the 2004 SCF households for both computations.[21] The current reverse mortgage program is less generous than the theoretical one. The current program gives markedly fewer younger retirees access to consumable housing equity—for example, only 51 percent of 62–69-year-olds versus 90 percent in the theoretical program—and the amounts of equity are also smaller.

A natural question to ask is how the recent trends in house values affected these results. Consumable housing equity will generally increase with greater house values. But, as already noted, the recent increase in house values was partly offset by increased debt. Table 4-4 explores how this process played out, focusing on the ratio of consumable net worth to standard net worth, by SCF year, using the theoretical reverse mortgage program from Table 4-1 (which generally overstates consumable housing

TABLE 4-3 Comparing 'Upper-Bound' and Actual 'Consumable' Housing Equity: 2004 Only

Age Category	Best-Case 'Consumable' Housing Equity		Reverse Mortgage 'Consumable' Housing Equity	
	% > 0	Median Value if > 0	% > 0	Median Value if > 0
25–61	36.1	44,006	0.00	0
62–69	89.5	80,110	51.2	67,768
70–79	93.7	90,497	85.7	79,875
80–89	100.0	119,776	94.7	102,961
90–94	100.0	113,128	100.0	97,810
Median if age ≥ 62	93.7	93,217	75.84	81,194

Source: Authors' computations.

Notes: In columns 2 and 3, best-case 'consumable' housing equity is defined as the amount of capital that could be extracted from a house by a risk-neutral mortgage lender in 2004 (given the owners' ages and genders and prevailing 30-year fixed mortgage rates), less the existing debt secured by the primary residence. In the last two columns, reverse mortgage 'consumable' housing equity is defined as the maximum amount of capital that could be extracted from a house by a reverse mortgage using the programs available in 2007, netting out the existing debt secured by the primary residence. These programs lend only to those aged 62 and older. Sample includes homeowners with houses with values less than $1 million, 2004 SCF.

equity). The fraction of net worth available for nonhousing consumption is at or near all-time highs for homeowners aged 62 or older. For those aged 62–69 in 1989, 69 percent of net worth was consumable; by 2004, that fraction rose to 80 percent. For 80–89-year-olds, the fraction of net worth that could be consumed rose from 83 percent in 1989 to 90 percent in 2004.

Underlying these results, the fraction of older households with *any* consumable housing equity generally declined from the relative house price peak of 1989 to the trough of 1995–8, and rose with house prices again through 2004. However, even in 2004, the fraction had not caught up to its level in 1989. This partly reflects the increased debt we observed in recent years. The turnaround in the *amount* of consumable home equity (conditional on being positive) began a little later, in 2001 or 2004, for households aged 62 and older. But by 2004, the median amounts of consumable housing equity were larger than in 1998, about double for households aged 62 and older. These recent trends reflect both the recent growth in house prices and the recent decline in interest rates.

TABLE 4-4 Ratio of Net Worth Available for Consumption to Standard Net Worth for Households with 'Consumable' Equity, Using 'Upper-Bound' Definition, by Age and Year

Age Category	Year						
	1989	1992	1995	1998	2001	2004	Median
25–61	0.50	0.57	0.58	0.61	0.62	0.65	0.59
62–69	0.69	0.73	0.73	0.74	0.76	0.80	0.74
70–79	0.77	0.82	0.79	0.79	0.80	0.83	0.80
80–89	0.83	0.85	0.85	0.86	0.88	0.90	0.86
90–94		0.90	0.88	0.91	0.89	0.96	0.91
Median if age ≥ 62	0.75	0.80	0.79	0.81	0.80	0.84	0.80

Source: Authors' computations.

Notes: 'Consumable' housing equity is defined as the amount of capital that could be extracted from a house by a risk-neutral mortgage lender (given the owners' ages and genders and prevailing 30-year fixed mortgage rates), less the existing debt secured by the primary residence. Net worth using 'consumable' housing equity replaces housing equity in the net worth calculation with 'consumable' housing equity. Sample includes homeowners with houses with values less than $1 million, 1989–2004 SCF.

Conclusions and Discussion

We have documented the evolution of the life-cycle profiles of net worth and of housing values, equity, and debt, from 1983 through 2004, using the SCF. We find that the recent increase in house prices increased the net worth of retirement-aged households, but less than one-for-one. This happened, in part, because other assets appreciated along with housing. In addition, households increased their housing debt, offsetting some of the increase in house value, and used some of the proceeds to invest in other assets. However, this latter explanation seems to be most prevalent among younger households and to a degree among the youngest elderly, but not among the oldest seniors who do not hold much housing debt. We also show that a large fraction of seniors' housing equity is not actually available for nonhousing consumption, especially for younger retirees. For example, for the median 62- to 69-year-old household, only 49 percent of housing equity or about $50,500 can actually be consumed, even using the theoretical upper-bound reverse mortgage; this excludes the 12 percent of such households with no consumable housing equity at all. Even for the median 90-year-old household, only 89 percent of housing equity is available, or about $103,000.

These results imply that consumable net worth is smaller than standard calculations of net worth. Even among households aged 62–69 who have consumable housing equity, median consumable net worth in the upper-bound case is only three-quarters of a standard measure of net worth. By age 90, the median household could spend only 91 percent of its net worth on nonhousing consumption. On the other hand, these fractions have increased in recent years, partly due to increased house values and partly due to lower interest rates. Overall, these results show that accounting for the trends in older households' ability to extract housing equity is important for obtaining an accurate picture of their consumable net worth and potential standard of living in retirement.

Acknowledgments

The authors are grateful for funding in part by the Zell-Lurie Real Estate Center at Wharton. Igar Fuki provided outstanding research assistance. We thank John Ameriks, Julia Coronado, and Olivia S. Mitchell for helpful comments.

Notes

[1] The baseline of no-moving (constant housing consumption) is not only conceptually attractive but also appears to be realistic. Households rarely tap housing equity by moving and, when they do, it appears to be largely in response to particular circumstances such as an adverse health event (Venti and Wise 1989, 1990, 2004; Megbolugbe, Sa-Aadu, and Shilling 1997). Nor do they appear to plan on selling their houses to finance retirement (Lusardi and Mitchell 2007). On the other hand, other researchers have found some evidence that households do reoptimize their housing equity (Coronado, Maki, and Weitzer 2007), or point out that households have a valuable option to do so (Skinner 2007). Our analysis will not capture the value of the *option* to reduce housing consumption. Still, even households that move (whether they downsize or switch to renting) will have to devote a large portion of the proceeds from the sale to cover the transactions costs plus future housing services. Another way to tap housing equity is to simply cut back on maintenance. (c.f. Davidoff 2006; Gyourko and Tracy 2006). We consider that to be similar to accessing capital through credit markets in that such households cannot tap *all* their housing equity and the amount they can access will depend on the number of years they expect to remain in their houses.

[2] Unlike other forms of housing debt, the borrower cannot default on a reverse mortgage and he offloads to the lender the risk associated with the uncertainty over how long he will stay in his home. In practice, reverse mortgages currently have high fees and interest rates and provide relatively little equity.

[3] Most prior studies add all of housing equity to net worth (e.g., Mitchell and Moore 1998; Poterba and Samwick 2001; Coronado, Maki, and Weitzer 2007). Others leave housing equity out altogether (Bernheim et al. 2000), or split the difference (Engen, Gale, and Uccello 1999). Venti and Wise (1991) find that a reverse

mortgage could increase nonhousing consumption by as much as 10 percent on average, but they do not express that number as a fraction of housing equity or net worth. Other research on the value of reverse mortgage products focuses on the potential size of the market for products, rather than the equity available to be tapped (Merrill, Finkel, and Kutty 1994; Rasmussen, Megbolugbe, and Morgan 1995).

[4] Of course, one can extend this line of reasoning to many other liabilities that are not measured, for instance households' expected food expenses. However, in such cases, there is no matching asset (or durable good) on the other side of the balance sheet that directly offsets the liability. Buying a house provides a hedge against changes in housing costs, potentially a perfect hedge for a household that never sells its house or otherwise has an infinite effective horizon. The example of long-term care insurance, discussed elsewhere in this volume, is related in that it hedges future long-term care expenses.

[5] Consistent with this implication, Campbell and Cocco (2005) find that the response of consumption to house prices increases with age.

[6] A more complete description of the survey can be found in Bucks, Kennickell, and Moore (2006).

[7] We also drop 22 households who report negative gross assets.

[8] We have 3,506 household-level observations in 1983, 13,962 in 1989, 17,235 in 1992, 18,768 in 1995, 19,210 in 1998, 19,854 in 2001, and 20,283 in 2004, for a total of 112,818. The 1989 through 2004 SCFs have five replicate observations per household.

[9] Naturally, we have relatively more data on households born between 1920 and 1969 as the members of those households are within the age range of 25–94 for more years of the survey. We have 1,751 observations on household heads born between 1900 and 1909; 6,735 for 1910–19; 13,915 for 1920–9; 16,988 for 1930–9; 24,496 for 1940–9; 26,199 for 1950–9; 17,130 for 1960–9; and 5,604 for 1970–9.

[10] We are grateful to Jeff Brown for sharing these tables with us.

[11] The definition of net worth follows Bucks, Kennickell, and Moore (2006). Assets include checking, savings, and money-market accounts; call accounts at brokerages; certificates of deposit; directly-held mutual funds; stocks; bonds; retirement accounts; savings bonds; the cash value of whole life insurance; trusts, annuities, and managed investment accounts; other financial assets such as royalties and loans made; vehicles; primary residence, other residential, and nonresidential real estate; business interests; and other nonfinancial assets such as jewelry and antiques. Debt includes debt on the primary residence and other residential and nonresidential real estate; credit-card debt; installment loans not for real estate or credit cards such as vehicle or student loans; and other debts such as margin loans or loans against life-insurance policies.

[12] Gale and Pence (2006) also find that the largest gains in wealth between 1989 and 2001 accrued to older households.

[13] Gyourko, Mayer, and Sinai (2006) show that the pattern of house price growth varies considerably across cities, so the national average is an imperfect proxy for the house price growth experienced by a given household in the SCF. Unfortunately, city of residence is not publicly available in the SCF and even region is made

available only in some surveys, so we cannot match external measures of house price appreciation to households in the SCF.

[14] For brevity, subsequent graphs will focus on the over-time life-cycle profiles.

[15] Coronado, Maki, and Weitzer (2007) compared two cohorts in the HRS, interviewed in 1992 and 2004, and concluded that households might have increased their housing debt in response to house appreciation in order to rebalance their portfolios.

[16] The corresponding cohort analysis (not shown) suggests the possibility of a significant cohort effect, in addition to the time effects just discussed. At any age, later birth cohorts have more debt than earlier cohorts. If this reflects some decline in aversion to housing debt for more recent birth cohorts, then one needs to be careful about extrapolating from today's seniors to future seniors. Future cohorts of seniors could arrive in retirement with less housing equity than do the current elderly.

[17] For example, consider a homeowner who purchased a house for $200,000, financed 100 percent with debt. The house is now worth $210,000. This homeowner's housing equity ($210,000 current value—$200,000 debt = $10,000) is entirely capital gain, and thus the household would have a ratio of one. If the homeowner had financed 80 percent with debt, he would have $50,000 in housing equity ($210,000 current value—$160,000 debt) and $10,000 in capital gain ($210,000 current value—$200,000 purchase price) and the ratio would be $10,000/$50,000 = 0.2.

[18] Unfortunately, we have a consistent CPI series only back to 1967, so households who purchased their homes prior to that date are omitted. Also, we cannot adjust for the length of ownership. Consider a household who purchased a house in 1970 and in 2002 sold it (with a large capital gain) and purchased a new house using the gain as a down payment. This household would appear to have relatively small housing capital gains in 2004 because it would have been in the new house for only two years and we cannot track the capital appreciation from its prior house.

[19] An alternative approach is to suppose that a household draws down its housing equity by selling its house and renting (through a long-term lease). Since the household's housing services are no longer being provided by an owned house, the household will have to reserve some of the proceeds from the house sale to pay for its future rents. A younger household that is expected to live a relatively long time would have to reserve more of the proceeds but an older household could reserve less, *ceteris paribus*. We use reverse mortgages to estimate the consumable portion of housing equity because, unlike rents for owner-occupied houses, mortgage interest rates are easily observable. In addition, reverse mortgage lenders absorb the uncertainty over length-of-life.

[20] It turns out that in every age group in the SCF, the median household with positive consumable housing equity has no housing debt. Thus it makes no difference whether we report consumable housing equity as a fraction of housing equity or house value.

[21] Even so, we still are comparing the 2004 SCF (with 2004 interest rates and expected inflation) to the actual 2007 program, so the match is imperfect.

References

Bernheim, B. Douglas, Solange Berstein, Jagadeesh Gokhale, and Laurence J. Kotlikoff (2000). 'How Much Should Americans Be Saving For Retirement?' *American Economic Review*, 90(2): 288–92.

Bucks, Brian, Arthur Kennickell, and Kevin Moore (2006). 'Recent Changes in U.S. Family Finances: Evidence from the 2001 and 2004 Survey of Consumer Finances,' *Federal Reserve Bulletin*, March 22: 1–38.

Campbell, John Y. and João F. Cocco (2005). 'How Do House Prices Affect Consumption? Evidence from Micro Data,' NBER Working Paper no. 11534. Cambridge, MA: National Bureau of Economic Research.

Coronado, Julia L., Dean Maki, and Ben Weitzer (2007). 'Retiring on the House? Cross-Cohort Differences in Housing Wealth,' in B. Madrian, O. S. Mitchell, and B. J. Soldo (eds.), *Redefining Retirement: How Will Boomers Fare?* Oxford: Oxford University Press, pp. 296–308.

Davidoff, Thomas (2006). 'Maintenance and the Home Equity of the Elderly,' Fisher Center for Real Estate and Urban Economics Paper No. 03–288. Berkeley, CA: University of California, Berkeley.

Engen, Eric M., William Gale, and Cori Uccello (1999). 'The Adequacy of Retirement Saving,' *Brookings Papers on Economic Activity*, #2: 65–165.

Gale, William and Karen M. Pence (2006). 'Are Successive Generations Getting Wealthier, and If So, Why? Evidence from the 1990s,' *Brookings Papers on Economic Activity*, #1: 155–234.

Gyourko, Joseph E., Christopher J. Mayer, and Todd M. Sinai (2006). 'Superstar Cities,' NBER Working Paper no. 12355. Cambridge, MA: National Bureau of Economic Research.

—— and Joseph Tracy (2006). 'Using Home Maintenance and Repairs to Smooth Variable Earnings,' *Review of Economics and Statistics*, 88(4): 736–47.

Lusardi, Annamaria and Olivia S. Mitchell (2007). 'Baby Boomer Retirement Security: The Roles of Planning, Financial Literacy, and Housing Wealth,' *Journal of Monetary Economics*, 54(1): 205–24.

Megbolugbe, Isaac, Jarjisu Sa-Aadu, and James Shilling (1997). 'Oh, Yes, the Elderly will Reduce Housing Equity Under the Right Circumstances,' *Journal of Housing Research*, 8: 53–74.

Merrill, Sally R., Meryl Finkel, and Nandinee Kutty (1994). 'Potential Beneficiaries from Reverse Mortgage Products for Elderly Homeowners: An Analysis of American Housing Survey Data,' *Journal of the American Real Estate and Urban Economics Association*, 22: 257–99.

Mitchell, Olivia S. and James Moore (1998). 'Can Americans Afford to Retire? New Evidence on Retirement Saving Adequacy,' *The Journal of Risk and Insurance*, 65(3): 371–400.

Poterba, James and Andrew Samwick (2001). 'Portfolio Allocations over the Life Cycle,' in S. Ogura, T. Tachibanaki, and D. Wise (eds.), *Aging Issues in the United States and Japan*. Chicago, IL: University of Chicago Press, pp. 65–103.

Rasmussen, Dennis, Isaac Megbolugbe, and Barbara Morgan (1995). 'Using the 1990 Public Use Microdata Sample to Estimate Potential Demand for Reverse Mortgage Products,' *Journal of Housing Research*, 6(1): 1–23.

Sinai, Todd and Nicholas S. Souleles (2005). 'Owner-Occupied Housing as a Hedge Against Rent Risk,' *Quarterly Journal of Economics*, 120(2): 763–89.

Skinner, Jonathan (2007). 'Are You Sure You're Saving Enough for Retirement?' NBER Working Paper no. 12981. Cambridge, MA: National Bureau of Economic Research.

Venti, Steven F. and David A. Wise (1989). 'Aging, Moving and Housing Wealth,' in D. A. Wise (ed.), *The Economics of Aging*. Chicago, IL: The University of Chicago Press, pp. 9–48.

—— —— (1990). 'But They Don't Want to Reduce Housing Equity,' in D. A. Wise (ed.), *Issues in the Economics of Aging*. Chicago, IL: The University of Chicago Press, pp. 13–32.

—— —— (1991). 'Aging and the Income Value of Housing Wealth,' *Journal of Public Economics*, 4: 371–97.

—— —— (2004). 'Aging and Housing Equity: Another Look,' in D. A. Wise (ed.), *Perspectives on the Economics of Aging*. Chicago, IL: The University of Chicago Press, pp. 127–75.

Part II

Retirement Payouts: Balancing the Objectives

Chapter 5

The Role of Individual Retirement Accounts in US Retirement Planning

Sarah Holden and Brian Reid

Individual Retirement Accounts (IRAs) are an important component of retirement savings in the USA, where the $4.2 trillion held in IRAs represented one-quarter of the $16.4 trillion of tax-deferred retirement saving (at year-end 2006; see Figure 5-1). IRAs have become an important pool of assets because of their key role in the retirement saving market (Brady and Holden 2007a, 2007b). Workers with earned income have the opportunity to make contributions to these accounts, and households can also use them to manage assets that they have transferred or rolled over from employer-sponsored retirement accounts such as 401(k) plan balances. In the US context, all IRAs provide investors with access to tax-advantaged saving; these tax incentives are intended to encourage individuals to use these accounts to save for retirement. At the same time, the tax advantages make IRAs an attractive vehicle for managing taxes in general. Federal laws and regulations place limits and restrictions on IRA contributions and on how individuals may take distributions from these accounts. Current tax law requires that individuals must begin taking distributions from their traditional IRAs at age $70^1/_2$, and generally the law imposes a 10 percent penalty on distributions taken prior to age $59^1/_2$.

This chapter examines how IRA holders manage these increasingly important retirement saving vehicles. Prior research has tended to report that people rarely tap into their IRA assets before retirement; they typically do so only as a last resort when faced with a financial shock. Further, the evidence has shown that people tend to postpone withdrawals from IRAs until required to do so by law. Our new results draw on data from the Federal Reserve Board's Survey of Consumer Finances (SCF), the Internal Revenue Service (IRS) Statistics of Income (SOI) Division data, and Investment Company Institute (ICI) household surveys of IRA owners. The findings confirm that few IRA owners take withdrawals prior to age $70^1/_2$ and withdrawals tend to be small. We also offer a multivariate analysis evaluating withdrawal patterns in more detail.

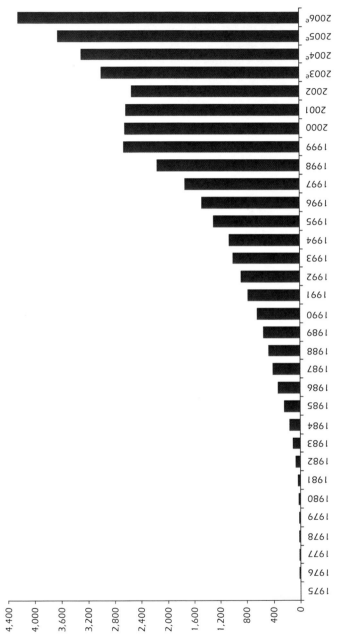

Figure 5-1. IRA assets, 1975–2006 (billions of nominal dollars). *Sources*: Investment Company Institute, IRS Statistics of Income Division, Federal Reserve Board, and American Council of Life Insurers. Derived from Brady and Holden (2007a). *Notes*: e = estimated, p = preliminary.

Prior Research

The long-term growth in account-based retirement saving has focused attention on how and whether households accumulate sufficient assets to fund retirement.[1] Previous research has studied the saving or accumulation phase of retirement planning,[2] but little analysis has been devoted to the withdrawal or distribution phase of these retirement accounts. Some analysts have examined the disposition of lump-sum distributions when workers change jobs and retire,[3] but few have looked at subsequent withdrawals from retirement accounts.

One reason there has been little comprehensive study of the withdrawal process is the limited availability of data, particularly with respect to IRAs. Nevertheless, some researchers have made headway on IRA withdrawal activity. For instance, Lin (2006) analyzes IRA withdrawal activity of HRS households; she shows that the probability of IRA withdrawals among older workers increases 3.6 percentage points within two years after an involuntary job loss. Using a panel of taxpayers from 1987 through 1996, Amromin and Smith (2003) study withdrawal activity among taxpayers younger than $59^1/_2$ and therefore, generally subject to the 10 percent penalty. They find that IRA withdrawals with penalty are more likely among households that experience adverse shocks (e.g., income shocks; demographic shocks, such as divorce; and lumpy consumption needs, such as education and housing). In addition, they find that the effect of adverse shocks is amplified for households with the lowest levels of financial wealth. They conclude that the empirical findings are consistent with the hypothesis that retirement assets are a financing resource of last resort. Bershadker and Smith (2006) analyze the same 10-year panel of taxpayers but examine the withdrawal activity of taxpayers aged 63–65 in 1987 and then follow them over the 10-year panel. About 40 percent of taxpayers were aged 63–69 when they first tapped their IRAs; 60 percent were aged 70 or older. These authors also study whether IRA-owning taxpayers started taking withdrawals prior to, near, or after retirement. They find that only 12 percent of IRA-owning taxpayers were 'early tappers', taking distributions more than two years prior to retirement. Another 42 percent of IRA-owning taxpayers were 'on-time tappers', first withdrawing from their accounts in the two-year window around retirement. The remaining 45 percent of IRA-owning taxpayers were 'late tappers', who waited until more than two years after retirement to tap into their IRAs.

In what follows, we build on this research by analyzing IRA withdrawal activity for a more recent time period using household survey and tax return information. This is informed by a brief history of IRAs, followed by IRA distribution rules and descriptive data on households who own IRAs. Next, we evaluate household surveys conducted by the ICI, which ask individuals to identify the reasons for their withdrawals. We also provide results from a multivariate model that examines several factors affecting IRA withdrawal activity. Controlling on a variety of demographic and other characteristics helps us to identify factors that increase the probability of households withdrawing money from their IRAs before they are required to do so.

A Brief History of Individual Retirement Accounts

Saving for retirement in the USA has long been encouraged with tax-advantaged saving plans. Some are sponsored by employers, such as defined benefit and 401(k) plans, while others are individual-based such as IRAs. The laws governing these plans are dynamic and change over time.[4] In 1974, Congress enacted the Employee Retirement Income Security Act (ERISA) to protect and enhance Americans' retirement security by establishing comprehensive standards for employee benefit plans. ERISA also allowed the first form of IRA, known as a 'traditional' IRA. From the start, traditional IRAs were designed to serve two purposes: as contributory retirement plans, and as the recipients of rollovers from employer-sponsored retirement plans when workers change jobs or retire.

Since 1974, Congress has changed the legal environment for IRAs many times, and it has also created new types of IRAs. Seeking to increase retirement plan coverage among small employers, the 1978 Revenue Act introduced the first employer-sponsored IRAs, known as Simplified Employee Pension (SEP) IRAs, which were later joined by Salary Reduction SEP IRAs (SAR-SEPs) in 1986, and then Savings Incentive Match Plan for Employees (SIMPLE) IRAs in 1996 (see Table 5-1).[5] To offer individuals a differently structured tax-deferred retirement savings vehicle, the Taxpayer Relief Act of 1997 introduced the Roth IRA, which is an IRA that accepts after-tax contributions but generally permits tax-free withdrawals (Internal Revenue Service 2006).

Rules regarding contribution limits and deductibility eligibility also have changed over time, with observable impact on contributions flowing into traditional IRAs. For example, with the goal of bolstering retirement saving, the Economic Recovery Tax Act of 1981 (ERTA) raised the annual IRA contribution limit from the lesser of $1,500 or 15 percent of compensation, to the lesser of $2,000 or 100 percent of compensation. Previously, an individual with retirement plan coverage at work faced restricted eligibility to make deductible traditional IRA contributions, but ERTA made traditional IRAs 'universal' by allowing any taxpayer under the age of $70^{1}/_{2}$ with earned income to make a tax-deductible contribution irrespective of retirement plan coverage at work. Deductible contributions to traditional IRAs increased sharply, rising from $4.8 billion in 1981 to $28.3 billion in 1982 (see Figure 5-2). During this time of simplified IRA rules and

TABLE 5-1 US Household Ownership of Individual Retirement Accounts (IRAs)

	Year Created	Number of Households with Type of IRA, 2006	Percent of Households with Type of IRA, 2006
Traditional IRA	1974		
	Employee Retirement Income Security Act	34.8 million	30.4
SEP IRA	1978		
	Revenue Act		
SAR-SEP IRA	1986		
	Tax Reform Act	7.9 million	6.9
SIMPLE IRA	1996		
	Small Business Job Protection Act		
Roth IRA	1997		
	Taxpayer Relief Act	14.4 million	12.6
Any IRA (total)		42.2 million	36.9

Source: Investment Company Institute (ICI 2007).

Note: Multiple responses included.

expanded eligibility, contributions rose and the number of individuals saving for retirement through IRAs increased, including those with lower incomes (Internal Revenue Service, Statistics of Income Division, 1989, 1984; Skinner 1992).

The Tax Reform Act of 1986 (TRA) eliminated universal deductibility eligibility, by re-establishing employer-sponsored retirement plan coverage as the basis for allowing tax-deductible contributions to traditional IRAs. In 1987, deductible contributions to traditional IRAs dropped to $14.1 billion, compared with $37.8 billion in 1986 (see Figure 5-2). Tax return data suggest that many taxpayers who remained eligible to make contributions stopped making them.[6] Deductible contributions to traditional IRAs edged downward over the ensuing years, decreasing after the introduction of Roth IRAs, and slipping further to $7.4 billion in 2001. The Economic Growth and Tax Relief Reconciliation Act (EGTRRA) of 2001 provided a much-needed boost, although it did not remove the eligibility rules. EGTRRA increased traditional IRA contribution limits for the first time in 20 years and introduced catch-up contributions for workers aged 50 or older. Traditional IRA contributions increased a bit in response to the changes introduced by EGTRRA.[7]

By year-end 2006, IRA assets totaled $4.2 trillion, with traditional IRAs holding the bulk of IRA assets: $3.8 trillion or nearly 90 percent of the

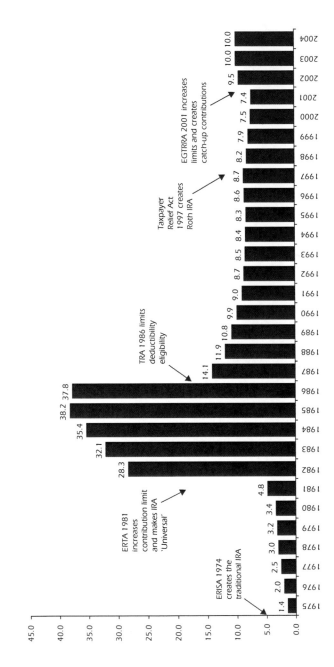

Figure 5-2. Deductible contributions* to traditional IRAs, 1975–2004 (billions of dollars). *Sources:* IRS Statistics of Income Division; Individual Income Tax Returns; Publication 1304, various years; and *SOI Bulletin*, various issues. *Note.* * Deductible IRA contributions reported on individual income tax returns (Form 1040).

Table 5-2 Most IRA Assets Are Held in Traditional IRAs (IRA assets by type, year-end, 1997–2006)

	Traditional[1]		SEP and SAR-SEP		Roth[2]		SIMPLE		Total
	Assets ($ billions)	Share[4] (%)	Assets ($ billions)	Share[4] (%t)	Assets ($ billions)	Share[4] (%)	Assets ($ billions)	Share[4] (%)	Assets[3] ($ billions)
1997	1,642	95	85	5	—	—	1	(*)	1,728
1998	1,974	92	115	5	57	3	4	(*)	2,150
1999	2,423	91	143	5	76	3	9	(*)	2,651
2000	2,407	92	134	5	78	3	10	(*)	2,629
2001	2,395	91	131	5	79	3	14	1	2,619
2002	2,322	92	117	5	78	3	16	1	2,533
2003	2,719[e]	91	145[e]	5	106[p]	4	23[p]	1	2,993[e]
2004	2,962[e]	90	165[e]	5	127[e]	4	3[e]	1	3,284[p]
2005	3,260[e]	90	185[e]	5	145[e]	4	40[e]	1	3,632[e]
2006	3,784[e]	89	219[e]	5	178[e]	4	51[e]	1	4,232[e]

Sources: Investment Company Institute and IRS Statistics of Income Division, derived from Brady and Holden (2007*a*).

Note: Components may not add to totals because of rounding.

[1] Traditional IRAs includes contributory and rollover IRAs.

[2] Roth IRAs includes contributory and conversion Roth IRAs.

[3] Total assets includes education IRAs, which were renamed Coverdell Education Savings Accounts (ESAs) in July 2001.

[4] Share is the percent of total IRA assets.

(*) = less than 1/2%.

e = estimated *p* = preliminary.

total (see Table 5-2). Despite having only been available since 1998, Roth IRAs represented 4 percent of all IRA assets, with $178 billion. Indeed, in each tax-year from 1999 through 2004, contributions to Roth IRAs have exceeded those to traditional IRAs.[8] Employer-sponsored IRAs (SEP, SAR-SEP, and SIMPLE) held the remaining 6 percent of IRA assets.

In addition to contributions and investment gains, asset transfers from employer-sponsored retirement plans have contributed significantly to the growth in traditional IRAs. When workers change jobs or retire, they are allowed to transfer (or roll over) in a lump sum the accumulations from their employer-sponsored retirement plans to IRAs to preserve the monies' tax-deferred status. Federal Reserve Board SCF data indicate that households identified about half of traditional IRA assets in 2004 as resulting from rollovers (Brady and Holden 2007*a*). In a 2005 survey of households owning IRAs conducted by ICI, 43 percent of households with traditional IRA assets indicated that their IRAs contained rollovers.[9] IRS-SOI data indicate rollovers into traditional IRAs were $204 billion in 2002 (see Table 5-3). These data highlight the long history of traditional IRAs as an accumulation vehicle, whether through contributions or rollovers. The IRS

TABLE 5-3 IRAs by Age of Taxpayer, Tax-Year 2002

	Total IRA Assets at Year-End 2001[a]		Total Contributions[b]		Rollovers		Roth Conversions		Withdrawals[c]		Total IRA Assets at Year-End 2002	
	Millions of Taxpayers (1)	Billions of Dollars (2)	Millions of Taxpayers (3)	Billions of Dollars (4)	Millions of Taxpayers (4)	Billions of Dollars (6)	Millions of Taxpayers (7)	Billions of Dollars (8)	Millions of Taxpayers (9)	Billions of Dollars (10)	Millions of Taxpayers (11)	Billions of Dollars (12)
All taxpayers, total	48.404	2,619.4	14.614	42.3	3.989	204.4	0.239	3.3	11.479	123.3	49.908	2,532.7
Under 20	0.266	1.1	0.199	0.3	—	—	0.002	0.0	0.027	0.2	0.341	1.1
20 under 25	0.745	2.0	0.572	0.9	0.061	0.2	0.017	0.1	0.063	0.2	0.968	2.6
25 under 30	1.770	8.1	0.995	1.8	0.208	1.0	0.014	0.0	0.173	0.6	2.036	8.4
30 under 35	3.055	27.1	1.425	3.3	0.346	4.0	0.024	0.1	0.323	1.6	3.348	28.7
35 under 40	4.146	63.9	1.617	4.3	0.398	7.5	0.026	0.2	0.441	2.8	4.409	61.0
40 under 45	5.233	133.4	1.928	5.5	0.458	10.9	0.023	0.4	0.446	4.7	5.539	123.9
45 under 50	6.122	215.7	2.095	6.6	0.478	18.0	0.030	0.4	0.538	6.0	6.256	202.0
50 under 55	6.108	292.2	2.095	7.1	0.451	28.5	0.033	0.4	0.588	8.6	6.269	291.9
55 under 60	5.649	363.8	1.786	6.3	0.552	40.1	0.024	0.6	0.624	12.7	5.818	394.9
60 under 65	4.802	426.3	1.213	3.9	0.448	49.6	0.027	0.5	1.035	18.1	4.865	447.0
65 under 70	3.740	386.6	0.549	1.8	0.290	23.0	0.014	0.4	1.048	19.0	3.712	362.8
70 under 75	3.164	421.0	0.113	0.4	0.182	14.0	0.006	0.1	2.757	26.0	3.007	370.6
75 under 80	2.290	202.4	0.020	0.1	0.081	5.2	0.0002	0.0	2.198	15.7	2.166	174.6
80 and over	1.315	75.7	0.006	0.03	0.037	2.4	—	—	1.219	7.2	1.174	63.3

Source: Derived from Bryant and Sailer (2006).

Note: Components may not add to totals because of rounding. All figures are estimates based on samples using a matched file of income tax returns, Forms 5498, and Forms 1099-R. The age classifications are based on each taxpayer's age at year-end 2002 for comparability across years.

[a] The total IRA assets at year-end 2001 are at fair market value.

[b] Includes deductible contributions reported on the Form 1040 and nondeductible contributions.

[c] Withdrawals are reported on Form 1099-R; does not include withdrawals for the purpose of rollovers to other IRA accounts if the transfer was made by the trustee; Roth conversions are shown separately.

has tracked distributions or withdrawals from IRAs, as well. In 2002, total withdrawals from IRAs were $123 billion and predominantly made by older taxpayers.

Traditional IRA Distribution Rules

The topic of retirement income management is one of substantial interest of late; for instance, Mahaney and Carlson (2008) explore the timing of the take-up of Social Security benefits, and Sharpe, Scott, and Watson (2008) highlight the importance of earmarking certain assets to cover future income needs with a 'lockbox' spending strategy. Our work [Investment Company Institute (ICI) 2000a, 2000b] shows that most defined contribution plan balances are rolled over into IRAs at retirement, underscoring the importance of IRA payouts as a key component in households' retirement withdrawal activity.

These payouts are governed by a variety of rules stipulating how households may withdraw or take 'distributions' from their IRAs. A withdrawal from a traditional IRA plan, if taken by an individual younger than age $59^1/_2$, is generally subject to a 10 percent penalty on the taxable portion of the withdrawal (in addition to the federal, state, and local income tax that may be due). Taxpayers older than $59^1/_2$ but younger than $70^1/_2$ may take distributions from a traditional IRA without penalty, but they are not required to take distributions until age $70^1/_2$. In general, someone aged $70^1/_2$ or older will be required under tax law to take withdrawals from his or her traditional IRA, so that these monies which had been allowed to accumulate on a tax-deferred basis are mainly used to finance retirement (rather than have them flow to heirs at the retiree's death). The required minimum distribution (RMD) must then be taken annually in an amount tied to life expectancy tables published by the IRS.

Over the years, however, Congress has relaxed the use of IRA assets, making it easier for individuals to withdraw money in special situations, without incurring the additional penalty. For example, under the TRA of 1986, Congress added one such exemption, which allows the taxpayer to set up a substantially equal periodic payment (SEPP) plan and avoid the 10 percent penalty (see Figure 5-3).[10] Prior to TRA 1986, the main exception to the 10 percent penalty was triggered if the IRA owner died or became disabled. Other exemptions allowing for IRA withdrawals without penalty have been added: for instance, in 1996, Congress first allowed IRA owners to take distributions to pay for certain medical and health insurance expenses.[11] The Taxpayer Relief Act of 1997 exempted withdrawals used to pay for qualified higher education expenses or for a first-time home purchase (up to $10,000) from the penalty. In 1999, penalty-free

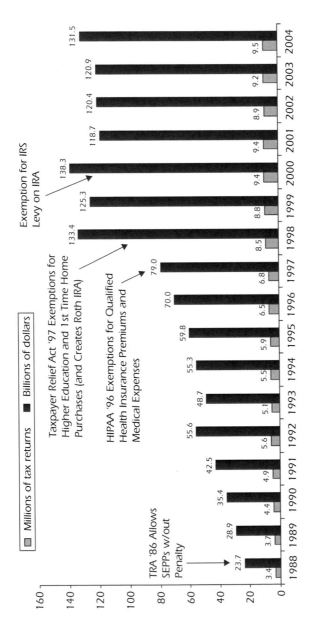

Figure 5-3. IRA distributions,* 1988–2004. *Sources*: IRS Statistics of Income Division, Individual Tax Returns, Publication 1304, various years; and Authors' Summary of Legislative Changes. *Notes*: *Total IRA distributions reported on Form 1040. Data include amounts converted to Roth IRAs.

distributions could be used to pay for an IRS levy on the IRA.[12] Recently, Congress permitted distributions for specific events (e.g., reservists called to active duty, hurricane damage) and placed time limits on when penalty-free withdrawals related to these events could occur.[13]

Characteristics of Traditional IRA Owners

Three different data sources are generally used to describe both the demographic and financial characteristics of households and individuals owning IRAs as well as the withdrawal behavior of traditional IRA owners.[14] Some of the data questions overlap, allowing comparisons, but many items are unique to a single datasource. The broad similarity of demographic and financial characteristics suggests that it is sensible to combine the separate results to glean a coherent story of traditional IRA ownership and withdrawal patterns.

One datasource is the IRS-SOI division, which reports IRA data from a variety of tax and information forms. In addition to *SOI Bulletin* articles,[15] the IRS constructs a public-use data file that contains weighted information from individual tax returns (IRS Form 1040; these are appropriately blurred to protect taxpayer anonymity). A second datasource is the Federal Reserve Board's SCF (for discussion see Bucks, Kennickell, and Moore 2006). We also use household surveys conducted by the ICI to determine both the incidence of IRA ownership and the characteristics and activity of IRA owners (e.g., West and Leonard-Chambers 2006*a*, 2006*b*).

Both the ICI and SCF data have been previously used to trace households' IRA ownership. SCF data from 2004 indicate that half of US households had some sort of 'retirement account' (see Table 5-4; Bucks, Kennickell, and Moore 2006). Retirement accounts are defined to include IRAs; Keogh accounts; and 401(k), 403(b), thrift saving, and other employer-sponsored retirement accounts from current and previous jobs. Social Security and employer-sponsored defined benefit plans are not included in retirement accounts. Finer analysis shows that about one-quarter of households held traditional IRAs in 2004; this agrees with ICI household surveys that include a representative sample of all US households IRA ownership. In 2006, these data show that 30 percent of households had traditional IRAs by 2006 (see Table 5-1).

The incidence of traditional IRA ownership varies across financial and demographic characteristics. Although households across all income groups hold IRAs, only 5 percent of households in the lowest income quintile[16] have traditional IRAs, compared with 58 percent of households in the top income decile (see Table 5-4).[17] Traditional IRA ownership tends to increase with age of head of household: fewer than 10 percent

TABLE 5-4 Family Holdings of Retirement Account Assets and Traditional IRAs, 2004 (percent of families, by selected characteristics)

Family Characteristic	Retirement Accounts[a]	Traditional IRAs	Traditional IRA Withdrawals	Traditional IRA Withdrawals Among Owners
All families	49.7	24.1	4.3	18.0
≤70	52.5	23.2	1.5	6.6
70+	33.4	28.9	20.6	71.4
Income percentiles				
<20	10.2	5.2	1.6	30.8
20–39.9	30.2	12.4	4.7	38.2
40–59.9	53.0	22.9	6.1	26.5
60–79.9	70.1	31.0	5.2	16.7
80–89.9	81.5	39.3	3.4	8.5
90–100	88.5	58.4	4.9	8.3
Age of head (years)				
<35	40.2	9.3	0.8	8.0
35–44	55.9	18.2	0.8	4.4
45–54	57.7	28.1	0.6	2.2
55–64	63.1	39.7	2.5	6.4
65–74	43.2	34.5	15.7	45.6
75+	29.2	25.7	17.1	66.8
Head's education				
No high-school diploma	16.2	5.2	3.5	67.2
High-school diploma	43.7	18.7	4.4	23.4
Some college	47.8	18.6	3.2	17.3
College degree	68.9	38.8	5.2	13.4
Race or ethnicity of respondent				
White non-Hispanic	56.2	29.6	5.5	18.7
Nonwhite or Hispanic	32.9	9.6	1.2	12.4
Head's current work status				
Working for someone else	57.1	21.3	1.2	5.5
Self-employed	54.6	36.9	3.6	9.7
Retired	33.0	26.6	13.3	50.0
Other not working	24.9	14.4	1.1	7.7
Housing status				
Owner	60.2	31.7	5.8	18.2
Renter or other	26.2	7.0	1.1	16.3
Percentiles of net worth				
<25	14.1	1.4	0.1	8.1
25–49.9	43.2	10.3	1.0	9.8
50–74.9	61.9	29.5	6.4	21.6
75–89.9	77.7	46.9	9.3	19.9
90–100	82.5	67.3	10.6	15.8

Sources: Authors' tabulations from Survey of Consumer Finances; Bucks, Kennickell, and Moore (2006).

[a] Retirement accounts include IRAs; Keogh, 401(k), 403(b), and other retirement accounts from current and past employers.

TABLE 5-5 Age Composition of Traditional IRA Owners

	Households with Traditional IRAs in 2005: ICI Survey Data		Taxpayers with Any IRAs in 2002: IRS SOI Form 5498 Data		Households with Traditional IRAs in 2004: SCF Data	
	Percent of Households[a]	Percent of Assets[a,b]	Percent of Taxpayers	Percent of Assets	Percent of Households[b]	Percent of Assets
Age of head (years)	100.0	100.0	100.0	100.0	100.0	100.0
<40	13.1	4.4	22.2	4.0	15.2	4.2
40–49	24.1	25.7	23.6	12.9	19.1	14.3
50–59	28.4	28.0	24.2	27.1	27.4	26.6
60–69	15.7	28.0	17.2	32.0	19.5	30.7
70+	18.7	13.8	12.7	24.0	18.7	24.2

Sources: Investment Company Institute, Federal Reserve Board Survey of Consumer Finances, and IRS Statistics of Income Division, derived from Bryant and Sailer (2006).

[a] Number of respondents varies.

[b] Components do not add to 100% because of rounding.

of households younger than age 35 have traditional IRAs, but about 40 percent of preretiree households (aged 55–64) have traditional IRAs. Incidence of IRA ownership is a bit lower among retiree households, reflecting in part a cohort effect. The incidence of traditional IRA ownership also rises with educational achievement of the head of household. Five percent of households with no high-school diploma hold traditional IRAs. About one-in-five households with a high-school diploma has a traditional IRA, as do households with some college. Two-in-five households with at least a college degree hold traditional IRAs. In addition, incidence of traditional IRA ownership rises with net worth percentile.[18]

Using IRS-SOI data, Bryant and Sailer (2006) report that IRAs are held by people across a range of ages and incomes. The most recent IRS-SOI data available cover year-end 2002, at which point 70 percent of the 49.9 million taxpayers with IRAs (of any type) are younger than age 60 (see Table 5-5). Under the traditional IRA rules, they would generally not be eligible to take a withdrawal or distribution without penalty. Another 17 percent of taxpayers with IRAs are 60–69 years old, who generally would be eligible to make penalty-free withdrawals from their IRAs. The remaining 13 percent of taxpayers with IRAs at year-end 2002 are aged 70 or older. Under traditional IRA rules, these taxpayers would have to take out at least the RMD amount.

Surveys also show that households across a wide range of ages (and incomes) hold traditional IRAs. For example, ICI surveys indicate that nearly 20 percent of households with traditional IRAs are headed by individuals aged 70 or older, as do the SCF data (see Table 5-5). The size of the IRA holdings also varies across household demographic and financial variables. The median traditional IRA holding tends to increase with income, net worth, and education level of households (see Table 5-6). Traditional IRA balances tend to increase with age, up to households in their late 60s and early 70s, but these tend to decline among older owners.

Traditional IRA Withdrawal Activity

Policymakers have sometimes worried that individuals might tap their IRAs before retirement, and accordingly, federal law imposes a tax penalty for early withdrawals. In practice, older individuals do account for most of the IRA owners taking withdrawals, suggesting that the penalties for early withdrawals work to discourage individuals from withdrawing money from their IRAs before reaching retirement. For example, in 2002, the IRS-SOI data reveal that more than half (54 percent) of taxpayers with IRA withdrawals were aged 70 or older, 18 percent were 60–69 years old, with the remaining 28 percent of taxpayers taking withdrawals being aged 59 or younger (see Table 5-3). A pooled cross-sectional analysis of ICI surveys from 2000 to 2005 shows a similar concentration of older households among those taking withdrawals between 1999 and 2004; some 54 percent of households making withdrawals from their traditional IRAs were aged 70 or older, 21 percent were aged 59–69, and 25 percent were younger than 59 years old (see Table 5-7). The SCF data on households making withdrawals in 2003 also have a similar age distribution.

The concentration of withdrawals among older Americans reflects a much lower incidence of withdrawals among younger individuals. The SCF data indicate that about 7 percent of IRA-owning households headed by an individual aged 70 or younger made a withdrawal, while 71 percent of households headed by individuals older than 70 made withdrawals (see Table 5-4). Half of retired households with traditional IRAs made withdrawals. The finding that incidence of IRA withdrawals is much lower among households under age 70 is not isolated to this particular SCF survey. The pooled cross-sectional ICI household survey data show a similar incidence of withdrawal activity between 1999 and 2004. Seventeen percent of households holding traditional IRAs in each survey year had either withdrawn some of the money (14 percent) or liquidated their traditional IRA (3 percent) in the year prior to the survey (see Table 5-7). Only 6 percent of households headed by individuals younger than age 59 made withdrawals, while 18 percent of households aged 59–69 took withdrawals, and 57 percent of households aged 70 or older had withdrawals.

Consistent with earlier research findings that younger households are more likely to tap their IRAs following some financial need, ICI household

TABLE 5-6 Family Holdings of Retirement Account Assets and Traditional IRAs, 2004 (median amounts)[a]

Family Characteristic	Retirement Accounts[b] ($)	Traditional IRAs ($)	Traditional IRA Withdrawals ($)
All families	35,200	35,300	3,000
≤70	35,000	36,000	6,000
70+	42,000	33,000	2,200
Percentiles of income			
<20	5,000	9,500	2,400
20–39.9	10,000	17,000	1,500
40–59.9	17,000	18,000	2,000
60–79.9	32,000	25,000	3,700
80–89.9	71,000	55,000	7,000
90–100	184,000	100,000	23,100
Age of head (years)			
<35	11,000	10,000	2,500
35–44	28,000	22,000	5,000
45–54	55,500	40,000	5,000
55–64	83,000	52,000	6,000
65–74	80,000	75,000	3,700
75+	30,000	25,000	2,000
Head's education			
No high-school diploma	12,400	14,000	1,300
High-school diploma	20,000	20,000	1,700
Some college	21,000	28,000	4,000
College degree	64,800	50,000	6,800
Respondent's race or ethnicity			
White non-Hispanic	41,000	40,000	3,000
Nonwhite or Hispanic	16,000	15,000	3,000
Head's work status			
Working for someone else	30,000	30,000	3,500
Self-employed	60,000	50,000	6,000
Retired	46,000	42,000	3,000
Other not working	31,000	28,000	2,500
Housing status			
Owner	46,000	40,000	3,000
Renter or other	11,000	14,000	2,400
Percentiles of net worth			
<25	3,000	3,000	2,400
25–49.9	11,700	8,000	3,000
50–74.9	34,000	17,000	1,500
75–89.9	95,000	50,000	3,100
90–100	264,000	122,000	10,000

Sources: Authors' tabulations from Survey of Consumer Finances and Bucks, Kennickell, and Moore (2006).

[a] Median calculated among households engaged in the financial activity indicated.

[b] Retirement accounts include IRAs; Keogh, 401(k), 403(b); and other retirement accounts from current and past employers.

TABLE 5-7 Traditional IRA Withdrawal Activity by Age of Head of Household, 1999–2004 (percent of traditional IRA owners taking withdrawals)[a]

	Households with Traditional IRA Withdrawals	Age of Head of Household (years)		
		Under 59	59–69	70 or Older
Reason for withdrawal[b]				
Take required minimum distribution	46	10	12	75
Pay living expenses	18	24	34	9
Pay for health care	8	9	9	8
Reinvest the money[c]	9	10	11	7
Buy a home	5	9	6	2
Make a large purchase	8	9	16	5
Pay for education	4	11	3	1
Other	16	22	23	11
Age of head of household				
<59	25	100	0	0
59–69	21	0	100	0
70+	54	0	0	100
Amount withdrawn[d]				
<$2,500	31	29	15	39
$2,500–$4,999	15	15	11	17
$5,000–$9,999	18	20	21	16
$10,000–$24,999	20	19	29	16
$25,000–$49,999	9	7	14	7
$50,000+	7	10	10	5
Mean ($)	15,100	17,100	19,600	12,200
Median ($)	5,000	5,000	10,000	4,000
Full or partial withdrawal from traditional IRA				
Withdrew some, but not all money	85	67	86	93
Withdrew all money	15	33	14	7
Overview				
Percent of traditional IRA owners[a]	17	6	18	57
Withdrew some, but not all money	14	4	15	52
Withdrew all money	3	2	3	5

Source: Investment Company Institute, Annual Tracking Survey (2000–5).

Note: Number of respondents varies.

[a] Seventeen percent of households either still holding traditional IRAs in the year of the survey and having withdrawn some of the assets (14%) or having liquidated (3%) their traditional IRA during the year prior to the survey are counted as having withdrawals. The denominator includes households still holding traditional IRAs and those households whose withdrawals in the previous year closed their traditional IRAs. Results are pooled over 2000–5 survey years covering withdrawal activity in 1999–2004.

[b] Multiple responses included.

[c] Households indicating they were buying investments outside IRAs and/or buying another type of IRA.

[d] Components may not add to 100% because of rounding.

IRA survey responses find that about one-quarter of households with the head of household under age 59 cited the need to pay living expenses as a reason for tapping their IRAs, and 9 percent cited paying health-care expenses (see Table 5-7). Buying a home and paying for education were other reasons for tapping the IRA among younger households, both of which are permitted without penalty under certain circumstances. About 10 percent of households headed by individuals aged 69 or younger cited the rules for RMD as a reason for withdrawal, which on the surface looks anomalous. Younger households may cite RMD as a withdrawal reason because another individual in the household could be aged $70^1/_2$ or older or some of these individuals may have inherited IRAs with RMDs occurring.

In addition to being concerned that individuals will tap their IRAs early, policymakers also express concern that households will use their IRAs or other retirement savings to make large discretionary expenditures. There are many legitimate reasons that retired individuals may make a large purchase, such as consumer durables, which will assist them in smoothing consumption during retirement. However, few households indicate that they took the money 'to make a large purchase' (see Table 5-7). And among those households aged 70 or older taking withdrawals, RMD was the most cited reason with 75 percent of households headed by individuals aged 70 or older giving this reason for withdrawing.

IRA withdrawals in a given year tend to be relatively small—whether measured as a percent of aggregate assets or measured as an individual dollar amounts. Comparing annual total IRA distributions to the previous year's total assets shows that withdrawals have been modest and appear to have trended down despite the new penalty exceptions (see Figures 5-3 and 5-4). The pop-up in 1998 to 7.7 percent of assets reflects the large conversion of $39.3 billion into Roth IRAs.[19] Amounts withdrawn by individual households also tend to be modest. Tabulation of the [Internal Revenue Service, Statistics of Income Division (IRS-SOI) 2002] tax return data shows that 36 percent of tax returns with taxable IRA distributions had a distribution of less than $2,500 (see Table 5-8). Similarly, the pooled cross-sectional ICI household survey information finds that 31 percent of households with traditional IRA withdrawals had withdrawn less than $2,500. And, the SCF traditional IRA withdrawals were less than $2,500 in 44 percent of households with traditional IRA withdrawals.

Multivariate Model of IRA Distribution Activity

The previous section has suggested that the current tax and penalty structures seem to discourage individuals from tapping their IRAs prior to retirement. Next, we set up and test a multivariate model to assess the

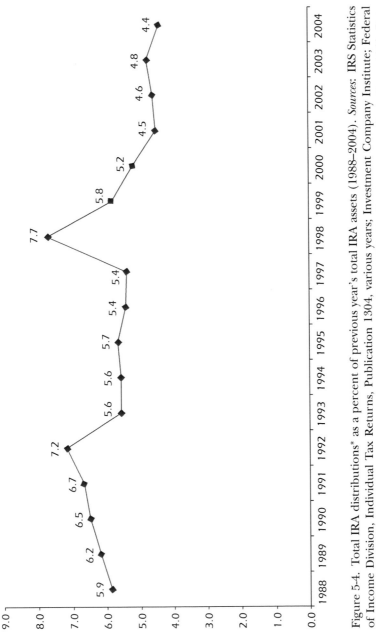

Figure 5-4. Total IRA distributions* as a percent of previous year's total IRA assets (1988–2004). *Sources*: IRS Statistics of Income Division, Individual Tax Returns, Publication 1304, various years; Investment Company Institute; Federal Reserve Board; and American Council of Life Insurers. *Notes*: *Total IRA distributions reported on Form 1040. Data include amounts converted to Roth IRAs.

TABLE 5-8 Traditional IRA Withdrawals Tend to Be Small (percent of traditional
IRA owners taking withdrawals)

	Traditional IRA Withdrawals: ICI 1999–2004[a] (percent of households)[c]	Taxable IRA Distributions:[b] SOI Form 1040 Data for 2002 (percent of tax returns)[c]	Traditional IRA Withdrawals: SCF Data for 2003 (percent of households)[c]
Amount withdrawn			
<$2,500	31	36	44
$2,500–$4,999	15	19	12
$5,000–$9,999	18	17	18
$10,000–$24,999	20	17	15
$25,000–$49,999	9	7	6
$50,000+	7	4	5
Mean[c] ($)	15,100	10,700	10,500
Median[c] ($)	5,000	4,200	3,000

Sources: Investment Company Institute, Annual Tracking Survey (2000–5); Tabulation of
IRS Statistics of Income Form 1040 Public-Use File Data, 2002; and Tabulation of Federal
Reserve Board 2004 Survey of Consumer Finances.

[a] Results are pooled over 2000–5 survey years covering withdrawal activity in 1999–2004.

[b] Taxable IRA distributions reported on the Form 1040 include conversions to Roth IRAs.

[c] The ICI and SCF tabulations are computed for households taking traditional IRA withdrawals. The SOI tabulations are computed for tax returns with taxable IRA distributions.

effectiveness of current tax incentive and penalty structures to encourage
individuals to use their IRAs as a retirement savings vehicle rather than
simply a tax-deferred savings pool. The IRA withdrawal decision is modeled
as a two-step process whereby in step 1 the household decides to take a
distribution/withdrawal or not, and in step 2, it decides how much to withdraw. Accordingly, we use a sample-selection (Heckman's two-step) model
to capture the probability of taking the withdrawal and the subsequent
amount taken if it is positive. The penalty structures included in the tax
code serve as a guide for determining the variables included in the first
step of the estimation process. In particular, withdrawals prior to age $59^{1}/_{2}$
generally are subject to a 10 percent penalty on the taxable portion of
the withdrawal, with two exceptions being when the proceeds are used
to pay health expenses or a first-time home purchase. If these policies
are effective, we would expect that being younger than 60, being in good
health, and not having a home mortgage would all reduce the probability
of taking a withdrawal from an IRA.

Table 5-9 lists the variables used for the first-step Probit analysis: household income; an indicator for the head of household being aged 60 or

TABLE 5-9 Variables for SCF Traditional IRA Withdrawal Analysis

	Type of Variable	Percentage of Traditional IRA Owning Households[a]
Income		
Household income	Continuous	
Age		
Possible penalty (Age ≤60)	Dummy; if ≤60, then = 1	78.5
Education of head of household		
No high-school diploma	Dummy	2.1
High-school diploma	Dummy; omitted category	21.4
Some college	Dummy	14.2
College degree[b]	Dummy	62.4
Race or ethnicity of respondent		
White non-Hispanic/nonwhite or Hispanic	Dummy; if nonwhite or Hispanic, then = 1	12.7
Health status of head of household		
Healthy/not healthy[c]	Dummy; if not healthy, then = 1	13.1
Current work status of head of household		
Working for someone else	Dummy; omitted category	62.1
Self-employed	Dummy	20.5
Retired[d]	Dummy	14.3
Other not working[e]	Dummy	3.2
Housing status		
Owns home with mortgage	Dummy	65.4
Owns home with no mortgage	Dummy; omitted category	25.4
Renter or other	Dummy	9.2
Financial assets		
Amount held in traditional IRA(s)	Continuous	
Amount held in nonretirement Financial assets	Continuous	

Source: Authors' tabulation from Federal Reserve Board Survey of Consumer Finances, 2004.

[a] Sample drawn from 2004 Survey of Consumer Finances consisting of households owning traditional IRAs with head of household aged 70 or younger.

[b] College degree includes two-year programs, any college degree, and graduate degrees.

[c] Self-assessed health variable. If respondent indicated 'excellent' or 'good' health, then classified as 'healthy.' If the respondent indicated 'fair' or 'poor' health, then classified as 'not healthy.'

[d] Retired includes retired and disabled, which includes students and homemakers and those aged 65 and older and not working.

[e] Other not working includes mainly those under 65 and out of the labor force.

younger ('possible penalty'); head's education level; respondent's race or ethnicity; head's self-assessed health status and current work status; housing status (in particular, also accounting for the presence of a mortgage); and household financial assets (amounts held in traditional IRAs and financial assets outside of tax-deferred retirement accounts). The multivariate analysis uses the 2004 SCF household survey data-set. As noted above, individuals responding to this survey are similar to those observed in the ICI household surveys and the IRS-SOI tax return and taxpayer data. Because the Internal Revenue Code (IRC) rules require IRA owners to make withdrawals after age $70^{1}/_{2}$, this analysis uses a limited sample of traditional IRA-owning households whose head of household is not aged $70^{1}/_{2}$ or older.

Table 5-10 reports the estimation results of the Probit analysis. First, we address variables suggested by the tax code, namely, being under age 60 ('possible penalty'), and, therefore, generally subject to the 10 percent penalty, decreases the probability of a withdrawal. The penalty exemption encompasses some medical and home purchase amounts; being in poor health or having a home mortgage increases the likelihood that a household makes a traditional IRA withdrawal. The health variable might also reflect a negative shock to the household and, consistent with Amromin and Smith (2003) and Lin (2006), could be interpreted as financial need increasing the likelihood of a withdrawal. Employment status also affects the probability of withdrawal, with those whose head of household is retired are more likely to tap their IRAs. If the head of the household has less than a high-school education, the probability of withdrawal is increased. With respect to the amount held in traditional IRAs, households with more IRA assets are less likely to take a withdrawal than households with fewer IRA assets, up to $11,000 in traditional IRA assets. Households with more than $11,000 in their traditional IRAs are more likely to withdraw the more they have in their IRAs.

The second stage of the analysis examines the factors that determine the amount of the withdrawal, in levels and as a percentage of the IRA assets held prior to the withdrawal.[20] The second stage of the estimation is based on a model that certain factors that affect the decision to make the withdrawal do not play a role in the amount of the withdrawal. Since the 10 percent penalty for early withdrawal generally applies regardless of the amount withdrawn, and the exceptions for health expenses and buying a first home are relatively generous, we assume that the amount of the withdrawal is not affected by the penalty or these two primary exceptions to the penalty. We also assume that race/ethnicity and education level do not affect the amount of the withdrawal once the decision to withdraw has been made. The variables included in the regression that explores the factors that affect the amount of the withdrawal are the age of the head of the household, their household income, their employment status,

TABLE 5-10 Probit Estimation of the Probability that Traditional IRA-Owning Household Made a Withdrawal[a]

Variable Name		Coefficient	Standard Error	Predicted and Marginal Effects Evaluated at Means of Independent Variables (%)
Predicted probability of withdrawal at means				2.0
Income	Constant/Intercept	2.577	1.702	
	ln(Household income)	−0.125	0.081	−0.06(+10)
Age	No penalty predicted (reference)			6.1
	Possible penalty (Age ≤60)	−0.675***	0.165	−4.8
Head's education	No high-school diploma	0.775*	0.401	+7.3
	High-school diploma predicted (reference)			1.7
	Some college	0.164	0.243	+0.8
	College degree[b]	0.035	0.201	+0.2
Respondent race or ethnicity	White non-Hispanic predicted (reference)			1.9
	Nonwhite or Hispanic	0.287	0.208	+1.8
Head's health status	Healthy[c] predicted (reference)			1.8
	Not healthy[c]	0.365**	0.182	+2.4
Head's work status	Working for someone else predicted (reference)			1.7
	Self-employed	−0.002	0.173	−0.01
	Retired[d]	0.512**	0.208	+3.6
	Other not working[e]	0.333	0.403	+2.0

Housing status	Owns home with mortgage	0.497**	0.172	+1.9
	Owns home with no mortgage predicted (reference)			1.0
Financial assets	Renter or other	0.026	0.330	0.1
	ln[Amount held in traditional IRA(s)]	−0.519*	0.280 $\Big\}$	+0.04(+10)
	ln[Traditional IRA(s)] squared	0.028**	0.013	
	ln(Amount held in nonretirement financial Assets)	−0.032	0.140 $\Big\}$	−0.03(+10)
	ln(Nonretirement financial assets) squared	−0.001	0.007	
	Observations	1,366		

Source: Authors' analysis of Federal Reserve Board Survey of Consumer Finances, 2004.

Notes: *: Significant at the 10% level, **: Significant at the 5% level, ***: Significant at the 1% level.

[a] Sample drawn from 2004 Survey of Consumer Finances consisting of households owning traditional IRAs with head of household aged 70 or younger.

[b] College degree includes two-year programs, any college degree, and graduate degrees.

[c] Self-assessed health variable. If respondent indicated 'excellent' or 'good' health, then classified as 'healthy.' If the respondent indicated 'fair' or 'poor' health, then classified as 'not healthy.'

[d] Retired includes retired and disabled, which includes students and homemakers and those aged 65 and older and not working.

[e] Other not working includes mainly those under 65 and out of the labor force.

their IRA assets, and their financial assets held outside of their tax-deferred retirement accounts.

Results from the conditional second stage (including only households headed by individuals under age 70) do not indicate that any of the factors are significant in explaining the amount withdrawn other than age and nonretirement financial assets. Among those taking withdrawals, the amount of the withdrawal increases with age until the head of the household reaches his or her mid-forties and then declines as his or her age increases (see Table 5-11). Households withdraw more from their IRAs the more they have in nonretirement financial assets, but the square of this variable is only significant at the 10 percent level. We also explore how these same factors affect the share or percentage households withdraw from their traditional IRA accounts. Only age has a significant effect on the share of the IRA account that households withdraw. Households increase the share of their traditional IRA withdrawn until the head of household reaches his or her mid-forties, after which the share declines.

All told, these results suggest that the current tax and penalty structures seem to provide incentives for individuals to use their IRAs as a dedicated pool of retirement saving by discouraging early withdrawals. However, once a household decides to take a withdrawal, the amount of the withdrawal is only related to age. Given that these accounts are important repositories for rollovers from employer-sponsored retirement plans, including 401(k) assets, the tax incentives for using IRAs seem to encourage people to consider them as retirement financing vehicles. While there is some leakage from these accounts, the leakage in large part seems in line with the exceptions that Congress has put in place.

Conclusions

The IRAs are a substantial and growing component of US retirement assets. Since their inception, federal law has provided tax incentives for individuals to use IRAs and tax penalties to discourage tapping of these accounts prior to retirement. This chapter tackles the question of whether these incentives are encouraging individuals to use their IRAs for retirement purposes. After a brief history of IRAs and an analysis of aggregate IRA data, we evaluate detailed information on IRA owners and their withdrawal activity. Our evidence indicates that few households tap their IRAs prior to retirement, even in the wake of several years of the loosening of withdrawal restrictions. In fact, RMDs are cited as the main reason for taking withdrawals. Overall it appears that most households are managing their withdrawal behavior in a manner consistent with policy motivations for these accounts.

TABLE 5-11 Heckman IRA Withdrawal Regression Results

	Dependent Variable: ln (withdrawal amount)		Dependent Variable: ln (percentage of account withdrawn)	
	Coefficient	St. Error	Coefficient	St. Error
Constant/Intercept	0.591	3.864	−4.073	2.963
ln(Household income)	−0.039	0.172	0.060	0.131
Age of head of household (years)	0.280**	0.112	0.185**	0.085
Age-squared	−0.003***	0.001	−0.002**	0.001
Working for someone else (omitted category)				
Self-employed	0.123	0.429	−0.065	0.339
Retired[b]	0.542	0.514	0.350	0.403
Other not working[c]	−0.302	0.883	−0.196	0.669
ln (amount held in traditional IRA)	0.834	0.727	0.381	0.530
ln [traditional IRA(s)] squared	−0.013	0.033	−0.034	0.024
ln (Amount held in nonretirement financial assets)	−0.682	0.483	−0.316	0.344
ln(Nonretirement financial assets) squared	0.038*	0.020	0.020	0.014
Mills Lambda	−0.710	0.543	−0.642	0.411

Source: Authors' analysis of Federal Reserve Board Survey of Consumer Finances, 2004.

Notes: *: Significant at the 10% level, **: Significant at the 5% level, ***: Significant at the 1% level.

[a] Sample drawn from 2004 Survey of Consumer Finances consisting of households owning traditional IRAs with head of household aged 70 or younger.

[b] Retired includes retired and disabled, which includes students and homemakers and those aged 65 and older and not working.

[c] Other not working includes mainly those under the age of 65 and out of the labor force.

The views expressed in this chapter are those of the authors and do not necessarily reflect those of the ICI or its members. The authors thank Michael Bogdan for data tabulations.

Appendix

This appendix provides a brief description of each data-set used in the analysis; the data are drawn from public and proprietary data sources.

Survey of Consumer Finances

The SCF is a triennial interview survey of US families sponsored by the Board of Governors of the Federal Reserve System and the US Department of Treasury. The sample design for the survey is driven by the need to measure a broad range of financial characteristics. The sample design has two parts: (*a*) a standard geographically based random sample and (*b*) a specially constructed oversampling of wealthy families. Weights are used to combine the two samples to represent the full population of US families. The 2004 SCF interviewed 4,522 families, which represent 112.1 million families. Data available on the Board's website are suitably altered to protect the privacy of individual respondents. Bucks, Kennickell, and Moore (2006) provide a comprehensive discussion of the SCF sampling and weighting procedures. Data, code book, and Federal Reserve Board analysis related to the SCF are available at the Board's website at www.federalreserve.gov/pubs/oss/oss2/2004/scf2004home.html.

Statistics of Income Division

The IRS-SOI Division publishes a series of tabulations based on Form 5498 and individual income tax returns (Form 1040). In addition, the IRS-SOI division makes available an SOI public-use tax file. Focusing on the former, Bryant and Sailer (2006) present the most recent Form 5498 tabulations published by the IRS-SOI division. Sailer, Weber, and Gurka (2003) explain the tax and information returns used to tabulate the data. Basically, the additional data from the information returns (such as IRA data reported on Form 5498) are linked to the individual tax return files, which are a representative sample of tax returns in the USA. Parisi and Hollenbeck (2004, 2005, 2006) report recent aggregate results from the individual tax returns. Turning to the IRS public-use tax file, this information is drawn from US federal individual income tax returns; the 2002 public-use tax file contains 131,307 records, weighted to represent statistical information for the 130.1 million federal individual income tax returns (Form 1040, Form 1040A, and Form 1040EZ) filed for tax-year 2002. The file is designed for making national-level estimates, and the data-set consists of detailed information taken from SOI sample records (the 'microdata file'). Individual names, Social Security numbers, and other personal identifying factors have been omitted. To preserve the character of the microdata file, while also protecting the identity of individuals, the public-use tax file is based on a subsample (less than one-third) of the microdata file and blurs some of the individual return items. Thus, individual records in the public-use tax file may or may not contain data from just one tax return, and never contain the full item content of any one tax return. The data in the public-use file do not provide access to individual taxpayer records.

Investment Company Institute Tracking and IRA Surveys

This chapter also relies on data tabulations from two ongoing ICI house-hold surveys: the Annual Tracking Survey and the IRA Owner Survey. The first relies on an annual survey of 3,000 randomly selected US households to determine the incidence of mutual fund ownership and IRA ownership (among other things). This chapter makes use of the IRA ownership inci-dence. The survey's standard error for the total sample is ±1.8 percent-age points at the 95 percent confidence level. The second datasource is the ICI IRA Owner Survey. West and Leonard-Chambers (2006a, 2006b) present results from the 2005 survey which interviewed 595 randomly selected households owning IRAs [including traditional, Roth, SEP, SAR-SEP, and SIMPLE IRAs; Coverdell education savings accounts (ESAs), for-merly called Education IRAs were not included]. The standard error is ±4.0 percentage points at the 95 percent confidence level.

Notes

[1] At year-end 1985, defined contribution plan and IRA assets comprised 32 percent of the $2.3 trillion US retirement market. By year-end 2006, defined contribution plan and IRA assets accounted for 51 percent of the $16.4 trillion US retirement market (Brady and Holden 2007b). In addition, some employees have an individual account in an employer-sponsored defined benefit plan (mainly in cash balance plans) and many can opt to receive a lump-sum distribution from their company defined benefit plans.

[2] See, for instance, Copeland (2007); Love, Smith, and McNair (2007); Poterba, Venti, and Wise (2007); Blitzstein, Mitchell, and Utkus (2006); Holden, Brady, and Hadley (2006); VanDerhei, Copeland, and Salisbury (2006); Holden et al. (2005); Holden and VanDerhei (2005, 2002a, 2002b); and Mitchell and Utkus (2004).

[3] For example, see Copeland (2005); Investment Company Institute (ICI) (2000a, 2000b); Sabelhaus (2000); Burman, Coe, and Gale (1999); Purcell (1999); Sabel-haus and Weiner (1999); Poterba, Venti, and Wise (1999, 1995); and Chang (1996).

[4] For more discussion, see Holden et al. (2005) and Holden, Brady, and Hadley (2006).

[5] The TRA of 1986 created SAR-SEP IRAs, but the Small Business Job Protection Act of 1996 halted further creation of new SAR-SEP IRAs.

[6] For example, see Joint Economic Committee (2004), which indicates that analy-sis of the IRS-SOI data suggests that the presence of income limits reduces partic-ipation rates at all income levels. Hrung (2004) cites literature analyzing the role that taxpayer confusion plays in the reduction in contribution activity. In addition,

Burnham (2003) finds that some lower-income individuals who are covered by employer-sponsored plans contribute to their IRAs as if they were constrained by the same contribution limits as higher-income individuals when they are not (analyzing 1997 IRS-SOI data). Smith (2002) finds lower participation rates among taxpayers in the phase-out ranges, which he suggests may be due to the complexity of calculating a partial deduction and/or the expectation of being above the income range in the future. Furthermore, some research suggests that a reduction in the promotion of IRAs after universality was removed also had an impact (see Hrung 2004 for additional references).

[7] Bryant and Sailer (2006) find that 53 percent of taxpayers making contributions in 2002 took advantage of the higher limits. West and Leonard-Chambers (2006a) report that a rising share of eligible households is making catch-up contributions over time.

[8] Contributions to Roth IRAs in 1999 were $10.7 billion compared with total contributions of $10.3 billion to traditional IRAs that year. In 2002, contributions to Roth IRAs were $13.2 billion, while total contributions to traditional IRAs were $12.4 billion (Bryant and Sailer 2006; Brady and Holden 2007a, 2007b).

[9] West and Leonard-Chambers (2006a) also found that IRAs with rollovers had higher average traditional IRA balances.

[10] TRA 1986 conformed the withdrawal restrictions for various tax-deferred arrangements (e.g., qualified plans, IRAs, 403(b) arrangements) and included the exception for SEPPs for any age, including owners younger than $59^1/_2$ years of age. The taxpayer would seek to qualify under IRC §72(t), which was made effective for distributions in tax years after 1986.

[11] The exemptions for health insurance premiums and medical expenses came under the Health Insurance Portability and Accountability Act of 1996 (HIPAA). The penalty is not assessed on distributions equal to or less than any qualified medical expenses in excess of 7.5 percent of adjusted gross income, or if to pay for health insurance premiums if the IRA owner is unemployed. See IRS, *Publication 590* for a complete description of the current rules.

[12] This exemption was part of the IRS Restructuring and Reform Act of 1998.

[13] For example, reservists who were called into active duty after September 11, 2001 and before December 31, 2007 and who took distributions from their IRA after being called into active duty could do so and not be subject to the penalty. Also, if a taxpayer's home was located in a disaster area resulting from hurricanes Katrina, Rita, or Wilma and the distribution was made before January 1, 2007 and the taxpayer sustained economic loss because of the hurricane, they are allowed to take up to $100,000 without incurring the penalty.

[14] A data appendix provides additional details on datasources used.

[15] These are described in Bryant and Sailer (2006) and Parisi and Hollenbeck (2006) among other publications.

[16] The income percentile breaks are those for the national SCF sample. As explained by Bucks, Kennickell, and Moore (2006), the income levels delineating the percentiles in 2004 were as follows: less than 20 percent ($18,900); 20–39.9 percent ($33,900); 40–59.9 percent ($53,600); 60–79.9 percent ($89,300); and 80–89.9 percent ($129,400).

[17] Households with IRA withdrawals are distributed across the income groups: 3.4 percent of households with IRA withdrawals are in the bottom income quintile (nationwide) of households; 6.4 percent are in the second income quintile; 17.5 percent are in the third income quintile; 26.8 percent are in the fourth income quintile; 18.9 percent are in the second-highest income decile; and 27.0 percent are in the top income decile.

[18] The net worth percentile breaks are those for the national SCF sample. As explained in Bucks, Kennickell, and Moore (2006), the net worth levels that delineate the percentiles in 2004 are: less than 25 percent ($13,300); 25–49.9 percent ($93,100); 50–74.9 percent ($328,500); and 75–89.9 percent ($831,600).

[19] See Campbell, Parisi, and Balkovic (2000). In 1998, the first year in which Roth IRAs were available, eligible taxpayers could spread the income tax owed on the conversion amount over four years, which boosted conversion activity in that year.

[20] IRA assets prior to the withdrawal are estimated by adding the withdrawal amount to the current year-end assets to approximate the IRA balance before the withdrawal was taken.

References

Amromin, Gene and Paul Smith (2003). 'What Explains Early Withdrawals from Retirement Accounts? Evidence from a Panel of Taxpayers,' *National Tax Journal*, 56(3): 595–612.

Bershadker, Andrew and Paul A. Smith (2006). 'Cracking Open the Nest Egg: IRA Withdrawals and Retirement Finance,' *National Tax Association Proceedings, 98th Annual Conference on Taxation, 2005*: 73–83.

Blitzstein, David, Olivia S. Mitchell, and Stephen P. Utkus (eds.) (2006). *Restructuring Retirement Risks*. Oxford: Oxford University Press.

Brady, Peter and Sarah Holden (2007*a*). 'The U.S. Retirement Market, 2006,' *ICI Fundamentals*, 16(3).

—— —— (2007*b*). 'Appendix: Additional Data on the U.S. Retirement Market,' *ICI Fundamentals*, 16(3A).

Bryant, Victoria L. and Peter J. Sailer (2006). 'Accumulation and Distribution of Individual Retirement Arrangements, 2000–2002,' *SOI (Statistics of Income) Bulletin*, Spring: 233–54.

Bucks, Brian K., Arthur B. Kennickell, and Kevin B. Moore (2006). 'Recent Changes in U.S. Family Finances: Evidence from the 2001 and 2004 Survey of Consumer Finances,' *Federal Reserve Bulletin*, March: A1–38.

Burman, Leonard E., Norma B. Coe, and William G. Gale (1999). 'What Happens When You Show Them the Money?: Lump-Sum Distributions, Retirement Income Security, and Public Policy,' Department of Treasury and The Brookings Institution, Report for the US Department of Labor (Final Report No. 06750-003).

Burnham, Paul (2003). 'Utilization of Tax Incentives for Retirement Saving,' *A CBO Paper*. Washington, DC: Congress of the United States, Congressional Budget Office.

Campbell, David, Michael Parisi, and Brian Balkovic (2000). 'Individual Income Tax Returns, 1998,' *SOI Bulletin*, Fall: 8–46.

Chang, Angela E. (1996). 'Tax Policy, Lump-Sum Pension Distributions, and House-hold Saving,'*National Tax Journal*, 49(2): 235–52.

Copeland, Craig. (2005). 'Lump-Sum Distributions,' *EBRI Notes*, 26(12): 7–17.

—— (2007). 'How Are New Retirees Doing Financially in Retirement?' *EBRI Issue Brief*, 302.

Federal Reserve Board (2004). 2004 Survey of Consumer Finances. Washington, DC. www.federalreserve.gov/pubs/oss/oss2/2004/scf2004home.html.

Holden, Sarah and Jack VanDerhei (2002*a*). 'Can 401(k) Accumulations Generate Significant Income for Future Retirees?' *ICI Perspective*, 8(3), and *EBRI Issue Brief*, 251.

—— —— (2002*b*). 'Appendix: EBRI/ICI 401(k) Accumulation Projection Model,' *ICI Perspective*, 8(3A).

—— —— (2005). 'The Influence of Automatic Enrollment, Catch-Up, and IRA Contributions on 401(k) Accumulations at Retirement,' *ICI Perspective*, 11(2), and *EBRI Issue Brief*, 283.

——, Kathy Ireland, Vicky Leonard-Chambers, and Michael Bogdan (2005). 'The Individual Retirement Account at Age 30: A Retrospective,' *ICI Perspective*, 11(1).

——, Peter Brady, and Michael Hadley (2006). '401(k) Plans: A 25-Year Retrospective,' *ICI Perspective*, 12(2).

Hrung, Warren B. (2004). 'Information, the Introduction of Roths, and IRA Participation,' *Contributions to Economic Analysis & Policy*, 3(1), Article 6: 1–17.

Internal Revenue Service (2006). *Individual Retirement Arrangements (IRAs), Publication 590*. Washington, DC: Internal Revenue Service.

Internal Revenue Service, Statistics of Income Division (1984). *1982 Individual Income Tax Returns, Publication 79 (10–84)*. Washington, DC: US Government Printing Office.

—— (1989). *1986 Individual Income Tax Returns, Publication 1304*. Washington, DC: US Government Printing Office.

—— (2002). *2002 Statistics of Income Public Use Tax File*. Washington, DC: Internal Revenue Service, Statistics of Income Division, Individual Statistics Branch.

Investment Company Institute (ICI) (2000*a*). 'Financial Decisions at Retirement,' *ICI Fundamentals*, 9(6).

—— (2000*b*). *Defined Contribution Plan Distribution Choices at Retirement: A Survey of Employees Retiring Between 1995 and 2000*. Washington, DC: Investment Company Institute.

—— (2007). *2007 Investment Company Fact Book*, 47th edn. Washington, DC: Investment Company Institute.

Joint Economic Committee (2004). *A Primer on Individual Retirement Accounts (IRAs)*. Washington, DC: Joint Economic Committee, United States Senate.

Lin, Emily (2006). 'Job Loss and Retirement Fund Distributions Among Older Workers,' *Working Paper*. Washington, DC: US Department of the Treasury.

Love, David A., Paul A. Smith, and Lucy C. McNair (2007). 'Do Households Have Enough Wealth for Retirement?' FEDS Working Paper no. 2007-17. Washington, DC: Board of Governors of the Federal Reserve System.

Mahaney, James I. and Peter C. Carlson (2008). 'New Approaches to Retirement Income Planning,' Chapter 7, this volume.

Mitchell, Olivia S. and Stephen P. Utkus (eds.) (2004). *Pension Design and Structure: New Lessons from Behavioral Finance*. Oxford: Oxford University Press.

Parisi, Michael and Scott Hollenbeck (2004). 'Individual Income Tax Returns, 2002,' *SOI Bulletin*, Fall: 8–45.

—— —— (2005). 'Individual Income Tax Returns, 2003,' *SOI Bulletin*, Fall: 9–49.

—— —— (2006). 'Individual Income Tax Returns, 2004,' *SOI Bulletin*, Fall: 8–46.

Poterba, James, Steven Venti, and David A. Wise (2007). 'Rise of 401(k) Plans, Lifetime Earnings, and Wealth at Retirement,' NBER Working Paper no. 13091. Cambridge, MA: National Bureau of Economic Research.

Poterba, James M., Steven F. Venti, and David A. Wise (1995). 'Lump-Sum Distributions from Retirement Saving Plans: Receipt and Utilization,' NBER Working Paper no. 5298. Cambridge, MA: National Bureau of Economic Research.

—— —— —— (1999). 'Pre-Retirement Cashouts and Foregone Retirement Saving: Implications for 401(k) Asset Accumulation,' NBER Working Paper no. 7314. Cambridge, MA: National Bureau of Economic Research.

Purcell, Patrick J. (1999). 'Lump-Sum Distributions and Retirement Income Security,' *Journal of Pension Planning & Compliance*, 26(3): 27–59.

Sabelhaus, John (2000). 'Modeling IRA Accumulation and Withdrawals,' *National Tax Journal*, 53(4), Part 1: 865–75.

——, and David Weiner (1999). 'Disposition of Lump-Sum Pension Distributions: Evidence from Tax Returns,' *National Tax Journal*, 52(3): 593–613.

Sailer, Peter J., Michael E. Weber, and Kurt S. Gurka (2003). 'Are Taxpayers Increasing the Buildup of Retirement Assets? Preliminary Results from a Matched File of Tax Year 1999 Tax Returns and Information Returns,' *National Tax Association Proceedings, 95th Annual Conference on Taxation, 2002*: 364–369.

Sharpe, William F., Jason S. Scott, and John G. Watson (2008). 'Efficient Retirement Financial Strategies,' Chapter 9, this volume.

Skinner, Jonathan (1992). 'Individual Retirement Accounts: A Review of the Evidence,' *Tax Notes*, January 13: 201–211.

Smith, Paul A. (2002). 'Retirement Saving Over the Long Term: Evidence from a Panel of Taxpayers,' *Working Paper*. Washington, DC: Department of the Treasury and Federal Reserve Board.

VanDerhei, Jack, Craig Copeland, and Dallas Salisbury (2006). *Retirement Security in the United States: Current Sources, Future Prospects, and Likely Outcomes of Current Trends*. Washington, DC: Employee Benefit Research Institute.

West, Sandra, and Victoria Leonard-Chambers (2006a). 'The Role of IRAs in Americans' Retirement Preparedness,' *ICI Fundamentals*, 15(1).

—— —— (2006b). 'Appendix: Additional Data on IRA Ownership in 2005,' *ICI Fundamentals*, 15(1A).

Chapter 6

Retirement Distributions and the Bequest Motive

G. Victor Hallman

Planning for and managing retirement assets as well as the payouts from these revolve around securing adequate retirement income and assuring the continuity of such income for as along as retirees (and their spouses) live. Most people are concerned about a possible lack of adequate retirement income and the risk that they will outlive their assets. Often advisers suggest that a logical and efficient strategy to deal with these issues for risk-averse retirees is to annuitize the retiree's assets or benefits over his or her lifetime (or if married, over the joint and last survivor lifetimes of the retiree and spouse). Another suggested strategy is to use a combination of life annuitization and an installment withdrawal plan. These approaches are indeed efficient for providing lifetime retirement income. They are based, however, on the implicit assumption of limited resources for retirement income, and hence they presume the need to disburse, and probably consume, those resources over the lifetimes of the retiree and his or her spouse.

Despite the logic of annuitization or the combination approach, we are left with the so-called 'annuity puzzle,' which notes that relatively few retirees actually purchase immediate life annuities or choose life annuitization for their retirement benefits. One reason (of several) cited for this 'annuity puzzle' is the bequest or inheritance motive.[1] This chapter explores the nature, limitations, and strategies used in implementing the bequest motive as part of a retiree's decision-making about how to manage his assets in retirement.

In what follows, we first discuss what we mean by the bequest motive and how current law permits tax-favored transfers to heirs. Next, we turn to the constraints limiting these transfers, and finally discuss current strategies making these more feasible. We conclude that US tax law provides tax incentives to encourage the provision of retirement income via minimum distribution rules. In practice, however, these rules and other tax law provisions now permit significant tax-favored wealth transfer and charitable giving strategies.

Nature and Significance of the Bequest Motive

By the bequest or inheritance motive, we mean using income-tax-favored (i.e., tax-deferred or tax-free growth) retirement plans as vehicles to pass wealth to heirs (usually children and grandchildren) of the retiree and spouse, or to charity after the last of their deaths. To accomplish this, the retiree (participant in the case of qualified retirement plans, and owner in the case of individual retirement accounts and annuities) and spouse *during their lifetimes* plan to draw down the balance of their retirement plans as little as permitted by the tax law (and by their personal needs) so that assets can continue to grow tax-deferred or tax-free (in the case of Roth IRAs) for as long as possible. They also seek to arrange plan beneficiary designations so that after their deaths their beneficiaries have the opportunity to maintain income-tax-deferral or tax-free growth for as long as possible (generally over the beneficiaries' life expectancies). This is the so-called 'stretch' IRA strategy.[2] As US tax law and Internal Revenue Service (IRS) regulations now stand, with proper planning, such income-tax-deferral or tax-free growth can easily continue for 50 or more years and extend over the life expectancies of the owner, his or her spouse, and their children (and possibly grandchildren)—in other words, over two or more generations.

Some researchers contend that, even if assets are needed during retirement (beyond the minimum distributions required by law), it is preferable from an income tax standpoint to first take such distributions from taxable investment accounts (investment portfolios held outside of tax-advantaged plans), and only later from tax-advantaged retirement accounts.[3] This is the strategy of tax-efficient *sequencing of lifetime distributions* from different categories of accounts. While such sequencing does seem somewhat to increase asset values, we conclude that it may not be a quantitatively significant strategy for wealth transfer.[4]

Retirement plan distributions are also a highly tax-efficient way to fulfill a person's charitable giving objectives, as they represent gross income for federal income tax purposes both to the retiree during the retirement years and to plan beneficiaries after the retiree's death. They are income in respect of a decedent (IRD). But since charities are tax-exempt, they realize no income tax liability when such distributions are payable to them. Charitable gifts at death are also deductible for federal estate purposes. As a result, some suggest that retirement plan assets, and other IRD items for that matter, should be used to fulfill a person's charitable objectives (Hoyt 2002a). While charitable giving may be, in itself, a socially desirable motivation, again we see the tax-driven use of retirement assets for purposes other than providing retirement income to the participant or owner and spouse. It may also be noted that in the case of tax-deferred retirement assets made

TABLE 6-1 Number of and Growth in High Net Worth
Individuals: North America 2001–5

	High Net Worth Individuals (millions)	Change over Previous Year (%)
2001	2.2	—
2002	2.2	0
2003	2.5	13.5
2004	2.7	8.0
2005	2.9	7.4

Source: Capgemini and Merrill Lynch (2004: 2; 2006: 4–5, 31).

payable to (or rolled over to) tax-exempt charities, the government never collects income taxes on the deferred amounts.

Accordingly, the bequest or inheritance motive can involve many complex goals, including the deferral of distributions from retirement plans for long periods so that income-tax-deferred (or tax-free) assets pass to at least one generation beyond that of the original participant or owner; and the use of retirement assets to make otherwise desired charitable gifts.[5] Of course, implied in the planning for these goals is the notion that the original participant or owner has sufficient wealth, income, and other resources so that he need not consume most of the retirement assets during retirement; in other words, he is probably a reasonably high net worth individual. Table 6-1 indicates that the number of high net worth individuals (defined as persons holding $1 million or more in financial assets) doubled in the first five years of the twenty-first century.

The significance of retirement assets (qualified retirement plans and IRAs) in the gross estates of decedents whose estates filed federal estate tax returns is also growing over time.[6] Table 6-2 indicates that such percentages have doubled over the 1990s. One explanation for this trend is the emergence of individual account-type plans that enable participants to leave retirement assets to heirs. In the future, decedents will

TABLE 6-2 Retirement Assets as a Percentage of
Gross Estates for Federal Estate Tax
Returns Filed: 1992, 1995, and 2001

	Male Decedents (%)	Female Decedents (%)
1992	5.8	2.3
1995	7.8	3.2
2001	11.2	5.5

Source: Johnson and Mikow (1999) and Eller (2005).

increasingly be able to leave more account balances from these types of plans in their gross estates. Further, the substantial increases in qualified plan contribution and benefit limits, compensation limits, section 401(k) employee elective contribution limits, and IRA contribution limits, enacted in the Economic Growth Tax Relief Reconciliation Act (EGTRRA) of 2001 and made permanent by the Pension Protection Act (PPA) of 2006, are enabling higher net worth individuals to contribute significant amounts to tax-advantaged plans. Of course these changes have benefited from the long trend of generally favorable economic and investment performance, particularly for common stocks, producing good investment returns for many individual account plans.

These factors have combined to generate growing retirement assets in the hands of individuals who can afford to delay taking benefits during their retirement, and who can also consider using a portion of these assets to satisfy charitable giving objectives. This development, paired with tax law complexity regarding retirement plan distributions, has led to considerable planning activity among estate planners and wealth management professionals to aid clients in arranging for the distribution of retirement plan assets (Hoyt 2002*a*; Choate 2004, 2006).

Tax and Economic Constraints on Wealth Transfer

Before discussing specific planning strategies that may be used to enable tax-advantaged retirement plans to fulfill bequest or charitable motives, it is useful to briefly describe the tax rules intended to assure that these retirement benefits will, in fact, be used for retirement. Possible economic constraints on using these benefits for wealth transfer purposes are also noted.

Tax Rules Affecting Timing of Retirement Plan Distributions

One philosophy guiding tax law holds that income tax advantages to retirement plans are intended to encourage their adoption to provide retirement income (rather than for wealth transfer or estate planning purposes). In practice, the idea would be that retirement plan distributions should be taken neither too early (presumably for current consumption or other nonretirement purposes) nor too late (presumably for wealth transfer purposes). The specific rules that embody this policy objective include the 10 percent penalty tax on 'premature distributions'; age limits on distributions from plans such as Roth IRAs and 401(k) plans; and the required beginning date (RBD), minimum distribution rules, and 50 percent penalty tax on insufficient distributions [i.e., less than the minimum required distributions (MRDs)].

The 10 percent penalty tax (also called the section 72(t) penalty) is levied on retirement plan distributions to participants or owners who are younger than age $59^1/_2$. There are a number of exceptions to this penalty tax, but they do not change the fundamental purpose just noted. The minimum distribution rules apply to qualified retirement plans, section 403(b) plans, IRAs, and section 457 plans. For lifetime benefits of participants or owners, minimum distributions must begin by an RBD which is specified as the first of April of the calendar year following the year in which the person attains age $70^1/_2$. The person must take MRDs for the year in which he or she attains age $70^1/_2$ and for each subsequent year (by December 31 of that year).[7]

During the participant's or owner's lifetime, the MRDs are based on his or her life expectancy from a Uniform Lifetime Table as stipulated by the Federal Government (see Appendix Table 6-A1). To calculate the MRD for a particular year, the account balance at the end of the previous year (or plan year) is divided by the distribution period shown in the Table for his or her attained age in that distribution year. The distribution periods decline with age but never reach zero. Thus, they are recalculated each year since that year's life expectancy becomes the applicable divisor.[8] The effect of this is that MRDs will continue over the person's lifetime, although the amounts will normally increase with time. The distribution periods under the Uniform Lifetime Table are based on the joint life expectancies of the participant or owner and a theoretical person (beneficiary) 10 years younger. This generally is true regardless of whom the beneficiary may be.[9]

The Uniform Lifetime Table is beneficial for the bequest motive. It will call for relatively low MRDs for many years after a person attains the RBD. Depending on the investment return inside the plan, this means retirement plan account balances may continue to grow, and hence be available for beneficiaries, for many years after minimum distributions must begin. For example, assuming plan assets have a 6 percent investment return, the MRD will not exceed that year's investment return inside the plan until the participant or owner reaches age 83. If plan assets can earn 8 percent, the corresponding age is 89.

Roth IRAs are not subject to the minimum distribution rules for distributions during the *owner's* lifetime; they do apply, however, to *plan beneficiaries* after the owner's death. This lifetime treatment is also very beneficial for the bequest motive. It means Roth IRA account balances can grow tax-free without any diminution for an owner's entire lifetime, which may be 20, 30, or more years after retirement, before passing to a beneficiary at the original owner's death. Roth IRAs have grown significantly since they were first introduced in 1997. For example, in 2002 taxpayers *contributed* ~$42.3 billion to individual retirement arrangements of which about $13.2 billion or 31.2 percent were contributions to Roth IRAs. Such Roth contributions have increased about 14.1 percent from the year 2000 when such data for IRAs were first produced. In addition, in 2000, 3,989,390 taxpayers *rolled over* ~$204.4 billion into traditional IRAs. Of course, when the total fair market value of IRA assets in 2002 of about $2.6 trillion are considered, Roth IRA assets represented only about 3.0 percent because Roth plans are of such recent origin (Bryant and Sailer 2006).

Recent legislative developments are likely to increase the proportion of assets in Roth plans. For one, the Tax Increase Prevention and Reconciliation Act of 2005 eliminated (for years after December 31, 2009) the $100,000 or less modified adjusted gross income eligibility requirement for conversion of a traditional to a Roth IRA. Thus, for 2010 and thereafter, persons with modified adjusted gross incomes in excess of $100,000 will be able to convert some or all of their traditional IRAs to Roth IRAs by paying income tax on the converted amount. This should increase such conversions substantially because higher income persons are more likely to be able to afford the income tax on conversion and to benefit from the tax-free investment growth and no minimum distribution requirements during their lifetimes than lower income traditional IRA owners. In addition, the PPA of 2006 made Roth 401(k) and 403(b) plans permanent. These Roth plans were created by EGTRRA in 2001 for 2006 and thereafter, though the provision for these (along with the rest of EGTRRA) was to 'sunset' in 2011. In 2006, the PPA nullified the 'sunset' as to the pension and IRA provisions of EGTRRA, in effect making them permanent. It is possible that many employers may have hesitated to add a Roth 401(k) option to their benefit plans, possibly because of the greater administrative cost, but more likely because they were unsure that this option would survive by 2011. Now they are.

The minimum distribution rules are different for distributions to plan or IRA beneficiaries after a participant's or owner's death: in particular, they depend on who the beneficiary is and whether the participant or owner died before or after his or her RBD. In general, if the only beneficiary is a 'designated beneficiary,' who would be an individual, two or more individuals, or a see-through trust (defined later as one having only individual beneficiaries), the benefits can be made payable over the beneficiary's life expectancy using the Single Life Table (as in Appendix Table 6-A1). The *individuals* (persons) for this purpose may be either a surviving spouse or individuals other than a surviving spouse. Minimum distributions to a see-through trust are based on the life expectancies of the individual beneficiaries of the trust.

In general, if a *surviving spouse* is the only designated beneficiary of a plan, let us assume an IRA, he or she can: (*a*) leave the IRA in the name of the deceased spouse and treat it as an 'inherited IRA'; taking minimum distributions usually over the surviving spouse's life expectancy using the Single Life Table but recalculating the remaining life expectancy at the surviving spouse's age each year;[10] or (b) treat the IRA as his or her own, naming his or her own beneficiaries, not having to begin distributions until the surviving spouse's RBD (aged 70½), and using the Uniform Lifetime Table with its much slower MRDs. The second choice is usually preferable for deferral purposes.

If the designated beneficiary is an *individual or individuals other than a surviving spouse*, the account balance generally can be payable over the beneficiary's life expectancy or the life expectancy of the oldest beneficiary in the case of multiple beneficiaries (without separate accounts) using the Single Life Table but with a fixed-term or 'reduce-by-one' approach (no recalculation). This may be less advantageous for deferral purposes.

Finally, if there is *no designated beneficiary* (which might occur, e.g., if the beneficiary is a trust that is not a see-through trust, a charity, the decedent's estate, or multiple beneficiaries when at least one is not an individual), the no-designated-beneficiary rule applies. In this case, if death occurs before the participant's or owner's RBD, a five year rule applies and the account balance must be paid out by the end of the fifth anniversary of the decedent's death. If death occurs on or after the RBD, the account balance must be paid out at least over the deceased participant's or owner's remaining life expectancy using the Single Life Table with no recalculation (i.e., applying the fixed-period method). These 'no-DB' rules are the least favorable for deferral purposes.

As noted previously, after a Roth IRA owner's death, the post-death minimum distribution rules just described also apply to Roth IRA beneficiaries. Of course, the distributions to them are tax-free just as they were during the original owner's lifetime.

Economic Constraints on the Bequest Motive

The bequest advantage from 'stretching' retirement plan payouts depends almost entirely on income-tax-deferral or income-tax-free investment growth of the payouts. Therefore, a fair question is how valuable income-tax-deferral is from an economic or investment viewpoint.

Qualified dividends on stocks and long-term capital gains are currently taxed at a top rate of 15 percent (at least through 2010); by contrast, distributions from qualified retirement plans, traditional IRAs, and other retirement plans are taxed as ordinary income. Further, most capital assets get a stepped-up income tax basis at death, while most retirement plan distributions are IRD. Accordingly, some commentators have questioned the economic value of deferral in retirement plans versus direct after-tax ownership of assets.[11] But deferral in a retirement plan will always be advantageous, assuming that the applicable income tax rate at the time of contribution is the same as at the time of distribution, and that the asset allocations inside the plan and outside the plan are such that the *before-tax* total returns are the same for both, while *after-tax* investment returns outside the plan are less than the returns inside the plan (because the outside return is subject to income taxation). This is true, in essence, because the retirement plan participant or owner is getting tax-deferred investment income on money that otherwise would be paid in taxes; he is in a sense investing the government's money. But the *degree* of this advantage depends on a host of factors including the length of the period of deferral, whether there is a rising or declining stock market, the level of interest rates and other investment returns, turnover of common stocks outside the plan, and the availability of investment products (such as index mutual funds) that affect such turnover, whether there will be step-up in basis at death, investment expenses, and others.

Another economic question is what income tax rates will be at the time of the retirement plan distributions. At present, individual income tax rates are at a historically low level. Yet conventional wisdom argues that income tax rates during a person's retirement years tend to be lower than during the working years. As a rule, higher tax rates at distribution rather than during the contribution phase would favor tax-free investment growth (Roth plans) and be relatively disadvantageous for tax-deferral plans. The reverse would be true for lower rates at distribution than at contribution.

Finally, contributions to tax-advantaged retirement plans involve inflexibilities (due to plan requirements and tax law contribution limits), lack of liquidity (due to tax law limits on distributions), possible penalty taxes, and the risk of possible future disadvantageous changes in the tax law. Participants and owners also may forgo other tax advantageous uses of plan contributions and assets, such as making gift-tax-free transfers to children and grandchildren.

Strategies for Wealth Transfer and Charitable Giving with Retirement Benefits

Various strategies may be used to make tax-effective transfers of retirement assets within the family and as charitable gifts. In our overreview, we assume that the participant or owner has a substantial qualified retirement plan or IRA individual account balance at retirement.

The 'Stretch IRA' Concept with Spouse as a Designated Beneficiary

This is the simplest and most effective tax-deferral strategy. The participant or owner names a spouse as a beneficiary of the qualified plan or IRA account balance, with perhaps the children or trusts for the children as contingent beneficiaries. Upon the participant's or owner's death, the surviving spouse normally rolls over the participant's qualified plan account balance to an IRA, or elects to treat the decedent's IRA as an own rollover IRA.[12] The surviving spouse then may name a beneficiary or beneficiaries for the IRA, often the children (or trusts for the children). The original beneficiaries (the children) also may name successor beneficiaries in case they do not outlive their life expectancies. This spousal rollover IRA strategy can result in the deferral of taxable distributions (in the case of traditional IRAs) or continuation of tax-free investment growth (in the case of Roth IRAs) under the minimum distribution rules for the spouse's lifetime and then over the life expectancies of the children. This is the classic 'stretch IRA' approach-distributing benefits over one or more life expectancies.

An Example of a Spousal 'Stretch IRA'

As an example, assume that Homer Smith is about to retire from the XYZ Corporation and he is 65 years old (his birthday is February 1). He and his wife, Mary, aged 61, have two children: Homer Jr., aged 35, and Hortense, aged 28. They all are in good health. Homer and Mary appear to be happily married, have no prior spouses, and both are competent in investing and property management (Mary having been a successful accountant for many years). Their nonretirement asset picture is summarized in Table 6-3.

TABLE 6-3 Nonretirement Assets of Homer and Mary Smith: A Hypothetical Example

Assets and Ownership	Value ($)
Principal residence (owned by Homer and Mary as joint tenants with right of survivorship)	600,000
Summer home (owned by Homer and Mary as joint tenants with right of survivorship)	400,000
Individually owned securities (common stocks, bonds, and CDs) owned by Homer	1,000,000
Individually owned securities (common stocks, bonds, and CDs) owned by Mary	500,000
Cash and other assets (owned by Homer and Mary as joint tenants with right of survivorship)	100,000

Source: Author's computations.

As Homer's retirement approached, Homer and Mary have determined that their asset allocation (other than their real estate) should be 50 percent in a diversified portfolio of common stocks (selected conservative individual stocks and mutual fund shares), 45 percent in bonds and CDs (diversified as to maturity, issuer, and credit quality), and 5 percent in cash equivalents. In light of good *asset location planning*, they decide to hold their taxable bonds and CDs in tax-deferred or tax-free retirement accounts, and their common stocks, tax-exempt bonds, taxable bonds, and their cash equivalents individually. They expect an average annual total return on their common stock portfolio of 8 percent (3 percent qualified dividends and 5 percent long-term capital gains) and an annual current yield on their bonds and CDs of 6 percent. They also plan to rebalance their portfolio periodically to maintain their desired assert allocation. Homer's employer, the XYZ Corporation, has a defined benefit (DB) pension plan covering both retirees (under a qualified joint-and-survivor annuity form) and a 401(k) plan. Homer and Mary will also receive government social security benefits. Mary also has a vested pension promise from a previous employer that will commence when she reaches age 65. Homer and Mary will be eligible for Medicare and XYZ Corporation at present has a retiree medical plan that will cover them.

Homer's and Mary's objectives are to maintain their living standards during retirement, to protect themselves against medical expenses and possibly custodial care expenses during retirement, to have an emergency fund, possibly to make lifetime (annual exclusion) gifts to their children, and possibly to make gifts to charity. Assuming that these objectives can be met from their pension, social security, and individually held investment income (as it would appear they can), at the last of their deaths they would like to leave as much as possible to their children (and hopefully grandchildren) with as little tax shrinkage as possible.

Given this scenario, assume that Homer has a $1.5 million 401(k) account balance in his XYZ Corporation plan and decides to *directly transfer (roll over)* this account balance to his own traditional IRA at age 65. He names Mary as a designated beneficiary of the IRA. Homer and Mary plan to take only the MRDs from this IRA so that it can continue to grow tax-deferred for as long as possible for the benefit of their children. Homer need not take any distributions from the IRA until the *required beginning date* at age 70$^1/_2$ (in about five years).[13] Using the Uniform Lifetime Table, Homer's distribution period (life expectancy) at age 70 is 27.4 years, which in effect requires a minimum distribution of 3.6496 percent of the IRA account balance as of the end of the previous year.[14] If we assume that account balance is $2,007,338 ($1.5 million at 6 percent for five years), the minimum distribution for Homer's 70$^1/_2$ years is $73,260, which is substantially less than the 6 percent interest income (of \$120,440) from the IRA for that year.[15]

Homer continues to take increasing minimum distributions until his *death* which we shall assume to be at age 86. To the extent that the minimum distribution for the year of his death was not taken by Homer, it must be taken by Mary as a beneficiary. Assuming Homer's estate plan calls for an 'optimal marital deduction' strategy (use of the marital deduction only until it reduces the federal estate tax on Homer's estate to zero and then the balance of his estate to a credit-shelter or by-pass trust or gift—a 'reduce to zero formula'), there will be no federal estate tax payable at Homer's death. The IRA account balance payable to Mary will qualify for the federal estate tax marital deduction and hence will be deductible for federal estate tax purposes.[16]

As a general principle, making income-tax-deferred retirement plan account balances payable to a surviving spouse also is an efficient estate tax strategy because they represent IRD and so the distributions will be taxable as ordinary income to the beneficiary (the surviving spouse). Therefore, the income tax payable on those distributions (which must be paid in any event) comes from the surviving spouse's assets and hence will not be in his or her gross estate when the surviving spouse subsequently dies, thereby reducing his or her federal estate tax liability.

After Homer's death, as the designated beneficiary of his IRA, Mary elects to treat the IRA as her own and names her two children as equal beneficiaries. She must begin taking minimum distributions in the year following Homer's death since she then would be age 83 (beyond her RBD). Her distribution period at age 83, using the Uniform Lifetime Table (since she is treating the IRA as her own), is 16.3 years, so she effectively must withdraw (and pay tax on) 6.1350 percent of the account balance (calculated as of the end of the year of Homer's death) by December 31 of the year following his death. She then must continue taking increasing minimum distributions until the year after her death. Assuming further that Mary also dies at age 86 (four years after Homer's death), the remaining IRA account balance is payable equally to her and Homer's two children as designated beneficiaries of Mary's IRA.[17] Since they are designated beneficiaries, the account balance may be paid out to them over their life expectancies using the Single Life Table and fixed-period (one year less) method.

At Mary's death, the remaining IRA account balance will be included in her gross estate for federal estate tax purposes. It normally will also result in a federal estate tax in her estate unless she has remarried and names a surviving spouse as a beneficiary or leaves it to charity (which seem unlikely in this case). Her will normally should specify (in a tax clause) that any death taxes attributable to the tax-advantaged retirement account should be payable from other assets in her estate so the full amount of the retirement account can continue to grow tax-deferred (in this case) or tax-free (in the case of a Roth IRA).

The IRA now will be payable to the two children as an inherited IRA. As of Mary's death, Homer Jr. will be age 60 and Hortense will be 53. When IRAs are payable to multiple beneficiaries, the general rule is that the account balance must be paid out over the fixed-period life expectancy of the oldest beneficiary, which here is Homer Jr. But if separate accounts are established for each beneficiary by December 31 of the year following the year of Mary's death, each beneficiary can use his or her own life expectancy in calculating MRDs. Assuming such separate accounts are created, under the Single Life Table Homer Jr.'s life expectancy would be 24.4 years (at age 61) and Hortense's life expectancy would be 30.5 years (at age 54), as of the year following the year of their mother's death when they must begin taking minimum distributions. In that year, the percentage withdrawals would be 4.0984 percent and 3.2787 percent, respectively. The applicable divisor (life expectancy) for each would then be reduced by one each year thereafter. Therefore, the IRAs must be exhausted (entirely distributed) by the 25th and 31st years, respectively.

The IRA distributions will be taxed as ordinary income to the children. However, since there was federal estate tax attributable to the IRA account balance paid by Mary's estate, and the distributions to the children are IRD, the children are entitled to an itemized income tax deduction each year for the pro rata share of the federal estate tax paid on their retirement plan distributions. This is to avoid double taxation of distributions of IRD items.

Given this example then, Table 6-4 shows the periods of income-tax-deferral made possible by this 'stretch IRA' strategy in this situation starting

TABLE 6-4 Periods of Income-Tax-Deferral for the Smith Example: The Spousal 'Stretch IRA' Strategy

Distributee and Age	Period of Deferral
Homer: the ages of 65 through 69: no distributions	5 years
Homer: age 70 through 86: minimum distributions using Uniform Lifetime Table	17 years
Mary: age 83 through 86: minimum distributions using Uniform Lifetime Table	4 years
Homer Jr.: age 61 through 85+: minimum distributions using Uniform Lifetime Table (fixed period)	24+ years
Hortense: age 54 through 84+: minimum distributions using Uniform Lifetime Table (fixed period)	30+ years

Source: Author's computations; see text.

with Homer's retirement at age 65. It is interesting to observe that in this rather straightforward example, income-tax-deferrals continue for more than 30 years after the deaths of the original plan participant, Homer, and his spouse, Mary. This was actually a longer deferral period than applied during the lives of the participant and his spouse.

If any part of this retirement plan had been a Roth IRA, no distributions from the Roth would be required over Homer's or Mary's lifetimes since there are no MRDs from a Roth IRA for the owner's lifetime. In this case, it would result in 26 years of tax-free investment growth. At Mary's death, the Roth IRA account balance would be in her gross estate for federal estate tax purposes and would be an inherited Roth IRA for the children for income tax purposes. Thus, the children must begin taking minimum distributions at this point over their life expectancies (normally using separate accounts) under the fixed-period method. These distributions would be income-tax-free (not IRD), so no itemized deductions for federal estate tax paid on the retirement account would be available. Clearly the 'stretch' Roth IRA approach offers substantially more income-tax-advantaged bequest potential than even the 'stretch' traditional IRA.

Possible Problems with Spousal Rollover 'Stretch IRAs'

While this approach normally can provide the best purely tax-driven deferral (bequest) potential, it is not without possible nontax problems. First, the retirement account is made payable to the spouse as a designated beneficiary and so this spouse *controls the account* after the original owner's death. Hopefully, the surviving spouse will follow the just described rollover 'stretch IRA' strategy and also name the deceased spouse's children as beneficiaries of the survivor's rollover IRA. However, there may be a number of practical impediments to this actually happening. It may be a second (or more) marriage and the survivor may not be willing to designate the deceased spouse's children of a prior marriage as beneficiaries of his or her rollover IRA. Similarly, the surviving spouse may remarry and have a new family to consider in planning for the retirement account.

A second concern is that management of the rollover IRA will be in the hands of the surviving spouse and he or she may not be experienced or competent concerning investments and wealth management. Further, the surviving spouse may decide that deferral is not for him or her and for various reasons (good or bad) take the retirement money now, despite paying higher taxes (the consumption motive). But there also may be valid estate planning reasons for taking more than the required minimum distributions, such as the need for funds to make annual exclusion (or other gift-tax-free) gifts to children or grandchildren or for charitable contributions.

These same issues may apply to children named as beneficiaries of the original IRA or the spousal rollover IRA.

Additionally, when retirement benefits constitute the bulk or a large part of an estate, and the estate is large enough to attract potential federal estate taxation, there may not be enough non-retirement-plan assets (directly owned assets) to fund fully a credit-shelter or by-pass trust (or gift) when executing an optimal marital deduction strategy. Assuming no lifetime taxable gifts, at an estate owner's death the optimal marital deduction calls for an amount equal to the applicable exclusion amount to be placed in a credit-shelter or by-pass trust (or gift) that does not qualify for the marital deduction in the decedent's estate and is not included in a surviving spouse's gross estate. The remainder of the decedent's estate is left so as to qualify for the marital deduction. This reduces the federal estate tax on the estate of the first spouse to die to zero and diminishes the tax on the estate of the second spouse to die by the tax that otherwise would be payable on the amount in the by-pass trust or gift. When retirement plan assets are needed (and used) to fund the credit-shelter or by-pass trust, they are not available for a spousal rollover 'stretch IRA', which offers the best income-tax-deferral result. The result can be a planning dilemma between maximum income-tax-deferral (saving) and maximum estate tax saving.

This complexity can be illustrated with the Homer Smith example. If Homer were to die soon after he retired at age 65 (in 2007), his gross estate for federal estate tax purposes would be $3,050,000 (ignoring his DB plan). Assuming funeral expenses, estate administration expenses and debts of the estate total $50,000, the net value would be $3,000,000. An optimal marital (reduce to zero formula clause in his will) then would cause $2,000,000 to be placed in a by-pass trust (presumably with Mary and the children as beneficiaries) or gift and $1,000,000 would pass to Mary so as to qualify for the marital deduction (of which $550,000 would be from their two homes and other jointly owned assets). But Homer's probate estate only has $1,000,000 of assets (individually owned securities) with which to fund the by-pass trust and pay the estate's debts and expenses. Therefore, if the by-pass trust (or gift) is to be fully funded, Homer (or Mary by disclaimer) will need to have about $1,050,000 of his IRA account balance payable to the by-pass trust (or payable to their children or to trusts for their children) to make up the full $2,000,000 now permitted at his present asset values. In such a situation, a decision must be made either to give up part (or all) of the income-tax-deferral (or tax-free growth) advantages of a spousal rollover IRA and fully fund the by-pass trust, or to maintain the entire IRA account balance as a spousal rollover IRA with its income tax advantages but to underfund the by-pass trust or gift which may result in higher estate tax at the surviving spouse's subsequent death.[18] Naturally, this issue will depend on the size of the applicable exclusion amount at the person's death, which is uncertain at this time; the proportion of the gross estate consisting of retirement assets; and even the status (existence) of the federal estate tax itself.

The 'Stretch IRA' Concept with Other Individuals as Designated Beneficiaries

Individual beneficiaries other than a surviving spouse also may take minimum distributions over their life expectancies, but they must use the Single Life Table and the fixed-period (one year less) method. Other individual beneficiaries cannot roll over a qualified plan to their own IRA or treat a decedent's IRA as their own, but they may have 'inherited IRAs' payable over their life expectancies. This can allow them considerable 'stretch' opportunities, depending on their ages. These individuals often would be children, but they also might be grandchildren, siblings, other family members, or domestic partners or companions.

Returning to the case of Homer Smith, for example, if for some reason Mary were not in the picture (previous death, divorce, or more than adequate assets of her own), Homer could name his two children as beneficiaries of his 401(k) savings plan or of his rollover IRA. If Homer were tragically to die early, say at age 65, and assuming separate accounts are established for each child, Homer Jr.'s life expectancy at his age 36 (one year after Homer's death) would be 48.5 years (or a 2.0618 percent minimum required distribution) while Hortense's life expectancy at age 29 would be 54.3 years (or a 1.8416 percent minimum distribution). Thereafter, their expectancies would decline by one each year until the account balance for each would be exhausted in the 49th year for Homer Jr. (his age 85) and in the 55th year for Hortense (her age 84) regardless of whether they lived longer than those ages.

At Homer's death (assumed at age 65 here), if he had not yet rolled over his 401(k) qualified savings plan account balance to his own IRA and his children were the equal beneficiaries of the 401(k) plan, under the provisions of the PPA of 2006, the children (as nonspouse individual beneficiaries) could transfer their account balances to an 'inherited IRA' for each with each IRA being in Homer's name as decedent but payable over the child's life expectancy as beneficiary. If Homer had done a rollover to his own IRA prior to his death, the IRA custodian would treat each child's separate account as an 'inherited IRA' in Homer's name (as decedent) but payable over each child's life expectancy as beneficiary.

Naturally, if Homer were to die at a more likely age, such as the previously assumed age 86, his children's life expectancies would be shorter—age

57 and 27.9 years for Homer Jr. and age 50 and 34.2 years for Hortense. However, substantial income-tax-deferral (or tax-free growth) still would be possible. Grandchildren (none are assumed in the Homer Smith example) could also possibly be named as individual beneficiaries. However, they would be 'skip persons' to the participant or owner and so the generation-skipping transfer tax would have to be considered.

As noted earlier, children or other individual beneficiaries may have some of the same practical problems with 'stretch IRAs' as a surviving spouse as beneficiary. Wealth management professionals often comment anecdotally that children beneficiaries may want the money now (even though taxed) rather than being 'dribbled out' over their life expectancies.

Trusts as Beneficiaries

It sometimes is desirable to have retirement benefits payable to a trust as beneficiary rather than to a spouse, children, or other individuals. This can be for all the estate planning, family, control, investment management, and allowance for discretion reasons that trusts are generally used. But when retirement benefits are made payable to trusts, income-tax-deferral and other advantages often are sacrificed at least to some degree for trust administration. Thus there are income tax and other trade-offs in using retirement benefits to fund trusts.

Trade-offs with Trusts as Beneficiaries

One such trade-off is that income-tax-deferral often is reduced. The general minimum distribution rule is that retirement plan account balances payable to other than individual designated beneficiaries must be paid out by the end of the fifth anniversary of the participant's or owner's death. This rule applies to trusts unless a trust meets the tax law requirements to be a see-through trust.

Under the minimum distribution rules, a *see-through trust* as beneficiary allows distributions to be paid from the plan (normally an IRA) over the life expectancy of the oldest trust beneficiary (using the Single Life Table without recalculation) or over the separate life expectancy of each trust beneficiary if a separate subtrust is named for each trust beneficiary in the *plan's* beneficiary designation form (the separate accounts rule). To be a see-through trust, all trust beneficiaries must be individuals, they must be identifiable from the trust instrument, the trust must be irrevocable and valid under state law, and the trustee must supply certain documentation to the retirement plan administrator.

Another possibility is to make a trust a *conduit trust*. To be such a trust, the trust instrument must require the trustee to distribute to an individual trust beneficiary any distribution the trustee receives from the retirement plan. In other words, unlike a see-through only trust, the trustee cannot accumulate plan distributions in the trust to be distributed later under the terms of the trust and perhaps in the trustee's discretion. For minimum distribution purposes, a conduit trust beneficiary is treated as if he or she had been named individually as the sole plan beneficiary. Therefore if, for example, a surviving spouse is beneficiary of a conduit trust, the MRDs would be over his or her life expectancy, using the Single Life Table but with recalculation. If any other person is beneficiary, the MRDs would be over his or her life expectancy but without recalculation (i.e., the fixed-period method). For a surviving spouse, this does not produce nearly the deferral possibilities as the spousal rollover 'stretch IRA'.

Another trade-off is that the effective trust income tax rates normally will be higher than those actually applying to individual beneficiaries.[19] Therefore, retirement plan distributions to trusts that are accumulated in the trust (i.e., not paid out currently to trust beneficiaries) normally will be taxed at a higher rate. Other trade-offs are trustees' fees (although these percentage charges may be roughly equivalent to the expense ratios of most mutual funds) and the time and costs of creating trusts. Further, if married participants of most qualified retirement plans are involved, spousal consent to any beneficiary designation other than the spouse will be required under the Retirement Equity Act of 1984 (REA).

Qualified Terminable Interest Property (Q-TIP) Trusts as Beneficiaries

To illustrate how alternative trust structures might work, we alter Homer Smith's situation to assume that Homer has been married before; he has a daughter, Abigail, from his first marriage; and he is divorced from his first wife. Let us further assume that Mary and her stepdaughter do not get along at all. Under these circumstances, Homer may fear that Mary will not name Abigail as an equal beneficiary (along with *their* two children) of any rollover IRA of Mary's if he names Mary as outright beneficiary of his qualified plan or IRA (the control factor). However, Homer does want his retirement plan account balance (or part of it) to qualify for the federal estate tax marital deduction.

A classic estate planning solution for this kind of situation is to leave property to the spouse (here, Mary) in a qualified terminable interest property (Q-TIP) trust with trust income payable to the spouse (Mary) for life, and at Mary's death the remainder (the trust corpus) presumably going to Homer's three children equally in this case. Such a Q-TIP trust qualifies for the marital deduction at Homer's death and so is deductible by his executor in determining any federal estate tax liability (which will be reduced to zero under the previous assumptions), but leaves to Homer (in drafting the trust terms) where the property goes after Mary's death.

The difficulty with having an IRA account balance (as opposed to other, non-IRD property) payable to a Q-TIP trust is a significant loss of income-tax-deferral (or tax-free growth).[20] For example, assume Homer does name such a Q-TIP trust as beneficiary of his IRA (i.e., life income to Mary remainder to his three children), and the trust is a *see-through trust* but not a conduit trust. In this case, if Homer dies at age 86 with Mary being age 83 the next year, the MRDs would be based on Mary's life expectancy under the Single Life Table on a fixed-period basis (no recalculation). Therefore, the IRA account balance at Homer's death would have to be paid out to the trust in only 8.6 years. Further, MRDs in excess of the income earned inside the IRA would be taxed to the trust at its likely higher tax rate.[21] But under this scenario, these after-tax excess MRDs will accumulate in the trust and be available for distribution to the remainder beneficiaries (the children) after the surviving spouse's death. Therefore, there will be a bequest potential here, but once the distributions leave the IRA, there will no longer be income-tax-deferral or tax-free growth advantages.

If, however, the Q-TIP trust is structured as a *conduit trust,* all distributions from the IRA will be passed through the trust to the surviving spouse. The advantages of this are somewhat longer deferral (because the MRDs are calculated using the Single Life Table but *with recalculation*) and probably lower income tax rates because the distributions all will be taxable to the surviving spouse.[22] But the disadvantage here from a bequest point of view is that, assuming the surviving spouse lives a reasonable period of time, very little will be left in the Q-TIP trust at his or her death to go to the remainder beneficiaries (the children).

By-Pass Trusts as Beneficiaries

As noted previously, it may be necessary for estate tax reasons to have retirement plan benefits payable to a by-pass or credit-shelter trust. But the disadvantages of doing so are that income-tax-deferral likely will be substantially reduced, higher trust income tax rates may apply, and any income tax paid by the trust on IRA distributions that are not currently paid out as income to trust beneficiaries (i.e., are accumulated in the trust) will reduce trust corpus and hence lessen the estate tax skipping advantage of these trusts.

How fast MRDs must be paid to any see-through trust depends on who the trust beneficiaries are. In general, the MRDs will be based on the life expectancy of the oldest trust beneficiary (unless there are subtrusts for each beneficiary). For many by-pass trusts, the beneficiaries will be the surviving spouse and the children and so the surviving spouse normally will be older and his or her life expectancy under the Single Life Table without recalculation will govern the amounts of the MRDs. This is because in most cases (e.g., like that of Homer Smith) the estate is not so large that a surviving spouse can live comfortably on just the income from the marital share and his or her own assets. Planners often want the income (and perhaps the corpus subject to an independent trustee's discretion or an ascertainable standard) of the by-pass trust at least available to a surviving spouse. In the instant case, if Homer dies at age 86 and Mary is 83 in the next year, the IRA would have to be emptied into the trust in 8.6 years.

If only the children are beneficiaries of a see-through by-pass trust, the life expectancy of the oldest child would govern (unless subtrusts are created). For example, if Homer Smith were to die at age 86, and had named only Homer Jr. (age 57 the next year) and Hortense (age 50 the next year) as beneficiaries of his by-pass trust, Homer Jr.'s life expectancy under the Single Life Table with no recalculation would govern and the IRA would have to be paid out to the trust over 27.9 years. This offers substantially more deferral than when Mary was also a beneficiary but possibly at the price of Mary's economic security.

This discussion illustrates how naming Q-TIP trusts or by-pass trusts for spouses and children can very substantially reduce 'stretch possibilities'. Therefore, such trusts may not be desirable beneficiaries for retirement plan accounts. Yet dependent on the circumstances, their use may be a necessary trade-off of income-tax-deferral for other estate planning or family advantages.

Trusts for Other Individuals (Children) as Beneficiaries

Such see-through trusts are governed by the same general principles as just described for by-pass trusts for children only. They really offer essentially the same deferral (or tax-free growth) opportunities as when children are named directly. As noted above, the naming of comparatively young (and healthy) children directly or in see-through trusts as beneficiaries can offer very substantial income-tax-subsidized bequest opportunities.

Charitable Remainder Trusts (CRTs) as Beneficiaries

An attractive deferral strategy, in some situations, would be to have retirement plan benefits payable to a CRT at the participant's or owner's death with individuals (children, spouse and children, or others) as the unitrust or annuity trust noncharitable income beneficiaries during their lifetimes. A charity will then be the remainder beneficiary after the death of the last noncharitable income beneficiary. The CRT strategy can be particularly attractive when there are at least some younger noncharitable beneficiaries who are in reasonably good health and the participant or owner is charitably inclined. Thus, a CRT can provide income, for example, over the lifetimes (not just life expectancies) of a spouse (who may be older) and then of children who normally will be younger.

This strategy provides deferral because when the participant or owner dies, the retirement plan account balance is paid to the CRT, which is a tax-exempt entity, and hence no income tax is payable. Thus the full account balance remains undiminished in the CRT to provide a unitrust or annuity trust income to the noncharitable beneficiaries for their lifetimes. A unitrust income interest from a charitable remainder unitrust (CRUT) is a fixed percentage of each year's value of the trust corpus, while an annuity trust interest from a charitable remainder annuity trust (a CRAT) is a fixed dollar amount each year. CRUTs generally are more flexible, and if the investment performance of a CRUT is good, the unitrust amount may increase over time thus providing some protection to the beneficiary against long-term inflation.[23] The unitrust rate must be at least 5 percent and cannot be more than 50 percent. When a CRT is created (at the death of the participant or owner), the actuarial value, using IRS tables, of the charity's remainder interest must be at least 10 percent of the trust's value. When the income interest is paid out to the beneficiaries, it is taxable to them under a four tier system. This normally results in the income being taxable as ordinary income when retirement plan benefits are used to fund a CRT.

For illustrative purposes, let us return to the Smith case. Now suppose Homer is charitably inclined and decides to leave $500,000 of his rollover IRA to a 6 percent CRUT payable to Mary for her lifetime and then to their children for their lifetimes; finally, when the last noncharitable beneficiary has died, the remainder is to go to a charity (e.g., the University of Pennsylvania). He does this instead of naming a by-pass trust as beneficiary.[24] At Homer's death, say at age 86, 6 percent of the CRUT corpus (initially $30,000) will be payable as ordinary income to Mary for as long as she actually lives (not just for her 8.6 years life expectancy as assumed in the by-pass trust example).[25] Then upon Mary's death, say at age 86, the CRUT payout will continue for the children's lifetimes. If each child dies, say, at age 90, this will be for 37 more years since Hortense will be 53 at Mary's death. This would result in deferral for Homer's surviving family of 41 years.

Retirement plan benefits may also be made payable to a charitable gift annuity plan. This approach would provide the noncharitable human beneficiary(ies) with a fixed life-annuity income (guaranteed by the charity) and based on the ages of the noncharitable beneficiaries and the gift annuity rates offered by the charity.

Lump-Sum Distributions from Qualified Plans Containing Appreciated Employer Securities

This strategy can be attractive and defer considerable wealth when a participant's qualified retirement plan individual account contains a substantial amount of appreciated employer securities. While some income tax must be paid at the time of the distribution, there can be substantial deferral of tax on most of it and the part represented by net unrealized appreciation (NUA) of employer securities will be taxed as long-term capital gains (rather than ordinary income) when the securities are finally sold. NUA is the difference between the value of the employer securities at distribution and their *basis to the plan* (value when acquired by the plan for the participant's account).

As an example, let us assume that Homer Smith's 401(k) account balance is allocated $250,000 in a bond fund, $250,000 in a guaranteed investment contract (GIC), and $1,000,000 in his employer's (XYZ Corporation's) common stock. The basis of this employer stock to the plan is $300,000. Homer has no income tax basis in his qualified retirement plan account balance because none of his contributions (made before-tax), employer matching contributions, or investment earnings on his account have ever been taxed to him.

At age 65, Homer decides to take a lump-sum distribution of his entire 401(k) plan account balance in one taxable year. The tax result of this would be as follows:

Lump-Sum Distribution	$1,500,000
Less:	0
Homer's Basis in Plan Account	−700,000
Net Unrealized Appreciation (NUA)	$800,000
on Employer Securities	
($1,000,000 − $300,000)	
Potentially Taxable Amount	

However, Homer also is able to do a partial rollover of the non-XYZ stock portion of the total distribution (or $500,000) to his own traditional IRA.[26] Thus, assuming such a partial rollover, Homer would only be taxed (as ordinary income) on $300,000 (the basis to the plan of the XYZ stock) in the year of the total distribution. He would have received $1,000,000 worth of XYZ stock with an income tax basis to him of $300,000 (because he paid tax on this amount) and $500,000 in a traditional rollover IRA (which he could 'stretch' as discussed previously). Presumably, he would take the tax on the $300,000 of ordinary income from other non-retirement-plan assets so his rollover IRA could remain undiminished for future tax deferral and he would not have to sell any of the XYZ stock now and recognize capital gains.

Homer could then hold the XYZ stock as long as he wished and would only recognize tax on the NUA (and any subsequent appreciation) when he sold the stock and then at long-term capital gains rates, assuming he held the stock for more than one year. If Homer dies before selling the XYZ stock, it does not get a stepped-up income tax basis at death. Therefore, his heirs also will recognize long-term capital gain when they later sell the stock. Thus, there could be a long period of tax deferral possibly extending into future generations.

Charitable Rollovers and Other Charitable Giving

The PPA of 2006 introduced an interesting approach to allowing direct lifetime transfers of retirement assets to qualified charities. For 2006 and 2007 only, the law allows persons aged $70^{1}/_{2}$ or older to distribute up to $100,000 per year from their IRAs to qualified charities without recognizing taxable income, but also without being able to take a charitable income tax deduction for the contribution. Such distributions also count toward the person's minimum required distribution for that year. Whether this lifetime charitable giving provision will be extended beyond 2007 is uncertain. It is strongly favored by the nonprofit charitable community.

In addition to CRTs and charitable rollovers, participants and owners can name charities as beneficiaries or partial beneficiaries of non-Roth retirement plan account balances. As noted previously, this is perhaps the most tax-efficient way to make desired charitable contributions at death because (other than Roth IRAs) the retirement plan death benefits are IRD. Thus, when payable to non-tax-exempt beneficiaries, they are included in the decedent's gross estate for federal estate tax purposes and are also ordinary income when paid out to the beneficiaries (with an itemized income tax deduction for any estate taxes paid on the benefit). In contrast, most capital assets get a stepped-up income tax basis at death and hence pass no accumulated capital gains to heirs.

Conclusions

The general objective of present tax law is to use tax incentives to encourage the provision of retirement income, not for tax-subsidized wealth transfer or charitable giving. The main mechanism for enforcing this policy is the minimum distribution rules. In practice, however, these rules and other tax law provisions now permit significant tax-favored wealth transfer and charitable giving strategies. Hence, once there are adequate resources for retirement, these strategies often are important in planning retirement plan distributions. Strategies for using tax-favored retirement plans as wealth transfer devices include spousal and nonspousal rollover 'stretch IRAs' strategy with its possible income-tax-deferral (or tax-free growth) over two or more generations. Also, as minimum distribution rules do not apply to Roth IRAs during the owner's lifetime, this greatly enhances their tax-free growth potential. Making retirement plan distributions payable to charities or charitable entities can also offer substantial tax advantages. These and other interesting options have been extended by the 2006 PPA.

Appendix

TABLE 6-A1 Life Tables Used for Computing Minimum Required Distributions

Single Life Table		Single Life Table Cont.		Uniform Lifetime Table	
Age	Life Expectancy	Age	Life Expectancy	Age of Employee	Distribution Period
0	82.4	20	63.0	70	27.4
1	81.6	21	62.1	71	26.5
2	80.6	22	61.1	72	25.6
3	79.7	23	60.1	73	24.7
4	78.7	24	59.1	74	23.8
5	77.7	25	58.2	75	22.9
6	76.7	26	57.2	76	22.0
7	75.8	27	56.2	77	21.2
8	74.8	28	55.3	78	20.3
9	73.8	29	54.3	79	19.5
10	72.8	30	53.3	80	18.7
11	71.8	31	52.4	81	17.9
12	70.8	32	51.4	82	17.1
13	69.9	33	50.4	83	16.3
14	68.9	34	49.4	84	15.5
15	67.9	35	48.5	85	14.8
16	66.9	36	47.5	86	14.1
17	66.0	37	46.5	87	13.4
18	65.0	38	45.6	88	12.7
19	64.0	39	44.6	89	12.0

TABLE 6-A1 (*Continued*)

Single Life Table		Single Life Table Cont.		Uniform Lifetime Table	
Age	*Life Expectancy*	*Age*	*Life Expectancy*	*Age of Employee*	*Distribution Period*
40	43.6	76	12.7	90	11.4
41	42.7	77	12.1	91	10.8
42	41.7	78	11.4	92	10.2
43	40.7	79	10.8	93	9.6
44	39.8	80	10.2	94	9.1
45	38.8	81	9.7	95	8.6
46	37.9	82	9.1	96	8.1
47	37.0	83	8.6	97	7.6
48	36.0	84	8.1	98	7.1
49	35.1	85	7.6	99	6.7
50	34.2	86	7.1	100	6.3
51	33.3	87	6.7	101	5.9
52	32.3	88	6.3	102	5.5
53	31.4	89	5.9	103	5.2
54	30.5	90	5.5	104	4.9
55	29.6	91	5.2	105	4.5
56	28.7	92	4.9	106	4.2
57	27.9	93	4.6	107	3.9
58	27.0	94	4.3	108	3.7
59	26.1	95	4.1	109	3.4
60	25.2	96	3.8	110	3.1
61	24.4	97	3.6	111	2.9
62	23.5	98	3.4	112	2.6
63	22.7	99	3.1	113	2.4
64	21.8	100	2.9	114	2.1
65	21.0	101	2.7	115+	1.9
66	20.2	102	2.5		
67	19.4	103	2.3		
68	18.6	104	2.1		
69	17.8	105	1.9		
70	17.0	106	1.7		
71	16.3	107	1.5		
72	15.5	108	1.4		
73	14.8	109	1.2		
74	14.1	110	1.1		
75	13.4	111+	1.0		

Source: Federal Register (2002).

Notes

[1] See, for example, Horneff et al. (2007: 1) where the authors view life annuities, phased withdrawal plans, and blended portfolios of annuities and withdrawal plans as means of converting retirement assets into income flows 'so as not to exhaust their funds too soon'. Also see Bernheim (1991) and Hurd and Smith (1999) for data on anticipated bequest motives of the elderly.

[2] As discussed later, the income-tax-deferral ('stretch') strategy in some circumstances may come into conflict with estate planning goals that may call for retirement benefits to be payable to a trust or trusts at the owner's death. Thus, income-tax-deferral may have to be sacrificed for estate tax savings or trustee administration and control in some cases.

[3] Reichenstein (2006) does not couch the analysis in terms of wealth transfer, but rather focuses on lengths of possible lifetime distributions assuming the retiree's objective is to spend down a specified inflation-adjusted, after-tax annual amount over an ~30-year period. Interestingly, the strategy of sequencing lifetime distributions, first from taxable accounts and then from retirement accounts, does produce longer distribution periods under the study's 'base case' assumptions after about 30 years. But the difference in periods between (*a*) taxable first, then retirement plan distributions second (for a period of 30 years); and (*b*) retirement plan first, then taxable second (for a period of 27.4 years) turns out to be 2.6 years (or about 8.67 percent less than the 30 years); this gap does not seem particularly great to the present author considering the time period involved. Further, when Reichenstein changes his assumptions, so that common stocks are passively invested (in index mutual funds or exchange traded funds) and assuming no stock turnover (with no realized and recognized capital gains) until the end of the 30-year period, the difference in periods narrows to 1.9 years or about 6.33 percent less than 30 years.

[4] This conclusion is reinforced by the author's work using a model projecting accumulated wealth from age 65 to 95, starting with portfolios of $2 million in a traditional IRA and $2 million in a taxable account containing stocks and bonds; both accounts were allocated 60 percent to stocks and 40 percent to bonds, respectively. The model assumed a 9 percent average annual return on stocks (6 percent long-term capital gains and 3 percent qualified dividends) and 6 percent return on bonds, a 35 percent tax rate on ordinary income, a 15 percent rate on qualified dividends and long-term capital gains, 75 percent unrealized capital gains on the common stocks as of age 65, a 100 percent turnover rate on the stocks over the first 20 years with none thereafter, a step-up in basis at death at age 95, and no MRDs for the sake of convenience. We assumed that the retiree needed a $400,000 after-tax distribution for some purpose at age 65 from one of these accounts. We found that the sequencing of the distribution from the taxable account and not from the IRA (rather than the reverse) produced the best wealth accumulation results, but the difference was only 4.22 percent more by age 95. This difference would have been even less, if required minimum distributions had been taken from the IRA.

[5] A combination of these elements lies in having retirement plan assets payable to a charitable remainder trust (CRT) with family members the noncharitable unitrust or annuity trust beneficiaries. This approach is described *infra*.

[6] A federal estate tax return must be filed by the executor or administrator of the estate of a deceased US citizen or resident alien when the value of his or her gross estate exceeds a threshold amount, which is the applicable exclusion amount for the year of death less any taxable gifts made after 1976. In recent years, this applicable exclusion amount has ranged from $600,000 in 1987; $1,000,000 by 2002; $2,000,000 in 2006, 2007, and 2008; and is scheduled to increase to $3,500,000 in 2009, with the estate tax being repealed in 2010, and then the estate tax returning in 2011 with an applicable exclusion amount of $1,000,000, unless there are legislative changes in the meantime. Thus, the number of estate tax returns actually filed has declined over these years.

[7] The person may take his or her first MRD by December 31 of the year in which he or she attains age $70^1/_2$ (his or her first distribution calendar year) or wait until April 1 of the following year in which case he or she must take two distributions that year.

[8] The minimum distribution rules apply to defined benefit (DB) plans as well as defined contribution (DC) plans. However, the life-annuity payouts under DB pension plans typically meet these rules.

[9] If the actual sole beneficiary is the participant's or owner's spouse, who is more than 10 years younger than the participant or owner, the MRD may be calculated using a Joint and Last Survivor Table that will produce lower divisors (hence lower MRDs) than the Uniform Lifetime Table.

[10] If the deceased spouse died before his or her RBD, distributions to the surviving spouse beneficiary must begin by the later of December 31 of the year following the year of the decedent's death or December 31 of the year the decedent would have attained age $70^1/_2$. If the deceased spouse died on or after his or her RBD, distributions to the surviving spouse must begin by December 31 of the year following the decedent's death and may be payable over the longer of the surviving spouse's life expectancy or what would have been the decedent's life expectancy. It may also be noted that the tax law and the IRS do not use the term 'inherited IRA' in the case of a spousal beneficiary. But that term is commonly used in the case of any individual beneficiary and is so used here.

[11] See, for example, Kennedy, Kent, and Weger (2006); Blyskal (1993); and Hoyt (2005).

[12] Only a *surviving spouse* can roll over or treat as his or her own account balance as just described. Other *individual (nonspouse) beneficiaries* can transfer a decedent's qualified plan account balance to an inherited IRA for the beneficiary (potentially payable over the beneficiary's fixed period single life expectancy) but in the name of the decedent, or can have the decedent's IRA treated as an inherited IRA for the beneficiary in the same fashion. But for nonspouse beneficiaries, this is not the same as the spouse's rolling over to or treating as his or her own IRA.

[13] Homer could wait to take his first minimum distribution until April 1 of the calendar year following his $70^1/_2$ years and then take another distribution for that year by December 31 of that year. However, he decides not to 'double up' distributions for that year and to take his first minimum distribution by December 31 of his $70^1/_2$ years.

[14] This is simply one divided by the applicable distribution period or 27.4 at age 70.

[15] Using the favorable Uniform Lifetime Table, in this case the required minimum distributions will be less than the 6 percent investment return from the IRA until Homer reaches age 83. This will be true as long as 100 divided by the investment return inside the IRA is less than the applicable distribution period. In this case, $100 \div 6 = 16.67$. The distribution period for age 82 is 17.1 years.

[16] As is discussed later under the heading 'Possible Problems with Spousal Rollover "Stretch IRAs",' since the IRA balance represents such a large part of Homer's gross estate for federal estate tax purposes, it is possible that there will not be enough nonretirement probate assets in his estate to fund fully the credit-shelter trust for an optimal marital in this case. As described later, this represents a planning dilemma and the solution may be either to use some of the retirement assets to fund the credit-shelter trust or gift (and thus not have them payable to the surviving spouse) or to underfund the credit-shelter trust or gift.

[17] It may be noted that while we assume both Homer and Mary died at age 86 (which was their life expectancy at age 65), and left a substantial IRA account balance for their children, had they lived beyond age 86 and continued taking minimum distributions, they would never have completely exhausted the IRA. This is because under the Uniform Lifetime Table their life expectancy is recalculated at each age.

[18] Still another possibility under these circumstances is for the amount (or part of the amount) of retirement plan assets that otherwise would go into a by-pass or credit-shelter trust to be made payable to a CRUT or annuity trust (CRAT) with the surviving spouse and then the children as noncharitable beneficiaries of the charitable remainder trust for their respective lifetimes (Hoyt 2002b).

[19] Trust income tax rates are the same as individual rates, except trusts do not have a 10 percent bracket. However, trust income tax brackets are very compressed and so the taxable income of trusts reaches the top 35 percent rate much more quickly than for individual taxpayers. For example, as of 2007 trust tax rates reach the top 35 percent rate after only $10,450 of taxable income, while individuals do not reach the top bracket until after $349,700 of taxable income.

[20] In this case, Homer probably would roll over his qualified 401(k) plan account balance to his own IRA before naming the Q-TIP trust as beneficiary. IRAs are not subject to REA so Mary would not have to consent to a beneficiary designation other than herself.

[21] The trustee of the Q-TIP trust must withdraw each year from the IRA the larger of the MRD or the income inside the IRA for that year for estate tax reasons. The surviving spouse must receive the larger of the income inside the IRA or the trust's income. However, at Mary's age the MRDs would likely exceed the IRA income.

[22] In this case, the surviving spouse will receive the larger of the MRD or the income inside the IRA each year, and at Mary's age this will very likely be the MRD.

[23] Of course, if the reverse is true, the CRUT income stream will decline.

[24] A CRUT can be made to qualify for the federal estate tax marital deduction if the surviving spouse is the only noncharitable beneficiary. It then can be used instead of, say, a Q-TIP trust. But in this case a charity and not the children would be the remainder person after the spouse's death. If the children are also named as CRT beneficiaries as just described, there would be no marital deduction for the CRT at

Homer's death, but there would be a small estate tax charitable deduction for the actuarial value of the charitable remainder interest as of the date of Homer's death. Thus, planners may recommend a CRUT for spouse and children as a substitute for a by-pass trust since a by-pass trust does not qualify for the marital deduction anyway. See Hoyt (2002*b*). Of course, if the estate is not large enough to attract federal estate tax, this factor does not matter.

[25] If the net investment income inside the CRUT (which would be income-tax-free to the CRUT) exceeds the unitrust payout (6 percent assumed here), the value of the CRUT corpus will grow and so will future unitrust payouts. But if CRUT net investment income does not match payouts, CRUT corpus will be used to make up the difference, and the reverse will be true. Thus, there is some investment risk, as well as opportunity, in this strategy.

[26] After the Pension Act of 2006, he could also roll over part or all of this amount to a Roth IRA, if he meets the eligibility requirements to convert to a Roth, but then he would be taxed on the amount being rolled over to the Roth.

References

Bernheim, Douglas (1991). 'How Strong Are Bequest Motives? Evidence Based on Estimates of the Demand for Life Insurance and Annuities,' *Journal of Political Economy*, 99(5): 899–927.

Blyskal, Jeff (1993). 'Questionable Assumptions,' *Worth*, July/August: 70.

Bryant, Victoria L. and Peter J. Sailer (2006). 'Accumulations and Distributions of Individual Retirement Arrangements, 2001–2002,' *Statistics of Income Bulletin*. Washington, DC: Internal Revenue Service, Spring: 233–54.

Capgemini and Merrill Lynch (2004). *World Wealth Report 2004*. New York: Capgemini.

—— —— (2006). *World Wealth Report 2006*. New York: Capgemini.

Choate, Natalie. (2004). 'The 100 Best and Worst Planning Ideas for Your Client's Retirement Benefits,' Presentation before the Philadelphia Estate Planning Council, September 21.

—— —— (2006). *Life and Death Planning for Retirement Benefits*, 6th edn. Boston, MA: Atax Publications.

Eller, Martha B. (2005). 'Which Estates Are Affected by the Federal Estate Tax?: An Examination of the Filing Population for Year-of-Death 2001,' *Statistics of Income Bulletin*. Washington, DC: Internal Revenue Service, Summer: 191.

Federal Register (2002). 'Life Expectancy and Distribution Period Tables,' Rules and Regulations § 1.401(a)(9)–9. US Government Printing Office: National Archives and Records Administration: 67(74) April 17. 67(74): 19012.

Horneff, Wolfram, Raimond Maurer, Olivia S. Mitchell, and Ivica Dus (2007). 'Following the Rules: Integrating Asset Allocation and Annuitization in Retirement Portfolios,' *Insurance: Mathematics and Economics*, 42(1): 396–408.

Hoyt, Christopher (2002*a*). 'Family and Charitable Planning with Retirement Accounts,' Presentation for the Joint Fall CLE Meeting. Section of Taxation and Section of Real Property, Probate & Trust Law. Boston, MA.

Hoyt, Christopher (2002*b*). 'Solution for Estates Overloaded with Retirement Plan Accounts: The Credit Shelter CRUT,' *Trust & Estates*, May: 21–29, 53–62.

—— (2005). 'Why Not to Invest in Non-Deductible IRAs.' *Trusts & Estates*, September: 70–74.

Hurd, Michael and James Smith (1999). 'Anticipated and Actual Bequests,' NBER Working Paper no. 7380, Cambridge, MA: National Bureau of Economic Research.

Johnson, B. W. and J. M. Mikow (1999). 'Federal Estate Tax Returns 1995–1997,' *Statistics of Income Bulletin*, Summer: 77.

Kennedy, Michael, Bernard Kent, and Karl Weger (2006). *PricewaterhouseCoopers Guide to Tax and Financial Planning 2006*. Hoboken, NJ: John Wiley & Sons, Inc.

Reichenstein, William (2006). 'Tax-Efficient Sequencing of Accounts to Tap in Retirement,' *TIAA-CREF Institute Trends and Issues*, October: 5–21.

Chapter 7

Rethinking Social Security Claiming in a 401(k) World

James I. Mahaney and Peter C. Carlson

Much has been written about the value of taking Social Security at an early age versus delaying the initial start date to a later age. This chapter explores the premise that the full value of delaying Social Security has not been properly measured due to a lack of inclusion of the tax benefits, survivor benefits, projected Cost-of-Living-Adjustment (COLA) benefits, and spousal benefits available under the Social Security provisions and the Senior Citizens' Freedom to Work Act of 2000. Additionally, the lack of expenses charged to an individual during retirement when higher Social Security benefits are chosen should be factored into the evaluation, as the private sector has moved to a 'Do-It-Yourself' retirement structure. Longevity risk, inflation risk, investment risk, and the financial risk caused by the death of a spouse are all now more widely borne by the individual. In addition, two emerging risks have been created in the new 'Do-It-Yourself' retirement model; expense risk and tax risk. We will discuss these emerging risks in this chapter and how these emerging risks should be incorporated into the discussion of the Social Security take-up debate.

As the risks of providing retirement income security have shifted from the employer to the individual, Social Security take-up decisions should be more closely analyzed. Fewer individuals are retiring with a traditional defined benefit pension, and as more retirees choose lump sum options from defined benefit and defined contribution plans, the importance of Social Security as part of a retiree's financial security has greatly increased. The challenge for US retirees is that they themselves are responsible for making decisions about how and when to tap their primary retirement income sources to ensure a secure retirement. Importantly, they appear to receive incomplete or inaccurate information about how to make a decision about when to begin Social Security benefits. Intermediate and long-term interest rates remain below historical averages and many financial experts are predicting lower returns than historical averages in the near future in equity and fixed income markets. Accordingly, Social Security should be more widely recognized as providing valuable financial security to the majority of retirees. Traditional 'break-even' points should be revisited in light of higher Full Retirement Ages (FRAs), increased longevity, and the additional risks to retirement security that are now borne more heavily by individual retirees.

In the future, Social Security benefits will become increasingly valuable due to their tax-favored status, inflation protection, survivor protection, and longevity protection. Conversely, IRA income faces investment risk, expenses, and purchasing power erosion and involves self-insuring at a high cost. Income from an IRA (or similar individual account products) may also run out and leave surviving spouses more vulnerable to financial risk. Essentially, when an individual chooses to delay Social Security versus taking Social Security early, that individual will be trading higher IRA income for higher Social Security income over the course of his or her retirement. This is even more salient with the changes brought on by the Senior Citizens' Freedom to Work Act of 2000, permitting spouses to initiate spousal benefits even when the primary worker is delaying Social Security benefits. Thus far this development has not been well understood, appreciated, utilized, or brought into the traditional break-even analysis.

For simplicity, we will assume in what follows that the primary worker is male and the spouse is female, although Social Security is not sex specific. While reading on, one can assume that the spouse with the higher Social Security benefit is the 'worker' and is married to the 'spouse'. Benefits that the spouse collects on her own benefit will be referred to as the spouse's 'worker benefit'. Benefits she collects on the primary's record will be referred to as the 'spousal benefit'.

Related Literature

The Social Security Administration (SSA) (2005) notes that most individuals still take Social Security retirement benefits early; 72 percent of current Social Security retirement income recipients receive reduced benefits because they started their benefits prior to their FRA. A number of studies have been completed in recent years regarding Social Security take-up decisions, including Coile and Gruber (2000). Gustman and Steinmeier (2002) note that many individuals have a strong time preference for receiving Social Security benefits earlier rather than later, even when lifetime benefits may be higher if claiming of Social Security is delayed. Jennings and Reichenstein (2001) present a way to estimate the present value of Social Security benefits both before taxes and after taxes. Their work argues that after-tax income is what really matters to a retiree and therefore taxation of retirement income is a critical part of the equation on how to structure a financial plan to take retirement income.

We build on the Jennings/Reichenstein approach to show that the taxation of Social Security benefits is largely misunderstood, such that the after-tax present value of Social Security wealth is in general higher than what has previously been discussed. In addition, we point out that a new option to take spousal benefits resulting from the Senior Citizens' Freedom to Work Act of 2000 greatly increases the value of delaying Social Security benefits for a married couple. Changes in the FRA and the value of COLA benefits to a retiree and worker are presented by Muksian (2004). We extend this research by incorporating tax considerations and expenses into the equation of whether a financial planner should recommend that clients should take Social Security earlier rather than delaying the start of benefits.

Postretirement Risks in a 'Do-It-Yourself' Retirement World

Much heard in recent circles is the phrase of an 'ownership society'. What this means is that individuals should decide how and where they should invest their assets for retirement, including Social Security wealth. Arguably, in the retirement income world of the private sector, an ownership society already exists outside of Social Security. That is, the shift from defined benefit to defined contribution plans allows the retiring individual to retire with a lump sum that he or she must manage to provide income for as long as it is needed. Additionally, many employers have switched to cash balance plans where the majority of workers choose a lump sum distribution. Finally, many individuals are choosing to retire from traditional defined benefit plans with a lump sum.

Retirees who leave a qualified retirement plan with a lump sum must now make sure that needed income flows continue to be generated for the life of the retiree (and the spouse, if married). Of course, these periods are unknown and longevity risk may be misunderstood and frequently underestimated by retiring individuals. With the lack of annuitization occurring, many more individuals will likely run out of money due to their longevity and lack of appropriate planning. McKinsey & Company (2005) reports that a 65-year-old couple has a greater than 50 percent chance that one partner will live into their 90s.

Individuals who elect a lump sum option under their retirement plans also bear investment risk. A majority of individuals retiring from defined contribution and cash balance plans roll their lump sums into IRAs and take on investment risk. According to the United States General Accounting Office (GAO) (2003), an increasing number of individuals are doing the same under the lump sum option of traditional defined benefit plans. In such cases, three actions must occur to have a positive outcome.

First, financial markets must cooperate and provide adequate investment returns, especially in the critical years immediately preceding and after retirement. Second, individuals must choose mutual funds which will perform well (as defined by approaching or exceeding broader market returns). Finally, individuals must not buy and sell across funds at the wrong time. As the Dalbar study (2004) shows, the average mutual fund investor struggles with this, as fear and greed drive behavior. For instance the S&P 500 produced average annual returns of 12.98 percent from 1984 to 2003, but the average equity fund investor only received a return of 3.51 percent as individuals made poor decisions in timing their mutual fund purchases and redemptions. For those who chose to time the market and not invest the same amount each month, the return was actually -3.29 percent. Fixed income returns were even worse, as the average investor earned only 3.75 percent annually over the 20-year period, compared to the 11.16 percent average annual return of the Long-Term Government Bond Index.

Furthermore, Bengen (1994) and others argue that the sequence of investment returns on a lump sum nest egg will dramatically influence how long the nest egg will provide income. Thus Monte Carlo simulation techniques have emerged over the last decade to help determine a 'safe withdrawal rate'. Four main criticisms are directed at the use of Monte Carlo simulations by financial advisers. First, they tend to ignore investment and advice expenses (Kotlikoff and Burns 2004). Second, they ignore taxes, which can dramatically impact retirement security, as we will discuss below. Third, Monte Carlo techniques rely on returns drawn from historical averages. As investment returns during the early years of retirement dramatically impact the odds of the nest egg surviving for retirements that can last two or three decades, market returns of the next decade may disappoint investors and may not be properly positioned with Monte Carlo techniques. Indeed, Whitehouse (2005) polled some of the most widely recognized experts in the financial markets who predicted their expected real returns in the bond and stock markets over the next 40 years. The results, summarized in Table 7-1, do not approach historical averages. A final criticism of Monte Carlo simulation techniques is that it may be unrealistic to assume that retirees will have the fortitude to stay invested in equity markets as they get older and experience market losses.

Inflation risk is very real over retirement periods that can last 25 or more years. At a 3 percent inflation rate, the value of one dollar falls to $0.48 after 25 years. Historically, US inflation rates have averaged around 3.1 percent. Whether inflation returns to the hyperinflationary periods of the 1970s and early 1980s remains to be seen, but there are arguments that the coming demographics issues and budget deficits will cause higher inflation (Arnott and Casscells 2003; Kotlikoff and Burns 2004). Both the smaller number

TABLE 7-1 Projected Real Rates of Return (%) Anticipated Over the Next
40 Years

Financial Expert Name	Organization	Stocks (%)	Government Bonds (%)	Corporate Bonds (%)
William Dudley	Goldman Sachs	5.00	2.00	2.50
Jeremy Siegel	Wharton	6.00	1.80	2.30
David Rosenberg	Merrill Lynch	4.00	3.00	4.00
Ethan Harris	Lehman Brothers	4.00	3.50	2.50
Robert Shiller	Yale	4.60	2.20	2.70
Joseph LaVorgna	Deutsche Bank	6.50	4.00	5.00
Parul Jain	Nomura	4.50	3.50	4.00
John Lonski	Moody's	4.00	2.00	3.00
David Malpass	Bear Stearns	5.50	3.50	4.25
Jim Glassman	J. P. Morgan	4.00	2.50	3.00
	Average	4.81	2.80	3.33

Source: Whitehouse (2005); reprinted with permission.

Note: This table indicates that financial experts expect the investment returns of stocks and bonds to be below historical averages over the next several decades.

of workers left in the workforce and the cost of entitlement programs are likely to generate higher inflation as the bills become due.

The death of a spouse can cause a significant risk to a widow or widower as Social Security and pension benefits are significantly reduced. In addition, women can be much more vulnerable financially with defined contribution plans, compared to defined benefit plans, since they lose the protection provided under the defined benefit joint and survivor benefit option (Munnell and Sass 2005). In addition, women often marry older men and have longer life expectancies. Furthermore, many widows left the financial management of retirement to their spouses and, at widowhood, are faced with an overwhelming burden of becoming the investment manager and financial planner with little expertise.

Social Security: Subtle Changes with Major Impact

Changes enacted under Social Security reforms introduced in 1983 are now phasing in. Importantly, the FRA is now 66 for those who will become eligible for Social Security over the next several years and it will be going to 67 for the cohort born in 1960 and later. Changes to the FRA have increased the penalty for taking Social Security early. What was once a 20 percent decrease in the initial benefit amount when starting Social Security at age 62 is now a 25 percent decrease. The compounding effect of COLAs over longer life expectancies makes these cuts even deeper in nominal terms as the base amount on which COLAs are applied is reduced to a greater extent than it was when the FRA was 65. In addition, the 'reward' for delaying Social Security past the FRA is now 8 percent per year for those turning 62 in 2005 and later. Again, in nominal terms, the compounding effect of COLAs throughout retirement adds to the value of delaying compared to older cohorts who did not have an 8 percent Delayed Retirement Credit (DRC). It is also unlikely that most individuals realize that even when they are delaying benefits, they are receiving credit for COLAs during the period for which they are delaying the start of Social Security.

Consider an example. A worker turning 62 in 2006 has a final salary of $75,000 making her eligible for a $1,320 a month in Social Security benefits if she began immediately. If she delays Social Security benefits until age 70, her benefit will grow to $2,884, more than double what she would collect at age 62. Not only would she avoid the penalty for taking her benefits early, but she would also receive increased DRCs and all of the intermittent projected COLA credits projected in the Social Security Administration's trust report as of December 2006. Conversely, if she were to take the $1,320 at age 62, her benefit would grow only to $1,637 by age 70. A much higher initial benefit will receive much higher absolute dollar increases over time as the COLA rate is applied. Since these adjustments are compounding, the cumulative differences can be quite significant. Many individuals are likely not considering the impact of higher COLAs on a delayed benefit since the Social Security statement they receive does not illustrate the benefits of those higher COLAs. For example, in discussions with many retirees, we found that they use Excel spreadsheets to forecast their own break-even points and use the Social Security estimated benefits from the annual Social Security statement. By entering the age 66 amount and age 70 amount (which are in current dollars) into a formula that measures future dollar values, the analysis becomes skewed.

Value of COLAs

In nearly all break-even analysis, COLAs are ignored. Muksian (2004) points out that individuals often fail to account for the value of COLAs. Although the Social Security system is generally deemed to be actuarially fair whether taking benefits early, at FRA, or later, the value of COLA benefits, for those who are fortunate to live a long time (and vulnerable to inflation and longevity risk), during retirement can be dramatic. Although COLAs are not guaranteed by law, we believe that COLAs should be considered as part of the value proposition of weighing whether to delay Social Security benefits. Politically, it would be very difficult to cut COLA benefits for current retirees. Due to much longer life expectancies than in the past, the compounding value of COLAs should be considered, especially as these benefits often can be passed on to a widow at the death of the worker. When future projected COLAs are factored in, an individual retiring with a first Social Security check payable in 2006 at age 62 has a crossover age of 78 when comparing to waiting until age 70 to begin initial benefits.

What should be given strong consideration is that the longer the retiree lives, the higher the return delayed Social Security income provides. Benefits have 'snowballed' due to the DRCs and COLAs over many years. Conversely, consider that retirees tend to become more conservative with their own investments as they age and will often struggle to generate sufficient yield to make the income last for longer periods.

In recent years, inflation protection products such as Treasury Inflation Protected Securities (TIPs) and Inflation linked bonds (I-Bonds) have been introduced in the securities market. TIPs are now offered as 5-, 10-, and 20-year bonds but like other bonds, they can lose value in a rising interest rate environment. No matter what inflation rates occur in the future, COLAs on Social Security retirement benefits provide low-cost inflation protection that no private product can duplicate without significant cost. This is primarily due to the expense of providing similar benefits in the private market. As of this time, we believe only a couple of insurers are offering CPI-adjusted immediate annuities in the USA to allow individuals to transfer inflation risk to the insurer.

By taking Social Security early (while not purchasing a private inflation-adjusted annuity), a retiree 'chooses' to retain the inflation risk on the difference in annual income between the early Social Security amount chosen and the delayed Social Security income foregone. These dollars that must be made up are often much less tax efficient as they usually take the form of IRA withdrawals (taxed as ordinary income). Also, an individual picks up the expense of managing these dollars in the form of fees and expenses (commissions, management fees, 12B-1 fees, adviser charges, etc.).

Survivor Protection

The value of spousal and survivor benefits is another area where Social Security has not been adequately valued. The importance of spousal and survivor benefits is further enhanced as the protections provided by defined benefit retirement plans (with a spouse being forced to waive a joint and survivor annuity if one is not elected) disappear as defined contribution plans replace defined benefit plans in the private marketplace. The survivor protection offered under Social Security should be an important consideration in deciding when to take Social Security. Whenever a member of a married couple dies, the highest individual benefit at that point in time is the one that continues to be collected by the surviving spouse. In other words, it does not matter who dies first, the worker or the spouse, because the lower benefit drops off. Thus, when a primary worker delays Social Security, the higher delayed benefit plus any compounding COLAs are passed on to the widow at the worker's death, if that benefit is higher than the one she is currently receiving. If an individual still decides to start Social Security early at age 62, the potential benefit to his widow is also reduced at the higher penalty incurred with the FRA at 66 and climbing.

The fact that a higher, delayed retirement benefit can be passed on at death is often overlooked in break-even calculations. Mirer (1998) and Rose and Larimore (2001) explore the economic value of collecting Social Security early versus waiting until FRA, but both studies fail to put an economic benefit on the survivor benefit that continues on after the death of the retired worker. According to the Group Annuity Mortality Table of 1994 currently used by many insurers, given a couple who are both 65 years old, the odds that one of them will reach age 85 are 80 percent; age 90, 57 percent; and age 95, 28 percent. Therefore, there is a good chance of one of the spouses benefiting from a higher delayed Social Security amount for many years. Workers who are older than their spouses should give this special consideration, since their spouses are likely to survive them by several years.

Since the higher Social Security benefit is passed on to a surviving spouse at the worker's death and the lower spousal benefit is dropped, it is often more beneficial to start the spouse's benefits earlier (Jennings and Reichenstein 2001, Munnell and Soto 2005). Therefore, absent specific individual health considerations, it will often be beneficial to start the spouse's benefits first. To illustrate this, we first review what a spouse is eligible to receive according to Social Security rules. This provides the basis for our evaluation. The spouse of a worker is always able to receive whatever benefit she earns on her own record. In addition, if her own worker's benefit is less than half of her husband's primary worker benefit, then the spouse is also eligible to collect the excess of half of his primary benefit minus her own benefit. Both the worker benefit collected on her own record and the spousal benefit collected on his record receive reductions for taking the benefit before FRA. The spousal benefit reductions are greater than worker reductions. While the spouse's own worker benefit can receive DRCs if the benefit is postponed after FRA, her spousal benefit does not receive these credits. This clause in the Social Security rules, more fully explained below, is used to create a disincentive to delay receipt of benefits.

Under the old rules, Social Security policy prevented a wife from taking benefits based on her husband's primary worker benefit until he (the primary worker) became '*entitled*'. Although a worker might be *eligible* for full retirement benefits, say at age 66, he was not *entitled* until he filed for these benefits. And the spouse did not become *entitled to the spousal benefits* until the worker filed for those benefits. Therefore, since a spousal benefit did not receive DRCs and the spouse could only take those benefits once the worker files, it became clear that the value of delaying Social Security for a married couple was reduced if the worker is delaying Social Security and the spouse is *eligible* for benefits but not receiving them. The spouse would not receive any DRCs, and therefore 'left money on the table', if she continued to wait to start her benefits. Jennings and Reichenstein (2001) incorporated this into their present value calculations for Social Security options.

Recent changes to Social Security, however, have changed the dynamics of these outcomes and what married couples should now consider. In particular, the Senior Citizens' Freedom to Work Act of 2000 allowed seniors to 'file and suspend' their benefits upon reaching FRA, which enables the benefits of a worker to continue to accrue DRCs.[1] This ability to 'file and suspend' benefits is an option whether or not the primary worker is still working. Most importantly, it also allows the spouse to take Social Security benefits based on her spousal benefits even when her husband continues to delay his own benefit and receive DRCs. Thus, the disincentive to delay the primary worker's benefit due to spousal benefit concerns described above now impacts a much smaller percentage of beneficiaries, those cases where the spouse is older than the worker and eligible for spousal benefits.

Accordingly, the value of delaying Social Security for a primary worker (and eventually a potential widow) improved, since most of the time spousal benefits are not forfeited if the spouse is otherwise eligible to receive benefits. The Senior Citizens' Freedom to Work Act of 2000 provides more choice for the retirees and the decision on whether to collect Social Security benefits now becomes a separate one for the worker and the spouse in a married couple. It is critical that retirees and advisers understand these choices and their value if they are to make informed decisions to maximize the Social Security benefits available to them.

Given this flexibility, we have identified three primary strategies for couples when delaying Social Security. It is often in a couple's best interest to delay the primary benefit as late as possible, due to the fact that the benefit is passed on to the surviving spouse. The three options revolve around when the spouse takes her own worker's benefit. Scenario I involves the spouse starting benefits as early as possible. Under Scenario II, the spouse delays starting benefits until her FRA. With Scenario III, the spouse delays her benefits until age 70. While the full menu of options involve every month of age in between, these three key ages are chosen due to the change in the calculation of the timing of benefits formula that occurs at FRA.

Under all three scenarios, the primary worker will file and suspend upon reaching his FRA. Any benefit that the spouse is entitled to off the primary's record (the 'spousal benefit') will start at that time unless otherwise stated.

This new ability for the spouse to take spousal benefits at an earlier age is valuable because the lower (spousal) benefit will drop off once one of the married individuals dies. And, more importantly, the higher, delayed Social Security benefit is now 'stepped up to' by the widow and therefore can provide much higher survivor income protection. This especially holds true when a spouse is younger than the worker, as the younger the spouse (widow) is, the higher the present value of her projected benefits.

Table 7-2 identifies the actuarial present value of Social Security benefits for a married couple and compares beginning Social Security early at age 62 versus the three scenarios just described. For the purposes of this paper, the actuarial present value is defined as the survivorship-adjusted net present value of the cash flows. Cash flows are first multiplied by the probability of survival as determined by the 1994 Group Annuity Rates Mortality Table (GAR) and then discounted by the rate discussed below. The 1994 GAR table is chosen because it is designed to represent the mortality of those sufficiently healthy to work at the time the table is used. The primary worker is assumed to be entitled to an age 62 benefit of $1,414 per month. The three examples are based on the spouse being entitled to (*a*) no worker benefit on her own but a spousal benefit on the primary's record; (*b*) a $300 monthly worker benefit at age 62 and a smaller spousal benefit on the primary's record; and (*c*) a $1,000 monthly worker benefit at age 62 and no spousal benefit. For a discount rate, we chose to use the 15-year US treasury rate as of mid-January, 2007, the time all of the comparable market numbers were run. That rate was 4.9622 percent. Since Social Security is an obligation of the government, it is most appropriately discounted by the rate for other government securities.

It is helpful to break the Social Security decision into component parts. The first column of Table 7-2 calculates the actuarial value of the pretax cash flows for the primary worker (and surviving spouse conditional on the primary being the first death) if the worker elects to receive the benefits exactly at 62. The second column calculates the same value as of age 62 should the worker elect to delay the receipt of the benefits until age 70. The third through sixth columns relate to the decision around taking the spouse's benefits. Column 3 values the spousal benefit (and the spouse's worker benefit, if any) should the spouse elect to take benefits as early as possible. Column 4 (Scenario I) portrays the value to the spouse should she take benefits early while the primary delays. Remember, if the primary is delaying the benefit, the spousal piece collected off the primary's benefit cannot be collected until the primary reaches FRA.

TABLE 7-2 Actuarial Present Value of Social Security Benefits Under Alternative Retirement Strategies ($2006)

	Primary Worker		Spouse Delayed			
	Early at 62	Delayed at 70	Early at 62	Scenario I*	Scenario II**	Scenario III***
(a) $0 Spouse's worker benefit, spousal benefit only	344,896	397,144	108,634	114,816	N/A	N/A
(b) $300 Spouse's worker benefit and smaller spousal benefit	344,896	397,144	111,926	115,486	114,591	111,227
(c) $1,000 Spouse's worker benefit and no spousal benefit	344,896	397,144	164,630	164,630	162,081	150,867

Source: Authors' computations.

Note: Actuarial present value calculated using a 4.9622% net interest rate and the 1994 Group Annuity Rates mortality table for a couple both aged 62. In each example, Primary Worker is entitled to $1,404 per month. This table shows that the value of delaying Social Security benefits is increased due to the ability of the surviving spouse to inherit the higher delayed benefit upon the death of the primary worker. Due to the survivor benefit, the value to the spouse of her benefits is reduced if she waits past age 62 while the husband is delaying benefits.

* Spouse's worker benefit (if any) begins at age 62, spousal benefit (if any) begins at age 66.

** Spouse's worker benefit (if any) begins at age 66, spousal benefit (if any) begins at age 66.

*** Spouse's worker benefit (if any) begins at age 70, spousal benefit (if any) begins at age 66.

Columns 5 and 6 value the decision to take benefits under Scenarios II and III listed above.

As shown in Table 7-2, delaying the primary benefit until age 70 represents a greater present value option assuming a 4.9622 percent net interest rate and the 1994 GAR relative to taking the primary benefit early. In valuing the primary benefit, we used the probabilities that one member of the couple would still be alive to collect the higher, delayed benefit. This methodology is used because a surviving spouse may collect the primary's delayed benefit in the future if she is living and the primary worker has died. Choosing to delay the spouse's own worker benefits is a negative present value proposition because the formula for delaying is not actuarially equivalent for the spouse when one factors in the fact that both members of the couple must be alive in order for the spouse's benefit to be collected. This is illustrated from the $1,000 spouse's worker benefit [Example (c)] as one moves from Scenario I (starting the spouse's worker benefit at age 62) versus Scenario II (beginning the spouse's worker benefit at age 66). Conversely, the higher penalty for taking the spousal benefit on the primary record early makes the choice to delay receipt until FRA a positive one under these assumptions. This is shown through 'Example (a),' where the spouse has only a spousal benefit and no worker benefit of her own. The Present Value (PV) of taking the spousal piece at FRA (which is the earliest possible decision should the primary delay benefits) is higher than the PV of taking the spousal piece early. Thus, unless a couple has reason to believe their expected longevity is materially different than the longevity implied by the 1994 GAR table, Scenario I provides the best value. These figures do not include the effects of taxes and they also place no value on the peace of mind that comes from a higher guaranteed income level that will survive as long as one member is alive.

Additional Factors in the Take-Up Decision
Tax Treatment of Social Security Benefits

Social Security income is often much more tax efficient than IRA income under current tax law. In fact, we believe that the tax benefits of Social Security have been greatly underappreciated. Marginal tax rates may be much higher after retirement, as noted by Gokhale et al. (2001) and Gokhale and Kotlikoff (2003). Prior research such as Jennings and Reichenstein (2001) makes the assumption that Social Security income earned over the Combined Income thresholds will cause Social Security to be taxed at a rate of up to 85 percent of the benefits paid and that the source of income does not matter. Actually, this assumption will not necessarily hold true for the majority of individuals and mandates a closer look, especially in light of the question of when to initiate Social Security benefits.

The rules outlining the taxation of Social Security benefits can be found under section 126 of the Official Social Security Handbook [Social Security Administration (SSA) 2001]. A brief description is of use here. Law changes enacted in 1983 and later in 1993 provide that Social Security benefits received over certain thresholds of Combined Income are subject to taxation up to 85¢ of a Social Security dollar. The thresholds were determined in 1983 with the idea that only the wealthy would pay taxes on their Social Security benefits. After the first threshold, up to 50 percent of Social Security income is subject to taxation. After the second threshold, up to 85 percent of Social Security income is subject to taxation. The thresholds were not indexed for inflation, and currently as of 2007 stand at \$32,000/\$44,000 for married couples, and \$25,000/\$34,000 for single individuals. The threshold for 50 percent taxation was established effective for 1983, the 85 percent for 1994.

The Combined Income formula includes all of a retiree's income excluding Roth income together with 50 percent of their Social Security income. The amount of Social Security that is taxable is the minimum of three tests: 50 percent of the Combined Income amount over the first threshold plus 35 percent of Combined Income over the second threshold, *or* 50 percent of benefits plus 85 percent of Combined Income over the second threshold, *or* 85 percent of benefits. Combined Income counts all of the income that is normally taxable plus tax-free municipal bond income. Therefore a married couple which has saved diligently within a 401(k) can face a very high marginal tax rate on an additional dollar of IRA income. If the spouses are in a 25 percent tax bracket, they may pay 25¢ on the IRA dollar as ordinary income tax and another 21.25¢ on the Social Security dollar now subject to taxation at 85 percent (\$1 × .85 × 25 percent). The effective marginal tax rate on that dollar is therefore 46.25 percent. When current tax rates increase under the sunset provisions scheduled under current law, the effective rate will increase even higher and will exceed 50 percent. State taxes can push the marginal tax rate even higher.

Some financial journalists have dubbed this concept the 'tax torpedo'. But just as the tax torpedo can accelerate the taxes due on a retirement income strategy, *trading* IRA income for Social Security income can create a reverse tax torpedo and drastically reduce taxes. Commonly, a retiree will take Social Security early at age 62 and fund his remaining income needs with IRA withdrawals (which represent his qualified retirement savings). Many of these retirees will find themselves hit by the tax torpedo. Contrast, however, that an individual who delays taking Social Security and funds his needs out of his IRA or other qualified plan is, in essence, trading IRA income for higher Social Security income. This can provide distinct and measurable tax advantages. In lieu of just assuming that 85 percent of Social Security income will become taxable, it is important to recognize what type of income is being received. Since Social Security income only counts at a 50 percent rate into the Combined Income formula, much larger amounts of Social Security can be received before the Combined Income thresholds are met. Therefore, when trading an IRA dollar of income for a Social Security dollar, not only is the IRA dollar no longer present (and thus no tax is due), but less Social Security income is also subject to taxation.

A quick illustration is as follows: assume an IRA dollar is removed from the income pool and is added back in the form of Social Security. Removing the IRA dollar causes the Adjusted Gross Income (AGI) to reduce by one dollar. AGI is income including wages, interest, capital gains, and income from retirement accounts adjusted downward by specific deductions (including contributions to deductible retirement accounts), but not including standard and itemized deductions. The IRA dollar being removed also causes Combined Income to drop by a dollar. The Social Security dollar that is added back counts only half to Combined Income, netting a 50¢ decrease in the Combined Income amount. If, for example, we assume that the Combined Income amount is already over the second threshold, that 50¢ decrease results in an additional 42.5¢ reduction to AGI. This results in a total AGI reduction of $1.425. The total gross income has not changed, but AGI is reduced by $1.425.

In a 25 percent bracket, this saves $0.35625 in federal taxes on that dollar of income. If the beneficiary's state of residence also taxes Social Security, it functions the exact same way, albeit just with different tax rates. If the state does not tax Social Security, the lower IRA income still reduces state taxes. Of course, when enough dollars are shifted to Social Security (from an IRA), the retiree may slide into a marginal tax bracket lower than 25 percent. Therefore, additional retirement income such as Required Minimum Distribution amounts may also benefit from lower tax rates. Of course, additional income could be subject to the 'tax torpedo' as well.

Table 7-3 shows an example with $69,000 of pretax income. For a retired married couple both aged 72, having Social Security income of $24,000 plus IRA income of $45,000 results in AGI of $62,050. Conversely, the couple who delays Social Security and has Social Security income of $39,000 with a lower IRA income of $30,000 has the same pretax income of $69,000 but an AGI of only $40,675. The first couple has $21,375 more in AGI—52.5 percent higher and spends $3,206.25 more in federal income taxes alone for 2006. This same inefficiency occurs every year throughout their retirement once the higher Social Security benefits have started. That totals almost $100,000 in additional federal taxes over 30 years.

For a retiring individual with only 401(k) wealth (likely to be rolled into an IRA) and Social Security, to be able to afford delaying Social Security

TABLE 7-3 Tax Efficiency from Alternative Social Security Claiming Strategies ($2006)

	Strategy I	Strategy II
Social Security income	24,000	39,000
IRA yearly withdrawal	45,000	30,000
Other taxable income	0	0
Sum of income from all sources	69,000	69,000
Combined income	57,000	49,500
50% excess over 1st threshold +35% excess over 2nd	17,050	10,675
85% of benefits	20,400	33,150
50% of benefits +85% excess over 2nd threshold	23,050	24,175
Adjusted Gross Income (minimum of Combined Income Tests + IRA Income)	62,050	40,675
Federal taxes	6,060	2,854
State taxes	2,891	1,895
Other nontaxable income	0	0
Total after-tax income	61,703	65,321

Source: Authors' computations.

Note: This table indicates the tax efficiency of delaying Social Security once that higher income stream begins. The two columns compare taking the same amount of pretax income ($69,000) for a 72-year-old man with different amounts of Social Security and IRA income. The column on the right has a strategy that takes $15,000 more in Social Security income and $15,000 less in IRA income than the column on the left. As the right-hand column indicates, Adjusted Gross Income is reduced by approximately one third compared to the left-hand column because there is less IRA income and surprisingly, much lower taxable Social Security. State taxes are assumed to be 4.66%.

income, IRA income would need to be taken from the retiree's retirement date until the delayed Social Security start age. We will refer to this time period as the 'Bridge Period' and individuals will be receiving 'Bridge Income' from their IRA during this period. Although this IRA income is fully taxable as ordinary income and conventional wisdom holds that tax-deferred income is best delayed as long as possible, the benefits from delaying Social Security are often much greater. Many retirees will pay slightly higher taxes during the Bridge Period, but experience thousands of dollars in annual savings from the point that higher Social Security income begins. By decoupling when to take the majority of IRA income from the time one takes the majority of their Social Security income, much greater tax efficiency can be achieved.

Taken to an extreme, if a person were to convert all of his income into Social Security income, he would pay no taxes on the income. Social

Security, as a sole source of income, is tax-free up to $113,058 for 2006 for a married couple with the standard income tax deductions. (This number is indexed with inflation and tied to the tax brackets.) Thereafter for the next $28,000 of Social Security income, the marginal tax rate of another Social Security dollar is 4.25 percent. In reality, with the earnings cap, nobody can receive that much from Social Security. Two high-income earners who delayed to age 70 could total ~$60,000 in benefits in today's dollars.

As a planning strategy, however, pre-retirees could project their future Social Security benefits at age 70 and assume lower taxes will be paid on their income. Due to the wage indexing of Social Security benefits, many retirees will retire with significant Social Security benefits. Often, these benefits can be turned into tax-free income at age 70. Let us consider a higher than average earning dual income couple, both aged 55 and earning $75,000 a year. We assume the couple wants to retire at age 62. The Social Security Web site shows a future value of $20,400 for each worker if collecting at age 62, for a total of $40,800 for the couple. However, if the couple, while still retiring at age 62, waits to begin Social Security benefits until age 70, those benefits are projected to be ~$44,500 per person for a total of $89,000 of income beginning at age 70 eight years later. If they had no other income, the entire $89,000 of Social Security income would escape federal and state taxation.

As the Combined Income thresholds are not indexed for inflation, more and more individuals will be subject to the tax torpedo and therefore would benefit from this strategy. Munnell (2003) and others have discussed the increased taxation of Social Security benefits that is occurring over time, as individuals will be more likely to have income over these non-indexed Combined Income thresholds. The higher taxation can often be avoided when higher Social Security benefits are elected and IRA income is minimized. At very high amounts of other income, the tax benefits of trading for more Social Security dollars become limited to the 15¢ of every Social Security dollar that is always sheltered from taxes. Thus, there are always some tax benefits to this strategy, no matter what the income level is. Although it is not intuitive due to the lower Social Security taxation thresholds (starting at $25,000 and $32,000), our research shows that retirees receiving up to $90,000 per year in after-tax income can see significant tax savings once higher, delayed Social Security benefits begin.

When considering the after-tax dollars actually available for the retirement lifestyle, the break-even age for comparing early Social Security versus delayed Social Security is often lowered to somewhere between 75 and 76 years old. The actual age varies depending on the tax situation of the individual. It is important to note that the tax advantages created by delaying Social Security may be even more advantageous for a married couple after the death of the primary worker. Note that the surviving spouse will be in a single tax bracket and have a lower Combined Income threshold. With a strategy of 'early Social Security' and IRA withdrawals, the widow will likely see taxation of the IRA and much of her Social Security income. By evoking a strategy at the beginning of retirement of taking IRA income first and a higher delayed Social Security amount, a widow may see much lower taxes since most of the income is in the form of Social Security via the higher Survivor Benefit. And thus, as mentioned above, that income is treated more favorably and will likely see the Social Security taxation formula pick up the test which calculates 50 percent of the Combined Income amount over the first threshold plus 35 percent of Combined Income over the second threshold. Consider, a widow could have $50,000 of Social Security income (counting as $25,000) before hitting that first threshold for a single individual.

As mentioned above, many financial advisers advocate taking Social Security early and invoke a strategy to manage IRA withdrawals. Since longevity and investment risks are not often pooled via annuitization, a larger nest egg is needed to self-insure against these postretirement risks when additional income is needed above and beyond an 'early' Social Security benefit amount. Furthermore, expenses must be considered.

The Expense Advantage of Social Security

The 'safe withdrawal rate' initially introduced by Bengen (1994) uses Monte Carlo simulation of historical returns to predict the probability of successfully providing an income stream over a 20-, 30-, or 40-year retirement horizon. Unfortunately, investment expenses and fees are often ignored in this discussion. Pye (2001) concluded that investment expenses can have a profound impact on withdrawal rates. Since individuals increasingly bear the burden of providing income throughout retirement, expenses drained from a portfolio also will reduce future retirement income and thus have emerged as a risk to retirement security. Pye found that the safe withdrawal rate must be reduced by ratio of the expense rate divided by the expected rate of return of the portfolio. Therefore, a 30-year 'safe withdrawal rate' of 4 percent, which assumed a 7 percent average gross return with 2.5 percent expenses, would have to be reduced by 35.7 percent to 2.57 percent $[1 - (.025/.07) \times .04]$. In this example, over 35 percent of potential income is going to pay for expenses, yet many individuals appear not to be factoring in these expenses when calculating a safe withdrawal rate.

In Maxey (2005), Lipper reported that the average expense ratio of equity funds had risen to 1.56 percent. In addition, Karcinski, Livingston, and O'Neal (2004) found that the average equity mutual fund has an additional 96 basis points of hidden fees made up of brokerage costs and trading costs. Some retirees also pay up-front commissions to purchase mutual funds, while many others pay an asset-under-management fee of 1–1.5 percent to a financial adviser/planner. Therefore, total annual expenses for a retiree to hire professional assistance in a 'Do-It-Yourself' retirement world can easily amount to 3 percent or more.

By trading IRA income for higher, delayed Social Security income, a retiree transitions the expenses of managing his assets to the government. Although an individual has paid Federal Insurance Contributions Act (FICA) taxes during his or her working years, there is no additional cost based on the size of the chosen Social Security benefit. We assume a retiree elects delayed Social Security and receives $20,000 (adjusted annually for inflation) more of income from age 70 on. If the retiree had elected the lower Social Security amount ($20,000 less), a comparable safe withdrawal rate of 5 percent for the next 20 years may provide a high probability of income being provided for the full duration under a 60/30/10 stock/bond/cash split. Therefore, with no expenses, a lump sum amount of $400,000 could provide the 5 percent withdrawal of $20,000, which is income above and beyond the (early) Social Security benefit. However, once fees are brought in, the size of the lump sum needed grows tremendously. If one assumes 2.5 percent of expenses and an assumed 7 percent gross return, the safe 5 percent withdrawal amount is lowered to 3.215 percent $[1 - (.025/.07) \times .05]$. Therefore, to provide $20,000 of income, the lump sum amount grows from $400,000 to $622,083. This is a much more expensive strategy as evidenced that in the first year alone, $20,000 of income is provided but also expenses of $15,552 (2.5 percent $\times$ $622,083) are generated.

By delaying Social Security, the individual no longer bears the costs of providing that additional income. Since Social Security is 'expense free' during retirement, more dollars can be received by a retiree and not used to pay for investment/financial expertise.

Social Security Options and Customization Are Available

As defined contribution plans replace defined benefit plans, the role of the traditional Social Security benefit as an annuity will become relatively more important. Many retiring Americans will have a much greater fraction of wealth tied up in Social Security than from their own private retirement savings. Consider that a married high earner in 2006 would retire with over $25,000 of Social Security income between the worker and the nonworking spouse if they started collecting right away at age 62. Even assuming no fees, ignoring the tax efficiency, and assuming a 4 percent safe withdrawal rate, that couple would need $625,000 of saving just to provide a similar pretax benefit with 90 percent confidence that income will last 30 years.

Individuals have the ability to start different pieces of Social Security at different times. A working spouse could start her own worker benefits at age 62, add the additional spousal benefit when her husband reaches FRA, and then eventually assume an even higher widow's benefit at the death of her spouse. Another additional strategy can be used to maximize spousal benefits when the primary earning spouse is delaying Social Security as long as the lower earning spouse has already filed for benefits based on her work record. As Ruffenach (2007) noted, under this strategy, once the primary worker attains FRA, he files *only* for spousal benefits. He would be entitled to spousal benefits for the four-year period from age 66 to age 70. At age 70, once the higher benefit is claimed based on his own earnings history, the spousal benefits being paid to him would cease.

This tactic is unique since historically, the higher earning spouse may not have been thinking about claiming spousal benefits. The key to understanding this option is based on the earlier mention of the difference between being 'eligible' for a Social Security benefit and being 'entitled'. For example, an individual may be 'eligible' for full retirement benefits at age 66. But he only becomes 'entitled' to those benefits once he has filed for those benefits.

Accordingly, if an individual does not file for his Social Security benefits based on his own earnings, he is not 'entitled' to those earnings. Therefore, he may become 'entitled' to spousal benefits once he files for them (if his spouse has filed for benefits based on her work record and he is past FRA) since he is not yet 'entitled' to benefits based on his own work record. Prior to the FRA, an application for a spousal benefit is deemed to also be an application for the worker benefit. This is no longer the case once FRA is reached. Although these additional spousal benefits would add to the present value of Social Security benefits for those delaying Social Security, the figures in this chapter do not reflect these values.

Once individuals customize a strategy to optimize their potential Social Security benefits, they can structure an IRA strategy to provide income during the Bridge Period from retirement to the delayed Social Security date of the primary worker. For a married couple who started the spouse's Social Security benefit earlier, this income could be 'carved out' of the IRA income needed.

The Benefits of Delaying Social Security and Taking Bridge Income

Thus far we have explained the inflation benefits, tax benefits, expense benefits, and survivor benefits of delaying Social Security. Further, we have introduced the concept of decoupling IRA and Social Security income by drawing on IRA assets first during a Bridge Period to higher, delayed Social Security. In this section, we explore this strategy in more depth. Specifically, we assume that the Bridge Income is in the form of a period-certain annuity constructed to provide a steady stream of nominal income on an after-tax basis to the retirees. A period-certain annuity is an immediate annuity term vehicle that pays monthly income for a specified period. Once that period has expired, no further value exists in the annuity. Since the money has been rolled out of a qualified plan, the period-certain annuity is in the form of an IRA. Thus, all income is taxable when payments are received by the individual. The annuity will provide 3 percent annual increases to provide for some inflation protection during the Bridge Period. The annuity will be reduced proportionately for the married couple as the spouse begins to receive Social Security benefits. For the annuity, we used a 5 percent nominal interest rate, assumed typical annuity administrative expenses, and an assumed 4 percent distribution cost. Other investment vehicles could also be utilized during the Bridge Period including laddering CDs or bonds, as well as using an invested portfolio of assets. Below, we present the annuity due to the ability to customize exact cash flows.

Three different cases are presented. The first two cases reflect single workers, George and Marianne. Both are relatively high-income earners and are projected to receive $1,414 a month in Social Security benefits if they start at age 62. Since Social Security does not make any distinctions by sex, their benefits and taxes are identical; only their projected longevity is different. The third example is of a married couple, whom we will refer to as John and Linda, both assumed to be aged 62. Similar to Table 7-2 above, we examine various levels of spouse Social Security income for this general case.

In the first example, George has $247,000 of 401(k) assets which he is considering rolling over to an IRA. He wishes to retire at age 62, at which point he can begin collecting a pension benefit of $3,000 per month. (Note that the $3,000 pension income could be $3,000 of IRA withdrawals as both are taxed the same at the federal level). George considers taking Social Security at 62 and funding the remaining income he needs to live on by taking IRA withdrawals. Alternatively, he can take IRA income first during the Bridge Period and delay Social Security to age 70. He thus benefits from not taking the Social Security reduction, accumulating DRCs, and benefits from the intervening COLAs. By delaying Social Security, George can plan on much higher Social Security income versus IRA income during a retirement expected to last many years. Conversely, by taking early Social Security, George has higher IRA income. We make the same financial assumptions for Marianne, the single female.

To compare the two financial strategies, we develop a methodology that would match incomes on an after-tax basis. In this example for single retirees, George or Marianne will be providing themselves with $58,000 of inflation-adjusted net after-tax income for the rest of their lives. Our methodology is as follows:

- Project Social Security Benefits to age 100, assuming both take the benefits early versus at age 70. The projected COLAs in the 2006 Annual Social Security Trustees report are used to adjust the benefits annually.
- Project Tax Brackets using 2006 tax brackets and standard deductions for single individuals out to the year 2044, taking into account the current sunset provisions in the tax law. For state taxes, a flat rate is assumed (4.66 percent for married, 5.19 percent for single) and taxes are calculated as a percentage of AGI.
- Calculate the Cost of the Bridge Income during the Bridge Period under the delayed approach. Using these assumptions and the assumed pension income, we calculate the after-tax benefit of starting Social Security at age 70. We then discount that after-tax amount back to age 62 for inflation using a 3 percent step rate. Next, we solve for the gross income that would need to be taken from the IRA assets to generate that level of after-tax income. Then we price the eight-year period-certain annuity using the initial income level calculated in the previous step and increasing the payment by 3 percent to reflect Cost of Living increases. Last, we calculate the projected after-tax income for every year until age 100.
- Calculate the required IRA withdrawals that would need to be made under the early Social Security approach to match the after-tax income of the delayed approach for every year until age 100. IRA assets are presumed to grow at a 5.78 percent nominal rate (see Appendix Table 7-A1).

Once the cash flows are determined, we can then compare the two approaches.

The single premium annuity to provide the Bridge Income utilizes almost the entire $247,000 IRA balance. This can be viewed as the cost of 'purchasing' the income during the Bridge Period to affect this strategy. This is the number we use as the basis of our comparisons going forward. We then calculate present values of the income up until various points. In

TABLE 7-4 Present Value of Required Income ($): Single and Married Cases

Social Security Claim		Single		Married
		Marianne	George	John and Linda
	Total after-tax income	58,000	58,000	68,000
	Annual IRA withdrawals (non-delayed)	15,149	15,149	18,135
Delayed to 70	Cost of bridge income period-certain annuity	246,636	246,636	276,648
Early at 62	Until life expectancy	286,454	259,819	381,931
Early at 62	75% life expectancy	335,199	311,553	419,113
Early at 62	90% life expectancy	364,601	350,194	453,453
Early at 62	Cost of inflation-protected annuity	304,064	276,266	409,635
Early at 62	Pye Safe Withdrawal Approach	451,424	451,424	540,414

Source: Authors' computations.

Note: Values calculated as of December 2006/January 2007. IRA assets accumulate at a 5.78% rate. This table compares costs of two strategies. The first involves delaying Social Security of the primary worker until age 70 while taking IRA income first during a Bridge Period from retirement until delayed Social Security begins. This is compared to a second strategy which starts Social Security at age 62 and couples that income with IRA income beginning at the same time. To provide the same after-tax income as the first approach via IRA withdrawals (in addition to the 'early' Social Security), the present value of the needed IRA is indicated. Similar values are provided if the individuals wanted to ensure the same after-tax income until the 75th and 90th percentiles of life expectancy. In addition, if the IRA was invested in an inflation-adjusted annuity, the cost is provided as of January 2007. Finally, we calculate the cost if the IRA utilized a safe withdrawal strategy of an initial 4% and thereafter increasing for inflation while incorporating Pye's methodology of properly accounting for investment expenses. Pye's methodology utilizes 4% Safe Withdrawal Rate with a 60/30/10 stock mutual fund/bond mutual fund/cash mix. Expenses are assumed to be 150 bp for stock mutual fund, 75 bps for bond fund, zero for cash. Expected gross return is 7.10%.

calculating the value of this approach, we use income up to the assumed life expectancies similar to Jennings and Reichenstein (2001); this approach is superior to calculating a pure actuarial value, since actuarial values do not adequately reflect the risks an individual faces. An individual is either alive or not and thus is required to provide himself with the full amount of necessary income, or none at all. (Life expectancies can be found in Appendix Table 7-A1.) Results are shown in Table 7-4.

Using the 1994 Group Annuity Rate mortality table, Marianne has a life expectancy of 87, and George has a life expectancy of 84. We also present values at the 75th and 90th percentiles of longevity. This is important as one of the largest risks that retirees face is living a longer life than they perhaps expect and thus risk running out of an adequate amount of income. Financial plans that focus only on life expectancy have a 50 percent chance of falling short. The present value is calculated using the same 4.9622 percent net interest rate utilized earlier. It is much more expensive for Marianne, on an expected value basis, to finance her after-tax income needed by electing early Social Security at age 62 and taking IRA withdrawals. The IRA balance runs out quickly as the retiree must not only pay higher taxes but also must provide the 'foregone COLAs' (the difference between COLA awards between the early Social Security and delayed Social Security amounts) out of her IRA. For George, the values are not quite as large, but the approach is still more efficient. These projections do not account for the risks of investing for retirement on one's own including poor mutual fund selection, greater than projected fund expenses, and the effects of reverse dollar cost averaging. This analysis also sets aside investment risk—the probability of running out of money is much higher under these assumptions (effectively a 6.16 percent withdrawal rate) than under the safe withdrawal rates calculated by Pye (2001). Recall that under Pye's methodology, the safe withdrawal rate must be reduced by the annual expenses divided by the expected return. Thus, with the safe withdrawal rate driven down by expenses, the size of the required nest egg must increase substantially. Using the assumed returns and expenses utilizing Pye's methodology, one would need a little over $451,000 to have 90 percent confidence that George or Marianne could make the necessary withdrawals until age 92.

A better alternative to Pye's approach may be to purchase an inflation-protected annuity from a financial services company to provide desired income above and beyond this reduced, early Social Security benefit. This is the closest comparable financial product to the delayed Social Security plus Bridge Income approach. An initial income level of $1,262 a month would need to be purchased to roughly approximate the cash flow required. A quote received on January 23, 2007, was $276,265 for George and $304,063 for Marianne for inflation-protected, life-only income annuities (www.flagship.vanguard.com). Thus, to provide themselves with most of the protections and income that following the delayed Social Security approach would bring, George would need 12 percent ($30,000) more in assets, and Marianne would need over 23 percent ($58,000) more.

The benefits are also substantial for the married couple, John and Linda. We assume they have $277,000 in assets and a $3,000 a month Joint and 100 percent Survivor pension. We assume that John has a monthly Social Security benefit of $1,414 if he starts at age 62. Rather than examine all possible Social Security scenarios for the couple, we assume that Linda has a small worker's benefit of $300 per month and would be eligible to collect a spousal benefit based on John's work record as well. Scenario I has Linda starting her $300 per month benefit immediately at age 62 and then collecting an additional $586 (today's dollars) spousal benefit starting at age 66. This is deliberately the most complex situation, to illustrate a practical application of the various components of the Social Security decision. We follow the same procedures as used in the single example, but substitute the married tax brackets and standard deductions. Again, the annuity increases at a 3 percent rate to mimic Social Security annual increases but is reduced proportionately when spousal Social Security begins. Essentially, the spousal Social Security income is carved out of the annuity cash flow. In calculating the value of the approach, we use the cash flows calculated for a married couple until the joint first to die age, and then we use the cash flows calculated for a single individual until the joint last to die age. John and Linda's total after-tax real income approximates $68,000 per year in retirement.

Results appear in Table 7-4. For our married couple, the benefits of following a delayed Social Security approach are significant. To provide the same level ($68,000 after-tax) of income, John and Linda would need anywhere from $67,000 to $265,000 more in assets, depending on the methodology chosen and the certainty level desired. John and Linda would need additional outside income of ~$1,511 per month to have the same level of after-tax income that a delayed Social Security strategy would provide. This amount would drop by ~5 percent upon the first death, thus it approximately equates to a Joint and 95 percent survivor annuity with inflation adjustments. While not illustrated here, if Linda had no worker's benefit, the required cash flow would drop a bit more, equating to a Joint and 85 percent benefit.

While not portrayed in these examples, we note that for two-income households, delaying both the spouse and the primary's worker benefits can result in very significant tax savings. Retirees should consider the benefits in light of both partners' health and projected longevity to determine if it is worth delaying both. It is also useful to note that we only consider income motives in this chapter. The primary disadvantage of the delayed Social Security plus Bridge Income strategy is the fast spend-down of assets during the Bridge Period. While significant tax advantages and efficiencies exist, retirees need to live into their mid-70s or early 80s in order to truly benefit from the strategy relative to an early Social Security plus drawdown approach.

Conclusion

Our research shows that individuals should not just look at traditional 'break-even' points when evaluating when to begin Social Security retirement benefits. Instead, optimizing their potential Social Security payments over the next several decades can provide retirees with significant financial peace of mind. In particular, Social Security has undergone significant changes that make the value of delaying the receipt of Social Security benefits greater than in the past. Specifically, the increase in the FRA and DRCs can result in significantly greater benefits from delaying Social Security.

The tax efficiency of Social Security income and the 'tax torpedo' penalization of taking qualified retirement income serve to magnify these benefits. In the future, greater numbers of spouses will become eligible for their own worker benefits, but they should consider how those benefits integrate with their spouse's benefits to provide optimal survivor income protection. Additionally, changes made under the Senior Citizens' Freedom to Work Act of 2000 make delaying Social Security for the worker (the higher earning Social Security beneficiary within a married couple) even more attractive. With the additional benefits of survivor protection, inflation adjustments, low expenses, and customization options available, delaying Social Security (for at least one member of a retiring couple) and taking income from personal retirement savings during the Bridge Period becomes a very efficient strategy of providing retirement income. Conversely, the rates of return required to be generated by personal savings accounts such as IRAs and 401(k)s to pay for the additional taxes and expenses when choosing to take Social Security early exceed what many academics and professionals are projecting today. In sum, reasonably healthy individuals and couples may wish to take seriously the potential benefits of delaying Social Security, and first providing themselves with income from their qualified retirement saving.

Appendix

TABLE 7-A1 Life Expectancy Ages

	Marianne	George	Married (first to die)	Married (last to die)
Life expectancy	87	84	80	91
75% expectancy	93	90	86	95
90% expectancy	97	95	90	99

Source: Society of Actuaries (1995).

Note

[1] Since this information is not widely known, interested readers may secure more information in the Social Security *Program Operations Manual System* §§GN 02409.100 and GN 02409.110 [Social Security Administration (SSA) 2007].

References

Arnott, Robert D. and Anne Casscells (2003). 'Demographics and Capital Market Returns,' *Financial Analysts Journal*, 59(2): 20–9.

Bengen, William (1994). 'Determining Withdrawal Rates Using Historical Data,' *Journal of Financial Planning*, 7(10): 171–80.

Coile, Courtney and Jonathan Gruber (2000). 'Social Security and Retirement,' NBER Working Paper no. 7830. Cambridge, MA: National Bureau of Economic Research.

Dalbar, Inc. (2004). *Quantitative Analysis of Investor Behavior 2004*. Boston, MA: Dalbar, Inc.

Gokhale, Jagadeesh and Laurence Kotlikoff (2003). 'Who Gets Paid to Save?' in James M. Poterba (ed.), *Tax Policy and the Economy, Vol. 17*. Cambridge, MA: The MIT Press, pp. 111–40.

—— —— and Todd Neumann (2001). 'Does Participating in a 401(k) Raise Your Lifetime Taxes?' NBER Working Paper no. 8341, Cambridge, MA: National Bureau of Economic Research.

Gustman, Alan and Thomas L. Steinmeier (2002). 'The Social Security Early Entitlement Age in a Structural Model of Retirement and Wealth,' NBER Working Paper no. 9183, Cambridge, MA: National Bureau of Economic Research.

Jennings, William and William Reichenstein (2001). 'Estimating the Value of Social Security Retirement Benefits,' *Journal of Wealth Management*, 4(3):14–29.

Karcinski, James, Miles Livingston, and Edward S. O'Neal (2004). 'Portfolio Transactions Costs at U.S. Equity Mutual Funds,' Zero Alpha Group. www.zeroalphagroup.com/news/hiddenstudy111704.cfm.

Kotlikoff, Laurence and Scott Burns (2004). *The Coming Generational Storm*. Cambridge, MA: The MIT Press.

Maxey, Daisy (2005). 'How To Look At Mutual Fund Fees,' *The Wall Street Journal*, February 7: R1.

McKinsey & Company (2005). *The Retirement Journey*. New York, NY: McKinsey & Company.

Mirer, Thad W. (1998). 'The Optimal Time to File for Social Security Benefits,' *Public Finance Review*, November, 26: 611–36.

Muksian, Robert (2004). 'The Effect of Retirement Under Social Security at Age 62,' *Journal of Financial Planning*, January: 64–71.

Munnell, Alicia (2003). 'The Declining Role of Social Security,' *Just the Facts on Retirement Issues*, Center for Retirement Research Report #6. Boston, MA: Center for Retirement Research at Boston College.

—— and Mauricio Soto (2005). 'Why Do Women Claim Social Security Benefits So Early?' *Just the Facts on Retirement Issues*, Center for Retirement Research Report #35. Boston, MA: Center for Retirement Research at Boston College.

—— and Steven Sass (2005). '401(k) Plans and Women: A 'Good News/Bad News Story,' *Just the Facts on Retirement Issues*, Center for Retirement Research Report #13. Boston, MA: Center for Retirement Research at Boston College.

Pye, Gordon (2001). 'Adjusting Withdrawal Rates for Taxes and Expenses.' *Journal of Financial Planning*, April: 126–36.

Rose, Clarence and L. Keith Larimore (2001). 'Social Security Benefit Considerations in Early Retirement.' *Journal of Financial Planning,* June: 116–21.

Ruffenach, Glenn (2007). 'The Baby Boomer's Guide to Social Security,' *The Wall Street Journal,* November 17: R1.

Social Security Administration (SSA) (2001). *The Official Social Security Handbook.* Washington, DC: Social Security Administration.

—— (2005). *Annual Statistical Supplement to the Social Security Bulletin.* Washington DC: Social Security Administration.

—— (2007). *Program Operations Manual System.* Washington, DC: Social Security Administration.

Society of Actuaries (1995). '1994 Group Annuity Mortality Table,' *Transactions of Society of Actuaries,* 47: 886.

United States General Accounting Office (GAO) (2003). 'Private Pensions: Participants Need Information on Risks They Face in Managing Pension Assets At and During Retirement,' GAO-03-810, July 29.

Whitehouse, Mark (2005). 'Social Security Overhaul Plan Leans on a Bullish Market.' *The Wall Street Journal,* February 28: C1.

Chapter 8

Regulating Markets for Retirement Payouts: Solvency, Supervision, and Credibility

Phyllis C. Borzi and Martha Priddy Patterson

In the past, the American worker entitled to a retirement benefit under an employer-sponsored defined benefit (DB) plan could look forward to a stream of retirement income, usually payable monthly. Retirement plans typically paid 'pensions' using a DB payment formula where the former employee received guaranteed fixed periodic payments for life and, in many cases, these payments continued during the life of a surviving spouse (although often at a lower level). The worker and the retiree had no role in managing the portion of the overall pool of accumulated assets from which retirement benefits would be paid and, as long as inflation did not run rampant, a retiree had no responsibility for or concern about investing the pension assets over the long term, because each month, another check would be forthcoming to cover the expenses for that month. To the extent that the monthly pension payment was more than necessary to cover that month's expenses, retirees could continue accumulating assets for that proverbial 'rainy day' or unexpected or catastrophic expense.

During their work careers, individuals are frequently insured against a number of hazards. Through their employment, employees are often offered health insurance, disability insurance, and opportunities to save for retirement or to accrue retirement benefits partially subsidized by the employer. Because wages roughly follow inflation, workers are generally protected from the inflation risk, as well (Hess and Schweitzer 2000). But once the individual retires and the accrual stage of retirement saving typically ends, it is more difficult to insure against the new risks of aging and of managing one's own investments and savings. Risks of longevity, illness, and inflation become very real. In addition, developing hedges against those risks are growing more challenging. The Social Security system pays benefits for life and provides automatic payment increases based on inflation, and Medicare provides certain basic levels of health-care coverage to the elderly and disabled; both offer some protection against these risks. Although DB pensions did provide retirees a considerable percentage of replacement income for life, thus offering a hedge against longevity risk (but not against inflation), such plans are becoming increasingly rare.[1]

Members of the Baby Boomer generation will need to find protections against all these natural and inevitable risks. But they will also face one important risk that was not of much concern for their predecessors: namely, they will have to protect themselves against the risk of fraud. For many, their employer-provided retirement benefits will be paid in the form of a lump-sum benefit rather than a series of periodic payments. Unfortunately, the marketplace offers many opportunities to separate the unwary and the uninformed from their retirement plan cash distributions. When asked why he robbed banks, the famous Depression-era thief, Willie Sutton, answered, 'Because that's where the money is.' It was a sensible 'marketing' strategy for identifying potential robbery targets then, and it is likely to be just as pertinent a strategy today for those who would engage in investment fraud and other financial crimes.

The purpose of this chapter is to begin to identify and examine the legal and regulatory structures in the marketplace designed to protect individual investors from financial loss through the insolvency, fiscal mismanagement, and/or malfeasance of those entities to which they have turned to for help in managing and investing their retirement distributions. In addition, we are interested in the extent to which new products have begun to emerge in the marketplace designed to protect retirees from these risks or that would encourage investment in less risky alternatives. To accomplish these tasks, we utilize two approaches: (*a*) interviews with key thought leaders in the financial services industry, consumer advocates, and state and federal government officials to determine whether and to what extent they have focused on legal, regulatory, and industry protections for retirees and their pension distributions and what new developments were occurring that might enhance protections for retirees; and (*b*) traditional legal research to identify statutes, regulations, and self-regulatory approaches currently in place to address these concerns.

What is at Stake for Retired Individuals?

The average Baby Boomer who earns a retirement benefit through a 401(k) plan is estimated to have an account balance of just under $128,000 at age 50 and about $141,000 at age 60. [Investment Company Institute (ICI) 2006*b*]. While some might argue that these amounts are too small to be attractive to those who specialize in financial frauds, others would disagree. Less sophisticated investors may not be quick to identify the appropriate law enforcement authorities and this may enable fraud to go undetected for a longer period of time. But more importantly, an individual who loses 'only' \$128,000, which could represent most of the retirement nest egg, is likely to be far worse off than an individual who loses considerably more in dollar terms though less as a percentage of total net worth.

Unfortunately, fraud follows the money. So, will the 401(k) generation be especially vulnerable to investing in products that are too risky or inappropriate for their age or health status or vulnerable to placing their trust and future in the hands of incompetent investment advisers or other dishonest individuals? Evidence so far suggests it may be. George Gaberlavage, Associate Director of AARP's Public Policy Institute, has observed that 'victims [of financial fraud] used to be older retirees, but now the people who are being scammed are younger and younger. People in their 50s are going to state regulators to complain.'[2]

Most retiring individuals receiving a 401(k) account payout or other single-sum cash distribution from a retirement plan have never been faced with such a considerable amount of money to manage at one time. Nor have they been faced with the daunting challenge to make it last through the end of their lives. So what are people to do?

The financial industry is well aware of the significant amounts of money that will be available for management and investment as Baby Boomers retire. In response, they are developing and marketing new products designed to hedge many retirement income risks and to capture these retirement assets for management. Some of these products will be available only through employers who choose to offer their retiring employees access to the product.[3] Alternatively, the 401(k) plan itself may offer to act as a facilitator for the individual's 401(k) distribution by transferring the account balance to a third-party financial organization offering a product with unique features to former participants in an employer's plan.

Shift to Defined Contribution Plans Affects Nature of Risk in Retirement

As previously noted, the challenges faced by individuals in managing their assets in retirement are significantly affected by the continuing shift to defined contribution (DC) plans and the changing nature of the distribution options offered to retirees in traditional DB plans, since the form in which participants receive their benefits at retirement influences the asset management choices available to them. According to the Investment Company Institute (ICI 2006a), 25 years ago there were 30 million active participants in DB plans, 19 million in DC plans, and virtually none in 401(k) plans. But today the situation has changed dramatically: some 47 million workers participate in 401(k) plans, 8 million in other types of DC plans, and only 21 million in DB plans.

This shift in plan type is important since, at retirement, DC participants typically receive their benefits in a single-sum cash payment, while DB-covered workers typically draw their benefits in the form of a life annuity or other stream of payments. The historical tilt toward annuitization of DB plan distributions may largely be a function of two factors: (*a*) requirements under the Employee Retirement Income Security Act of 1974 (ERISA) imposed on DB plans to offer an annuity option at retirement are inapplicable to most DC plans; and (*b*) the fact that most workers accept the traditional view that pensions are supposed to yield a stream of payments for life.

Nevertheless, the predominance of annuitization under DB plan distributions is also changing. For instance, the United States Government Accountability Office (GAO 2003) has reported that all workers in DB plans have an annuity option, but about half of DB plans now offer workers the option at retirement to take their benefits in a single-sum cash distribution. By contrast, almost all DC-covered workers are offered a lump-sum option, and just over one-third can take their distribution in annuity form (certain types of DC plans, other than 401(k) plans, are required to provide benefits in the form of a qualified joint-and-survivor annuity). For a number of reasons, including uncertainty about the long-term economic viability of their companies and the willingness of employers to continue to stand behind their pension promises, as well as the fact that recently interest rates used to calculate lump sums have resulted in more valuable cash payments than annuities, more and more workers in DB plans, when given a choice, decide to take their pensions in lump sum (GAO 2003). For this reason, the number of workers who actually elect annuities when offered continues to decline. For example, some 60 percent of retirees selected annuities between 1992 and 2000, but more recently, retirees tend to elect a lump-sum distribution that is either rolled over to an individual retirement account (IRA) or left in the plan (GAO 2003). Moreover, the same GAO report found that plan sponsors and administrators indicate that most retirees do not select annuities when given payment option choices. For most of those who do so, this decision may also increase their risks of investment and loss, given the fact the Pension Benefit Guaranty Corporation (PBGC) insures private employer and multiemployer pension benefit payments of up to a maximum limit adjusted annually.[4] No such 'insurance' is available for benefits taken as a lump sum.

As a result, there is much concern about whether retirees possess the skills necessary to face the postretirement challenges in managing their income in light of longevity, investment, and other risks. This concern is not limited to those who have received lump-sum distributions from 401(k) plans, but it also extends more broadly to individuals who receive benefits in a single-sum cash distribution. One could argue that retirees who take lump-sum distributions from their DB plans may be potentially more vulnerable to problems managing their distributions than their counterparts in 401(k) plans, since they have not had the experience of facing similar investment management challenges during the accumulation phase of their retirement, unless they were lucky enough to have both DB and self-directed 401(k) plans available to them as workers.

There are little data available on what happens to cash distributions once retirees have received them; what there is, however, suggests that most individuals roll over their distributions to IRAs. In fact, the ICI reports that nearly half of IRA assets came from rollovers from employer-sponsored plans.[5] However, the likelihood of the distribution being rolled over increased with the age of the individual receiving the distribution until age 60 and the size of the distribution, before a substantial decline for older ages. Copeland (2005) notes that while 55.6 percent of recipients aged 51–60 rolled over their entire distributions, only 37.8 percent of recipients aged 65 or older did so.

Advising Retirees on Financial Matters and the Regulatory Structure

As we have noted, little attention has to date been devoted to the question of whether adequate regulatory safeguards are in place to assure that retirees are protected against fraud and insolvency in connection with the investment vehicles in which they place their trust to meet these conventional risks. A preliminary review of the legal and regulatory environment surrounding existing investment vehicles and the nature and extent of protection for retirees raises important questions regarding this question.

Matrix of Regulators for Retirement Investments

Most of the financial products available to those near or at retirement fall into either the guaranteed 'insurance' arena, which includes annuities and long-term care benefits, or the securities arena, which includes mutual funds and stocks that generally offer no guarantees.[6] One complication with regulating DC plan payouts (and lump sums from DB plans) pertains to the complexity of the US financial regulatory system. Specifically, investments designated as 'securities' are regulated by both the United States Securities and Exchange Commission (SEC) and the state agencies with jurisdiction over securities. Generally, investments designated as 'insurance' are regulated under state law by a state's department of insurance. In some states, the same agency regulates both securities and insurance, although usually through different offices.[7] In addition to governmental regulation, both securities and insurance products may also be regulated by self-regulatory organizations (SROs), such as the National Association of Securities Dealers (NASD), which have authority to develop and test monitoring standards.

As we show below, disputes about whether an investment is an 'insurance product' or a 'security' are becoming increasingly common, as more complex investments are brought to market. Such disputes over regulatory authority also create the potential for an environment that may encourage some unethical financial product marketers to argue that the product is a security when confronted with insurance regulators and, when questioned by security regulators, argue the same product is insurance. Thus a regulatory vacuum could be created that puts retirees at a substantial disadvantage without their even being aware that such a problem exists.

Microcosm of the Problem—Suitability Rules

Under US securities laws, the concept of 'suitability' of an investment for a potential purchaser is well established.[8] That is, the SEC requires that certain securities be marketed only to potential buyers meeting minimum income and net worth standards. Interestingly, however, this federal securities suitability law does not apply to insurance products. And as financial and investment products grow more complex and integrated, tensions are emerging with respect to who has authority to regulate these products. For instance, this question has arisen in the context of which agency should regulate annuity-type investment products such as variable annuities and equity indexed annuities.

In 2003, the National Association of Insurance Commissioners (NAIC) adopted the Senior Protection in Annuity Transactions Model Regulation [National Association of Insurance Commissioners (NAIC) 2003]. Since then, many states have adopted the Model Regulation or similar suitability regulations. In 2006, the NAIC's Life Insurance and Annuities Committee expanded the model's protections to cover all consumers. 'When we first drafted the model, senior citizens were the focus because that's where the complaints originated,' said Commissioner Jim Poolman of North Dakota. 'It's become increasingly clear that problems are now expanding to include people under 65' (NAIC 2006).

Should Regulators Consider More Uniformity?

As Boomers near retirement and move from the accumulation to the distribution phase of retirement, many more individuals will be receiving their entire pension benefit in a single-sum cash distribution. For some, at least some of those assets will reasonably be used to purchase annuities, to help control the risk of outliving their money. Nevertheless, the 50 different state insurance laws pose a significant barrier, both for those seeking to design and market annuities for this group of purchasers and for those potential purchasers seeking to understand the annuity products offered. NAIC has attempted to address these issues by creating a series of 'model' statutes in the hope that each state will adopt the NAIC standard. Such laws can encourage a wider market of insurance and investment products and greater risk pooling of those products, as well as provide a greater likelihood that consumers can compare similar products. In addition, these laws may also mitigate, or, in some cases, eliminate, expensive procedural legal battles over 'choice of law' rules before the purchaser and seller can get to the merits of the suit.

Advocates of more uniformity in insurance-type investments have urged the creation of an 'optional federal insurance charter', which would regulate certain types of insurance (including property and casualty, life, and health insurance) at the federal level, if insurers elected to be covered by certain specified requirements. In the 109th Congress, for example, bills were introduced that would have authorized the issuance of a federal charter for insurance or any other insurance operations to be regulated, 'to provide a comprehensive system for the regulation and supervision of national insurers and national agencies, to provide for policyholder protections in the event of an insolvency or impairment of a national insurer.'[9] No action was taken on these bills in the 109th Congress, but similar bills were again introduced in the 110th Congress. It should be noted that this approach has several powerful opponents. The very mention by the United States Secretary of the Treasury Henry Paulson that the idea was worth consideration was enough to generate prompt opposition to the concept by the Coalition Opposed to a Federal Insurance Regulator, a coalition of insurance companies, trade associations, and agents and brokers (Insurancenewsnet 2007).

Some state regulators note that the lack of parallel regulation of investments in areas where both the federal and the state governments have regulatory authorities is a significant problem. According to Wisconsin's Insurance Commissioner Patty Struck, it is unclear how the federal ERISA law governing employer-sponsored benefits will interact with state securities and insurance laws in regulating retirement product sales and other employer retirement plan distributions.[10]

Financial Advice

Recent Congressional attention has been focused on facilitating employers' ability to provide financial advice for active employees.[11] However, at no point in the lengthy and often contentious Congressional debate was the question raised about providing financial advice for persons who have already retired. Arguably, retirees could also benefit from financial counseling. Moreover, their need for advice is quite immediate and serious, since their ability to recover from investment misjudgments is severely limited.

Little is known about what assistance retirees have available to them once they retire, to help them determine how to manage and invest their distributions. Survey data suggest that although few had financial advisers before retirement, many retirees do discuss what to do with their money after retirement with financial and tax advisers. Nevertheless, there is significant distrust in the advice that these financial advisers give (Greenwald, Bryck, and Sondergeld 2006). In fact, to the extent that retirees have been responsible for investing their pension assets preretirement in their 401(k) plans, there appears to be little change in asset allocation for most retirees' postretirement (Greenwald, Bryck, and Sondergeld 2006). So in determining whether sufficient regulatory protection exists for the investment vehicles used by many retirees, one should begin by looking at what investment vehicles are being utilized.

A Brief Examination of the Regulatory Structure Applicable to Key Asset Products

The most recent EBRI/ICI data regarding where 401(k) assets are invested show that 38 percent of the assets are in equity funds, 11 percent in company stock, 10 percent in balanced funds (including lifestyle and lifecycle funds), and 39 percent in fixed-income securities [including 10 percent in bond funds, 13 percent in guaranteed investment contracts (GICs) and other stable value funds, and 4 percent in other money funds; data for 2005]. For purposes of this discussion, 'funds' include mutual funds, bank collective trusts, life insurance separate accounts, and pooled investment products primarily invested in the type of funds indicated above (Holden and VanDerhei 2006). With respect to IRA assets, some 45 percent are invested in mutual funds, 38 percent in brokerage funds, 9 percent in life insurance, and 7 percent in banks/thrifts (Copeland 2007).

In view of this concentration, we focus our exploration into the regulatory structure for monitoring fraud and solvency for four asset product categories: mutual funds, bank products, insurance company products (including annuities), and brokerage accounts. To this we turn next.

Overview of Regulation of Mutual Funds

Legally known as an 'open-end company,' a mutual fund is an investment company that pools money from many investors for investment by an investment adviser in stocks, bonds, short-term money-market instruments, and other instruments.[12] Mutual funds are generally organized under state law as corporations or business trusts.[13] Unlike a typical corporation, however, a mutual fund generally has no employees of its own. Rather, most funds are organized and operated by an investment adviser who supplies the fund with its officers and employees and, more often than not, selects the fund's initial slate of directors [United States Securities and Exchange Commission (SEC 2006)]. Congressional concern about the potential for abuse inherent in such a structure led to the enactment of the Investment Company Act of 1940 (the '1940 Act or Act'), 15 U.S.C. section 80a-1 *et seq.*[14] The thrust of the Act is on disclosure to the public of information about the fund and its investment objectives. The Act also includes detailed requirements concerning investment company structure and operations (SEC 2007*a*).

In addition to the detailed requirements contained in the 1940 Act, mutual funds are subject to the Securities Act of 1933 (1933 Act), which requires fund shares offered to the public to be registered with the SEC and regulates mutual fund advertising, and the Securities Exchange Act of 1934 (1934 Act), which regulates how funds are sold and requires persons distributing funds or executing fund transactions to be registered with SEC as broker–dealers. Finally, investment advisers to mutual funds are subject to the Investment Advisers Act of 1940 (IAA), which requires them to register with the SEC, imposes reporting requirements, and prohibits them from engaging in fraudulent, deceptive, or manipulative practices.

The SEC is responsible for the enforcement and administration of the federal securities laws, including the 1940 Act. The SEC oversees mutual funds by performing on-sight inspections of mutual funds' compliance with federal securities laws, reviewing disclosure documents, and engaging in other regulatory activities, such as rulemaking, responding to requests for exemptions from applicable federal securities laws, and providing interpretations of those laws (GAO 1997). The SEC is also responsible for investigating and prosecuting violations of securities laws by mutual funds (GAO 1997).

In addition to the federal securities laws discussed above, mutual funds are also subject to state regulation in those states in which it sells shares. While the National Securities Markets Improvement Act of 1996 (NSMIA) provided that, among other things, mutual funds registered under the 1940 Act are subject to exclusive federal jurisdiction with regard to regulatory requirements, the states may still impose notice requirements (Hazen 2005). The NSMIA also preserves states' enforcement jurisdiction with respect to fraud or deceit, or unlawful conduct by a broker or dealer, in connection with securities or securities transactions.[15] Notably, it was the then New York Attorney General, Eliot Spitzer, who first identified the recent trading abuses in the mutual fund industry and brought enforcement actions against a number of mutual fund companies.

Aside from that important example, little has been written about the effectiveness of this law, although its purpose was to reduce the multiplicity of regulation of securities and eliminate duplication and conflicts between state and federal regulatory efforts except in the narrow areas described above. Presumably, one expected effect of this delineation of authority was that state resources could now be redirected toward protecting consumers from fraudulent conduct by brokers and dealers, although most states do not appear to have followed the lead of New York and used the tools offered by NSMIA as did Attorney General Spitzer.

Reporting and Disclosure Requirements for Mutual Funds

The 1940 Act expressly recognizes that investors are adversely affected when mutual funds fail to provide adequate, accurate information on funds' securities.[16] Consequently, the Act contains detailed registration, reporting, and disclosure requirements. Before a mutual fund can begin to operate, it must first file a notification of registration with the SEC.[17] Mutual funds must then file a registration statement with the SEC within three months after the filing of the notification of registration.[18] The purpose of the registration statement is to provide information as to a fund's proposed activities for the protection of investors.[19] The registration statement must contain, among other things, a detailed description of the fund's investment policies, and those policies that the fund deems as matters of fundamental policy.[20] Once filed, the objectives and policies identified in the registration statement can only be changed with shareholder approval.[21]

In addition, the 1940 Act requires mutual funds to file periodic reports with the SEC and to send certain reports to shareholders.[22] In what one legal commentator (Hazen 2005) characterizes as a 'final safety net for investors', SEC regulations require that, 'in addition to the information expressly required to be included in a registration statement or report, there shall be added such further material information, if any, as may be necessary to make the required statements, in the light of the circumstances under which they are made, not misleading.'[23]

While the 1940 Act's disclosure regime is undoubtedly comprehensive, it appears that 401(k) participants might not necessarily receive the same level of disclosure as other mutual fund participants. According to Andrew J. Donohue, Director of the SEC's Division of Investment Management, '[d]ifferent 401(k) participants receive varying levels of information, from full prospectuses and shareholder reports to one-page charts containing limited data and information' (Donohue 2007). Mr. Donohue intends to address this issue by working with the U.S. Department of Labor on a standardized mutual fund disclosure document for 401(k) investors as part of SEC's current disclosure reform initiative (Donohue 2007).

Structural Requirements for Mutual Funds

The 1940 Act also requires mutual funds to have a board of directors that will 'protect the interests of the fund's shareholders' (GAO 2004a). In what has been described as the 'cornerstone' of the 1940 Act's effort to control conflicts of interest within mutual funds, the Act requires that at least 40 percent of a fund's board be composed of independent outside directors.[24] Specifically, the Act provides that, except in limited circumstances, no more than 60 percent of the members of the board may be 'interested persons' of the fund.[25] The term 'interested person' means the fund's investment adviser, principal underwriter, and certain other persons (including their employees, officers, or directors) who have a significant relationship with the fund, its investment adviser, or principal underwriter.[26] If, however, an investment adviser is affiliated with the principal underwriter of a fund, a majority of the board of directors must be independent of both the investment adviser and the principal underwriter.[27]

The Act assigns a number of special responsibilities, involving the supervision of management and financial auditing to disinterested directors. Disinterested directors must, for example, review and approve the contracts of the fund's investment adviser and principal underwriter.[28] In this regard, the Act requires that disinterested directors request 'such information as may reasonably be necessary to evaluate the terms of [the] contract.'[29] Disinterested directors are also required to select the accountants who prepare the fund's filings under the Act.[30] Finally, the Act vests disinterested directors with the authority to appoint other disinterested directors to fill vacancies resulting from the assignment of advisory contracts.[31]

The Act also limits who can serve as an officer, director, employee, investment adviser, or member of an advisory board of a mutual fund. For example, certain persons convicted of a felony or misdemeanor arising from a securities transaction within the past ten years, or anyone temporarily or permanently enjoined from effecting securities transactions, are prohibited from serving as an officer, director, employee, investment adviser, or member of an advisory board of a mutual fund.[32] In addition, mutual funds are precluded from indemnifying any director or officer against any liability to the fund or the fund's shareholders to which such director or officer would otherwise be subject by reason of willful misfeasance, bad faith, or gross negligence, in the performance of his or her duties.[33] Finally, mutual funds must safeguard their assets by placing them in the hands of a custodian and by providing fidelity bonding of officers and employees of the fund.[34] Under the Act, a person convicted of larceny and embezzlement from a mutual fund can be fined up to $10,000 or imprisoned up to five years.[35]

Prior to the enactment of the 1940 Act, Congress mandated a study of the investment company industry.[36] As the Supreme Court noted in *E.I. du Pont* v. *Collins*, 432 U.S. 46 (1977), one of the problems identified in that study was the numerous transactions between investment companies and persons affiliated with them, which resulted in a distinct advantage to the 'insiders' over the public investors.[37] In response to this problem, the 1940 Act prohibits conflict of interest transactions between the fund and affiliated persons.[38] For example, with limited exceptions, the Act prohibits an affiliated person, promoter, or underwriter of a fund from selling securities (or other property) to the fund.[39] These provisions are designed to preclude officers, directors, and principal underwriters, among others, from self-dealing in transactions to which the mutual fund is a party.

To enforce these provisions, the 1940 Act authorizes the SEC to seek injunctive relief against a mutual fund officer, director, adviser, or underwriter, among others, for a breach of fiduciary duty involving personal misconduct with respect to any fund for which such person serves or acts.[40] In addition, under the Act, an investment adviser is 'deemed to have a fiduciary duty with respect to the receipt of compensation for services' from a mutual fund.[41] This duty is in addition to the specific fiduciary responsibilities that are already imposed on investment advisers by the IAA of 1940. These requirements are important to investors because they emphasize the significant fiduciary duties that arise as a result of the legal relationship formed when an investor entrusts his or her assets and financial well-being to an individual whose job is to invest those assets in a prudent manner on his or her behalf. In order to create a climate of confidence for individuals to invest in mutual funds in the first place, conflicts of interests, self-dealing, and other similar activities that create opportunities for the mutual fund or its officers or employees to enrich themselves at the expense of the investor must be clearly prohibited. Just as importantly, situations in which these activities occur in violation of these rules must be dealt with swiftly and severely in a way that reinforces public confidence in the integrity and responsiveness of the enforcement regime created under the securities laws.

SEC Response to Mutual Fund Scandals

In recent years, there have been reports of mutual fund improprieties involving late trading of fund shares, inappropriate market timing activities, and the misuse of nonpublic information about fund portfolios. The SEC has brought enforcement actions against a number of mutual fund complexes and issued new rules designed to improve fund governance, ethical standards, and disclosure to investors.[42] As of May 31, 2005, the SEC brought 29 enforcement actions involving mutual fund complexes (and their employees) and 12 enforcement actions against broker–dealers (and their employees).[43] While moving forward to undertake this type of public enforcement activity by the SEC is important, the ultimate outcome of these actions (many of which are still in progress) and their success at deterring future wrongdoing remains unclear. Investor confidence that the SEC possesses the resources and will aggressively enforce existing laws will largely depend on the real and perceived success of these legal actions.

On the regulatory front, mutual funds and investment advisers must now establish internal compliance programs to ensure compliance with the federal securities laws.[44] As part of these compliance programs, funds and advisers must (a) implement written policies and procedures reasonably designed to prevent violation of the federal securities laws; (b) conduct an annual review of their policies and procedures; and (c) designate a chief compliance to administer the compliance program. The SEC has also adopted amendments to Form N-1A under the 1933 Act and 1940 Act to require mutual funds to disclose (a) market timing procedures; (b) practices regarding 'fair valuation' of portfolio securities; and (c) policies and procedures addressing disclosure of their portfolio holdings.[45] The SEC also issued new rules under the IAA of 1940 that require investment advisers to adopt written codes of ethics to ensure compliance with federal securities laws.[46] Such codes must, at a minimum, include a standard (or standards) of business conduct that reflects the fiduciary obligations of investment advisers.

These measures all focus on enhanced disclosure and improvements in corporate governance as a means to provide greater protection for investors. Although these are important and necessary regulatory actions, it remains to be seen whether the type of mutual fund abuses that affected ordinary investors (including those seeking to invest their pension distributions) will in fact be deterred by these measures, or whether new forms of malfeasance will occur despite these changes.

Overview of Insurance Regulation

For historical reasons, regulation of insurance in the United States has long been the exclusive domain of the states. States' authority to regulate insurance was affirmed by Congress in 1945 when it passed the McCarron-Ferguson Act, 15 U.S.C.A. section 1011-1015, which granted an antitrust exemption for insurance activities to the extent that they were regulated by state law. This Act held that 'the continued regulation and taxation by the several States of the business of insurance is in the public interest.' More recently, the Gramm-Leach-Bliley Act reaffirmed the preeminence of regulation of insurance by the states as granted by the McCarron-Ferguson Act. As a result, each state has its own statute governing insurance companies and the products they offer. While far from uniform, state insurance statutes generally contain, among other things, restrictions on insurance operations (including investment activities, agent licensing, and product filing requirements) and other requirements to ensure solvency and protect consumers. As discussed more fully below, the insurance laws of all states also establish life and health guaranty associations to protect policyholders against the insolvency of an insurance company.

Insurance companies offer a wide range of insurance/investment products to retirement plans. Two of the more common products found in 401(k) plans are GICs and variable annuities. A GIC is a fixed income investment option offered by insurance companies, which typically provides a guaranteed rate of return for a specified time period (McGill et al. 2004). The rate of return provided by GICs will generally be based on currently available market yields of a specified asset mix, which will generally be slightly lower than the rate of return on similar investments (McGill et al. 2004).

A variable annuity is a contract between the purchaser and an insurance company under which the insurer agrees to make periodic payments beginning either immediately or at some future date, and if the purchaser dies during the accumulation phase, a death benefit is paid to the purchaser's beneficiary [United States Securities and Exchange Commission and National Association of Securities Dealers (SEC/NASD 2004)]. A purchaser of a variable annuity allocates his or her contributions among the various investment options, which are generally contained in subaccounts. These investment options are, more often than not, mutual funds that invest in stocks, bonds, money market instruments, or some combination of the three (SEC 2007b). Unlike a fixed annuity, payment amounts under a variable annuity will depend on the performance of the underlying investment portfolio.

Variable annuity contracts are generally subject to federal securities laws.[47] Thus, absent an exemption from the registration requirements of the 1933 Act, variable annuities must be registered as securities with the SEC. One such exemption is contained in section 3(a)(2) of the 1933 Act for securities issued in connection with a stock bonus, pension, or profit-sharing plan which meets the requirements for qualification under section 401(a) of the Internal Revenue Code.[48] It is important to note, however, that the section 3(a)(2) exemption is from the 1933 Act's registration requirements. Marketers of variable annuities remain subject to the antifraud provisions of the federal securities laws.

Notwithstanding the classification of variable annuities as securities under the 1933 Act, states can and often do classify variable annuities under their own state securities and insurance laws. According to a recent study conducted by the Hawaii Legislative Reference Bureau, only 14 states classify variable annuity contracts as securities (Sugano 2006). This is significant because sales abuses involving variable annuities will only fall within the jurisdiction of the state securities commissioner if such contracts are classified as a security. In those states that do not classify variable annuities as a security, abuses surrounding the marketing and sale of those products would presumably fall within the jurisdiction of the state insurance commissioner.

To make matters more confusing, the insurance statutes in 40 states include language providing the state insurance commissioner with exclusive jurisdiction over the issuance and sale of variable insurance contracts (Sugano 2006). The author of the Hawaii study notes that this raises the question of 'whether insurance divisions get involved in enforcement activities in those states where variable annuities are not defined as 'securities' under the securities laws' (Sugano 2006). Interestingly, when the author of the Hawaii study posed this question to NAIC, whose membership is composed of the insurance commissioners of all of the states, an NAIC representative stated that NAIC does not track such information. The Hawaii study also notes that there may be problems of overlapping jurisdiction in those states that have securities statutes that classify variable annuities as securities, and insurance statutes that provide the insurance commissioner with exclusive jurisdiction over variable annuities (Sugano 2006).

State Guaranty Association Coverage

As noted above, every state has a guaranty association which protects policyholders against the insolvency of an insurance company operating in that state. While established under state law, guaranty associations are not state agencies (GAO 1993); this implies that the states do not guarantee that the guaranty associations themselves will have sufficient funds to cover their obligations (GAO 1993). When an insurance company is liquidated, state life and health insurance guaranty associations are triggered to provide coverage and benefits to policyholders living in their state [National Organization of Life and Health Insurance Guaranty Association (NOLHIGA) 2007a]. If the insolvent insurer does not have enough funds to meet its obligations, each state guaranty association assesses the member insurers in its state a share of the amount required to meet the claims of resident policyholders (NOLHIGA 2007a). The amount assessed is based on the amount of premiums each company collects in that state on the kind of business for which benefits are required (NOLHIGA 2007a). Table 8-1 summarizes different state practices.

While coverage varies by state, most guaranty associations cover direct individual or direct group life and health insurance policies as well as individual annuity contracts issued by the guaranty association's member insurers (NOLHIGA 2007b). State guaranty associations generally do not cover any portion of a policy in which the investment risk is borne by the individual, such as a variable annuity (NOLHIGA 2007b). Coverage of GICs, on the other hand, varies from state to state (NOLHIGA 2007b). Those states that exclude unallocated contracts from coverage generally do not cover GICs. Our review of state guaranty association statutes and information contained on the National Organization of Life and Health Insurance Guaranty Association's website indicates that some 30 states now provide some coverage for GICs.[49]

Overview of Regulation of Bank Investment Products

Bank-offered investment products are regulated by the federal banking agencies (the Federal Reserve Board, the Treasury Department's Office of the Comptroller of the Currency (OCC), and the Federal Deposit Insurance Corporation (FDIC; see GAO 2007). The Federal regulatory objectives in connection with bank-offered investment products are twofold: (a) to maintain the safety and soundness of the bank; and (b) to protect the interests of trust customers (GAO 1986).

In 2005, trust institutions held more than $20 million in fiduciary assets for retail and institutional clients (FDIC 2005). Trust institutions exercised investment discretion over almost 27 percent, or 4.9 trillion, of these assets. According to the FDIC (FDIC 2005), approximately half of all fiduciary assets are held in retirement accounts (employee benefit assets plus IRAs and Keoghs).

Bank regulators have the authority to grant or terminate the trust powers of banks and bank-holding companies and their bank and trust subsidiaries. Under 12 U.S.C. section 92a, the OCC is authorized to grant permission for a national bank to act as a fiduciary and to promulgate regulations governing the proper exercise of fiduciary powers. OCC supervises the trust activities of national banks under regulation 12 CFR part 9. The Federal Reserve and FDIC, in turn, supervise state banks' trust activities under regulations similar to OCC's. The Federal Reserve also supervises the trust company subsidiaries of bank-holding companies.

TABLE 8-1 State Guaranty Association Coverage

State	Statute	Coverage of GICs/Unallocated Annuity Contracts	Coverage of Variable Annuity Contracts
Alabama	Ala. Code §27-44-3(a)	[a]	Covers portion guaranteed by insurer
Alaska	Alaska Stat. §§21.79.020(b), (c)	Yes	Covers portion guaranteed by insurer
Arizona	Ariz. Rev. Stat. Ann. §20-682B	Yes[b]	Covers portion guaranteed by insurer
Arkansas	Ark. Code Ann. §§23-96-107(b); 23-96-106(a)	Yes	Covers portion guaranteed by insurer
California	Cal. Ins. Code §1067.02(b)(2)	No[c]	Covers portion guaranteed by insurer
Colorado	Colo. Rev. Stat. §10-20-104(2)(b)	No	Covers portion guaranteed by insurer
Connecticut	Conn. Gen. Stat. §§38a-860(f)(1), (2)	Yes	Covers portion guaranteed by insurer
Delaware	Del. Code Ann. §§4403(b)(1), 4403(b)(2)	Yes	Covers portion guaranteed by insurer
District of Columbia	D.C. Code Ann. §31-5402(b)(2)	No	Covers portion guaranteed by insurer
Florida	Fla. Stat. Ann. §631-713(3)	No	Covers portion guaranteed by insurer
Georgia	Ga. Code Ann. §§33-38-2(a); 33-38-2(c)	Yes	Covers portion guaranteed by insurer
Hawaii	Haw. Rev. Stat. §431:16-203(b)(2)	No	Covers portion guaranteed by insurer
Idaho	Idaho Code §41-4303(1), (2)	Yes	Covers portion guaranteed by insurer
Illinois	215 Ill. Comp. Stat. Ann. 5/531.03(2)(a), (b)	Yes	Covers portion guaranteed by insurer
Indiana	Ind. Code Ann. §§27-8-8-2-3(d), (e)	Yes	Covers portion guaranteed by insurer
Iowa	Iowa Code §§508C.3.2, 3.3	Yes	Covers portion guaranteed by insurer
Kansas	Kan. Stat. Ann. §§40-3003(b); 40-3008(n)(1)	No[d]	Covers portion guaranteed by insurer
Kentucky	Ky. Rev. Stat. Ann. §304.42-030(2)(b)	No	Covers portion guaranteed by insurer
Louisiana	La. Rev. Stat. Ann. §§22:1395.3B(1), (2)	Yes	Covers portion guaranteed by insurer

TABLE 8-1 (*Continued*)

State	Statute	Coverage of GICs/Unallocated Annuity Contracts	Coverage of Variable Annuity Contracts
Maine	Me. Rev. Stat. §§4603.1, 2	Yes	Covers portion guaranteed by insurer
Maryland	Md. Code Ann §§9-403(b)(1), (2)	No	Covers portion guaranteed by insurer
Massachusetts	Mass. Gen. Laws §146B(4)(B)(2)	No	Covers portion guaranteed by insurer
Michigan	Mich. Comp. Laws Ann. §500.7704(2)	Yes	Covers portion guaranteed by insurer
Minnesota	Minn. Stat. Ann. §§62B.19	Yes	Covers portion guaranteed by insurer
Mississippi	Miss. Code Ann. §83-23-205(2)(a), (b).	Yes	Covers portion guaranteed by insurer
Missouri	Mo. Ann. Stat. §376.717.3	No	Covers portion guaranteed by insurer
Montana	Mont. Rev. Code Ann. §33-10-201(4)	Yes	Covers portion guaranteed by insurer
Nebraska	Neb. Rev. Stat. Ann. §44-2703(2)(b)	No	Covers portion guaranteed by insurer
Nevada	Nev. Rev. Stat. Ann. §686C.035.1(a)	No	Covers portion guaranteed by insurer
New Hampshire	N.H. Rev. Stat. Ann. §§408-B:5.ll(a), (b)	Yes	Covers portion guaranteed by insurer
New Jersey	N.J. Rev. Stat. §§17B:32A-3.b, 3.c	Yes	Covers portion guaranteed by insurer
New Mexico	N.M. Stat. Ann. §59A-42-3A 59A-42-3B	ᵉ	Covers portion guaranteed by insurer
New York	N.Y. Ins. Law §§7703(a) 7703(b)	Yes	Covers portion guaranteed by insurer
North Carolina	N.C. Gen. Stat. §§58-62-21(b), (c)	Yes	Covers portion guaranteed by insurer
North Dakota	N.D. Cent. Code §§26.1-38.1-01.2, 1.3	Yes	Covers portion guaranteed by insurer
Ohio	Ohio Rev. Code Ann. §§3956.04(B)(1), (2)	Yes	Covers portion guaranteed by insurer
Oklahoma	Okla. Stat. Ann. §2025.B.2.	No	Covers portion guaranteed by insurer
Oregon	Or. Rev. Stat. §§734.790(1), (3)	Yes	Covers portion guaranteed by insurer
Pennsylvania	40 PA. Stat. §§991.1703(b)(1)	Yes	Covers portion guaranteed by insurer

(*cont.*)

TABLE 8-1   (*Continued*)

State	Statute	Coverage of GICs/Unallocated Annuity Contracts	Coverage of Variable Annuity Contracts
Rhode Island	R.I. Gen. Laws §§27-34.3-3(b)(1),(2)	Yes	Covers portion guaranteed by insurer
South Carolina	S.C. Code Ann. §38-29.40	No	Covers portion guaranteed by insurer
South Dakota	S.D. Codified Laws §58-29C-46B(2)	No	Covers portion guaranteed by insurer
Tennessee	Tenn. Code Ann. §56-12.204(b)(2)	No^f	Covers portion guaranteed by insurer
Texas	Tex. Ins. Code Ann. §463.202(c)(1)	Yes	Covers portion guaranteed by insurer
Utah	Utah Code Ann. §§31A-28-103(2)(a), (b)	Yes	Covers portion guaranteed by insurer
Vermont	Vt. Stat. Ann. tit. 8 §§4153(a) 4153(b)(1), (2)	Yes	Covers portion guaranteed by insurer
Virginia	Va. Code Ann. §38.2-1700C	No	Covers portion guaranteed by insurer
Washington	Wash. Rev. Code Ann. §48.32A.025	Yes	Covers portion guaranteed by insurer
West Virginia	W.Va. Code Ann. §33-26A-3(b)(1)	Yes	Covers portion guaranteed by insurer
Wisconsin	Wis. Stat. Ann. §646.01(1)(b)	No	Covers portion guaranteed by insurer
Wyoming	Wyo. Stat. Ann. §26-42-103(c)	No	Covers portion guaranteed by insurer

Source: Authors' compilation of state laws and National Organization of Life and Health Guaranty Associations summary of state statutes governing guaranty associations.

[a] Alabama's statute neither includes nor excludes GICs and/or unallocated annuity contracts.

[b] Arizona's guaranty association will only cover a GIC if the 'contract holder exercises an annuity option for individual persons' provided by the GIC on or before the date the life insurance company becomes subject to a delinquency proceeding. See Ariz. Rev. Stat. Ann. §20-682B.

[c] The California statute does, however, contain a limited exception to the exclusion. See Cal. Ins. Code §1067.02(b)(2).

[d] Coverage is, however, provided for unallocated annuity contracts issued to IRC §457 plans.

[e] New Mexico's statute neither includes nor excludes GICs and/or Unallocated annuity contracts.

[f] Coverage is, however, provided to unallocated annuity contracts issued to IRC §403(b) plans.

Provided certain requirements are met, collective investment funds are exempt from the registration, disclosure, and recordkeeping requirements of the 1940 Act.[50] They are not, however, exempt from the antifraud provisions of the 1933 Act and 1934 Act. Nor, for that matter, are they exempt from ERISA if the fund contains any account assets subject to ERISA. Thus, a collective investment fund in which one or more ERISA-covered employee benefit plans participate must comply with the myriad requirements imposed by ERISA, and participants of such funds are protected by ERISA (GAO 1986).

OCC regulations allow national banks to maintain and invest fiduciary assets in a collective investment fund. A collective investment fund is a trust managed by a bank or trust company that pools investments of retirement plans and other large institutional investors.[51] Participating interests in a collective investment fund are not FDIC-insured (United States Comptroller of the Currency (OCC) 2005). The regulations set forth detailed requirements concerning the need for a written plan, fund management (including the use of an outside adviser), fund valuation, admission and withdrawal, audit, and financial reports, and conflicts of interest, among other things. The regulations are intended to protect the interests of fiduciary accounts invested in collective investment funds (GAO 1986).

Collective Investment Fund Requirements

Part 9 of the regulations permit national banks to maintain and invest fiduciary assets in a collective investment fund 'where consistent with applicable law.' The term 'applicable law', as used in the regulations, refers to (*a*) the terms of the instrument governing a fiduciary relationship; (*b*) the law of a state or other jurisdiction governing a national bank's fiduciary relationships; (*c*) applicable federal law governing those relationships; or (*d*) any court order pertaining to the relationship.[52]

Section 9.18(b)(1) of the regulations requires that collective investment funds be established and maintained in accordance with a written plan, which must be approved by resolution of the bank's board of directors or by a committee authorized by the board. A copy of the plan must be made available to any person for inspection at the main office of the bank during banking hours. The written plan must, at a minimum, contain the following information regarding the manner in which the bank will operate the fund:

1. investment powers and policies with respect to the fund;
2. allocation of income, profits, and losses;
3. fees and expenses that will be charged to the fund and to participating accounts;

4. terms and conditions governing the admission and withdrawal of participating accounts;
5. audits of participating accounts;
6. basis and method of valuing assets in the fund;
7. expected frequency for income distribution to participating accounts;
8. minimum frequency for valuation of fund assets;
9. amount of time following a valuation date during which the valuation must be made;
10. bases upon which the bank may terminate the fund; and
11. any other matters necessary to define clearly the rights of participating accounts.[53]

A bank that administers a collective investment fund generally must have exclusive management of the fund, except as a prudent person might delegate to others.[54] The regulation also dictates the frequency in which a collective investment fund must be valued.[55] Specifically, a collective investment fund must determine the value of the fund's readily marketable assets at least once every three months. Collective investment funds must be valued at market value, or if such valuation is not readily ascertainable, at a fair value determined in good faith by the bank.[56] The regulations also require that collective investment funds must be audited at least once during each 12-month period by auditors responsible only to the bank's board of directors.[57]

Collective investment funds must issue an annual report that is intended both for the bank and the beneficiaries of participating accounts.[58] The report must disclose the fund's fees and expenses in a manner consistent with applicable law in the state in which the bank maintains the fund. The regulations also require that the report contain a list of investments in both cost and current market value, a summary of investment changes for the period reflecting purchases (with costs) and sales (with profit and loss), income and disbursements since the last report, and notation of any investments in default. The report may not contain predictions of future fund performance, but may include historical performance data.[59]

Banks that administer collective investment funds are subject to the following self-dealing and conflicts of interest rules: (*a*) the bank may not have an interest in the collective investment fund, except in its fiduciary capacity (this includes a prohibition on any creditor relationship between the bank and the fund or its participants); (*b*) the bank may not make a loan on the security of the participant's interest in the fund; (*c*) the bank may not lend, sell, or otherwise transfer assets of a fiduciary account to the bank, insiders, or affiliates; (*d*) no fund assets may be invested in the bank's stock or obligations.[60]

Banks may charge a 'reasonable fund management fee' if (*a*) the fee is permitted under applicable law (and complies with disclosure requirements, if any) in the state in which the bank maintains the fund; and (*b*) the amount of the fee does not exceed an amount commensurate with the value of legitimate services of tangible benefit to the participating fiduciary accounts that would not have been provided to the accounts were they not invested in the fund.

Bank Investment Contracts

A bank investment contract (BIC) is a stable-value investment product issued by a bank that guarantees to return the principal amount deposited by the contract holder on a specified date and at a specified rate of interest. Most BICs are insured by the FDIC (1988, 1989. Whether a particular BIC is insured by the FDIC depends on whether the BIC qualifies as a 'deposit'.[61] If a BIC is a deposit, FDIC insurance will apply. If, however, the BIC is not a deposit, no FDIC insurance will apply. While BICs are somewhat similar to GICs in that they may offer some insurance protection, BICs generally do not contain annuity provisions.

Overview of Self-Directed Brokerage Accounts

A relatively small number of 401(k) plans offer participants access to self-directed brokerage accounts. For example, about one-fifth of 401(k) plans report offering such accounts (Deloitte Consulting LLP 2006). Self-directed brokerage accounts offer plan participants the ability to invest in individual stocks and bonds in addition to mutual funds. Participants typically open an account with a brokerage firm of their own choosing, or, in some cases, the plan may offer a variety of brokerage firms from which participants may select.

The SEC shares oversight responsibilities over broker–dealers with the SROs (primarily NASD). The 1934 Act makes it unlawful for any broker or dealer to utilize interstate commerce 'to effect any transactions in, or to induce or attempt to induce the purchase or sale of, any security' unless such broker or dealer registers with the SEC.[62] In addition to registering with the SEC, brokers and dealers must also become members of an SRO.[63] The states also play an important role in the regulation of brokers and dealers.

Broker–dealers are subject to the 1934 Act's 'antifraud' provisions.[64] These provisions prohibit misstatements or misleading omissions of material facts, and fraudulent practices and conduct, among other things.[65] The 1934 Act also requires SROs to implement rules designed to prevent fraudulent and manipulative acts and practices.[66] One of the most important is NASD's rule imposing a 'suitability' obligation upon its member broker–dealers. The rule provides, in relevant part, that:[67]

(a) In recommending to a customer the purchase, sale or exchange of any security, a member shall have reasonable grounds for believing that the recommendation is suitable for such customer upon the basis of the facts, if any, disclosed by such customer as to his other security holdings and as to his financial situation and needs.

(b) Prior to the execution of a transaction recommended to a non-institutional customer, other than transactions with customers where investments are limited to money market mutual funds, a member shall make reasonable efforts to obtain information concerning:

(1)   the customer's financial status;
(2)   the customer's tax status;
(3)   the customer's investment objectives; and
(4)   such other information used or considered to be reasonable by such member or registered representative in making recommendations to the customer.

NASD has also issued guidance stating that broker–dealers have a 'fundamental responsibility for fair dealing' with their customers (NASD 2007b).

As noted above, broker–dealers are also subject to state regulation. Specifically, broker–dealers are subject to registration with, and antifraud enforcement by, states in which they do business.

The Securities Investor Protection Act of 1970 (SIPA)

The SIPA of 1970 created the Securities Investor Protection Corporation (SIPC), a private nonprofit corporation to protect investors from losses resulting from the financial failure of broker–dealers in whose custody the investors have placed cash or securities.[68] SIPC's mission is to promote confidence in securities markets by allowing for the prompt return of missing customer cash and securities held at a failed member-firm (GAO 2001: 6). SIPA gives SEC oversight responsibility over SIPC.[69] SIPC maintains a fund financed by annual assessments on all member firms and interest generated from its investments.[70] The SIPC fund amounted to $1.29 billion at year-end 2005 (SIPC 2005). This fund is used for advances to trustees for customer claims and to cover certain administrative expenses of a liquidation proceeding (GAO 2001).

Most broker–dealers registered under the 1934 Act must become members of SIPC.[71] There are, however, a number of important exceptions. Specifically, broker–dealers whose business consists exclusively of (a) the distribution of shares of mutual funds; (b) the sale of variable annuities; and (c) the business of insurance are not required to become members of

SIPC.[72] Thus, while shares of mutual funds are protected securities under SIPA, broker–dealers that deal exclusively in mutual funds are not SIPC members. Customers of such broker–dealers are, therefore, not protected by SIPC. SIPC provides coverage only if a member-brokerage firm goes bankrupt and does not have sufficient assets to settle its customer accounts. It does not protect investors against market risk or against losses due to poor performance of investments. SIPC does, however, cover individuals whose securities are stolen by a member-broker (SIPC 2007). To qualify for relief under SIPA, an investor must qualify as a 'customer' as defined by SIPA. Section 78lll(2) defines a 'customer' as follows [15 U.S.C.S. section 78lll(2)]:

Any person ... who has a claim on account of securities received, acquired, or held by the Debtor in the ordinary course of its business as a broker or dealer from or for the securities accounts of such person for safekeeping, with a view to sale, to cover consummated sales, pursuant to purchases, as collateral security, or for purposes of effecting a transfer. The term 'customer' includes any person who has a claim against the Debtor arising out of sales or conversions of such securities, and any person who has deposited cash with the Debtor for the purpose of purchasing securities.

SIPA sets coverage at a maximum of $500,000 per customer, of which no more than $100,000 may be in cash. In addition, a few insurance companies offer excess SIPC insurance, that is, private insurance that firms can purchase to cover claims in excess of the $500,000 limit under SIPA (GAO 2004*b*).

Does the Current Regulatory Structure Offer Sufficient Protection?

Our overreview of the key elements of the existing regulatory structure governing the four major types of assets that retirees are likely to utilize may lead the reader to believe that a sufficient layer of protection exists to safeguard individuals from serious fraud or insolvency. Nevertheless, little evidence exists regarding the effectiveness of these structures in preventing loss or ensuring that losses to investors are appropriately compensated.

It is one thing to note that if securities fraud occurs, investors have a right to sue to hold the wrongdoer accountable. As a practical matter, however, this right may be less than useful for the newly retired Enron employee whose 401(k) benefit is less than half what it should have been because corporate executives engaged in fraudulent activity. Similarly, state guaranty funds may be designed to compensate insurance policyholders for certain losses, but, as previously described, they typically operate after-the-fact:

after losses occur, the fund assesses each surviving insurer to make up the shortfall caused by an insurance company's failure. It can be months or years before policyholders receive compensation, yet during that period, retirees still have to pay their bills and go on with their lives. Additionally, resources for state enforcement and oversight are always in short supply.

Moreover, many of these statutory protections rely on various forms of disclosure as a mechanism to assure that investors are protected. The assumption seems to be that forcing public disclosure is an adequate substitute for traditional enforcement measures such as government auditing and monitoring. Yet disclosure that is neither understandable nor meaningful can be expensive for the entity required to undertake it, while nearly useless to the individual who was supposed to benefit from it. For instance, trying to make sense of a prospectus or a brokerage account or mutual fund statement is a daunting task for many individuals, and in fact may create more confusion and less likelihood the individual investor focuses on the most important information necessary to make a reasonable investment decision (Choi, Laibson, and Madrian 2006). While some in the Baby Boomer generation may be more financially literate than their parents, the degree of competence necessary to avoid potential dangers in evaluating the relative merits of a particular investment, understanding the dimensions of the financial risks one is facing, and managing income and investment decision-making is far from guaranteed or universal (Lusardi and Mitchell 2007).

Financial Advisers: New Training for New Challenges

Many retirees seek assistance from financial advisers to help them navigate the process of determining when, where, and how to invest their lump-sum retirement payouts, and how to manage their money in retirement. Providers of financial advice have a myriad of trade associations, credentialing organizations, and continuing education programs. But this multiplicity of education standards and credentialing creates considerable confusion among even financially knowledgeable individuals. Many of these designations do require extensive education and passage of lengthy examinations. Some of the organizations allow the public to access information about the individual credentialed by the organizations, including whether the individual remains in good standing with the organization.

The Coalition on Investor Education, consisting of North American Securities Administrators Association (NASAA), the Consumer Federation of America (CFA), the IAA, the Financial Planning Association (FPA), and the CFA Institute (provider of the Certified Financial Advisor designation), is one organization working on ways to clarify these various credentials.[73] They divide these players roughly into three groups: (*a*) investment advisers; (*b*) brokers; and (*c*) 'financial planners'.

'Investment adviser' and 'broker' are terms with specific legal definitions and defined responsibilities under securities laws (as discussed above). In contrast, 'financial planner' is not a legally defined term, but is a label commonly used to encompass all other suppliers of financial advice or products. The lack of clarity as to what type of background or experience an individual must have before acting as a financial planner or holding oneself out as some other type of an adviser in these matters in the marketplace is a source of concern, particularly for those who have well-recognized credentials and training in the business of providing financial education and investment advice. For instance, a subcommittee within the NASAA also is studying what action, if any, should be taken in defining and credentialing various state-recognized professional designations, such as 'elder adviser', so that consumers will have a better understanding about the competencies and training of these varying types of advisers. Newly retired individuals seeking advice on financial management and investment of their retirement distributions may be an easy target for those individuals in local communities who advertise their availability to assist individuals in these complicated and daunting financial tasks, even though these 'advisers' may have had little or no training or experience in these matters themselves.

It is also worth noting that providers of investment services and advice have differing legal obligations to their customers. As previously noted, whether the provider has a fiduciary duty to his or her customers can affect the advice the retiree might be given. Under the securities laws, investment advisers do have such a fiduciary duty and they are required to disclose their qualifications, how they are compensated, possible conflicts of interest and the existence of any pending disciplinary actions. In contrast, brokers are not generally bound by a fiduciary duty to their customers, nor are they required to disclose up-front conflicts of interest or their compensation structure. However, individuals providing financial advice may be registered or licensed investment advisers or brokers and therefore it may not be easy to determine what their legal duties and responsibilities to customers are. Although consumers may find out whether a person or firm is registered or licensed as an investment adviser or broker and review their disciplinary record by contacting NASAA or consulting their website, few retirees may even be aware that this is a problem, let alone how to investigate the credentials and record of the individual or firm interested in offering them advice.

The SEC has addressed the issue of fraud against retirement savings in a vigorous way through public awareness, using investor education, examinations, and enforcement.[74] During 2006, the Commission brought 23 lawsuits in the US federal courts involving fraud against seniors.[75] In addition, the Commission has partnered with state securities regulators, the New York Stock Exchange, and NASD to maximize enforcement and training resources.[76] Although this appears to be a step in the right direction in terms of recognizing the potential problem and the need for careful supervision of those who provide investment services and advice to seniors, it is far too early to evaluate the adequacy of these efforts.

The Role for Annuitization in a 401(k) World

Annuities can be offered as an investment alternative for participants in a 401(k) plan or as a form of payment when retirement assets are distributed from the plan. However, annuities have, to date, not yet become popular, either as an investment option in 401(k) plans or as a payout method.[77] But the retirement of the Baby Boomers may change that. Within the last few years, many financial product companies have entered this market by providing annuities as a 401(k) plan distribution product. In the past, plan sponsors may have been reluctant to include an annuity option for participants taking a distribution from a 401(k) plan.

The Regulatory Environment

One disincentive to 401(k) and other plan distributions in the form of annuities has been significantly reduced by section 625 of the Pension Protection Act (PPA) of 2006.[78] That section directs the Department of Labor to issue final regulations within one year of the Act's enactment to alter the applicability of its Interpretive Bulletin 95-1[79] to DC plans. In explaining what ERISA's fiduciary standards required, that Bulletin states that any employer-purchased annuity must be 'the safest available' annuity. The Bulletin was issued during the height of the Congressional and public debate over the safety and security of annuities purchased by terminating overfunded DB pension plans, and in particular the investigations and legal actions surrounding plan purchases of annuities offered by the Executive Life Insurance Company, placed in receivership by the California Insurance Department. The U.S. Department of Labor was apparently motivated to issue this directive by concern for participants in terminating overfunded DB plans, but its language appeared to sweep more broadly. The ordinary reading of the term 'safest' indicates that only a single annuity can meet that standard. Consequently, the practical meaning of the Interpretive Bulletin has been debated for more than a decade. During the recent consideration of pension legislation, Congress was told that as a result of the 'safest available annuity' rule, some DC plan sponsors avoided offering annuity options to their 401(k) participants because of concern about fiduciary liability in selecting a potential annuity carrier.

Section 625 of the PPA is an attempt to address that concern. It requires the Department to issue regulations clarifying that when a fiduciary selects an annuity as an optional form of distribution from an individual account (DC) plan covered by ERISA, that decision is not subject to the 'safest available annuity' requirement. However, all other fiduciary standards otherwise applicable under ERISA will still apply to the fiduciary's decision (e.g., the duty to prudently select the annuity carrier initially and monitor its performance once selected). Even after this change in the Department's Interpretive Bulletin 95-1 to clarify its limited applicability to DC plans, however, some plan sponsors may remain reluctant to enter into the role of offering various annuity payout options, in part because it still requires extra work on the part of the plan sponsor to identify, evaluate, and communicate the availability of a suitable annuity product.

The Employer Role in Offering 401(k) Annuity Products

Of late, a number of insurers have begun to develop and market annuity products for 401(k) plans, reviewed elsewhere in this volume (Ameriks et al. 2008). But from the perspective of individuals who will be receiving their benefits in the form of a lump-sum distribution, perhaps the most helpful marketplace development that is occurring is the effort to facilitate employer involvement in offering annuities as an optional form of distribution for benefits that would otherwise be paid as a single-sum cash payment. Keeping the plan sponsor of a DC plan engaged as a facilitator of the participant's ability to select an annuity at retirement and making the choice of an annuity a more attractive option could encourage a great number of individuals to annuitize and potentially reduce the chance of outliving their benefits.

Two interesting examples of this new approach of making it easier for sponsors of 401(k) plans to offer annuities are the products offered by Income Solutions, an annuity purchase program of Hueler Investment Services, Inc., and the program designed by the Expect to Live More (ELM) Income Group of Washington.[80] In both cases, the goal is to offer viable and affordable annuity options to retiring employees, while allowing the plan sponsor to avoid ERISA plan responsibilities for the products its former employees purchase. Income Solutions has brought a product to the market that enables plan sponsors to offer their retiring employees literally a supermarket of annuity providers who will compete for the retiree's business by supplying a bid to the retiree based on the same annuity features offered by its competitors participating on the site. The Income Solutions platform in effect enables the 401(k) plan participant to compare apples to apples as he or she decides whether to annuitize the 401(k) account balance at retirement and if so at what price. ELM Income Group of Washington is an outgrowth of a cooperative project undertaken by a number of large companies that banded together to use their combined marketplace leverage to challenge insurers to provide lower cost and more flexible annuity products for their employees and to the public at large. One unique feature of ELM's strategy that was required of insurance carriers with whom they contracted is that the insurers must make available the same products to the public (and to other employers) through their Internet website and toll-free numbers connected to salaried customer service representatives. ELM's first annuity offering involved fixed annuity products from Nationwide and The Principal Financial Group.

Conclusions

Many near-retirees confront the question of whether to receive their retirement benefits in a single-sum cash distribution or some other form. Most people facing this choice will be participants in DC plans with no other distribution option offered, but increasingly, participants in traditional DB plans may also affirmatively select a lump sum rather than an annuity. Yet once they have received their lump-sum distribution, the challenge of assuring that this sum will be sufficient to assure their financial security in retirement despite the longevity, illness, and inflation risks they will face is formidable.

While retirees who want to invest some or all of this single-sum retirement distribution have many financial products available to them, there are also many uncertainties as to whether adequate regulatory and enforcement structures exist in the marketplace to assure that their investments are protected from any financial loss they may suffer as a result of the insolvency or fraud of those individuals or entities to which they have entrusted their money. As we have shown, there is a detailed and complex regulatory structure governing the four major asset classes that most retirees use for their investments [mutual funds, bank products, insurance company products (including annuities), and brokerage accounts]. Nonetheless, there have been cases where individual investors have suffered losses, despite these regulatory protections.

In the past, financial risks to retirees were limited since the vast majority of them received their benefits in the form of an annuity—typically a monthly stream of income. Although purchasing annuities is not entirely risk-free, since the solvency of the annuity carrier is still a potential source of concern, at present the regulatory structure for guarding against fraud and insolvency of insurance carriers appears more developed and reliable than for the other types of investment opportunities. As previously noted, insurance is largely state-regulated and most states seem to be doing a good job in protecting annuity purchasers. But changes in the employer-sponsored plan marketplace have reduced the reliance on annuities as a hedge for the significant risks faced by retirees. Recently, however, as more and more attention has been paid to the challenges retirees must overcome in managing their single-sum pension distributions, there appears to be a renewed interest in annuitization and some heartening product development activity in the marketplace. We believe it unlikely that there will be a major resurgence of the traditional DB plan, but it is positive that some employers are beginning to believe that encouraging retirees to elect annuities may assist participants to avoid making investment and income mistakes in retirement.

Additional research is necessary in several areas. First, more analysis is needed on the regulatory structures covering the major asset categories relied on by individuals for investment of their retirement distributions. Although here we have only provided an overview of available protections, our research suggests that many experts are just beginning to focus on whether the currently regulatory system is resilient enough. It relies heavily on a combination of government regulation and peer-review standard-setting, and it is unclear if it is capable of providing the type of before-the-fact identification and prevention of potential solvency and fraud problems necessary to avoid large retiree losses—particularly when they may have no alternative income replacement mechanisms to rely on while the legal and regulatory tools available under the current system are used to compensate them for their loss.

Acknowledgment

The authors thank Joseph J. Shelton for his invaluable assistance in the research and preparation of this chapter.

Appendix: Federal Legal References

Burks v. *Lasker*, 441 U.S. 471, 482 (1979).

E.I. du Pont v. *Collins*, 432 U.S. 46, 54 (1977).

Green v. *Brown*, 276 F.Supp.753, 756 (S.D.N.Y. 1967).

SEC v. *Capital Gains Research Bureau, Inc.*, 375 U.S. 180 (1963).

SEC v. *Variable Annuity Life Insurance Company of America*, 359 U.S. 65 (1959).

SEC v. *Credit First Fund*, No. 05 Civ. 8741 (C.D. Cal. December 22, 2006).

SEC v. *U.S. Gas & Electric*, No. 06 Civ. 22440 (S.D. Fl. December 11, 2006).

SEC v. *Peter J. Dawson*, No. 06 Civ. 6360 (E.D. N.Y. November 30, 2006).

SEC v. *Spiro Germenis*, No. 06 Civ. 6153 (E.D. N.Y. November 21, 2006).

SEC v. *Viper Capital Management*, No. 06 SI 6966 (N.D. Cal. November 8, 2006).

SEC v. *Gari Aldridge*, No. 06 Civ. 5645 (N.D. Ill. October 18, 2006).

SEC v. *Joseph Y. Zumwalt*, No. 06 Civ. 61407 (S.D. Fl. October 3, 2006).

SEC v. *C. Wesley Rhodes, Jr.*, No. 06 Civ. 1353 (D. Or. September 28, 2006).

SEC v. *Seaforth Meridian*, No. 06 Civ. 4107 (D. Kan. September14, 2006).

SEC v. *Dennis Watts*, No. 02 Civ. 109 (N.D. Tex. September 8, 2006).

SEC v. *One Wall Street*, No. 06 Civ. 4217 (E.D. N.Y. September 5, 2006).

SEC v. *Jon W. James*, No. 06 Civ. 4966 (C.D. Cal. August 24, 2006).

SEC v. *Renaissance Asset Fund*, No. 06 Civ. 661 (C.D. Cal. July 17, 2006).

SEC v. *Pittsford Capital Income Partners*, No. 06 Civ. 6353 (W.D.N.Y. July 14, 2006).

SEC v. *ETS Payphones*, No. 00 Civ. 2532 (N.D. Ga. July 6, 2006).

SEC v. *Sherwin P. Brown*, (D. Minn. March 29, 2006).

SEC v. *Marion D. Sherrill*, No. 05 Civ. 21525 (S.D. Fla. May 26, 2006).

SEC v. *David L. McMillan*, No. 06 Civ. 0951 (D. Ariz. April 13, 2006).

SEC v. *Unlimited Cash*, No. 06 Civ. 594 (N.D. Tex. April 4, 2006).

SEC v. *Reinhard*, No. 06 Civ. 997 (E.D. Pa. March 6, 2006).

SEC v. *Edward S. Digges, Jr.*, No. 06 Civ. 137 (M.D. Fla. February 23, 2006).

SEC v. *Viatical Capital*, No. 03 Civ. 1895 (M.D. Fla. February 9, 2006).

SEC v. *Latin American Services*, Inc. No. 99 Civ. 2360 (S.D. Fla. Filed January 20, 2006).

Zell v. *InterCapital Income Securities, Inc.*, 675 F.2d 1041, 1047 (9th Cir. 1982).

Employee Retirement Income Security Act of 1974, 29 U.S.C. §1001 *et seq.*

Financial Services Modernization Act of 1999 (Gramm-Leach-Bliley Act), 15 U.S.C. §6801 *et seq.*

Glass-Steagall Act of 1933, 12 U.S.C. §36 *et seq.*

Investment Advisers Act of 1940, 15 U.S.C. §80b *et seq.*

Investment Company Act of 1940, 15 U.S.C. §80a *et seq.*

Pension Protection Act of 2006 (P.L. 109–280).

Securities Act of 1933, 15 U.S.C. §77a *et seq.*

Securities Exchange Act of 1934, 15 U.S.C. §78a *et seq.*

Securities Investor Protection Act of 1970. 15 U.S.C. §78aaa *et seq.*

12 C.F.R. Part 9 (2007).

17 C.F.R. Part 240 (2006).

17 C.F.R. Part 270 (2006).

17 C.F.R. Part 275 (2006).

Disclosure Regarding Market Timing and Selective Disclosure of Portfolio Headings, 69 Fed. Reg. 22,300 (April 23, 2004) (to be codified at pts. 239 and 274).

Suitability of Investment Advice Provided by Investment Advisers; Custodian Account Statements for Certain Advisory Clients, 59 Fed. Reg. 13464 (proposed March 16, 1994) (to be codified at 17 C.F.R. pt. 275).

United States Department of Labor, Interpretative Bulletin 95–1 (1995).

Federal Deposit Insurance Corporation Advisory Opinion Nos. 88–79 (1988).

Federal Deposit Insurance Corporation Advisory Opinion Nos. 88–79 (1989).

National Association of Securities Dealers Rule 2310 (2007a).

National Association of Securities Dealers Interpretative Material 2310–2 (2007b).

Notes

[1] According to the Employee Benefit Research Institute (EBRI 2007), the number of single-employer DB plans declined sharply from 112,208 in 1985 to 28,769 in 2005. In terms of participants, in 2005 the number of active participants in DB plans was 16.2 million, in contrast to 22.2 million in 1985. This decline in the number of DB plans reflects the termination of plans sponsored many small- and medium-sized employers.

[2] Personal communication with George Gaberlavage, Associate Director, AARP Public Policy Institute, February 21, 2007.

[3] For example, Income Solutions enables retiring employees of participating plan sponsors to go a website and seek competing bids from annuity providers.

[4] U.S.C. 1322 and 1322a. In 2007, single-employer plans will pay up to $49,500; multiemployer plan limits are calculated based on PBGC-established monthly rates multiplied by years of service.

[5] To date, the research on lump sums has largely focused on what individuals do when they leave their job and receive their benefits in cash. According to the Employee Benefits Research Institute (EBRI 2007), 46.7 percent of individuals receiving a lump-sum distribution reported rolling over at least some of their most recent distribution to some form of tax-qualified savings (an IRA or another qualified retirement plan), and 10 percent reported using some portion of the distribution for nontax qualified savings (Copeland 2005).

[6] With the enactment of the Gramm-Leach-Bliley Act of 1999 (P.L. 106-102), repealing the Glass-Steagall Act of 1933 (ch.89, 48 Stat.162), the ability of banks to conduct investment banking activities has further enlarged and complicated the financial markets and the products they may offer.

[7] Among these states are Michigan, Minnesota, North Carolina, Tennessee, Vermont, and Virginia.

[8] The SEC enforces this standard under the antifraud provisions of the Investment Advisers Act § 206, based on the advisers' status as fiduciaries. See discussion of proposed rules at 59 Fed. Reg. 13464 (March 16, 1994) and *SEC* v. *Capital Gains Research Bureau, Inc.*, 375 U.S. 180 (1963).

[9] H.R. 6225, introduced by Congressman Edward Royce of California and S. 2509, introduced by Senator Sununu of New Hampshire. No action was taken on either bill.

[10] Personal communication with Patricia D. Struck, Wisconsin Securities Division Administrator and President, February 5, 2007.

[11] Pension Protection Act of 2006, Public Law 109-280, §601 (August 17, 2006).

[12] U.S.C.S. §80a-5(a) (LexisNexis 2000 & Supp. 2005) (providing that an 'open-end' company is a management company which is offering for sale or has outstanding any redeemable security of which it is the issuer).

[13] Ibid; see also, 15 U.S.C.S. §80a-2(a)(8) (LexisNexis 2000 & Supp. 2005).

[14] *Zell* v. *InterCapital Income Securities, Inc.*, 675 F.2d 1041, 1047 (9th Cir. 1982).

[15] U.S.C.S. §77r(c)(1) (LexisNexis 1991 & Supp. 2005).

[16] U.S.C.S. §80a-1(b) (LexisNexis 1991 & Supp. 2005).

[17] U.S.C.S. §80a-8(a) (LexisNexis 1991 & Supp. 2005).

[18] C.F.R. §270.8b-5 (2006).

[19] *Green* v. *Brown*, 276 F.Supp. 753, 756 (S.D.N.Y. 1967).

[20] U.S.C.S. §80a-8(b) (LexisNexis 1991 & Supp. 2005).

[21] U.S.C. §80a-13(a) (LexisNexis 1991 & Supp. 2005).

[22] U.S.C.S. §80a-29 (LexisNexis 1991 & Supp. 2005).

[23] C.F.R. §270.8b-20 (2006).

[24] *Burks* v. *Lasker*, 441 U.S. 471, 482 (1979).

[25] U.S.C.S. §80a-10(a) (LexisNexis 1991 & Supp. 2005).

[26] U.S.C.S. §80a-2(a)(19)(A)(i)-(vi) (LexisNexis 1991 & Supp. 2005); see also, Government Accountability Office, Assessment of Regulatory Reforms to Improve the Management and Sale of Mutual Funds (GAO 2004a).

[27] U.S.C.S. §80a-10(b) (LexisNexis 1991 & Supp. 2005).

[28] U.S.C.S. §80a-15(c) (LexisNexis 1991 & Supp. 2005).

[29] U.S.C.S. §80a-15(c) (LexisNexis 1991 & Supp. 2005) (it should be noted that the fund's contract with its investment adviser must also be approved by the shareholders).

[30] U.S.C.S. §80a-31(a) (LexisNexis 1991 & Supp. 2005).

[31] U.S.C.S. §80a-16(b) (LexisNexis 1991 & Supp. 2005).

[32] U.S.C.S. §80a-9 (LexisNexis 1991 & Supp. 2005).

[33] U.S.C.S. §80a-17(h) (LexisNexis 1991 & Supp. 2005).

[34] U.S.C.S. §§80a-17(f), (g) (LexisNexis 1991 & Supp. 2005).

[35] U.S.C.S. §§80a-36, 80a-48 (LexisNexis 1991 & Supp. 2005).

[36] *E.I. du Pont* v. *Collins*, 432 U.S. 46, 54 (1977) (citing §30 of the Public Utility Holding Company Act, 49 Stat. 837, 15 U.S.C. §79z-4, which mandated that the SEC undertake such a study).

[37] Ibid.

[38] U.S.C.S. §80a-17(a) (LexisNexis 1991 & Supp. 2005).

[39] U.S.C.S. §80a-17(a)(1) (LexisNexis 1991 & Supp. 2005).

[40] U.S.C.S. §80a-35(a) (LexisNexis 1991 & Supp. 2005).

[41] U.S.C.S. §80a-35(b) (LexisNexis 1991 & Supp. 2005).

[42] Personal communication with Lori Richards, Director, Office of Compliance Inspections and Examinations, U.S. Securities and Exchange Commission, March 5, 2007.

[43] Ibid.

[44] C.F.R. §§270-83a-1, 275.206(4)-7) (2005).

[45] Disclosure Regarding Market Timing and Selective Disclosure of Portfolio Headings, 69 Fed. Reg. 22,300 (April 23, 2004) (to be codified at pts. 239 and 274).

[46] C.F.R. §275.204A-1 (2006).

[47] U.S.C.S. §77c(a)(8) (LexisNexis 1991 & Supp. 2005) (exempting certain insurance policies and annuity contracts from registration under the 1933 Act); see also *SEC* v. *Variable Annuity Life Insurance Company of America*, 359 U.S. 65 (1959) (holding that the variable annuity at issue was not an 'annuity' within the meaning of §3(a)(8) because the investment risk was assumed by the policyholder, not the insurer).

[48] U.S.C. §77c(a)(2) (LexisNexis 1991 & Supp. 2005).

[49] See Table 8-1, summarizing state guaranty association coverage for guaranteed investment contracts and variable annuity contracts.

[50] U.S.C.S. §80a-3(c)(11) (LexisNexis 1991 & Supp. 2005).

[51] C.F.R. §9.18(a)(2) (2006).

[52] C.F.R. §9.2(b) (2006).

[53] C.F.R. §9.18(b)(1)(i)-(xi) (2006).

[54] C.F.R. §9.18(b)(2) (2006).

[55] C.F.R. §9.18(b)(4) (2006).

[56] C.F.R. §9.18(b)(4)(ii) (2006).

[57] C.F.R. §9.18(b)(6) (2006).

[58] C.F.R. §9.18(b)(6)(ii) (2006).

[59] C.F.R. §9.18(b)(6)(iii) (2006).

[60] C.F.R. §9.18(b)(8) (2006) (note that banks are also subject to additional self-dealing and conflicts of interest rules under 12 C.F.R. §9.12).

[61] The term 'Deposit' is defined in the Federal Deposit Insurance Act, 12 U.S.C. §1813(l) to include, among other things, 'the unpaid balance of money or its equivalent received or held by a bank or savings association in the usual course of business and for which it has given or is obligated to give credit, either conditionally or unconditionally, to a commercial, checking, savings, time, or thrift account, or which is evidenced by its certificate of indebtedness, or other similar name...'. See also FDIC Opinion Nos. 88-79 (1988) and 90-46 (1990).

[62] U.S.C.S. §78o(a) (LexisNexis 1998 & Supp. 2005).

[63] U.S.C.S. §78o(b)(8) (LexisNexis 1998 & Supp. 2005).

[64] See, for example, 15 U.S.C.S. §§78i(a), 78j(b), 78o(c)(1), (2); see also 17 C.F.R. §240.15c1-2 (2006).

[65] U.S.C.S. §§78i(a), 78j(b), 78o(c)(1), (2) (LexisNexis 1998 & Supp. 2005).

[66] U.S.C.S. §78o-3(b)(6) (LexisNexis 1998 & Supp. 2005).

[67] National Association of Securities Dealers Rule 2310.

[68] U.S.C.S. §78aaa (LexisNexis 1998 & Supp. 2005).

[69]   U.S.C.S. §§78ccc (a)(2)(B), 78ggg (LexisNexis 1998 & Supp. 2005).

[70]   U.S.C.S. §78ddd(c) (LexisNexis 1998 & Supp. 2005).

[71]   U.S.C.S. §78ccc(a)(2)(A) (LexisNexis 1998 & Supp. 2005).

[72]   U.S.C.S. §78ccc(a)(2)(A)(ii). See also, 15 U.S.C.S. §78ccc(a)(2)(A)(i), (iii) (LexisNexis 1998 & Supp. 2005).

[73]   See their brochure for consumers, 'Cutting through the Confusion', that is designed to guide investors through the process of choosing an investment services provider by explaining the difference between brokers, investment advisers and financial planners and identifies key questions to ask when choosing an adviser (Coalition for Investor Education 2006).

[74]   Personal communication with Lori Richards, Director, Office of Compliance Inspections and Examinations, U.S. Securities and Exchange Commission, March 5, 2007.

[75]   *SEC* v. *Credit First Fund*, No. 05 Civ. 8741 (C.D. Cal. December 22, 2006); *SEC* v. *U.S. Gas & Electric*, No. 06 Civ. 22440 (S.D. Fl. December 11, 2006); *SEC* v. *Peter J. Dawson*, No. 06 Civ. 6360 (E.D. N.Y. November 30, 2006); *SEC* v. *Spiro Germenis*, No. 06 Civ. 6153 (E.D. N.Y. November 21, 2006); *SEC* v. *Viper Capital Management*, No. 06 SI 6966 (N.D. Cal. November 8, 2006); *SEC* v. *Gari Aldridge*, No. 06 Civ. 5645 (N.D. Ill. October 18, 2006); *SEC* v. *Joseph Y. Zumwalt*, No. 06 Civ. 61407 (S.D. Fl. October 3, 2006); *SEC* v. *C. Wesley Rhodes, Jr.*, No. 06 Civ. 1353 (D. Or. September 28, 2006); *SEC* v. *Seaforth Meridian*, No. 06 Civ. 4107 (D. Kan. September 14, 2006); *SEC* v. *Dennis Watts*, No. 02 Civ. 109 (N.D. Tex. September 8, 2006); *SEC* v. *One Wall Street*, No. 06 Civ. 4217 (E.D. N.Y. September 5, 2006); *SEC* v. *Jon W. James*, No. 06 Civ. 4966 (C.D. Cal. August 24, 2006); *SEC* v. *Renaissance Asset Fund*, No. 06 Civ. 661 (C.D. Cal. July 17, 2006); *SEC* v. *Pittsford Capital Income Partners*, No. 06 Civ. 6353 (W.D.N.Y. July 14, 2006); *SEC* v. *ETS Payphones*, No. 00 Civ. 2532 (N.D. Ga. July 6, 2006); *SEC* v. *Sherwin P. Brown*, (D. Minn. March 29, 2006); *SEC* v. *Marion D. Sherrill*, No. 05 Civ. 21525 (S.D. Fla. May 26, 2006); *SEC* v. *David L. McMillan*, No. 06 Civ. 0951 (D. Ariz. April 13, 2006); *SEC* v. *Unlimited Cash*, No. 06 Civ. 594 (N.D. Tex. April 4, 2006); *SEC* v. *Reinhard*, No. 06 Civ. 997 (E.D. Pa. March 6, 2006); *SEC* v. *Edward S. Digges*, Jr., No. 06 Civ. 137 (M.D. Fla. February 23, 2006); *SEC* v. *Viatical Capital*, No. 03 Civ. 1895 (M.D. Fla. February 9, 2006); *SEC* v. *Latin American Services*, Inc. No. 99 Civ. 2360 (S.D. Fla. Filed January 20, 2006).

[76]   While this would seem to be an obvious partnership to forge, various barriers to state and federal cooperation on regulatory enforcement can exist. Planning and coordination of different applicable laws can require careful organization and cooperation at both levels of government.

[77]   The EBRI/ICI Participant-Directed Retirement Plan Data Collection Project, which describes its work as the world's largest collection of information about individual 401(k) plan participant accounts, does not separately list annuities as an investment.

[78]   Pension Protection Act of 2006, Public Law 109-280 (August 17, 2006).

[79]   This Interpretive Bulletin can be found on the Department of Labor's Employee Benefits Security Administration's website [United States Department of Labor (DOL 1995)].

[80]   See Hueler Investment Services, Inc (2007) and ELM Income Group (2007).

References

Ameriks, John, Andrew Caplin, Steven Laufer, and Stijn Van Nieuwerburgh (2008). 'Annuity Valuation, Long-term Care, and Bequest Motives,' Chapter 11, this volume.

Choi, James J., David Laibson, and Brigitte Madrian (2006). 'Why Does the Law of One Price Fail? An Experiment on Index Mutual Funds,' NBER Working Paper no. 12261.

Coalition for Investor Education (2006). *Cutting through the Confusion: Where to Turn for Help with Your Investments.* North American Securities Administration Association. Washington, DC: NASAA.

Copeland, Craig (2005). 'Lump Sum Distributions,' *EBRI Notes*, 26(12): 7–13. Washington, DC: EBRI.

—— (2007). 'IRA Assets, Contributions, and Market Share,' *EBRI Notes*, 28(1): 8–14. Washington, DC: EBRI.

Deloitte Consulting LLP (2006). *Annual 401(k) Benchmarking Survey: 2005/2006 Edition.* New York: Deloitte Development LLC.

Donohue, Andrew (2007). 'Speech by SEC Staff: Remarks Before the American Bar Association Section of Business Law Spring Meeting,' March 16, 2007. Washington, DC: U.S. Securities and Exchange Commission.

ELM Income Group (2007). 'Expect to Live More (ELM),' ELM Income Group Homepage. www.elmannuity.com.

Employee Benefit Research Institute (2007). *Fast Facts from EBRI.* FFE no. 41, February. Washington, DC: EBRI.

Federal Deposit Insurance Corporation (2005). '2005 FDIC Trust Report,' Washington, DC: Federal Deposit Insurance Corporation.

Greenwald, Mathew, Sally Bryck, and Eric Sondergeld (2006). *Spending and Investing in Retirement: Is There a Strategy?* New York: LIMRA International, Inc. and the Society of Actuaries.

Hazen, Thomas Lee (2005). *The Law of Securities Regulation.* St Paul, MN: West Group.

Hess, Gregory D. and Mark E. Schweitzer (2000). 'Does Wage Inflation Cause Price Inflation,' Policy Discussion Papers, no. 10, April. Cleveland, OH: Federal Reserve Bank of Cleveland.

Holden, Sarah and VanDerhei, Jack (2006). '401(k) Plan Asset Allocation, Account Balances and Loan Activity in 2005,' *EBRI Issue Brief*, August, 296. Washington, DC: EBRI.

Hueler Investment Services, Inc (2007). 'About Us: Hueler Investment Services, Inc.,' Hueler Investment Services Website. www.incomesolutions.com/abouthueler.asp.

Insurancenewsnet (2007). 'Insurance Coalition Responds to OFC Comments,' February 2, 2007. Washington, DC.

Investment Company Institute (ICI) (2006a). *Research Perspective, 401(k) Plans: A 25-Year Retrospective.* November 2006. Washington, DC: ICI.

—— (2006b). *Research Perspective, EBRI/ICI Participant-Directed Plan Data Collection Project, Appendix: Additional Figures for the EBRI/ICI Participant-Directed Retirement Plan Data Collection Project for Year-End 2005.* Web-Only Edition, August 2006, 12(1A). Washington, DC: ICI.

Lusardi, Annamaria and Olivia S. Mitchell (2007). 'Financial Literacy and Retirement Preparedness: Evidence and Implications for Financial Education Programs,' Pension Research Council Working Paper 2007–04. Philadelphia, PA: The Wharton School.

McGill, Dan M., Kyle N. Brown, John J. Haley, and Sylvester J. Schieber (2004). *Fundamentals of Private Pensions*. Oxford: Oxford University Press: 782–5.

National Association of Insurance Commissioners (NAIC) (2003). *California, Florida, Texas Agree to Uniform Standards on Annuity Products*. Press release, December 9. Kansas City, MO: NAIC.

—— (2006). *NAIC Committee Expands Suitability Standards*. Press release, March 6. Kansas City, MO: NAIC.

National Organization of Life and Health Insurance Guaranty Association (NOLHIGA) (2007a). *Policyholder Information: The Safety Net at Work*. Herndon, VA: NOLHIGA.

—— (2007b). *Policyholder Information: Frequently Asked Questions*. Herndon, VA: NOLHIGA.

Securities Investor Protection Corporation (SIPC) (2005).*Annual Report 2005*. Washington, DC: SIPC.

—— (2007). *How SIPC Protects You: Understanding the Securities Investor Protection Corporation*. Washington, DC: SIPC.

Sugano, Dean (2006). *Variable Annuity Contracts Under State Statutes Relating to Securities and to Insurance*. Report No. 4, 2006. Honolulu, HI: Hawaii Legislative Reference Bureau.

United States Comptroller of the Currency (OCC) (2005). *Comptroller's Handbook: Collective Investment Funds*. Washington, DC: U.S. OCC.

United States Department of Labor (DOL) (1995). 'Interpretive bulletin relating to the fiduciary standard under ERISA when selecting an annuity provider,' 29 CFR 2509.95-1. Washington, DC: Department of Labor.

United States Government Accountability Office (GAO). (1986). *Functional Regulation: An Analysis of Two Types of Pooled Investment Funds*. GAO-86-63. Washington, DC: GPO.

—— (1993). *Private Pensions: Protections for Retirees' Insurance Annuities Could be Strengthened*. GAO-93-29. Washington, DC: GPO.

—— (1997). *Mutual Funds: SEC Adjusted its Oversight in Response to Rapid Industry Growth*. GAO-97-67. Washington, DC: GPO.

—— (2001). *Securities Investor Protection: Steps Needed to Better Disclose SIPC Policies to Investors*. GAO-01-653. Washington, DC: GPO.

—— (2003). *Participants Need Information on Risks They Face in Managing Pension Assets at and during Retirement*, GAO-03-810. Washington, DC: GPO.

—— (2004a). *Mutual Funds: Assessment of Regulatory Reforms to Improve the Management and Sale of Mutual Funds*. GAO-04-533. Washington, DC: GPO.

—— (2004b). *Follow-Up on Recommendations Concerning the Securities Investor Protection Corporation*. GAO-04-848. Washington, DC: GPO.

—— (2007). *Private Pensions: Increased Reliance on 401(k) Plans Calls for Better Information on Fees*. GAO-07-530. Washington, DC: GPO.

United States Securities and Exchange Commission (SEC). (2006). 'Invest Wisely: An Introduction to Mutual Funds,' Washington, DC: SEC.

—— (2007*a*). 'The Investor's Advocate: How the SEC Protects Investors, Maintains Market Integrity, and Facilitates Capital Formation,' Washington, DC: SEC.

—— (2007*b*). 'Variable Annuities: What You Should Know,' Washington, DC: SEC.

United States Securities and Exchange Commission and National Association of Securities Dealers (SEC/NASD). (2004). 'Joint Report on Examination Findings Regarding Broker-Dealer Sales of Variable Insurance Products,' June 9, 2004. Washington, DC: SEC.

Part III

Financial Products for Retirement Risk Management

Chapter 9

Efficient Retirement Financial Strategies

William F. Sharpe, Jason S. Scott, and John G. Watson

Today's retirees are making increasingly complex financial decisions. Gone are the days when one could rely solely on government or corporate pensions. The freezing or elimination of pension plans, combined with the rapid introduction of defined contribution plans, has forced retirees to rely more and more on their own investments to fund their retirement spending. Retirees are not only expected to fund a larger portion of their retirement spending, but early retirement and increased longevity imply their assets must support potentially longer retirements as well. To address this responsibility, a retiree has either implicitly or explicitly adopted an *investment strategy* to govern his investment decisions and a *spending strategy* to govern his spending decisions. A pair of investment and spending strategies constitutes a *retirement financial strategy*.

Economists have long explored the issue of optimal spending and investment strategies (Merton 1971). A major theme of their work is that optimal or *efficient* solutions are only achieved when investment and spending decisions are made in tandem as part of a complete retirement financial strategy. Economists use a standard framework in which the retiree's goal is to maximize expected utility in a *complete market*. However, solving such a utility maximization problem requires detailed knowledge about the retiree's preferences. Moreover, one must make assumptions about the trade-offs available in capital markets. Not surprisingly, financial advisers rarely embrace this approach; rather they rely on 'rules of thumb'. For example, one popular rule suggests annually spending a fixed, real amount equal to 4 percent of initial wealth and annually rebalancing the remainder to a 40–60 percent mix of bonds and stocks. The goal of this chapter is to consider whether the advice suggested by financial planners is consistent with the approach advocated by financial economists. More specifically, we examine some rules of thumb to see if they are consistent with expected utility maximization, for at least some investor in a standard market setting. If a rule is consistent, we say it is efficient and refer to the underlying utility as the investor's *revealed* utility.

In what follows, we make several key assumptions—the assumptions of our *canonical setting*. Regarding retiree preferences, we assume they are well modeled by additively separable utility functions.[1] Moreover, we assume that spending preferences take into account mortality estimates and the retiree's attitudes concerning his spending relative to that of any beneficiaries, and that the amounts to be spent under the plan will go either to the retiree or to beneficiaries. Further, we assume, as do many rules advocated by financial planners, that no annuities are purchased. Our assumptions about asset prices are consistent with a condition associated with models of asset pricing such as the Capital Asset Pricing Model and a number of Pricing Kernel Models—only risk associated with the overall capital market is compensated. More specifically, we assume that there is no compensation in higher expected return from taking nonmarket risk (Cochrane 2005; Sharpe 2007). Further, to keep the mathematics as simple as possible, we will develop our results using a simple *complete market* consisting of a riskless asset and a risky asset. Our risky asset tracks the market portfolio, which is assumed to follow a *binomial* process.

In the remainder of this chapter, we first provide the details of our canonical setting and formulate the financial economist's problem—find the investment and spending strategies that maximize a retiree's expected utility. We then develop conditions and tests to determine whether an arbitrary retirement strategy is optimal or efficient, and the equations for its revealed utility, when it exists. We then introduce the simple complete market to be used for illustrative purposes. Next we describe a fundamental spending strategy that employs *lockboxes*. We discuss three efficient lockbox strategies and their revealed utilities. We next look at two popular rules of thumb used by financial planners. We show that the first rule, the investment *glide-path* rule, is efficient provided it is paired with a very specific spending rule. We show that the second rule, the constant 4 percent spending rule, is only efficient when all investments are in riskless securities. Finally, we conclude with a summary of results and some topics for further investigation.

Revealed Utility and Retirement Spending

A retiree, who maximizes his expected utility, is faced with the following problem. For each year in the future, and for all states of the world in each year, our investor must optimally choose how much to consume and an investment policy to support that consumption. If markets are complete, our retiree can purchase contingent claims on the future states, and cash in these securities to pay for consumption. We assume that markets are complete, so that the investment alternatives are known, and only the consumption values are to be determined. Let 't' index future years, 's' index future states, and the pair 't, s' index a state that occurs at time 't'. We denote consumption by $C_{t,s}$, the probability that a state occurs by $\pi_{t,s}$, the current price of a contingent claim by $\psi_{t,s}$, utility from consumption at time t by $U_t(C)$, and initial wealth by W_0. Our investor must choose consumption values that maximize the function:

$$\max \sum \pi_{t,s} \cdot U_t(C_{t,s}) \tag{9-1a}$$

and also satisfy the budget constraint:

$$W_0 = \sum C_{t,s} \cdot \Psi_{t,s} \tag{9-1b}$$

In Equation (9-1), the summations are with respect to all states and times. Note that we have assumed that all states occurring at time t have the same utility function U_t, and that this utility is only a function of consumption at time t. The maximand in Equation (9-1a) is the expected utility of the consumption plan, which is assumed to be time separable. We assume that the utility functions $U_t(C)$ are increasing and concave, that is, $U'_t(C) > 0$ and $U''_t(C) < 0$. In other words, we assume that investors always prefer more to less and are risk averse. We term this the *canonical retiree problem*: given an initial wealth, to find the set of consumptions at every time and state in the future that will maximize expected utility, where these consumptions are provided by investments in state-contingent claims. Throughout, we assume that the retiree has a known separable utility function, knows the probabilities of future states, and knows the prices of contingent claims.

Many economists will find our canonical retiree problem both familiar and sensible, though most practitioners are likely to consider it beyond the pale. How many retirees know their utility functions? Very few, at best. But by choosing a particular retirement financial strategy, a retiree has either made a mistake or revealed something about his preferences. When we examine some popular strategies, in each case we seek to determine (*a*) whether the strategy is consistent with expected utility maximization; and (*b*) if so, what the characteristics are of the associated utility function. A strategy that meets condition (*a*) will be said to *reveal utility* in the sense that we can, if desired, answer question (*b*)—that is, determine the characteristics of the utility function for which the strategy would be optimal.

The relevant equations for this task are derived from the first order equations for the maximization problem. The full set of such equations includes the budget constraint and the following equations for each time t and state s:

$$U'_t(C_{t,s}) / U'_0(C_{0,0}) = \Psi_{t,s} / \pi_{t,s} \tag{9-2}$$

In Equation (9-2), the right-hand side is the ratio of the state-price to state-probability, sometimes termed the state's price-per-chance (PPC).[2] For any given time in the future, a retirement strategy prescribes a set of consumption values—one for each state. Using these choices and a model that specifies the PPC for each state, we can infer the marginal utility function $U'_t(C)$ for that time period, if it exists. Such a function exists if two conditions are met. First, the strategy must provide a single consumption value for each time and state. Second, in order to recover a concave utility function, consumption must be higher in states with lower PPC and the same in all states with the same PPC. More succinctly, if for a given time we rank the states in order of increasing consumption, this must be equivalent to ranking the states in order of decreasing PPC. If such an ordering is possible, we can then integrate the marginal utility function to get a revealed utility function. We note that the revealed utility functions $U_t(C)$ are not completely unique; for each time we can add an arbitrary integration constant, and all times can have a common positive multiple, namely $U'_0(C_{0,0})$. Fortunately this nonuniqueness is economically immaterial.

A key ingredient in our analyses is a model of the characteristics of asset prices. Since contingent claims prices are not observable, we need to make an assumption about the nature of equilibrium in capital markets. We adopt a multiperiod generalization of the results obtained with several standard models of asset pricing, such as the Capital Asset Pricing Model, some Pricing Kernel models, and the binomial model employed below. In particular, we assume that the explicit or implicit contingent claim prices at any given time t are a decreasing function of the cumulative return on the overall market portfolio from the present time to that time period. Equivalently, if for a given time we rank the states in order of increasing market return, this must be equivalent to ranking the states in order of decreasing PPC. This is the market setting for our canonical retiree problem.

For the remainder of the chapter, we will consider a state 's' at time 't' to be synonymous with cumulative market return at time 't'. So a retirement strategy must predict a single consumption value for any particular market return and be independent of prior market returns, that is, the particular *paths* that lead to the final cumulative return. Further, since we assume that the PPC is a decreasing function of market returns, the existence of a revealed utility requires that consumption be an increasing function of market return. Although our illustrations utilize a binomial process, the results apply in other settings as well.

Not all retirement strategies have revealed utilities. Three straightforward tests can be used to identify obvious violators. First, the retirement strategy cannot lead to multiple values of consumption for the same cumulative market return. Consumption must be path independent. Second, the present level of wealth for every state (before or after consumption) must also be path independent. If not, either consumption will ultimately be path dependent (a violation of the first test), or it must be the case that for one or more paths not all wealth will have been spent (a violation of optimality).

The third test used to identify violators is nonobvious, subtle, and exceedingly powerful. We term it the principle of *earmarking*. If knowledge of a state provides knowledge of consumption, and state prices exist, then at any point in time, the retiree's portfolio can be subdivided into assets that are earmarked for consumption in that state and time. It follows that assets allocated to all states at a given time can be aggregated so that our retiree can also identify the assets earmarked to support spending in any given year. Maximizing expected utility implies that our retiree knows at any point in time how much wealth is currently earmarked for consumption at each future date. If the wealth allocated to consumption at a specific time is uncertain, this uncertainty must translate to uncertainty regarding consumption in at least one state at that time, which necessarily violates maximizing expected utility.

A Simple Complete Market

In this section, we describe the simple *complete market* we use in the remainder of this chapter. Generally, a market is complete if the set of all contingent claims can be constructed using its assets. Our simple market has just two assets, a deterministic risk-free asset and a stochastic risky asset. The yearly returns on the risk-free asset are assumed constant, while the returns on the risky asset will track the returns of the total market portfolio. We assume that in any year the market is equally likely to move up or down, that the characteristics of the movements in each year are the same, and that the movement in any year is independent of the actual movements in prior years. More succinctly, the market moves are independent and identically distributed coin-flips, and thus the total number of up-moves (or down-moves) over a span of years has a *binomial distribution*.[3]

Given the above assumptions, our complete market is specified by three parameters: (*a*) the total annual market return R_u for an up-move; (*b*) the total annual market return R_d for a down-move; and (*c*) the total annual return R_f on a risk-free asset. All three of these annual returns are assumed to be real. For example, the values $R_u = 1.18$, $R_d = 0.94$, and $R_f = 1.02$ give a market portfolio with an annual expected real-rate of return of 6 percent, a volatility of 12 percent, and a Sharpe Ratio of 1/3. These values roughly correspond to an aggregate market portfolio made up of 40 percent bonds and 60 percent equities.

We take the initial value of the market portfolio to be 1, which is the value at the root of the binomial tree. After one year, the market value is equal to $\mathbf{V}_{m,1} = \mathbf{R}_{m,1}$. This value, the random total market return for the first

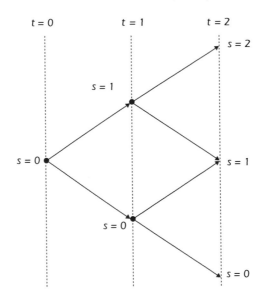

Figure 9-1. An illustration of a two-year binomial tree. *Source:* Authors' conception. *Note:* Each successive year (t) has one more possible market state (s). In the second year ($t = 2$) the middle state ($s = 1$) can be reached by either following the up-down path or down-up path.

year, can equal either R_u or R_d. In Figure 9-1, we draw two paths emanating from the initial market value, one up and one down, that connect the initial value to the two possible values at $t = 1$. After two years, the market value is equal to the random product $\mathbf{V}_{m,2} = \mathbf{R}_{m,1} \cdot \mathbf{R}_{m,2}$. It can have one of three possible values $\{R_u^2, R_u \cdot R_d, R_d^2\}$, but there are now four different, equally likely paths, {up-up, up-down, down-up, down-down} connecting the initial value with the three final values. The up-down path and the down-up path lead to the same market return, namely $R_u \cdot R_d$, and this value is twice as likely as either of the two possible paths that lead to it. After t years, the market value $\mathbf{V}_{m,t} = \mathbf{R}_{m,1} \cdot \mathbf{R}_{m,2} \cdots \mathbf{R}_{m,t}$ can have one of $(t + 1)$ possible values, $\{V_{t,s} = R_u^s \cdot R_d^{t-s} | 0 \le s \le t\}$, where the parameter '$s$' is the total number of 'up-moves'—a useful parameter for indexing the market values. On the other hand, there are 2^t paths between the initial state and the final states. The number of paths that have the market value indexed by s at time t will equal the binomial coefficient for 't-choose-s.' Hence, the state probability $\pi_{t,s}$, the probability that the market's value is equal to $V_{t,s}$, is given by the expression:

$$\pi_{t,s} = \frac{t!}{s! \cdot (t - s)!} \cdot 2^{-t} \tag{9-3}$$

In Equation (9-3), an exclamation point is used to denote a factorial.

Associated with every path of the binomial tree is the price today of a security that pays \$1 if and only if that path is realized. We term these securities path-contingent claims. We can use standard arbitrage pricing techniques to compute any such price. The price of a claim to receive \$1 at a given time and state is the cost of a dynamic strategy using the market and the risk-free asset that will provide this amount and nothing at any other time and state. For example, the current option price f_u for the first period up-move path and the current option price f_d for the first period down-move path are the following functions of R_f, R_u, and R_d:

$$f_u = \frac{R_f - R_d}{R_f \cdot (R_u - R_d)} \tag{9-4a}$$

$$f_d = \frac{R_u - R_f}{R_f \cdot (R_u - R_d)} \tag{9-4b}$$

The inequality $R_d < R_f < R_u$ is a necessary condition for positive prices. The prices for the two period paths can be written in terms of the one-period prices: $f_{uu} = f_u^2$, $f_{ud} = f_{du} = f_u \cdot f_d$, and $f_{dd} = f_d^2$. More generally, for a t-year path, the price is equal to $(f_u^s \cdot f_d^{t-s})$, where s is the number of up-moves. Hence, the option price for all paths that end at the market state 's' are the same, and depend only on the total number of up-moves and down-moves, not on the particular sequence of up-moves and down-moves. Thus today's price $\psi_{t,s}$ of a state claim that pays \$1 if and only if state s occurs is equal to the number of paths to the state times the price of each path:

$$\psi_{t,s} = \frac{t!}{s! \cdot (t-s)!} \cdot f_u^s \cdot f_d^{t-s} \tag{9-5}$$

We assume that markets are complete, or at least sufficiently complete, so dynamic strategies involving the market and the risk-free asset can replicate any state-claim. Finally for a fixed value of t, the sum of all the state prices is equal to $1/R_f^t$, the price of a risk-free dollar, t-years from now. This must be the case, since purchasing all the state claims available at year t guarantees the investor a dollar in year t, no matter which state is realized.

We are now in a position to show that for our binomial model, the PPC is a decreasing function of cumulative market return. First, the PPC and the cumulative market value are given by the formulas:

$$\psi_{t,s}/\pi_{t,s} = 2^t \cdot f_u^s \cdot f_d^{t-s} \tag{9-6a}$$

$$V_{t,s} = R_u^s \cdot R_d^{t-s} \tag{9-6b}$$

If we take the logarithm of each equation, we obtain two equations that are linear in s. After we eliminate the parameter s from this pair, we get the following simple relation between PPC and cumulative market return:

$$\psi_{t,s}/\pi_{t,s} = a^t / V_{t,s}^p \tag{9-7a}$$

In Equation (9-7a), the power p and time-factor a are constants defined by:

$$p = \ln\left(\frac{R_u - R_f}{R_f - R_d}\right) \div \ln(R_u/R_d) \tag{9-7b}$$

$$a = 2 \cdot f_d \cdot R_d^p \tag{9-7c}$$

Generally, p and a are positive, and so PPC is a decreasing function of total cumulative market return. In our numeric example, $p = 3.05$ and $a = 1.08$.

Lockbox Spending Strategies

Next, we introduce and illustrate *lockbox* strategies, an approach to spending which divides a retiree's initial wealth among separate accounts, one account for each future year of spending. The assets in each account are dynamically managed according to the account's exogenous investment rule. When an account reaches its target year, our retiree cashes out its investments, closes the account, and spends all of its proceeds. The accounts can be real or virtual, and we collectively call them lockboxes—a term that emphasizes the retiree's implicit obligation to yearly spend all the assets from the target account and to never comingle or spend the assets of any of the remaining accounts.

All efficient strategies adhere to the earmarking principle and have a lockbox formulation; however, there are inefficient lockbox strategies. The test for efficiency is simple: each lockbox's value must be a path-independent, increasing function of the cumulative market. For example, lockboxes that alternate investments in the risk-free and market assets are obviously path dependent and inefficient. In the remainder of this section, we pair three different investment strategies with lockbox spending. For each pair, we show that the resulting retirement strategy is efficient and derive its revealed utility.

Consider the lockbox strategy where each lockbox is invested in the market portfolio. Suppose our retiree has a planning horizon of T years, and has assigned F_0 dollars for today's consumption, placed F_1 dollars in the first lockbox, F_2 in the second and, more generally, F_t in the tth year lockbox. The total assigned dollars will sum to the initial wealth, that is, $W_0 = F_0 + F_1 + \ldots + F_T$. At the end of each year, the consumption from the

tth lockbox will equal F_t times the cumulative return of the market:

$$C_{t,s} = F_t \cdot V_{t,s} \tag{9-8a}$$

Note that for each state at each time there will be a unique amount of consumption, and this will be an increasing function of the market value. We see immediately that this investor has a revealed utility. The revealed marginal utility follows from Equations (9-2) and (9-7):

$$U_t'(C) = a^t \cdot (F_t/C)^p \tag{9-8b}$$

To obtain Equation (9-8b), we set $U_0'(C_{0,0})$ equal to 1, since the entire set of an investor's utility functions can be multiplied by a constant without changing the implied optimal strategy. This strategy is thus optimal for an investor with a utility function that exhibits constant relative risk aversion, generally abbreviated as constant relative risk aversion (CRRA), with risk-aversion parameter p. Further, our investor's attitudes toward consumption in future states relative to the present are revealed by the dollars assigned to the lockboxes.

Now, suppose that instead of investing solely in the market, our retiree invests $F_{m,t}$ dollars of lockbox t in the market and $F_{f,t}$ dollars in the risk-free asset, with the sum of the dollars invested equal to W_0. Once the initial allocation is made, our investor adopts a buy and hold investment strategy. In practice, this investment strategy could be implemented by purchasing a zero-coupon bond and a market exchange-traded fund for each lockbox. When the tth lockbox is opened and cashed out, the consumption will be:

$$C_{t,s} = F_{f,t} \cdot R_f^t + F_{m,t} \cdot V_{t,s} \tag{9-9a}$$

As long as at least some dollars are allocated to the market, consumption will be an increasing function of market returns. Solving for the revealed marginal utility we obtain:

$$U_t'(C) = a^t \cdot \left(\frac{F_{m,t}}{C - F_{f,t} \cdot R_f^t}\right)^p \tag{9-9b}$$

In this case, the strategy is optimal for an investor with a HARA utility function—one that exhibits hyperbolic absolute risk aversion. In effect, the investor requires a minimum subsistence level equal to the amount provided by the allocation to the risk-free asset and has CRRA with respect to the amount provided by the allocation to the market.

Our third example has lockboxes invested in constant-mix, constant-risk portfolios. Specifically, we annually rebalance a lockbox's assets so that a fraction β is invested in the market portfolio and the remaining fraction $(1 - \beta)$ is invested in the risk-free asset. We impose a no-bankruptcy condition; hence the total return must be positive in either an up or down state, and so β is limited to the range:

$$-R_f/(R_u - R_f) = \beta_{\min} < \beta < \beta_{\max} = +R_f/(R_f - R_d) \qquad (9\text{-}10a)$$

For our parameter choices, the bounds are $\beta_{\min} = -6.38$ and $\beta_{\max} = 12.75$. The total annual returns of the mix follow a binomial model, and the cumulative return $M_{t,s}(\beta)$ of the mix at time t and in state s is given by:

$$\mathbf{M}_{t,s}(\beta) = \left[(1 - \beta) \cdot R_f + \beta \cdot R_u\right]^s \cdot \left[(1 - \beta) \cdot R_f + \beta \cdot R_d\right]^{t-s} \qquad (9\text{-}10b)$$

Again, s denotes the number of up-moves in the path to time t.

As before, we let F_t's be the amounts of initial wealth allocated to the lockboxes, and we introduce β_t's as the constant mixes for the lockboxes. Although the risk in any given lockbox is constant, the risks among all the lockboxes are allowed to vary. It follows that the spending from a constant-mix lockbox is given by:

$$C_{t,s} = F_t \cdot \mathbf{M}_{t,s}(\beta_t) \qquad (9\text{-}11a)$$

We see from the previous equations that consumption will be an increasing function of s, provided the market exposures are nonnegative. But Equation (9-6a) showed that PPC is a decreasing function of s. Thus for a constant mix strategy, consumption at time t will be a decreasing function of PPC. Therefore the investor's utility function for that period will be revealed. Moreover, Equation (9-6b) showed that market return is an increasing function of s. Thus a constant-mix strategy will have no nonmarket risk and will be efficient.

Using Equations (9-6b) and (9-10b), we can eliminate the parameter s from Equation (9-11a) and write $C_{t,s}$ as an increasing function of $V_{t,s}$. The revealed marginal utility then follows:

$$U_t'(C) = a_t^t \cdot (F_t/C)^{\gamma_t} \qquad (9\text{-}11b)$$

$$\gamma_t = \ln\left[\frac{R_u - R_f}{R_f - R_d}\right] \div \ln\left[\frac{(1 - \beta_t) \cdot R_f + \beta_t \cdot R_u}{(1 - \beta_t) \cdot R_f + \beta_t \cdot R_d}\right] \qquad (9\text{-}11c)$$

$$a_t = 2 \cdot f_d \cdot \left[(1 - \beta_t) \cdot R_f + \beta_t \cdot R_d\right]^{\gamma_t} \qquad (9\text{-}11d)$$

Again, our retiree has a CRRA utility, but in this case, the retiree's choice for the exposures β_t determines the risk-aversions γ_t. Both the exposures β_t and initial allocations F_t determine the retiree's relative preference for consumption today, versus the future. We note if all the exposures are equal to one, the market exposure, then Equation (9-11b) reduces to Equation (9-8b), the result for the market only strategy.

The above three examples illustrate efficient financial retirement strategies and their revealed utility functions. Since financial economists often use CRRA or HARA models for utility, they may likely suggest one of our example strategies to a retiree. On the other hand, financial planners, who tend to rely on rules of thumb for investing and spending, would rarely advise one of the above combinations of investing and spending strategies. In the next two sections, we evaluate the efficiency of two of the most common rules.

Glide-Path Investment Strategies

Many advisers recommend that retirees annually adjust their portfolios by decreasing their exposure to equities, and thus reducing their overall risk. This rule of thumb, often called a *glide-path* strategy, is an age-based investment strategy. A classic example is the oft-quoted 100 – age rule for the percentage of assets allocated to equities, for example, 60-year-olds should hold 60 percent of their assets in bonds and 40 percent of their assets in equities. Many retirees follow a glide-path strategy by investing in *life-cycle funds*—age-targeted, managed funds intended to serve as the sole investment vehicle for all of a retiree's assets. In recent years, interest in life-cycle funds has exploded. Jennings and Reichenstein (2007) analyzed the policies of some leading life-cycle funds and found that a 120 – age equity allocation describes the typical management rule. An earlier chapter by Bengen (1996) suggested that the target equity allocation should equal 128 – age for clients up to age 80 and 115 – age afterward. The advocates of glide-path strategies often pair this investment rule with one or more options for a spending rule. However, there is only one spending rule that makes the complete retirement strategy efficient, and that rule is the focus of this section.

The investing rules described above specify equity percentages, but our market model deals more conveniently with market fractions. However, there is a simple linear relationship between the two descriptions. For example, our sample parameters roughly correspond to a market of 60 percent equities. In this case, the equity mix is 0 percent when $\beta = 0$, is 60 percent when $\beta = 1$, and is 100 percent when $\beta = 5/3$. Now, consider a 65-year-old retiree following the 120 – age rule. This retiree has the annual equity percentage targets of 55, 54, 53 percent, etc., and the annual market fraction targets of 55/60, 54/60, 53/60, etc. Because age-based rules are easily translated into a market-fraction time series, we generally use the latter to describe a glide path.

Consider the generic glide-path investment and spending strategy. At the beginning of each year, some portion of the portfolio is spent; the fraction β_t of the remainder is invested in the market, and the rest is invested in the risk-free asset. When this total portfolio strategy is efficient, it has a lockbox equivalent. We use this equivalence principle to derive the optimal spending rule. We start by choosing any one of the lockboxes, say the jth box, and virtually combine its contents and the contents of all succeeding lockboxes. Initially, the jth combined portfolio will have value $F_j + \ldots + F_T$, where the F_t's are again the initial lockbox allocations. The future values of a combined portfolio must satisfy two requirements. First, they must evolve in a path-independent manner, just like the values of the constituent lockboxes. Second, since the jth combined portfolio *is* the total portfolio for the jth year, this combined portfolio must have the glide path's market fraction β_j in the jth year, independent of the market state. Now, as we saw in the previous section, a constant-mix portfolio with market exposure β_j satisfies both of these requirements; in fact, it can be shown that every combined portfolio is a constant-mix portfolio. If we let the random variable $\Sigma_{j,t}$ be the value of the jth combined portfolio at year $0 \leq t \leq j$, then we have:

$$\Sigma_{j,t} = \left(F_j + \ldots + F_T\right) \cdot \mathbf{M}_t\left(\beta_j\right) \tag{9-12a}$$

where $\mathbf{M}_t(\beta)$ is the random cumulative return at year t for the constant-mix portfolio with market weight β; its value in state s at time t is given by Equation (9-10a).

Given the combined portfolios for an efficient glide path, the individual lockbox holdings follow immediately. First, the lockbox for T is just the combined portfolio for T; a constant-mix portfolio with exposure β_T and initial allotment F_T. The remaining lockbox portfolios are obtained by differencing successive combined portfolios. Let the random variable $\Lambda_{j,t}$ be the value of jth lockbox at time t:

$$
\begin{aligned}
\Lambda_{j,t} &= \Sigma_{j,t} - \Sigma_{j+1,t} \\
&= \left(F_j + \ldots + F_T\right) \cdot \mathbf{M}_t\left(\beta_j\right) - \left(F_{j+1} + \ldots + F_T\right) \cdot \mathbf{M}_t\left(\beta_{t+1}\right) \\
&= F_j \cdot \mathbf{M}_t\left(\beta_j\right) + \left(F_{j+1} + \ldots + F_T\right) \cdot \left[\mathbf{M}_t\left(\beta_j\right) - \mathbf{M}_t\left(\beta_{t+1}\right)\right]
\end{aligned} \tag{9-12b}
$$

The initial lockbox holds cash, the last lockbox holds a constant-mix portfolio, and the middle lockboxes hold a combination of assets; the first is a constant-mix asset, and the second is a 'swap' between two constant-mix assets. Finally, the efficient spending is given by $C_t = \Lambda_{t,t}$, or in terms of states:

$$
C_{t,s} = \begin{cases}
F_0, & t = 0 \\
F_t \cdot \mathbf{M}_{t,s}\left(\beta_t\right) + \left(F_{t+1} + \ldots + F_T\right) \cdot \left[\mathbf{M}_{t,s}\left(\beta_t\right) - \mathbf{M}_{t,s}\left(\beta_{t+1}\right)\right], & 0 < t < T \\
F_T \cdot \mathbf{M}_{T,s}\left(\beta_T\right), & t = T
\end{cases} \tag{9-12c}
$$

It is tedious, but straightforward, to directly verify that the above spending rule, coupled with its glide-path investment rule, is efficient. Further, though there is no simple function to describe the revealed utility, its values can be easily computed numerically.

Glide paths may well reflect the desires of many retirees to take less risk concerning their investments as they age, but these retirees' retirement strategies will be inefficient unless spending follows Equation (9-12c). Glide-path rules are ubiquitous, but their complementary spending rules are rare. In fact, we are unaware of any retiree that computes his annual spending according to the above rule. As an alternative to the glide-path strategy, we recommend the constant-mix lockbox strategy discussed in the previous section. If a retiree decreases the market fractions for successive lockboxes, then his total portfolio risk will tend to decrease over time. Thus, a retiree can retain the desired feature of the glide path, but can have a much simpler spending rule.

The Four Percent Rule

Many recent articles in the financial planning literature have attempted to answer the question: 'How much can a retiree safely spend from his portfolio without risking running out of money?'. Bengen (1994) examined historical asset returns to determine a constant spending level that would have had a low probability of failure. He concluded that a real value equal to ~4 percent of initial wealth could be spent every year, assuming that funds were invested with a constant percentage in equities within a range of 50–75 percent. Cooley, Hubbard, and Walz (1998) used a similar approach and found that a 4 percent spending rule with inflation increases had a high degree of success assuming historical returns and at least a 50 percent equity allocation. Later, Pye (2000) concluded that with a 100 percent allocation to equities, the 4 percent rule would be safe enough if equity returns were log-normally distributed with a mean return of 8 percent and a standard deviation of return equal to 18 percent.[4] Based on this research, there is a growing consensus that newly retired individuals with funding horizons of 30–40 years can safely set their withdrawal amount to 4 percent of initial assets and increase spending annually to keep pace with inflation. This is the foundation for the now common *4 percent rule* of thumb for retirement spending.

An efficient retirement strategy must be totally invested in the risk-free asset to provide constant spending in every future state.[5] However, the generic 4 percent rule couples a risky, constant-mix investment strategy with a riskless, constant spending rule. There is a fundamental mismatch between its strategies, and as a result it is inefficient. The following simple example illustrates these points. Consider a retiree who, whether the market goes up or down, wants to spend only $1 next year. He can achieve this goal by investing $1/R_f$ dollars in the risk-free asset. On the other hand, if he uses the market asset, he must increase his investment to $1/R_d$ dollars, so that if the market goes down, the investment pays the required $1. However, if the market goes up, the investment pays (R_u/R_d) dollars, and there is an unspent surplus. So, if our retiree truly requires just $1, then investing in the market is less efficient than investing in the risk-free asset because of the greater cost and the potential unspent surplus.

We can use the above argument to investigate a more general case. Suppose a retiree wants to support a constant spending level $C_{t,s} = f \cdot W_0$ for T years from a portfolio with initial wealth W_0 that is invested in a possibly, time-dependent strategy, for example, a glide path. Further, let D_t equal the minimum total return of the portfolio in year t. These minimums will correspond to down (up) moves for portfolios with positive (negative) market fractions β_t. Then to insure against the worst-case scenario, a safe spending fraction f must satisfy the equation:

$$\frac{1}{f} = 1 + \frac{1}{D_1} + \frac{1}{D_1 \cdot D_2} + \ldots + \frac{1}{D_1 \cdot D_2 \cdot \ldots \cdot D_T} \qquad (9\text{-}13)$$

The most efficient investment will yield the largest spending fraction f, which corresponds to maximizing the minimum returns D_t. However, in any period, the best of the worst is achieved by investing in the risk-free asset, and thus $\beta_t = 0$. For example, suppose a retiree has a planning horizon of 35 years and invests in the risk-free asset, then $D_t = R_f = 1.02$ and $f = 3.85$ percent. On the other hand, if the retiree insists on investing in the market portfolio, then $D_t = R_d = 0.94$ and $f = 0.77$ percent, a fivefold decrease in spending. For the risk-free asset $(D_t > 1)$, each successive year is cheaper to fund, but for the market portfolio $(D_t < 1)$, each successive year is more costly.

The safe spending fraction satisfies Equation (9-13). With this spending level, all scenarios, other than the worst-case scenario, will have an unspent surplus. If we raise the spending fraction just a bit, then the worst-case scenario will be underfunded and the spending plan will collapse if this path is realized. As we continue to raise the level, more and more scenarios will be underfunded, a few may be spot on, and the remaining will have a surplus. If our example retiree insists both on investing in the market and increasing his spending fraction to 4 percent, then $\sim$10 percent of scenarios will be underfunded and the remaining 90 percent of scenarios result in an unspent surplus. Further, more than 50 percent of the scenarios will have a surplus more than twice initial wealth! It is very unlikely that this retiree, who desired a riskless spending plan, would find such an eschewed-feast or -famine plan acceptable.

This type of analysis generalizes to any given desired spending plan. With complete markets, any given spending plan has a unique companion investment plan that delivers the spending at minimum cost. With state-contingent securities, the minimum cost investment plan involves simply purchasing the contingent claims that deliver the desired spending. Given our simple complete market, the contingent claims must be translated into dynamic strategies utilizing the market and riskless assets. Deploying this minimum required wealth using any other investment strategy necessarily results in surpluses and deficits relative to the desired spending plan. Extra wealth must then be introduced to eliminate all deficits.

The preceding assumed individual preferences were consistent with a fixed spending plan and demonstrated the inefficiency of a market investment plan. If we instead assume the investment plan is indicative of preferences, then we need to find a spending plan consistent with a market portfolio investment plan. This problem was previously analyzed, and the spending solution is reported in Equation (9-8a). If a market investment plan is indicative of preferences, then all efficient spending plans require spending that is proportional to cumulative market returns.

The 4 percent rule does not generate a revealed utility because the investment and spending rules do not correspond to an efficient retirement strategy. Retirees interested in fixed retirement spending should invest in the risk-free asset. Anyone who chooses to invest in the market should be prepared for more volatile spending. Either can adopt an efficient strategy. However, a retiree who plans to spend a fixed amount each period, while investing some or all funds in the market, faces a very uncertain future. Markets could perform well, and his wealth would far exceed the amount needed to fund his desired spending, or they could perform poorly, and his entire spending plan would collapse.

Conclusion and Discussion

Virtually all retirees have an explicit or implicit retirement spending and investment strategy. What is striking is the gulf that exists between how financial economists approach the problem of finding optimal retirement strategies and the rules of thumb typically utilized by financial advisers. Aside from identifying this gap, our objective with this chapter has been to evaluate the extent to which several popular retirement spending and investment strategies are consistent with expected utility maximization. This evaluation has two stages. First, is the given rule of thumb consistent with expected utility maximization for *any* investor? Second, if it is, how must the rule's investment and spending strategies be integrated to achieve and maintain efficiency?

By and large, we find that the strategies analyzed fail one or more of our tests. Investment rules suggesting risk glide paths pass the first assessment in that they are not per se inconsistent with expected utility maximization. However, the conditions on the implied spending rule required by efficiency seem onerous and unlikely to be followed by virtually any retirees. While risk glide paths only specify suggested investments, the 4 percent rule is fairly explicit about both the recommended spending and investment strategy. Unfortunately, the 4 percent rule represents a fundamental mismatch between a riskless spending rule and a risky investment rule. This mismatch renders the 4 percent rule inconsistent with expected utility maximization. Either the spending or the investment rule can be a part of an efficient strategy, but together they create either large surpluses or result in a failed spending plan.

While most of our results are obtained using a simple binomial model of the evolution of asset returns, many hold in more general settings, as we intend to show in subsequent research. Our results suggest a reliance on lockbox spending strategies, a very different type of retirement financial strategy than those currently advocated by practitioners. To an extent, this may be attributable to the assumptions we have made concerning both the nature of the capital markets and the objectives of the retiree. It is at least possible that one or more of the standard rules may be appropriate if prices are set differently in the capital markets and/or the investor has a different type of utility function. For example, one might posit that returns are not independent, but negatively serially correlated. Or one might focus on the efficiency of a strategy for an investor whose utility for consumption at a given time depends on both the consumption at that time and the consumption in prior periods. However, we suspect that it may be difficult to prove that the practitioner rules we have analyzed are efficient even in such settings.

Much of the analysis in this chapter relates to identifying problems with existing rules of thumb, but thus far, we have only hinted at ways to remedy the situation. An interesting line of inquiry would address this gap by finding an efficient strategy that strictly dominates an inefficient strategy such as one of those advocated by practitioners. There are two types of inefficiencies that could be introduced. First, a given retirement strategy could inefficiently allocate resources. That is, the same set of outcomes could be purchased with fewer dollars.[6] Given this inefficiency, a revised strategy could be constructed that strictly dominates the original strategy in that the revised strategy would increase spending in at least one state without decreasing spending in any state. A second type of inefficiency occurs when a strategy entails multiple spending levels for a given market return. If the total present value allocated to purchase the multiple spending levels were instead used to purchase a single spending amount, then as long as the expected returns in all such states are the same, any such replacement would be preferred by any risk-averse investor (formally, the revised set of spending amounts would exhibit second-degree stochastic dominance over the initial set). By making all such possible replacements, an inefficient strategy could be converted to a dominating efficient strategy. Another line of inquiry involves the examination of the properties of the revealed utility function associated with any efficient strategy, whether advocated initially or derived by conversion of an inefficient strategy. Such examination might reveal preferences that are inconsistent with those of a particular retiree and hence the strategy, while efficient, would not be appropriate in the case at hand.

Overall, our findings suggest that it is likely to be more fruitful to clearly specify one's assumptions about a retiree's utility function than to establish the optimal spending and investment strategy directly. Of course, one should take into account more aspects of the problem than we have addressed in this chapter. Annuities should be considered explicitly, rather than ruled out *ex cathedra*. Separate utility functions for different personal states (such as 'alive' and 'dead') could be specified rather than using a weighted average using mortality probabilities, as we have assumed here. Yet our analysis suggests that rules of thumb are likely to be inferior to approaches derived from the first principles of financial economics.

Acknowledgments

The authors thank John Ameriks, Olivia S. Mitchell, and Stephen Zeldes for many valuable comments on an early draft of this chapter. We also thank our colleagues at Financial Engines Wei Hui and Jim Shearer for their insights and support.

Notes

[1] We are assuming that for each time period, there is a utility function that gives the utility *measured today* as a function of the amount consumed in that period. Moreover, we assume that the investor prefers more to less and is risk-averse, so the utility function for a time period increases with consumption at a decreasing rate. The expected utility of consumption in a time period is simply the probability-weighted average of the utilities of the amounts consumed in different scenarios at the time. Finally, the expected utility of the retirement plan is the sum of the expected utilities for each of the time periods.

[2] Sharpe uses the term price-per-chance or PPC for the ratio of a state's price to its probability (Sharpe 2007). As discussed by Cochrane (2005), this quantity is also called the marginal rate of substitution, the pricing kernel, a change of measure, and the state-price density.

[3] Although our binomial model for annual market returns may appear highly restrictive, similar models using shorter time periods are often used in both the

academy and financial sector for pricing options and predicting the results of investment strategies.

[4] Pye (2000) also shows that a 60 percent initial allocation to Treasury Inflation Protected Securities (TIPS) improves the allowable withdrawal to 4.5 percent, while simultaneously lowering the measured downside-risk.

[5] As the market fraction β approaches zero, constant-mix lockboxes are invested in just the risk-free asset and provide constant spending. Further, the risk-aversion parameter of the underlying CRRA utility approaches infinity in this limit. Alternatively, state-independent spending can be viewed as the limit of the buy and hold lockbox for which all wealth is allocated to the risk-free asset and none in the market asset. Here, the subsistence levels of the underlying HARA utility exhaust the budget.

[6] Dybvig (1988a, 1988b) explored inefficient portfolio strategies in a pair of chapters. His approach is very useful for analyzing retirement strategies such as the 4 percent rule.

References

Bengen, William P. (1994). 'Determining Withdrawal Rates Using Historical Data,' *Journal of Financial Planning*, 7(4): 171–80.

—— (1996). 'Asset Allocation for a Lifetime,' *Journal of Financial Planning*, 9(4): 58–67.

Cochrane, John H. (2005). *Asset Pricing: Revised Edition*. Princeton, NJ: Princeton University Press: 3–147.

Cooley, Phillip L., Carl M. Hubbard and Daniel T. Walz (1998). 'Retirement Savings: Choosing a Withdrawal Rate That Is Sustainable,' *The American Association of Individual Investors Journal*, February: 16–21.

Dybvig, Phillip H. (1988a). 'Distributional Analysis of Portfolio Choice,' *Journal of Business*, 61: 369–93.

—— (1988b). 'Inefficient Dynamic Portfolio Strategies or How to Throw Away a Million Dollars in the Stock Market,' *Review of Financial Studies*, 1:67–88.

Jennings, William W. and William Reichenstein (2007). 'Choosing the Right Mix: Lessons From Life Cycle Funds,' *The American Association of Individual Investors Journal*, January: 5–12.

Merton, Robert C. (1971). 'Optimum Consumption and Portfolio Rules in a Continuous-Time Model,' *Journal of Economic Theory*, 3: 373–413.

Pye, Gordon B. (2000). 'Sustainable Investment Withdrawals,' *The Journal of Portfolio Management*, 26(4): 73–83.

Sharpe, William F. (2007). *Investors and Markets: Portfolio Choices, Asset Prices, and Investment Advice*. Princeton, NJ: Princeton University Press: 74–100.

Chapter 10

The Impact of Health Status and Out-of-Pocket Medical Expenditures on Annuity Valuation

Cassio M. Turra and Olivia S. Mitchell

The primary purpose of annuities is to protect people against the risk of outliving their financial resources in old age. Prior analysts have reported that annuities should be of substantial value to risk-averse people who face an uncertain date of death (Yaari 1965), yet relatively few people seem to purchase annuities at the point of retirement (Johnson, Burman, and Kobes 2004). A growing body of research has explored factors that may explain this puzzle, including retirees' desire to leave bequests, the existence of adverse selection in the annuity market, the overannuitization of retirement wealth, and the need for liquidity. Further, researchers have also found that people use private information about their survival chances to make the decision of purchasing an annuity, and those who anticipate living longer are more likely to buy an annuity (Petrova 2003). In any event, there is still little understanding of how private information regarding own health status may be related to the demand for annuities. Some researchers have tried to address this gap in knowledge (Sinclair and Smetters 2004), but empirical investigations of this kind have been hampered by the multidimensional aspect of health, and the absence of long-term nationally representative panel data on health at older ages.

In this chapter, we contribute to the literature on health status and annuity valuation by describing how differences in retirees' health status might influence the decision to purchase a life annuity. To do this, we use dynamic discrete choice estimation in the context of an economic model of behavior. We propose two approaches to incorporate the effect of health differentials on annuitization valuation. One incorporates the effect of health via differences in survival throughout the life cycle. Yet this approach does not consider precautionary savings that might be motivated by uncertain out-of-pocket medical expenses. Accordingly, our second model posits that retirees in different health states consider the effects of both uncertain out-of-pocket medical expenses and uncertain survival, when making their annuitization choice. We compare the optimal level of annuitization and the insurance value of a life annuity for people in different health states at the point of annuity purchase.

Compared to prior studies, our work is distinguished by its effort to measure the impact of *anticipated* poor health on annuity valuation. This is important in the retirement context since there is substantial risk of becoming disabled after age 65. For instance, the 70-year-old must anticipate that he may have severe functional limitations for about one-quarter of his remaining lifetime, and 70 percent of his remaining years will, on average, be spent with at least some functional difficulty (Crimmins, Hayward, and Saito 1994). The greater prevalence of disability among the elderly also brings with it much higher health spending: people with severe functioning limitations have annual Medicare costs $7,000 higher than nondisabled persons (Cutler and Meara 2001). Our study is therefore informative about the potential for development of an impaired annuity market that would provide higher payouts for consumers in poor health.

Understanding how health status affects annuity markets is also important for policy analysts, in particular those who propose personal Social Security retirement accounts (c.f. Cogan and Mitchell 2003). Recent research has suggested that mandating annuitization for all participants in a personal accounts scheme would imply transfers from high-mortality risk groups to low-mortality risk groups (c.f. Brown 2003). Health and mortality are also strongly associated, particularly among the elderly (Hurd, McFadden, and Merrill 2001). Consequently, understanding how health influences the insurance value of annuities may help insurers fashion annuity offerings under Social Security reform plans, so as to make a larger proportion of the participants better off.

The Context

Defined contribution (DC) pension plans now cover over 70 percent of those workers with a pension [United States Department of Labor (U.S. DOL 2004)]. As more employees reach retirement with large DC pension accruals, they are increasingly allowed to receive their savings as a lump sum, rather than annuitizing the saving as under conventional defined benefit (DB) plan. The concern is that, by taking their accumulated DC assets in a lump sum, participants may exhaust their pension assets before dying (Mitchell, Gordon, and Twinney 1997).

One way to protect against such longevity risk is to purchase a life annuity. A long economic literature has shown that risk-averse individuals with no bequest motives should strongly favor converting all their DC pension assets to private annuities. For instance, Mitchell et al. (1999) show that age-65 retirees with access to an actuarially fair annuity market would be predicted to fully annuitize at age 65. Further, that study estimated that people lacking access to an annuity market would be willing to forgo between 30 and 40 percent of their wealth at age 65, in order to purchase actuarially fair annuities. Brown (2003), using the same approach, shows how cross-group mortality differentials can influence life-annuity insurance values. He finds that annuities provide considerable longevity insurance to all groups, regardless of their race, ethnic group, or educational attainment, and even when annuity premiums are actuarially unfair, those facing high mortality (e.g., blacks with low education) would still be predicted to value a life annuity. These studies confirm the pioneering theoretical work of Yaari (1965) who showed that people lacking a bequest motive and facing an uncertain date of death would choose to fully annuitize.[1]

Overall, then, the theoretical literature suggests that that there should be substantial growth in the demand for life annuities, as more workers retire with large investments in DC plans. Yet this has not been the case to date. Thus Johnson, Burman, and Kobes (2004) used 10 years of data from the Health and Retirement Study (HRS)[2] to evaluate how persons aged 55+ disposed of their DC and Individual Retirement Account (IRA) funds. That study reports that only 4 percent of workers with DC plans annuitized their assets when they retired, and only 13 percent of those who took their accumulations from IRAs converted the resources to private annuities. Further, the market for individual life annuity in the USA remains small, amounting to less than 10 percent of the size of the life-insurance market (in 1999, Brown et al. 2001).

Several hypotheses have been offered to explain the low demand for private annuities, though considerable uncertainty about this puzzle remains. Some attribute the problem to adverse selection in annuity markets: for instance, only people with very low mortality might tend to purchase annuities, increasing the premium cost for people with average mortality prospects (e.g., Mitchell and McCarthy 2002). Nevertheless, although adverse selection does generate low rates of return in annuity contracts for persons of average mortality, annuity pricing seems to have little empirical impact on how consumers value life annuities (Brown 2003). Another explanation offered is that the elderly are overannuitized in the form of Social Security, and thus they may not need to purchase additional annuitization to insure against longevity risk. Empirical studies, however, tend to suggest that the elderly would be better off by purchasing additional private annuity contracts (Brown 2001a; Brown and Warshawsky 2001). Recently, Petrova (2003) uses the HRS to ask whether perceived mortality influences the desire to purchase a life annuity; this work confirms that private information on longevity has a strong influence on the decision to purchase a life annuity.

Information on health status is a key component of private information on longevity, and therefore is a determinant of subjective survival probabilities (Hurd, McFadden, and Merril 2001). Earlier studies have investigated how uncertain health and, therefore, uncertain medical expenses affect consumption and saving decisions at older ages (e.g., Hubbard, Skinner, and Zeldes 1995; Davis 1998; Palumbo 1999). One study, in particular, predicts that health shocks can reduce the value of a life annuity for risk-averse individuals (Sinclair and Smetters 2004). In what follows, we offer new empirical evidence of the effect of health status on annuity decision-making. We find that an economic model which ignores anticipated health problems tends to overestimate both the level of desired annuitization and the insurance value of the life annuity. Our results suggest that retirees who face uncertain health would prefer to partially annuitize and maintain some assets in liquid form, so they can buffer the negative effect of unexpected out-of-pocket medical expenses on future consumption.

Valuing Life Annuities

In this section, we first lay out the general multiperiod model of annuity purchase with uncertain survival, and we then extend the approach to incorporate uncertain out-of-pocket medical expenses as well as uncertain survival. Next, we discuss parameterization of the models as well as data sources used to evaluate key outcomes.

Model 1: A Yaari-Type Model

We begin by extending Yaari's classical life-cycle approach with uncertain lifetimes (1965), as further developed by Brown (2003, 2001*b*) and Mitchell et al. (1999). To do so, we posit that, at retirement at, say, age 65, the individual decides how much of his starting wealth should be annuitized. This is a maximization problem: that is, given current and future conditions (e.g., interest rate and mortality distributions), the consumer maximizes the value function by selecting the amount of annuity which provides the largest discounted sum of expected future utility. The model posits that consumers are rational and understand the consequences of their choices for future consumption, even though the exact outcomes are probabilistic. That is, while one's date of death is uncertain, a forward-looking retiree can evaluate his mortality distribution based on his health status at the age of annuity purchase.

The consumer's problem is solved using backward recursion; first the terminal period problem is solved, and then we work backward to find the value function at age 65. In the terminal period, $t = 95$, the future value function is equal to 0 since death is certain by the next period $(t+1)$.[3] As in Brown (2001*b*), and assuming no bequest motive, the retiree would maximize utility while consuming all remaining wealth, W_t; the period t single immediate life annuity, A_t; and preexisting real annuity (e.g., Social Security benefits) S_t:

$$V_t(c_t) = \max[u(c_t)], \qquad (10\text{-}1)$$

subject to the following constraints:

$$
\begin{aligned}
s.t. \quad & W_0 \; given \\
& W_t \geq 0 \quad \forall t \qquad\qquad\qquad (10\text{-}2)\\
& W_{t+1} = (W_t - C_t + S_t + A_t)(1+r)
\end{aligned}
$$

where r is the interest rate. Knowing the optimal consumption decision in period t allows one to find the optimal consumption decision that maximizes the value function in period $t-1$. The same logic is used subsequently in each previous period to choose the consumption that maximizes the Bellman equation:

$$V_{t-1} = u(c_{t-1}) + \beta_1 p_{t-1}[V_t(c_t)] \qquad (10\text{-}3)$$

where β is the discount factor, and $_1 p_{t-1}$ is the probability of surviving from period $t-1$ to t for an individual of health status j at the age at annuity purchase. We approximate optimal consumption paths by making wealth discrete and testing a large number of values between arbitrary minimum and maximum values that are consistent with the initial conditions of the model.

We seek to learn both the optimal level of annuitization at age 65 and the value of a life annuity in the life-cycle model. Following Mitchell et al. (1999), we perform a counterfactual exercise with two scenarios. First, we estimate the value function assuming people have full access to the annuity market; in other words, we choose the optimal level of annuitization that maximizes the value function, ranging from 0 to full annuitization. Next, we estimate the value function in an alternative scenario where people have no access at all to the annuity market, and we ask how much additional starting wealth (W_0) they would have to receive to make them as well off, as in the first scenario with the annuitization option. The insurance value of a life annuity is computed by comparing the two scenarios and computing the Annuity Equivalent Wealth measure (AEW), which indicates how much W_0 in the second scenario needs to be increased to produce the same value function in both scenarios.

Model 2: Out-of-Pocket Medical Expenses

The second model, we assess, takes into account that uncertainty regarding medical expenses may offer a reason for a retiree to maintain additional wealth instead of annuitizing all his assets. Here, the retiree is presumed to consider the effects of both uncertain future medical expenses and uncertain survival when choosing an optimal consumption path. Specifically, at the age of annuity purchase, we posit that he has private information regarding his future health status. He uses this information to evaluate the distribution of future health transitions, although his exact future health outcomes remain probabilistic. Each period (year) from age 65–95 or death, the individual learns whether he will incur out-of-pocket medical expenses. The probability of incurring out-of-pocket medical expenses is posited to be a function of the retiree's health status, age, and sex. The model has the intuitive implication that people cannot precisely predict their future medical expenses, but they know their out-of-pocket medical expenses at each age and can use that information when deciding about optimal future consumption.

The individual's problem in each period now has several possible outcomes. The expected value function is calculated by considering all possible combinations of health status and out-of-pocket medical expenses. The individual is posited to solve for consumption which maximizes utility for each possible path. At each period, the value function is the weighted sum of all solutions found, where the weights are the probabilities for each possible combination of health status and medical expenses:

$$V_{t-1}(c_{t-1}, h_{t-1}, M_{t-1}) = \sum_{y=1}^{k} g_{y,t-1} \max[u(c_{t-1}, h_{t-1}, M_{t-1})$$
$$+ \beta_1 p_{t-1} V_t(c_t, h_t, M_t)] \qquad (10\text{-}4)$$

subject to the constraints:

$$s.t. \quad W_0 \; given$$
$$W_{t-1} \geq 0 \quad \forall t \qquad (10\text{-}5)$$
$$W_t = (W_{t-1} - C_{t-1} - M_{t-1} + S_{t-1} + A_{t-1})(1 + r), \quad if \; M_{t-1} > 0$$

where h_{t-1} is health status at $t-1$, M_{t-1} is period $t-1$ out-of-pocket medical expenses, and g_{t-1} denotes the probabilities for the k possible combinations of health status and medical expenses. Following earlier studies (e.g., Hubbard, Skinner, and Zeldes 1995; Palumbo 1999), we assume medical expenses are not a consumption good and that individuals cannot borrow against the future. Therefore, a retiree who incurs out-of-pocket medical expenses is constrained to consume only the resources that remain after paying for medical care in each period. We also use the simplifying assumption that medical expenses in each period are not correlated with health status and mortality in the next period.[4]

The solution approach first involves choosing the optimal solution for the terminal period, $t = 95$, and then we continue recursively to find the value function at the age 65. In a fashion identical to that described above, the optimal consumption path is calculated at all values of annuitization and we choose the one that gives the largest discounted sum of expected future utility. We then compute AEW in order to estimate the insurance value of a life annuity in the context of uncertain out-of-pocket medical expenses. Results for both models are compared.

Model Parameterization

To implement the model, we adopt the popular isoelastic CRRA utility function of the form:

$$U(c) = \frac{C^{1-\gamma} - 1}{1 - \gamma}, \tag{10-6}$$

where γ is the coefficient of risk aversion (Hubbard, Skinner, and Zeldes 1995; Brown 2001b;). Since the third derivative of this function is positive, it implicitly allows for precautionary saving that arise from having uncertain out-of-pocket medical expenses in our second model (Deaton 1992). Consistent with earlier studies (e.g., Hubbard, Skinner, and Zeldes 1995), we assume a value for γ of three in our main analysis, and we also present sensitivity analyses using alternative values for γ of one and five.[5] Further, we assume a value of 3 percent for the rate of time preference, β, and a real 3 percent rate of interest per year, consistent with earlier studies (Mitchell et al. 1999; Brown 2001b; Petrova 2003).

We must also specify the probabilities of dying at each age, conditional on the health status at the age of annuity purchase (assumed to be 65). For example, suppose we are solving the models for an individual in good health at age 65. We need to know his age-specific probabilities of dying at ages 65–95, given he was in good health 1–30 years previously. The ideal data-set to estimate these would offer as many years of observation as the life spans modeled. Unfortunately, no nationally representative panel data on long-term health and mortality have been collected. Consequently, we instead use a multistate model (Schoen and Land 1979; Palloni 2001) to mimic the dependence of mortality on initial health states. This allows us to follow a hypothetical cohort from age 65 onward, and to calculate the probabilities of dying at each age, assuming persons at age 65 were in a specific state of health j. Each age-specific probability of dying is then posited to reflect health status as of the entry age of 65.

The use of a multistate model requires the estimation of forces of decrement between states of health. We use the HRS from 1993 to 2000 to estimate these decrements, since that survey reports mortality and health changes every two years stayed in the same state of health for up to five years. Using cohort data is an improvement, compared to cross-sectional forms of the multistate model, since we can reasonably approximate some of the effects of duration on the forces of transition (Schoen 1988). The duration-specific probabilities are specified as a multinomial logit model of the following form:

$$\ln\left(\frac{p_j}{p_J}\right) = a_j + \beta_j^{Age} x_1 + \beta_j^h x_2 + \beta_j^h x_3 \quad j = 1, \ldots, J-1, \quad (10\text{-}7)$$

where p_j is probability that an event j (health transition or death) occurs; p_J is the probability that a baseline event occurs; and x_i are indicators of the individual's health status in earlier waves.

As noted by many analysts, health is a multidimensional concept that can be measured in many different ways. Our previous study evaluated predictors of old-age mortality among several self-reported health indicators measured at the point of retirement (Turra 2004), and we concluded that functional status, smoking, and self-assessed health are good predictors of death patterns over the age of 70+. Accordingly, for the present analysis, we derive results using three states of health based on functional status data: no functioning problems, IADL limitations,[6] and activities of daily living (ADL) limitations.[7]

Table 10-1 summarizes estimates calculated from the mortality model described above in the HRS data, where we show life expectancy at age 65 for both men and women, conditional on health status at age 65. Not surprisingly, age-65 health differences have important implications for differences in life expectancy. For example, women with no functional limitations as of retirement age can expect to live 6.71 more years at age 65 than can women with ADL limitations. Among men, the difference of 5.7 years is smaller but still substantial.

TABLE 10-1 Life Expectancy at Age 65, HRS
(1993–2000)

	Women	Men
No functioning problems	21.04	16.78
IADL limitations	18.89	14.20
ADL limitations	14.33	11.06

Source: Author's calculations as described in the text.

Assuming no loading and no taxes, the expected present value of the payment stream from a single immediate life annuity is given by Brown (2001b) as:

$$A_t = \frac{W_0 \times a}{\displaystyle\sum_{j=1}^{35} \frac{\displaystyle\prod_{j=1}^{t}(1 - q_j)}{\displaystyle\prod_{k=1}^{j}(1 + r_k)(1 + \pi_k)}}, \qquad (10\text{-}8)$$

where q_j is the age-specific probability of dying, r_k is the real interest rate, and π_k is the inflation rate. The proportion of starting wealth (W_0) held in single immediate life annuity, a, indicates the optimal level of annuitization and is determined by the model.

To investigate the effects of adverse selection in the annuity market, we calculate optimal annuitization patterns under two approaches to annuity pricing. A first set of estimates assumes that retirees have access to actuarially fairly priced annuities[8]: in this case, we use the mortality distributions discussed above to calculate single immediate life-annuity payments for someone in each health status. A second set of estimates assumes that all purchasers pay uniform prices; in this case, we use the same mortality distribution for everyone to calculate the annuity payments irrespective of health status. The second scenario uses the annuitant life table from the Society of Actuaries (SOA 1999).

Table 10-2 presents money's worth values, or estimated expected discounted values of annuity payments per premium dollar. These values assume that all purchases pay uniform pricing, and they indicate how annuity payouts vary across people in different health states. The findings show that the value-per-premium dollar is always below one, regardless of sex and discount rate. These results confirm findings by Turra (2004), who showed that annuitant mortality is slightly lower than mortality of healthy individuals in the population. This explains why the results in Table 10-2 are always less than 1. The money's worth values are especially low for men, overall, and for retirees with ADL limitations—between 0.65 and 0.70. These estimates therefore imply that there would be significant adverse selection in the private annuity market, so that the decision to purchase a life annuity implies payouts well below the actuarially fair value, especially for retirees in poor health.

Another important economic parameter is the amount of starting wealth invested in a preexisting real annuity; for instance, this could include DB pension benefits and Social Security payments. The larger is the starting wealth in a preexisting real annuity, the smaller will be the amount remaining that the retiree can use to purchase the life annuity. For many

TABLE 10-2 Annuity Values per Premium Dollar for a Fixed Immediate
Real Annuity Purchased at Age 65 (before tax)

Sex & Discount Rate (%)	Health at the Age of Annuity Purchase		
	No Functioning Problems	IADL Limitations	ADL Limitations
Men			
3	0.89	0.76	0.60
5	0.91	0.79	0.63
7	0.92	0.81	0.66
Women			
3	0.97	0.88	0.69
5	0.98	0.90	0.71
7	0.98	0.91	0.74

Source: Authors' calculations.

Notes: Each entry shows the expected present discounted value of the annuity payouts per dollar of annuity premium. All calculations assume premium costs calculated based on the Annuitant Mortality Life Table (SOA 1999); no loads as per Mitchell et al. (1999).

simulations, we assume that half of initial wealth is held in a preexisting real annuity, a stylized description of the Social Security system (Mitchell and Moore 1998; Moore and Mitchell 2000). For sensitivity analyses, we also assume that the preexisting real annuity is either 25 or 75 percent of total retirement wealth.

Our empirical approach handles out-of-pocket medical expenses as a percent of the retiree's preexisting real annuity (pension or Social Security income), for two reasons. First, using relative rather than dollar values for out-of-pocket medical expenses avoids having to estimate dollar values for other model parameters, that is, all values are given in relative terms (e.g., relative to $W_0 = 100$). Second, by making medical expenses a function of retirement income, this implicitly assumes that the amount that the elderly spend on health care depends on income levels, which is a reasonable way to represent the distribution of health-care costs by socioeconomic group. Estimating out-of-pocket medical expenses requires calculating: (*a*) the distribution of health status at each age; (*b*) the value of medical expenses (as a proportion of Social Security income); and (*c*) the probabilities of incurring medical expenses by age and health. To derive the distribution of health status by age, we use the multistate life table model discussed above to calculate the probability of being in each health state by age, conditional on the health state at the age of annuity purchase (assumed to be 65). Figure 10-1 summarizes the results for men, and the graphs show the distribution of health status by age among male survivors, given their

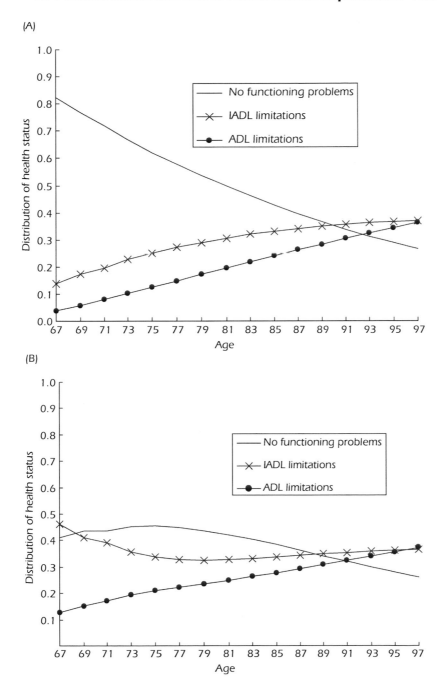

Figure 10-1. (*cont.*)

(C)

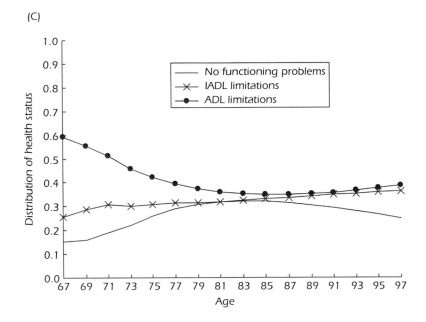

Figure 10-1. Distribution of health status by age, conditional on health status at the age of 65, men: no functioning problems at the age of 65. (A) No functioning problems at the age of 65. (B) IADL limitations at the age of 65. (C) ADL limitations at the age of 65. *Source:* Authors' calculations using the Health and Retirement Study.

functional status at age 65. As expected, the distributions of health states are very different at early ages, but they become more similar at very old ages, as health deteriorates for all people regardless of their initial state of heath.[9]

Next, we calculate the value of out-of-pocket medical expenses as a proportion of Social Security income. Here we rely on estimates provided by RAND[10] based on data from the HRS for the years 1998 and 2000. In the data-set, out-of-pocket medical expenses include expenditures not covered by health insurance in services such as hospital stays, nursing home stays, doctor visits, prescription drugs, dental care, home health care, outpatient surgery, and other services. In addition, we include total costs of premium for health insurance coverage.[11] For each respondent aged 65+, we calculate the ratio of out-of-pocket medical expenses to Social Security income. For purposes of analytical tractability, we then create a discrete distribution of the ratios by dividing them into 11 categories of expenses, anchored at 0 and ranging to ≥ 300 percent of Social Security income. Table 10-3 summarizes the distribution of observations in each of these categories, in the year 2000. As is clear, most of the individuals who incurred out-of-pocket expenses spent less than 25 percent of their annual Social Security income.

TABLE 10-3 Distribution of Out-of-Pocket Medical Expenses (as a proportion of Social Security income)

Categories (% of social security income)	Median Value ($)	Frequency (%)
0	0	20.12
0–25	11.79	48.87
25–50	43.53	16.20
50–75	68.58	6.52
75–100	96.04	2.76
100–125	122.25	1.48
125–150	139.19	0.92
150–175	168.02	0.64
175–200	194.13	0.44
200–300	268.32	0.81
300+	489.34	1.25

Source: Authors' calculations as described in the text using HRS 2000.

Nevertheless, about 5.5 percent of the elderly above age 65 did devote more than 100 percent of their Social Security income to out-of-pocket medical expenses.

To calculate the probability of incurring out-pocket-medical expenses in each category, we use a multinomial Logit model which controls for health status two years earlier, age, and sex. Table 10-4 presents the results from fitting the model for five categories of medical expenses.[12] The estimated coefficients give the partial effects of the explanatory variables on the log-odds of being in each category of medical expenses relative to the lowest category (of 0–25 percent of Social Security income). A positive coefficient indicates that the explanatory variable increases the probability of being in each category relative to the comparison category. It is apparent from Table 10-4 that the probability of incurring medical expenditures is significantly higher for women and persons in poor health status. The partial effects further indicate that age is significantly associated with the probability of incurring the highest category of medical costs (300+ percent of Social Security income).

These probabilities of incurring out-of-pocket medical expenses are combined with the distributions of health status by age as described before, to compute the probability of each possible consumption path by age and health. Finally, to represent the value of out-of-pocket medical expenses and health, we use the median ratio in each category of out-of-pocket medical expenses (see Table 10-3).

TABLE 10-4 Maximum Likelihood Estimation Results of the Probability of Incurring Out-of-Pocket Medical Expenses Between 1998 and 2000, Age 65+

Condition in 1998	Log (L2/L1)	Log (L4/L1)	Log (L6/L1)	Log (L8/L1)	Log (L10/L1)
Constant	−2.024**	−4.414**	−4.556**	−8.656**	−10.938**
	(0.335)	(0.730)	(1.279)	(1.905)	(1.079)
Age	0.005	0.002	−0.016	0.046	0.073*
	(0.004)	(0.010)	(0.017)	(0.025)	(0.013)
Female	0.272**	0.644**	0.835**	−0.030	0.455**
	(0.061)	(0.145)	(0.256)	(0.372)	(0.229)
Health status					
No functioning problems (omitted)					
IADL limitations	0.251**	0.391*	0.441	−0.015	0.932**
	(0.065)	(0.154)	(0.256)	(0.461)	(0.288)
ADL limitations	0.239**	0.935**	0.845**	1.010*	1.736**
	(0.089)	(0.174)	(0.301)	(0.446)	(0.291)
Log-likelihood = −13,110					
Sample size = 9,038					

Source: Authors' calculations from HRS (1998, 2000).

Notes: Categories of Medical Expenses computed as % of Social Security Income: L1 = 0–25%, L2 = 25–50%, L4 = 75–100%, L6 = 125–150%, L8 = 175–200%, L10 = 300+%. Standard errors in parentheses; *p < 0.05; **p < 0.01.

Empirical Findings

As is standard in economic models of annuity valuation, we present both the optimal annuitization level generated by the model and also the AEW for a variety of cases. The AEW refers to the amount of additional wealth that the retiree would require, if he did not have access to an annuity market, to achieve the lifetime utility level that he could achieve with access to an annuity market.

First, we compute the AEW for people who face no uncertain medical expenses. For each state of health, we provide the optimal choices under uniform pricing and actuarially fair risk pricing. We assume a preexisting real annuity worth 50 percent of initial wealth, and three alternative degrees of risk aversion. Focusing for discussion purposes on a risk-aversion level of three, it appears that there are utility gains from purchasing a nominal annuity; see Table 10-5. This is consistent with previous empirical analyses (e.g., Mitchell et al. 1999; Brown 2003). Full annuitization

TABLE 10-5 Annuity Equivalent Value and Optimal Annuitization, Model 1, Fixed Nominal Annuity (inflation = 3.2%)

	CRRA = 1		CRRA = 3		CRRA = 5	
	Annuity Equivalent Wealth	Optimal Additional Annuitization (% wealth)	Annuity Equivalent Wealth	Optimal Additional Annuitization (% wealth)	Annuity Equivalent Wealth	Optimal Additional Annuitization (% wealth)
Women						
No functioning problems						
Actuarially fair premium	1.172	50	1.244	50	1.245	50
Uniform pricing	1.152	50	1.222	50	1.224	50
IADL limitations						
Actuarially fair premium	1.241	50	1.340	50	1.359	50
Uniform pricing	1.122	50	1.220	50	1.229	50
ADL limitations						
Actuarially fair premium	1.435	50	1.629	50	1.675	50
Uniform pricing	1.043	39	1.170	50	1.230	50
Men						
No functioning problems						
Actuarially fair premium	1.261	50	1.395	50	1.437	50
Uniform pricing	1.156	50	1.277	50	1.366	50
IADL limitations						
Actuarially fair premium	1.379	50	1.570	50	1.639	50
Uniform pricing	1.096	46	1.248	50	1.311	50
ADL limitations						
Actuarially fair premium	1.550	50	1.852	50	1.980	50
Uniform pricing	1.022	26	1.167	50	1.263	50

Source: Author's calculations as described in the text.

is the optimal solution even when retirees lack access to an actuarially fair contract. Yet there is a much larger dispersion in the AEW values across population subgroups, as compared to earlier studies. Our figures vary between 1.17 and 1.85, and they depend heavily on the interaction between health status and annuity pricing. In the case of women with ADL limitations, for example, the AEW falls from 1.85 when annuities are actuarially fair to only 1.17 under uniform pricing. In other words, adverse selection in annuities appears to impose high opportunity costs for people in poor health, and it also reduces considerably the insurance value of a nominal annuity. The effects of adverse selection are also strong at the lower-risk-aversion level of one. In this case, the results in Table 10-5 show that women with ADL limitations and men with IADL or ADL limitations will choose partial annuitization. For example, men with ADL limitations will invest only half of available wealth in private annuities. Not surprisingly, the insurance value of annuities also falls considerably: AEW is 1.02 and 1.04, respectively, for men and women with ADL limitations.

Table 10-6 assumes that annuities provide consumers with a constant real payout stream; these results continue to ignore uncertain medical expenses. Compared to previous findings in the nominal annuity case, the actuarial pricing results indicate a slight increase in the utility gains from purchasing a real annuity. This pattern holds for people in good health, as well as for people in poor health with access to actuarially fair annuity premiums. Under uniform pricing, however, the opposite results obtain. Both men and women with ADL limitations would be worse off if they purchased a real rather than a fixed nominal annuity. This result is due to the fact that these individuals have a low probability of surviving to the oldest ages. Since a fixed nominal annuity offers higher real payouts early on, as compared to a real annuity, the utility gains for the less healthy are higher in the first case. These findings suggest that insurers can mitigate the effects of adverse selection for people in poor health, and increase the demand for private annuities, by providing annuities that offer higher payments in earlier years of the contracts.

We now shift attention to the results of our extended model to show how desired annuitization and AEW values change when people face both uncertain survival and uncertain out-of-pocket medical expenses. Table 10-7 reports the figures for each state of health and three values of preexisting real annuity: 25, 50, and 75 percent of wealth. We focus on the case of a fixed nominal annuity under uniform pricing, and a risk-aversion level of three. Here we see that both optimal annuitization and utility gains from purchasing a nominal annuity are lower when people face out-of-pocket medical expenses. In the case of a preexisting real annuity

TABLE 10-6 Annuity Equivalent Value and Optimal Annuitization: Model 1, Real Annuity

	CRRA = 1		CRRA = 3		CRRA = 5	
	Annuity Equivalent Wealth	Optimal Additional Annuitization (% wealth)	Annuity Equivalent Wealth	Optimal Additional Annuitization (% wealth)	Annuity Equivalent Wealth	Optimal Additional Annuitization (% wealth)
Women						
No functioning problems						
Actuarially fair premium	1.187	50	1.290	50	1.322	50
Uniform pricing	1.154	50	1.255	50	1.285	50
IADL limitations						
Actuarially fair premium	1.255	50	1.387	50	1.439	50
Uniform pricing	1.110	44	1.230	50	1.270	50
ADL limitations						
Actuarially fair premium	1.451	50	1.681	50	1.776	50
Uniform pricing	1.030	25	1.151	42	1.220	44
Men						
No functioning problems						
Actuarially fair premium	1.273	50	1.441	50	1.510	50
Uniform pricing	1.139	46	1.280	50	1.359	50
IADL limitations						
Actuarially fair premium	1.393	50	1.616	50	1.727	50
Uniform pricing	1.075	35	1.228	45	1.309	50
ADL limitations						
Actuarially fair premium	1.563	50	1.903	50	2.073	50
Uniform pricing	1.011	16	1.140	38	1.233	43

Source: Author's calculations as described in the text.

TABLE 10-7 Annuity Equivalent Value and Optimal Annuitization Under Uniform Pricing and Uncertain Survival: With and Without Out-of-Pocket (OOP) Medical Costs and Fixed Nominal Annuity

	Preexisting Real Annuity Worth 25% of Wealth		Preexisting Real Annuity Worth 50% of Wealth		Preexisting Real Annuity Worth 75% of Wealth	
	Annuity Equivalent Wealth	Optimal Additional Annuitization (% wealth)	Annuity Equivalent Wealth	Optimal Additional Annuitization (% wealth)	Annuity Equivalent Wealth	Optimal Additional Annuitization (% wealth)
Women						
No functioning problems						
Model 1: Uncertain survival	1.229	75	1.222	50	1.195	25
Model 2: Uncertain survival w/OOP costs	1.221	75	1.160	46	1.066	16
IADL Limitations						
Model 1: Uncertain survival	1.229	75	1.220	50	1.220	25
Model 2: Uncertain survival w/OOP costs	1.207	75	1.129	36	1.017	13
ADL Limitations						
Model 1: Uncertain survival	1.221	75	1.170	50	1.068	25
Model 2: Uncertain survival w/OOP costs	1.183	67	1.051	27	0.985	−3
Men						
No Functioning Problems						
Model 1: Uncertain survival	1.332	75	1.277	50	1.193	25
Model 2: Uncertain survival w/OOP costs	1.301	75	1.196	36	1.061	15
IADL Limitations						
Model 1: Uncertain survival	1.309	75	1.248	50	1.139	25
Model 2: Uncertain survival w/OOP costs	1.282	69	1.135	31	1.019	12
ADL Limitations						
Model 1: Uncertain survival	1.276	75	1.167	50	1.046	18
Model 2: Uncertain survival w/OOP costs	1.230	64	1.042	19	0.987	−3

Source: Authors' calculations as described in the text.

Notes: Model 1: Only Uncertain Survival; Model 2: Both Uncertain Survival and Out-of-Pocket Medical Costs. Both models assume inflation = 3.2% and CRRA = 3.

worth 50 percent of wealth, we find that people would forgo less of their wealth to purchase a nominal annuity. When uncertain medical expenses are accounted for, the AEW values fall from 1.17 to 1.04 for men with ADL limitations, and from 1.27 to 1.19 for men with no functioning problems. Similar results are observed for women. These results suggest that AEW is overstated 5–11 percent ignoring out-of-pocket medical expenses. Not surprisingly, the largest differences are for people with functional limitations, since they have the highest probability of remaining in poor health and therefore have the highest risk of incurring out-of-pocket medical expenses over the life cycle.

The effect of uncertain out-of-pocket medical expenses is more evident when we compare optimal levels of annuitization. Previous studies have indicated that people in poor health rarely annuitize (Brown 2001*b*; Johnson, Burman, and Kobes 2004). Indeed, our findings rationalize this empirical evidence, since because of precautionary motives, full annuitization is unlikely to be an optimal solution. In contrast to earlier studies and our simpler model, we now predict that all retirees, regardless of health status, will only partially annuitize at age 65. As expected, those in poorest health would be expected to convert the smallest amount of their wealth into an annuity. Table 10-6 shows that among men with ADL limitations, the optimal annuitization of additional wealth (conditional on Social Security being half of total wealth) is 19 percent, while among women in the same health status, the figure is 27 percent.

Finally, it is of interest to explore sensitivity analysis for other parameters. Increasing the levels of Social Security and DB pensions to 75 percent of wealth further reduces the optimal levels of annuitization and AEW values. Two factors explain this additional reduction. First, when more initial wealth is held as a preexisting real annuity, the insurance value of additional annuitization is reduced. Second, as discussed earlier, out-of-pocket medical expenses are measured as a proportion of Social Security benefits. Therefore, increasing the value of preexisting real annuity automatically increases the nominal value of out-of-pocket medical expenses, and therefore it produces more precautionary savings in our model. Although this is only one way to formulate the problem, it is illustrative in showing that private annuities can become worthless for people in poor health who are overannuitized and face the risk of incurring large out-of-pocket medical expenses.

Discussion and Conclusions

In this analysis, we have examined how retirees' health status may influence their decisions to purchase payout life annuities. Our main contribution is to show that the insurance value of a life annuity may be smaller than that reported in prior studies. The findings suggest that differences in health and anticipated health-care expenses can help explain why many people do not fully annuitize at retirement. While prior research suggested that an average person would forgo about 40 percent of his wealth to purchase a life annuity (Mitchell et al. 1999), our work indicates that this may not hold for the majority of the population. For someone with health problems, a life annuity priced using annuitant mortality rates implies expected payouts well below the actuarially fair value for that retiree. We provide evidence that adverse selection in annuities reduces the annuity equivalent wealth from values greater than 1.5, to values close to 1.17 for people in poor health, and 1.28 for people in good health. Prior studies have also ignored precautionary savings motivated by uncertain out-of-pocket medical expenses. Our stylized life cycle model with uncertain out-of-pocket medical expenses shows that annuities become less attractive to people facing such medical expenses. Thus, regardless of health status and medical shocks, full annuitization would still be optimal, if annuity markets were truly complete and were both life and health contingent (Davidoff, Brown, and Diamond 2005). Nevertheless, when both adverse selection and uncertain medical expenses are accounted for and annuity markets are incomplete, we show that annuity equivalent wealth values are fairly low for people in poor health, and about 25 percent higher for people in good health.

Some implications of our analysis are worth noting. First, earlier investigations have used annuity equivalent wealth measures as explanatory variables in models predicting retirees' probability of annuitizing (Brown 2001*b*; Petrova 2003). Although such models control for health status (Brown 2001*b*), our study indicates that they should also account directly for health differentials in the AEW measures. Second, our results also imply that offering higher payouts for consumers in case of a medical shock could make annuities more attractive for many, and perhaps even most, of the retiring population. Future research should evaluate how insurers might fashion annuity contracts that better fit the needs of the older, perhaps unhealthy, population. Finally, our model predicts that most retirees would be made worse off by requiring full annuitization, if uniform pricing were involved. These results are important in the context of Social Security reforms proposing personal retirement accounts with mandatory annuitization. Indeed, mandatory annuitization should integrate risk classification providing actuarially fair annuities to people in different health states.

Future research can extend our work by taking into account additional heterogeneity between people in different health states. In addition, it would be of interest to incorporate correlation between medical expenses and future mortality as well as bequest motives.

Acknowledgments

This research received support from the Social Security Administration via the Michigan Retirement Research Center at the University of Michigan and the Pension Research Council at the Wharton School of the University of Pennsylvania. Additional support was provided to the first author by Grant AG10168 from the National Institute on Aging, Samuel H. Preston, Principal Investigator. The authors are grateful to Jeffrey Brown for sharing his optimization code and for useful suggestions. Helpful comments were also provided by Irma Elo, Silvia Matos, Alex Muermann, Samuel Preston, Sara Rix, and members of the Wharton IRM Seminar series.

Notes

[1] Davidoff, Brown, and Diamond (2005) recently extended Yaari's model and derived conditions for optimal full annuitization in a more general setting. They show that when markets are complete, full annuitization is optimal even if some assumptions of Yaari's model are relaxed, such as additively separable utility. The value of annuities lessens if annuity markets are incomplete, but some annuitization is still optimal as long as there is a positive premium for annuitizing wealth and conventional markets are complete.

[2] The HRS is a nationally representative study of the non-institutionalized population over age 50 and their spouses/partners (regardless of age). The HRS data-set contains detailed data on health, financial status, retirement, and family support. Cohorts were interviewed in different waves from 1992 to 2002 (hrsonline.isr.umich.edu).

[3] This is the maximum age for which we can estimate reliable parameters based on actual data. Using an older age for the terminal age does not affect our conclusions since the probability of surviving beyond age 95 is low.

[4] Health status and mortality in period t depend on health status in period $t-1$, and the probability of incurring medical costs is a function of health status in period $t-1$. For this reason, part of the correlation between medical expenses and health status or survival in period t is indirectly accounted for in our model. Future work will explore alternative formulations.

[5] Previous studies have suggested that risk aversion may vary across population subgroups; thus Halek and Eisenhauer (2001) find that risk aversion in the HRS increases with education and is higher among natives and non-Hispanics; also self-reported depressed individuals have 13 percent lower risk aversion than the average individual. In future research we will evaluate the sensitivity of results to the hypothesis that people in poor health have lower risk aversion than those in good health.

⁶ IADLs refer to Instrumental Activities of Daily Living which include difficulties in performing at least one of the following activities: managing the money, making phone calls, preparing a hot meal, and shopping for groceries.

⁷ ADLs refer to Activities of Daily Living which include difficulties in performing at least one of the following activities: bathing/showering, dressing, eating and using the toilet, and getting in and out of bed.

⁸ An actuarially fair premium is one in which the premium equals the present discounted value of expected annuity payments.

⁹ In general, results for women are similar, although the proportion of female survivors with functional limitations is higher than that of men (results available upon request).

¹⁰ We use the 2004 RAND SSA-HRS datafile (www.rand.org/labor/aging/dataprod/#randhrs).

¹¹ Total premiums includes premiums for employer-provided health insurance, private health insurance, long-term care insurance, Medicare through a Health Maintenance Organization, and Medigap.

¹² We present only results for five categories for clarity; results for the omitted categories are consistent with those presented in Table 10-4.

References

Brown, Jeffrey R. (2001*a*). 'Are the Elderly Really Over-annuitized? New Evidence on Life Insurance and Bequests,' in D. A. Wise (ed.), *Themes in the Economics of Aging*. Chicago, IL: University of Chicago Press, pp. 91–126.

—— (2001*b*). 'Private Pensions, Mortality Risk, and the Decision to Annuitize,' *Journal of Public Economics*, 82(1): 29–62.

—— (2003). 'Redistribution and Insurance: Mandatory Annuitization with Mortality Heterogeneity,' *Journal of Risk and Insurance*, 70(1):17–41.

—— and Mark J. Warshawsky (2001). 'Longevity-Insured Retirement Distributions from Pension Plans: Market and Regulatory Issues,' National Bureau of Economic Research Working Paper no. 8064.

——, Olivia S. Mitchell, James M. Poterba, and Mark J. Warshawsky (2001). *The Role of Annuity Markets in Financing Retirement*. Cambridge, MA: MIT Press.

Cogan, John F. and Olivia S. Mitchell (2003). 'The Role of Economic Policy in Social Security Reform: Perspectives from the President Commission,' *Journal of Economic Perspectives*, 17(2): 149–72.

Crimmins, Eileen M., Mark D. Hayward, and Yasuhiko Saito (1994). 'Changing Mortality and Morbidity Rates and the Health-Status and Life Expectancy of the Older Population,' *Demography*, 31(1): 159–75.

Cutler, David M. and Ellen Meara (2001). 'The Concentration of Medical Spending: An Update,' in D. A. Wise (ed.), *Themes in the Economics of Aging*. Chicago, IL: University of Chicago Press, pp. 217–40.

Davidoff, Thomas, Jeffrey R. Brown, and Peter Diamond (2005). 'Annuities and Individual Welfare,' *American Economic Review*, 95(5): 1573–90.

Davis, Morris A. (1998). 'The Health and Financial Decisions of the Elderly,' Ph.D. Dissertation in the Department of Economics, University of Pennsylvania.

Deaton, Angus (1992). *Understanding Consumption.* New York: Clarendon Press.

Halek, Martin and Joseph G. Eisenhauer (2001). 'Demography of Risk Aversion,' *Journal of Risk and Insurance,* 68(1): 1–24.

Hubbard, R. Glenn, Jonathan Skinner, and Stephen P. Zeldes (1995). 'Precautionary Saving and Social Insurance,' *Journal of Political Economy,* 103(2): 360–99.

Hurd, Michael D., Daniel McFadden, and Angela Merrill (2001). 'Predictors of Mortality among the Elderly,' in D. A. Wise (ed.), *Themes in the Economics of Aging.* Chicago, IL: University of Chicago Press, pp. 171–98.

Johnson, Richard W., Leonard E. Burman, and Deborah I. Kobes (2004). 'Annuitized Wealth at Older Ages: Evidence from the Health and Retirement Study,' Final Report to the Employee Benefits Security Administration, U.S. Department of Labor. Washington, DC: The Urban Institute.

Mitchell, Olivia S. and David McCarthy (2002). 'Estimating International Adverse Selection in Annuities,' *North American Actuarial Journal,* 6(4): 38–42.

—— and James F. Moore (1998). 'Can Americans Afford to Retire? New Evidence on Retirement Saving Adequacy,' *Journal of Risk and Insurance,* 65(3): 371–400.

——, Michael S. Gordon, and Mark M. Twinney (1997). 'Introduction: Assessing the Challenges to the Pension System,' in M. S. Gordon, O. S. Mitchell and M. M. Twinney (eds.), *Positioning Pensions for the Twenty-First Century.* Philadelphia, PA: University of Pennsylvania Press, pp. 1–11.

——, James M. Poterba, Mark J. Warshawsky, and Jeffrey R. Brown (1999). 'New Evidence on the Money's Worth of Individual Annuities,' *American Economic Review,* 89(5): 1299–318.

Moore, James F. and Olivia S. Mitchell (2000). 'Projected Retirement Wealth and Savings Adequacy,' in O. S. Mitchell, P. B. Hammond, and A. M. Rappaport (eds.), *Forecasting Retirement Needs and Retirement Wealth.* Philadelphia, PA: University of Pennsylvania Press, pp. 68–94.

Palloni, Alberto (2001). 'Increment-Decrement Life Tables,' in S. H. Preston, P. Heuveline, and M. Guillot (eds.), *Demography: Measuring and Modeling Population Processes.* Malden, MA: Blackwell Publishers, pp. 256–72.

Palumbo, Michael G. (1999). 'Uncertain Medical Expenses and Precautionary Saving near the End of the Life Cycle,' *Review of Economic Studies,* 66(2): 395–421.

Petrova, Petia (2003). 'The Annuity Puzzle Gets Bigger,' Center for Retirement Research Working Paper BC01-D02A0403F, Boston College.

Schoen, Robert (1988). *Modeling Multigroup Populations.* Plenum Series on Demographic Methods and Population Analysis. New York: Plenum Press.

—— and Kenneth C. Land (1979). 'General Algorithm for Estimating a Markov-Generated Increment-Decrement Life Table with Applications to Marital-Status Patterns,' *Journal of the American Statistical Association,* 74(368): 761–76.

Sinclair, Sven H. and Kent A. Smetters (2004). 'Health Shocks and the Demand for Annuities,' Technical Paper 2004–9, July. Washington, DC: Congressional Budget Office.

Society of Actuaries (1999). 'Exposure Draft: The Rp-2000 Mortality Tables,' Working Paper. Schaumburg, IL: Society of Actuaries.

Turra, Cassio M. (2004). 'Living and Dying at Older Ages: Essays on the Hispanic Mortality Paradox and the Annuity Puzzle in the U.S.,' Doctoral Dissertation in the Graduate Group in Demography, University of Pennsylvania.

United States Department of Labor (U.S. DOL) Pension and Welfare Benefits Administration. (2004). *Abstract of 1998 Form 5500 Annual Reports.* Private Pension Plan Bulletin No. 12, Summer 2004. Washington, DC: USGPO.

Yaari, Menahem E. (1965). 'Uncertain Lifetime, Life-Insurance, and the Theory of the Consumer,' *Review of Economic Studies*, 32: 137–50.

Chapter 11

Annuity Valuation, Long-Term Care, and Bequest Motives

John Ameriks, Andrew Caplin, Steven Laufer, and Stijn Van Nieuwerburgh

This chapter develops a formal framework for understanding how existing financial instruments impact retirement security and considers new instruments that might be devised to enhance such security. Our framework draws on a model developed by Ameriks et al. (2007) which allows for both bequest and precautionary motives. Bequest objectives have to do with the desire to leave some assets to one's heirs. Precautionary motives include the desire to avoid being simultaneously bankrupt and in need of long-term care (LTC)—which here we term 'Medicaid aversion'. The model is used to characterize how households might value stand-alone life-contingent life annuities, where their valuation is seen to depend on household characteristics, including bequest motives and Medicaid aversion. Because such standard life-contingent immediate annuities are shown to be of limited value for most middle-class households, we then discuss alternative 'contingent' annuity designs that involve delayed payouts to better target longevity risk, and/or contain elements of long-term care insurance by including higher payments for those who are losing the ability to conduct one or more 'activities of daily living'.[1] Our findings have implications for the design of new financial instruments that permit family concerns to impact bequest and precautionary motives.

Lifetime Annuities and Precautionary Motives

Economists have shown that life-cycle consumers with uncertain lifetimes have strong incentives to annuitize wealth so as to be assured that resources will support an adequate level of lifetime consumption.[2] In practice, the voluntary usage of immediate annuity products in the USA is low. For instance, sales of standard annuities involving fixed payments in 2006 amounted to less than $6 billion of the estimated $236 billion in deferred and immediate annuity sales in 2006 [Life Insurance Marketing Research Association (LIMRA 2006)]. The picture changes little even if one includes immediate 'variable' life annuities that capture all or part of the equity premium, whose importance is stressed by Milevsky and Young (2007), but for which sales remain low outside the TIAA-CREF retirement system.

A large literature explores reasons for lack of consumer interest in standard fixed immediate annuities. Friedman and Warshawsky (1988, 1990); Mitchell et al. (1999); and Brown et al. (2001) examine pricing of immediate annuity contracts in the USA relative to hypothetical zero-cost 'actuarially fair' annuity contracts. They document persistent and significant costs of private annuity contracts above such a zero-cost benchmark, as well as significant cross-sectional variation in pricing across insurance providers. Yet their work suggests that insurance loads observed in practice (markups of roughly 7–15 percent relative to the benchmark zero-cost annuity, assuming annuitant mortality) would still result in substantial annuity demand among older individuals in the context of a basic life-cycle model. These findings are moderated by institutional constraints. For instance, the generosity of Social Security benefits is mentioned by Dushi and Webb (2004) as the major reason why voluntary annuitization rates are so low. Another institution important in this regard is the family: Kotlikoff and Spivak (1981) estimate that informal risk pooling of longevity/mortality risk within families can provide half or more of the insurance benefit obtainable in a world with complete annuity markets.

A more fundamental question concerning annuities is whether they address the most important risks retirees believe they face. Research on retiree spending suggests they may not, since many older households with high retirement assets tend to spend down very slowly in practice (De Nardi, French, and Jones 2006). In other words, such households are relatively immune to longevity risk in the standard sense, because their resources are virtually certain to last long enough to finance normal consumption expenditures in old age. One group of analysts, beginning with Kotlikoff and Summers (1981), contends that households spend little in retirement because of bequest motives; more recently Abel (2003) also suggested that bequest motives may help to explain low demand for annuities. Yet Davidoff, Brown, and Diamond (2005) point out that this depends critically on the form of the bequest motive, and in particular how risk averse the retiree is with respect to bequests. Moreover, empirical studies offer no clear evidence of an offset between annuitization and bequest motives; for instance Brown (2001) uses the 1992 HRS and finds no significant relationship between peoples' stated desire to leave bequests and their stated intention to annuitize a DC plan upon retirement. Johnson, Burman, and Kobes (2004) use the 2000 HRS where they determine that older adults with no children are no more likely to annuitize DC balances than others with children (and presumably stronger bequest motives).

Laitner and Juster (1996) also uncover no significant difference in bequest motives among households with and without children, though they do find a relationship between stated desires to leave an estate and the selection of certain immediate annuity refund features.

An alternative reason that people may not annuitize is that they may prefer to keep their assets liquid for precautionary purposes, in case they need the money for health expenses (Hurd 1987; Palumbo 1999). To this we turn next.

How Health Expenses and Medicaid Aversion Matter

To further explain how health costs and health preferences influence the demand for annuities, we build on recent studies including French and Jones (2004) and De Nardi, French, and Jones (2006). The issue of how health might influence interest in annuities is unclear; as Davidoff, Brown, and Diamond (2005) note, the demand for annuities will depend critically on the timing of health shocks and 'the illiquidity of annuities may be relevant if the risk occurs early in life, but not toward the end of life.' Turra and Mitchell (2008), however, show that relative to the high value of annuities typically found in a basic life-cycle framework, annuities are significantly less valuable for households facing uncertain age- and health-related medical care shocks. Sinclair and Smetters (2004) simulate a rich model of medical costs in later life and also reach a generally negative verdict on interest in annuities. Under the parameterizations outlined in that study, income annuities are avoided by consumers with wealth levels that would be seriously depleted were a medical shock to occur. This is because they see annuities as a 'risky asset', since health shocks simultaneously raise expenses and reduce the value of future annuity payments.

Prior research by Brown and Finkelstein (2004) examines the link between health considerations and demand for annuities, taking as its starting point the crucial role that actual and potential LTC expenses play for retirees. In the USA, the government pays for some long-term care costs under both the Medicare and Medicaid programs. The former does not cover all LTC costs, while the latter is the provider of last resort, being means tested. Currently, over 60 percent of LTC expenses are absorbed by Medicaid as provider of last resort, yet those with high wealth must absorb substantial long-term care expenses because of the means testing format. As a result, more than one-third of LTC expenditures are paid for out of pocket, nearly double the proportion of expenditures in the health sector as a whole covered out of pocket (National Center for Health Statistics 2002; Congressional Budget Office 2004).

The motivation to save for precautionary reasons depends critically on how consumers weigh Medicaid as a substitute for private LTC. If it is perceived as a good substitute, households with a low bequest motive will maintain high old-age consumption levels, and rely on Medicaid to pick up the tab should they need care in later life. Pauly (1990) argues that this is an important behavioral pattern in his explanation of why the long-term care insurance market has failed to thrive in the USA. Yet many people argue the opposite—indeed the implicit assumption of Sinclair and Smetters (2004) and Turra and Mitchell (2008) is that Medicaid is actually a very poor substitute for private care. A lack of evidence on this subject motivates our research reported in the next section.

Theoretical Model

Our model posits that the older household consists of a single individual who has just retired at age 65 (following Ameriks et al. 2007) and assumes that the maximum length of his retirement period is 35 years (to age 100). His stochastic mortality probability evolves over the retirement period in the manner defined below. The individual is assumed to maximize his remaining lifetime utility based on the excess of each period's consumption C over a subsistence level, C_{SUB} (see the Technical Appendix for more model details).[3] The consumer also receives an end-of-life utility from a bequest which is comprised of all assets held at death. The parameter ϖ indicates how strongly the retiree values bequests (and if wealth is negative at death, the bequest is zero). Here, bequests are left solely because of the satisfaction the retiree derives from leaving assets behind. In particular, our formulation eliminates any motives related to a desire to use the prospect of a bequest at death to influence the behavior of others while alive. It should also be noted that our bequest motive is difficult to distinguish from other explanations for saving (see Carroll 2007) such as hoarding, or simply 'wealth in the utility function.'[4]

With respect to functional form, we follow De Nardi (2004) in parameterizing the bequest utility with two parameters, one (ϖ) reflecting the strength of the bequest motive, and the other (φ) measuring the degree to which bequests are a luxury good (see the Appendix). To simply illustrate how these parameters work, consider a case where the retiree starts with wealth of X dollars, lives for exactly n years, and then dies. In each year of life, the individual would consume c dollars and, upon death, bequeaths the remaining $b = X - nc$. In this simple case, the problem is to choose a bequest that maximizes total (nondiscounted) utility. Given our functional forms for utility, the individual will optimally leave an inheritance to cover ϖ years of spending at an annual expenditure level, the amount by which lifetime consumption exceeds the threshold φ. If X proves insufficient to allow the individual to consume such an amount each year, no bequest is left.

More generally, the retiree starts with some nonnegative wealth amount and anticipates a constant stream of real annual 'Social Security' income each year Y for as long as he lives.[5] There is posited to be one risk-free asset in which the individual can invest and which yields a constant real rate of interest (the household is not allowed to borrow against future income). The individual may be in one of four health states in our model: state 1 is good health, in state 2 he has medical problems but no need for long-term care, in state 3 long-term care of some form is required, and state 4 is death. The individual is initially endowed with a health state, and thereafter his health state follows a Markov chain with an age-varying, one-period state transition matrix. A retiree reaching age 99 dies with probability one the following year. Together, the initial health state and the Markov transition matrices enable us to compute future probabilities attached to all health states, including death. Rather than include the retiree's health state directly in his utility function, we instead focus on the costs associated with alternative health states. Each state has associated with it a necessary and deterministic health cost. Paying these costs removes any utility penalty that would otherwise be associated with the health state.

In view of the fact that medical expenses might exceed available wealth, we need to include the possibility of bankruptcy in our model. Accordingly, an individual is forced to declare bankruptcy when he cannot afford to pay for medical costs and the subsistence level of consumption. Therefore, his consumption and end-of-period wealth in a period of bankruptcy depends on his medical state. In states 1 and 2, an individual who declares bankruptcy is left with sufficient assets to consume at a minimum level $C_{BAN} > C_{SUB}$, with end-of-period wealth remaining at zero. In the long-term care state, treatment of bankruptcy is related to the institutional reality of Medicaid. An individual declaring bankruptcy in the long-term care state forfeits all wealth to the government (end-of-period wealth is zero) and enters a Medicaid facility, receiving in that period the Medicaid level of consumption $C_{MED} > C_{SUB}$. In the period following bankruptcy, the individual's income continues on its deterministic path and there are no further implications of having been previously bankrupt. The Medicaid level of consumption, C_{MED}, has a powerful impact on the strength of the precautionary motive. If C_{MED} is very close to subsistence, there is a strong incentive for households to retain sufficient wealth to retain the private care option. If it is closer to annual consumption in the pre-Medicaid period, then the incentive will be to run down wealth and use the Medicaid subsidy in place of saving.

Model Parameterization

An important goal of our analysis is to illustrate how demand for various financial products varies, as a function of the strength of the precautionary motive and the bequest motive, ϖ. To this end, we fix all other preference parameters at conventional, calibrated values, with wealth and income numbers derived from survey evidence (c.f. Ameriks et al. 2007 and the Appendix).

With these values and the health and longevity dynamics described above, the model generates a median value for lifetime medical expenses of $18,000 for men ($56,000 for women), with a mean of $79,000 ($137,000). Importantly, long-term care costs make up 92 percent of all medical expenses. For the 61 percent of males who never enter long-term care, mean lifetime medical costs are only $7,900. Men (women) face a 26 percent (41 percent) chance of facing lifetime medical costs greater than $100,000 and a 10 percent (20 percent) chance of costs greater than $250,000.

Bequest and Medicaid Aversion Parameters

To parameterize retirees' bequest and Medicaid aversion coefficients, we draw from a survey designed to separately identify these two within a narrow range (Ameriks et al. 2007). In what follows, we provide both point estimates of median values and confidence bands. The median level of Medicaid aversion was around −5 (corresponding to a consumption equivalent of Medicaid of ~$10,000) while our best estimate of the population median level of the bequest motive was roughly 26. Yet there is substantial heterogeneity in our estimates: over one-quarter of respondents said they felt Medicaid to be so undesirable that it barely exceeded subsistence income of $5,000 (by less than $1,000). Over half of the respondents valued the consumption equivalent of Medicaid at below $10,000. On the other hand, some 30 percent of respondents display little or no such Medicaid aversion, treating a year in a Medicaid facility as equivalent to an annual consumption flow of $20,000 or more. This heterogeneity must be borne in mind when interpreting the figures that follow.

Turning to survey evidence on bequest motives, we again find substantial heterogeneity. More than one-quarter of the sample had strong bequest desires ($\varpi > 40$), with a very strong bequest preference ($\varpi > 90$) estimated for some 10 percent of the sample. Accordingly, based on our survey questions, it would appear that many individuals do place a high priority on bequests. We also show that wealth is not significantly related to estimated bequest parameters.

Implications for the Demand for Standard Life Annuities

Given this model setup, we next calculate the value of lifetime annuities for various different types of retirees. Our model predicts that the demand for annuities is positively associated with wealth, similar to that reported by Sinclair and Smetters (2004). For a given level of wealth and income, demand for annuities also varies according to the retiree's bequest and precautionary parameters. To quantify these effects, we develop and graph iso-valuation lines that indicate the amount per dollar of actuarially fair value that an individual would be willing to pay to purchase a given insurance contract. The excess of the indicated value above 1 can be interpreted as the maximum 'load' that an individual would be willing to pay for the given contract. For example, an iso-valuation of 1.20 means that the individual with the indicated combination of bequest and precautionary motives at that point on the graph would pay at most a 20 percent load to obtain the contract. These calculations are conditional on given wealth and income levels, chosen to represent a hypothetical, 'typical' participant in an employer-sponsored pension plan.

To construct the baseline case, we assume the following 'median' respondent: female, age 65, in good health, having disposable (real) lifetime income of $15,000 per year, and initial wealth of $200,000. Figure 11-1 shows how much this baseline respondent would be willing to pay for a $5,000 annual annuity stream (actuarially equivalent to a present value of $86,000 under our parameterization). The horizontal 'Bequest Motive' axis of Figure 11-1 (and all subsequent figures) is straightforward to interpret. The vertical 'Medicaid aversion' axis plots the log of the marginal utility of C_{MED}, a function of C_{MED} that describes the strength of the precautionary motive, so that the precautionary savings motive strengthens from bottom to top. Note that a Medicaid aversion value of zero on this axis corresponds to a low value for C_{MED} of $6,000, or only $1,000 above the subsistence level; a value of -5 indicates a value for C_{MED} of just over $10,000; and a value of -10 indicates a value for C_{MED} of some $30,000. The bottom left corner of Figure 11-1 depicts a retiree with no bequest motive and essentially no aversion to Medicaid. As expected, such an individual has a strong desire for annuities; her willingness to pay for this annuity is 2.2, meaning that the product would be demanded even for a 120 percent load. However, this willingness drops quickly as the strength of either motive increases. At typical values of the bequest motive and Medicaid aversion, the retiree would only purchase the annuity if it were priced at a load of less than 10 percent. At higher levels of Medicaid aversion, the annuity remains attractive only if priced at a load of less than 3 percent. Accordingly, for many retirees, a standard annuity is of minimal value given with typical loads of 7–15 percent.

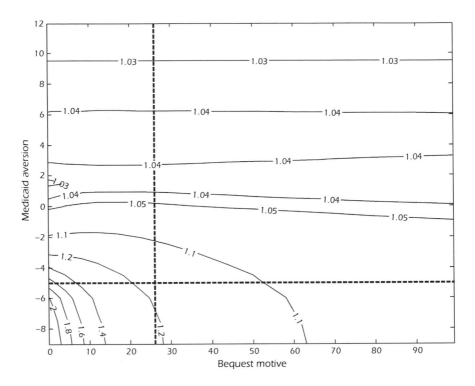

Figure 11-1. Baseline estimates of willingness to pay for a $5,000 fixed annuity by level of Medicaid aversion and strength of bequest motive. *Source*: Authors' calculations. *Notes*: The contour lines in this figure represent various levels of the ratio of the retiree's estimated willingness to pay to the zero-cost, risk-neutral present valuation of the annuity contract. For example, for all combinations of Medicaid aversion and bequest motives on the line marked '1.2' in the figure above, the retiree is willing to pay (up to) 20 percent above the cost of the contract in order to obtain the contract. For this figure, the retiree is assumed to be a healthy, 65-year-old female, with $200,000 in total wealth and preexisting (real) annuity income of $15,000 per year. Estimates of the median values of the strength of the bequest motive and Medicaid aversion within the surveyed population are indicated by the grey dashed lines on the chart.

Figure 11-2 presents the same analysis for a larger annuity: $10,000 annually instead of $5,000. The results are similar to Figure 11-1, though everywhere the retiree is less willing to pay per dollar of cost. The reason such a retiree is willing to pay less per dollar is straightforward: while the annuity payments are higher, the cost of the annuity is also twice as high ($172,000 compared to $86,000 for the $5,000 annuity in our parameterization), requiring the annuitant to relinquish even more

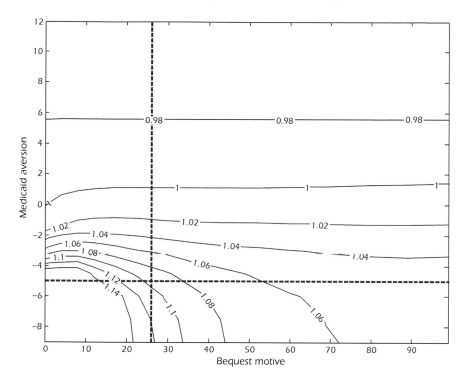

Figure 11-2. Baseline estimates of willingness to pay for a $10,000 fixed annuity by level of Medicaid aversion and strength of bequest motive. *Source*: Authors' calculations. *Note*: See Figure 11-1.

liquid wealth. This leaves her much more exposed to the risk that an LTC shock will force bankruptcy and/or seriously deplete assets remaining for a bequest.

Figure 11-3 presents the willingness-to-pay results for the smaller $5,000 annuity again, but now we assume that the retiree has less annual income and more liquid wealth. This reinforces the intuition just given above: with greater wealth, the risk subsides of bankruptcy due to LTC costs or depletion of the intended bequest, making the individual more willing to pay for the annuity. Relative to Figure 11-1, the wealthier retiree of Figure 11-3 is slightly more willing to pay for the annuity at virtually all combinations of Medicaid aversion and bequest motive.

Figure 11-4 presents the analysis for a retiree with both less income (here only $10,000 annually) and less wealth than in our baseline case ($100,000 vs $200,000 previously). At all levels of bequest motive and Medicaid aversion, this retiree is significantly less willing to pay for the $5,000

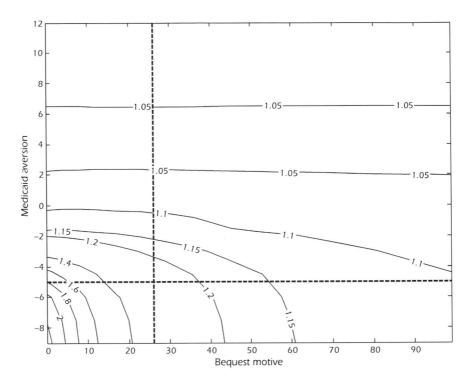

Figure 11-3. Higher liquid wealth estimates of willingness to pay for a $5,000 fixed annuity by level of Medicaid aversion and strength of bequest motive. *Source*: Authors' calculations. *Notes*: See Figure 11-1. For this figure, the retiree is assumed to be a healthy, 65-year-old female, with $286,000 in total wealth and preexisting (real) annuity income of $10,000 per year. Estimates of the median values of the strength of the bequest motive and Medicaid aversion within the surveyed population are indicated by the grey dashed lines on the chart.

annuity. Contrary to arguments on the demand or 'need' for annuities, our analysis suggests that as wealth decreases, demand decreases as well, as annuitization exposes the less wealthy retirees to a greater risk of ending up on Medicaid or sacrificing their bequests.

Figure 11-5 shows that the shape of the iso-value curves is very different for those with high wealth. This figure is for a woman at age 65, in good health, with disposable income of $25,000 and total wealth of $500,000, who roughly corresponds to the 90th percentile of empirical income- and wealth-distributions. Given these parameters, willingness to pay for annuities for the wealthy increases as Medicaid aversion increases, especially among those with strong bequest motives.

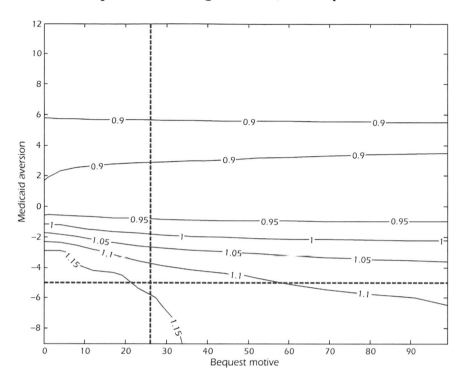

Figure 11-4. Lower-wealth and -income estimates of willingness to pay for a $5,000 fixed annuity by level of Medicaid aversion and strength of bequest motive. *Source*: Authors' calculations. *Note*: See Figure 11-3.

We also explore the effect of risk aversion over bequests by changing the standard formulation of the bequest motive to one in which the retiree cares only about the expected value of the bequest and disregards the odds of the ultimate bequest being higher or lower than expected (being 'risk neutral'). This specification of the bequest motive produces results similar to Figure 11-5, leading us to conclude that our overall analysis is not generally sensitive to whether retirees are described as risk averse or risk neutral over the size of their bequests.

We conclude that the strength of the bequest and precautionary motives are important determinants of interest in annuities. For a retiree who has no bequest motive and regards Medicaid as a good substitute for private LTC, annuities are a valuable form of insurance against longevity. However, as the desire to leave a bequest and avoid government-financed LTC increases, holding liquid assets becomes more important and interest in annuities wanes. This conclusion naturally suggests that we consider alternatives to standard life annuities.

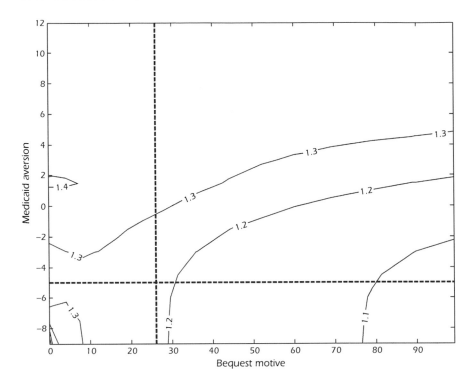

Figure 11-5. Higher-wealth and -income estimates of willingness to pay for a $5,000 fixed annuity by level of Medicaid aversion and strength of bequest motive. *Source:* Authors' calculations. *Note:* See Figure 11–1. For this figure, the retiree is assumed to be a healthy, 65-year-old female, with $500,000 in total wealth and preexisting (real) annuity income of $25,000 per year. Estimates of the median values of the strength of the bequest motive and Medicaid aversion within the surveyed population are indicated by the grey dashed lines on the chart.

Implications for Alternative Annuity Structures

Next, we outline and evaluate three annuity structures that would appear to be better targeted to the retirees we model. The first is a *reversible annuity*, which allows the holder to exchange the future income flow for its current cash value upon entering the LTC state. This is a straightforward response to the concern that purchasing the annuity depletes one's liquid wealth, which is particularly valuable when the retiree faces the high cost of LTC. The second is a *longevity insurance contract*, in which an individual makes up-front, irreversible payments in exchange for a promise that an insurer will pay an annual income for life beginning only if and when the annuitant reaches a prespecified, advanced age. While such a product addresses some of the issues that would seem to limit interest in conventional annuities, we believe it is of limited relevance in the context of our model. What is needed to significantly impact market interest in our framework is the introduction either of long-term care insurance features or some form of life-insurance features. Because life-insurance contracts and life annuities are offsetting financial contracts, most interesting for us are arrangements involving explicit tie-ins with LTCI. The third contract we examine is of this form, *combining a standard life annuity with extra payments in the LTC state.*

Intriguingly, these three are not products currently attracting the interest of households and financial designers. At the end of this section we outline actual developments in annuity markets. Why these changes are taking place and how they differ from the next steps that follow from application of richer life-cycle models is a crucial research subject, as outlined in the final section.

Reversible Annuity

The value of flexibility in terms of liquidity is demonstrated in Figure 11-6, which shows the willingness to pay for a *reversible annuity* of $5,000 annually. Reversibility here simply means that the annuitant could obtain the present value of any remaining annuity payments (adjusted for current age, mortality, and health status) when she needs LTC. This type of reversibility is not generally a feature of real-world annuity contracts; however, we show that if such a feature could be offered at relatively low additional cost, demand for annuities would increase quite substantially, especially among those with strong Medicaid aversion. Compared to the standard annuity, the reversibility option increases the willingness pay by up to 16 percent for the most Medicaid averse retiree depicted. For those with a strong bequest motive, the reversibility feature adds little to the value of the annuity (which is sensible; being able to reverse the annuity has no value at death, which is the state of greatest relevance to those with high bequest motives).

Longevity Insurance

While this product is sometimes deemed an innovation, it is effectively a highly restrictive contingent deferred annuity with a zero surrender/cash value and a constraint on when annuity income payments may begin. Nevertheless, it could potentially be structured such that the premium payments required are individually small and occur over a number of years, rather than as a single lump sum. In a world in which uninsurable, health-related expense shocks can occur and borrowing is costly or impossible, the ability

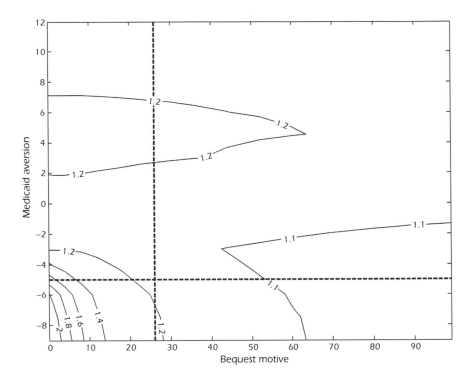

Figure 11-6. Baseline estimates of willingness to pay for a reversible $5,000 fixed annuity by level of Medicaid aversion and strength of bequest motive. *Source*: Authors' calculations. *Notes*: See Figure 11-1. For this figure, the retiree is assumed to be a healthy, 65-year-old female, with $200,000 in total wealth and pre-existing (real) annuity income of $15,000 per year. Estimates of the median values of the strength of the bequest motive and Medicaid aversion within the surveyed population are indicated by the grey dashed lines on the chart. The annuity used in this figure is different from those used in Figures 11-1 through 11-5, as this annuity can be 'reversed' (in other words, cashed-in or refunded) at any time.

to spread the cost of the annuity out over many periods' future periods may be of some value.

We model this product as a sequence of equal mortality-contingent payments that must be made in order to obtain income benefit beginning at a later date. The contract has no cashable value, but simply provides an annuity benefit late in life at little up-front cost at the point of retirement. Figure 11-7 illustrates our baseline retiree's willingness to pay for such a contract. Specifically, we consider a policy that pays annual benefits of $10,000 starting at age 85 in exchange for constant annual payments from the current age of 65 through age 84. Under our parameterization,

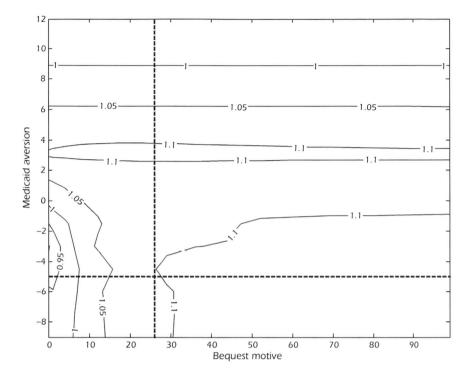

Figure 11-7. Baseline estimates of willingness to pay for $10,000 'longevity insurance' annuity by level of Medicaid aversion and strength of bequest motive. *Source*: Authors' calculations. *Notes*: See Figure 11-1. For this figure, the retiree is assumed to be a healthy, 65-year-old female, with $200,000 in total wealth and preexisting (real) annuity income of $15,000 per year. Estimates of the median values of the strength of the bequest motive and Medicaid aversion within the surveyed population are indicated by the grey dashed lines on the chart. The annuity used in this figure is different from those used in Figures 11-1 through 11-6. This annuity is a 'longevity insurance' policy that pays annual benefits of $10,000 starting at age 85 in exchange for level, constant annual payments from the current age of 65 through age 84.

actuarially fair payments for this contract are $1,560 per year. Relative to Figure 11-2 (the standard $10,000 annuity for the same retiree), we see that this contract structure modestly enhances willingness to pay for those with strong bequest motives and for those with Medicaid aversion in the middle of the range graphed. For those with low levels of both Medicaid aversion and bequest motive, there is actually less willingness to pay for the product, probably because it ultimately provides less protection against pure longevity risk than the standard annuity.

Combining Annuities with LTC Insurance

An LTC/life-annuity combination was discussed by Pauly (1990), and more recently by Murtaugh, Spillman, and Warshawsky (2001), Spillman, Murtaugh, and Warshawsky (2002), and Warshawsky, Spillman, and Murtaugh (2003). Here the idea is a straightforward combination of a life annuity with a disability type 'pop-up' benefit triggered by LTC needs. The specific product proposed by Murtaugh, Spillman, and Warshawsky (2001) combines a lifetime immediate annuity of $1,000 (nominal) per month, with a 'pop-up' payment of an additional $2,000 monthly for annuitants with 2 ADL (Activity of Daily Living or severe cognitive) impairments, plus another $1,000 monthly if the annuitant had 4 ADL impairments. Those authors argue that this combination product could alleviate adverse selection/pricing problems in both the LTC and annuity markets, and they estimate the cost of such a combination policy at about 3 percent less than if the two products were purchased separately.

The mechanics of such a policy are straightforward. Assuming actuarial fairness and complete information, suppose that a LTC policy which would pay X dollars per month in the LTC state costs Y dollars per month. Assume also a standard immediate life-annuity paying A dollars per month costs B dollars under the same assumptions. Purchasing the 'combination' policy then consists of paying B dollars to obtain a life annuity, and using Y dollars of the annuity payments to obtain LTC benefits X. Hence the 'combination product' pays a monthly benefit of $(A - Y)$ in non-LTC, non-death states, and $(A + X)$ dollars in the LTC state (assuming premiums cease once the individual claims LTC benefits), and nothing at death.

Figure 11-8 shows demand for the hypothetical LTC/annuity policy that pays a standard $5,000 annual annuity and an additional $10,000 per year of long-term care. The fair cost of this policy is $102,700, of which $86,300 is used to cover the annuity component and the remaining $16,400 covers LTC benefits. The figure illustrates that consumer demand for such a product would be expected to be strong and rise with Medicaid aversion, primarily due to the LTC component of the policy. For a retiree with no bequest motive or Medicaid aversion, LTC insurance is undesirable because it consumes resources and delivers benefits in states that are not of great concern. For all other parameter values, our calculations predict that there should be a tremendous demand for LTC insurance, even if offered at very high loads. For the most Medicaid averse, our model predicts that individuals would purchase the LTC component at loads of up to 300 percent! For those who dislike Medicaid or fear the depletion of their bequest, the LTC element offers insurance against the risk that most strongly threatens their security and so is the most appealing product. The reason these tremendous demands do not appear in the willingness to pay for the hybrid

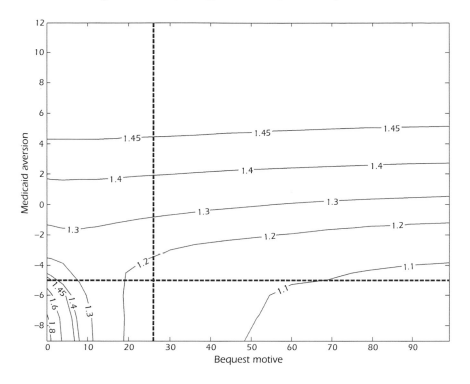

Figure 11-8. Baseline estimates of willingness to pay for a 'pop-up' LTCI/annuity combination by level of Medicaid aversion and strength of bequest motive. *Source*: Authors' calculations. *Notes*: See Figure 11-1. For this figure, the retiree is assumed to be a healthy, 65-year-old female, with $200,000 in total wealth and preexisting (real) annuity income of $15,000 per year. Estimates of the median values of the strength of the bequest motive and Medicaid aversion within the surveyed population are indicated by the grey dashed lines on the chart. The annuity used in this figure is different from those used in Figures 11-1 through 11-6. This annuity is a hypothetical LTCI/annuity policy that pays a standard $5,000 annual annuity and an additional $10,000 in each year of LTC.

product is the annuity component, which consumes most of the premium and remains relatively undesirable as described above. When compared to their willingness to purchase the annuity and LTC components separately, we find that people would be willing to pay only 96–99 percent of the combined value for the hybrid product. Our interpretation for this finding is that the two forms of insurance complement each other, so the combination suffers from simple decreasing returns to scale. In other words, having purchased the annuity component, the LTC element becomes slightly less valuable and vice versa. Nevertheless, the clear conclusion of this exercise is that any attempt to market a credible LTC insurance product, either alone or coupled with an annuity, should receive great interest among retirees.

Innovations in Annuity Design

Many suggestions about annuity and LTC combination products have been circulating among academics and policymakers, and several commercial firms have offered annuities with LTC riders. To date, these contracts offer LTC coverage paid for by periodic withdrawals from cash surrender values from an associated deferred annuity contract. Because deferred annuity contracts retain significant cash value, we posit that this type of product does not provide the ideal combination of longevity insurance and LTC protection; one product is described by Milliman Consultants (2004). It is possible that the commercial success of such policies may have been hampered by a variety of practical issues. For example, until recently, annuity owners were unable to convert preexisting accumulations on deferred annuity contracts to a combination type product that offers an insurance rider without triggering a taxable event.

Of course, it may be that policies with particular designs, for instance those involving large up-front costs/premiums, are avoided for other psychological reasons. And much product innovation in the annuity area seems to have psychological as much as economic origins. There is increasing awareness on the part of financial service providers concerning the perceived limitations of stand-alone annuities. The basic problem appears to be consumer discomfort with relinquishing large lump sums in exchange for future promises to pay. Given such discomfort, many if not most immediate annuity products are now sold with 'refund features' or other options that effectively amount to the addition of a saving/investment vehicle to the insurance product. For example, between two-thirds and three-quarters of the immediate life annuities purchased by retiring TIAA-CREF participants included of some form of 'refund' feature at the time of purchase, guaranteeing at least a minimum number of future payments in all states, regardless of realized longevity (Ameriks 2002). Of course, for insurance to be effectively provided (and for insurers to remain solvent in an equilibrium), resources must be relinquished by the insured in some states or contingencies, so that they can be transferred in some way to provide benefits in other states/contingencies. If consumers are unwilling to 'pay premiums' in states where risks do not materialize, there is no scope to provide benefits above those that could be achieved absent insurance in states where risks do materialize.

In recent years, so-called 'living benefits' riders have become popular in many deferred annuity contracts. For example, some 70 percent of new deferred annuity contracts are issued with riders that provide 'guaranteed minimum withdrawal' benefits, where a certain minimum level of income is promised in each year for a specified term (or for life), while the contract holder retains the ability to access a lump-sum/cash value at any time during that term. The lifetime versions of such products amount to the remittance of small periodic insurance premiums in exchange for the purchase of contingent lifetime annuity payments received only in states of world in which resources have been exhausted according to a minimum payment schedule and the annuitant is alive. The vast bulk of premiums paid for such contracts are represented by the value of the investments held on the contract; the embedded annuity amounts to a small fraction of the contract's initial value. These contracts apparently have wide appeal, but they can be quite complicated to analyze and price as illustrated by Milevsky (2006). It remains unclear why products have developed in this domain while remaining so limited in others. There are surely legal and regulatory constraints that make more innovative products costly to bring to market, especially if the innovative firm that finally breaks through the regulatory barrier cannot in some way exclude others from quickly following.

Promising Research Avenues

Next we turn to a brief discussion how research can help in the development of security-enhancing financial instruments for retirees. We do not discuss issues related to the definition of retirement, such as those highlighted by Chan and Huff Stevens (2008) concerning returns to work. Rather, we focus on areas in which improved understanding and practice are needed in order for those who are fully retired to face improved prospects.

LTC and Bequests as Family Matters

Our approach has emphasized the critical importance of LTC costs for retirement security, and we have suggested that insurance against these costs would be of great value to retirees. In practice, however, real-world sales of LTC insurance products are almost as low as sales of immediate annuities, which suggests that current LTC insurance contracts may be perceived by consumers as failing to provide effective insurance for retirees. More appealing long-term care products must respond to the reality that family members today bear the bulk of private long-term provision, implying that is vital to understand how families can and do contribute to long-term care arrangements for elders. Estimates of the incidence of caregiving within families vary across studies and datasets, but the National Alliance for Caregiving and AARP (2004) estimate that 44.4 million Americans are caregivers and provide that care in 22.9 million households in the USA (21 percent of households). The annual value of the services provided by such caregivers has been estimated at $257 billion (Arno 2002), which, if correct, would dwarf the value of formal LTC services.

These types of informal care arrangements may be a particularly important manifestation of the various problems that afflict the LTC insurance market (Consumer Reports 2003; Duhigg 2007). Among the most important defects of existing LTC policies is that typical LTC contracts are built on a standard reimbursement model, in which care expenses are incurred and submitted either by the policyholder or the care provider directly for reimbursement. These contracts hence involve some degree of risk that the insurer may deem some expenses/claims ineligible for coverage. Given the dynamic nature of medical science and treatment standards, in such long-term policies, how can one be assured that technological advances or the emergence of new or alternative treatments will be covered if needed? There is even some risk that the insurer will fail, although Lopes and Michaelides (2007) suggest that this factor alone is insufficient to explain low use of LTC services. However, if all such contracting problems taken together are perceived by retirees as significant, the only possible responses are to conserve resources and to rely in large part on the kindness of others to assist when the time comes.

In some cases, retaining assets may be in part a strategy that enables at least some compensation for informal caregivers who may be more willing to provide care if they do not have to do it 'for free.' Norton and Van Houtven (2005) conclude that parents providing inter vivos wealth transfers tend to provide those transfers to children who provide them with care. Clearly, one interpretation is that the transfers are informal, at least partial, payment for care services rendered; the older parent's transfer of wealth while alive may give care recipients some degree of control over how resources are spent.

If it is true that informal care arrangements are, in fact, how most of the infirm elderly receive care, it suggests that insurance arrangements better suited to supporting this existing infrastructure would be valuable. Research is needed to better understand how family structure feeds into the care-bequest complex, as this is a vital ingredient not only in financial innovation but also in public policy, where allowing for transfers to family members in exchange for care offers the potential to reduce the burden on the public purse.

The Role of Housing Wealth

Retirees must make many important portfolio decisions, some of which pertain to the general level of risk they bear; annuity products can have an important incentive effect in this regard (Milevsky and Kyrychenko 2008). Another issue pertains to the use of one's home to finance long-term care. Many retired households hold the majority of their wealth in the form of housing, and there is debate on the extent to which this should be treated as available for consumption in case of medical emergencies. In a recent study, Walker (2004) uses three waves of the Aging and Health Dynamics (AHEAD) survey data (1995, 1998, and 2000) to sharpen understanding of the circumstances under which housing equity is released by the elderly. She confirms that there are large declines in ownership rates for both married and single households late in the life cycle. For example, for married households with a younger spouse aged 80–81 at baseline, the rate of homeownership fell by 23 percentage points between 1995 and 2000. Particularly large declines were associated with demographic and health states such as ill health, nursing home stays lasting over 100 days, and death. These patterns suggest that there may be an intimate connection between the possible need for care and the need the elderly feel to own their homes 'free and clear'.

Psychological Factors

Psychological factors play an important role in retirement, with one of the most significant relating to decision-making competence. For instance, as noted above, one way to deliver resources for LTC care involves cash payments to qualified beneficiaries; this is appealing to many as it eliminates having to deal with insurers. On the other hand, beneficiaries can also be exploited by those who take over their decision-making authority (Stone 2001). (It is not clear that fears of abuse would be different in a reimbursement framework.) Some policymakers and consumer advocates worry that cash benefits provided to those with a condition requiring LTC services may not ultimately end up being used to obtain care, if unscrupulous service providers or even ill-intentioned relatives abuse the structure. Of course, this neglects the other side of the coin, which is the disregard of personal preference and limitation of individual choices.

Conclusions

Retirement security, and indeed financial security more generally, can be summed up simply as 'having the resources you need, when you need them.' Standard immediate life annuities are effective at providing a part of the resources needed in retirement, as they can help meet routine expenditures as long as the retiree is alive and healthy. But such products do little to deal with retirees' need for resources when emergencies arise, and they can even exacerbate financial distress in exigent situations. We have argued that better retirement security requires new mechanisms to enable retirees to bring additional resources to bear in emergencies, particularly given health shocks. Given the potential for a decline in the ability to make a choice among those who need LTC at the time they need it, the real design challenge is how to write effective contracts that work today to anticipate potential future decline, with sufficient safeguards and flexibility for change at later date. Clearly much research is required in this important area.

Acknowledgment

The authors are grateful to David McCarthy for helpful comments and suggestions.

Appendix

This appendix describes some technical details of our model. The interested reader should also consult Ameriks et al. (2007).

1. Preferences over consumption are described by a standard exponentially discounted, time-separable utility function with constant relative risk aversion based on the excess of consumption C over a subsistence level, C_{SUB}: $u(C) = (C - C_{SUB})^{1-\gamma}/(1 - \gamma)$. We set $C_{SUB} = 5$ (equivalent to \$5,000, as we measure dollar amounts in thousands) and $\gamma = 3$, and set the subjective time discount factor to 0.98.

2. End-of-life utility from bequests defined by the function $v(b)$:

   $v(b) = (\varpi/(1 - \gamma))((\varphi - C_{SUB}) + (b/\varpi))^{1-\gamma}$. We use the same coefficient of CRRA, $\gamma = 3$, over bequests as over consumption. We set $\varphi = 12$. [Note that Ameriks et al. (2007) use $\varphi = 6$ so that the values of ϖ here are analogous but not identical to those reported in that chapter.]

3. For consumption in non-LTC bankruptcy, we set $C_{BAN} = 8$. We assume all saved assets grow at a constant real rate of 2 percent per year, and we do not allow individuals to borrow (Ameriks et al. 2007 include a risky asset).

4. The age-dependent transition matrix for health states is calibrated to national data via 16 parameters (we do this exercise once for men

and once for women). The state of good health has no costs, the 'sick' state (sickness that does not require long-term care) has cost of $6,000 annually, long-term care costs are set to $50,000 annually, and we assume zero costs associated with death.

Notes

[1] Related work includes studies by Murtaugh, Spillman, and Warshawsky (2001); Warshawsky, Spillman, and Murtaugh (2002); and Spillman, Murtaugh, and Warshawsky (2003).

[2] The standard references are Yaari (1965) and Davidoff, Brown, and Diamond (2005).

[3] All cash flows are assumed to be in real, inflation-adjusted dollars; we do not model inflation risk.

[4] This approach is similar to the 'warm glow' specification of Andreoni (1989) with a Constant Elasticity of Substitution (CES) parameter matching that for consumption rather than the dynastic altruistic formulation implied by concern with children's utility per se.

[5] Taxes are ignored and we assume no income in the year of death.

References

Abel, Andrew (2003). 'Comment on Michael Hurd: "Bequests: By Accident or by Design?",' in A. H. Munnell and A. Sunden (eds.), *Death and Dollars: The Role of Gifts and Bequests in America.* Washington, DC: The Brookings Institution, pp. 118–26.

Ameriks, John (2002). *Recent Trends in the Selection of Retirement Income Streams Among TIAA-CREF Participants.* TIAA-CREF Research Dialogue, Issue no. 74.

—— Andrew Caplin, Steven Laufer, and Stijn Van Niewerburgh (2007). 'The Joy of Giving or Assisted Living? Using Strategic Surveys to Separate Bequest and Precautionary Motives,' NBER Working Paper no. 13105.

Andreoni, James (1989). 'Giving with Impure Altruism: Applications to Charity and Ricardian Equivalence,' *Journal of Political Economy*, 97:1447–58.

Arno, Peter S. (2002). 'Economic Value of Informal Caregiving,' Presentation before the Annual Meeting of the American Association of Geriatric Psychiatry. Orlando, FL, February 24.

Brown, Jeffrey (2001). 'Private Pensions, Mortality Risk, and the Decision to Annuitize,' *Journal of Public Economics*, 82(1): 29–62.

—— and Amy Finkelstein (2004). 'The Interaction of Public and Private Insurance: Medicaid and the Long-Term Care Insurance Market,' NBER Working Paper no. 10989.

——, Olivia S. Mitchell, James Poterba, and Mark Warshawsky (2001). *The Role of Annuity Markets in Financing Retirement.* Cambridge, MA: MIT Press.

Carroll, Christopher (2007). 'Why Do the Rich Save So Much?' Johns Hopkins Working Paper.

Chan, Sewin and Ann Huff Stevens (2008). 'Is Retirement Being Remade? Developments in Labor Market Patterns at Older Ages,' Chapter 2, this volume.

Congressional Budget Office (2004). *Financing Log-Term Care for the Elderly.* CBO Report. Congressional Budget Office: Washington, DC, April.

Consumer Reports (2003). 'Do You Need Long Term Care Insurance?' 68(11): 20–4.

Davidoff, Thomas, Jeffrey Brown and Peter Diamond (2005). 'Annuities and Individual Welfare,' *American Economic Review*, 95, December 2005: 1573–90.

De Nardi, Mariachristina (2004). 'Wealth Distribution, Intergenerational Links, and Estate Taxation,' *Review of Economic Studies*, 71(3): 743–68.

——, Eric French, and John Bailey Jones (2006). 'Differential Mortality, Uncertain Medical Expenses, and the Saving of Elderly Singles,' NBER Working Paper no. 12554.

Duhigg, Charles (2007). 'Aged, Frail and Denied Care by Their Insurers,' *The New York Times*, March 26: A1.

Dushi, Irena and Anthony Webb (2004). 'Household Annuitization Decisions: Simulations and Empirical Analyses,' *Journal of Pension Economics and Finance*, 3: 109–43.

French, Eric and John Bailey Jones (2004). 'On the Distribution and Dynamics of Health Care Costs,' *Journal of Applied Econometrics*, 19(6): 705–21.

Friedman, Benjamin M. and Mark J. Warshawsky (1988). 'Annuity Prices and Saving Behavior in the United States,' in Z. Bodie, J. Shoven, and D. Wise (eds.), *Pensions in the US Economy*. Chicago, IL: University of Chicago Press, pp. 53–77.

—— —— (1990). 'The Cost of Annuities: Implications for Saving Behavior and Bequests,' *Quarterly Journal of Economics*, 105(1): 135–54.

Hurd, Michael D. (1987). 'Savings of the Elderly and Desired Bequests,' *American Economic Review*, 77(3): 298–312.

Johnson, Richard W., Leonard E. Burman, and Deborah I. Kobes (2004). *Annuitized Wealth at Older Ages: Evidence from the Health and Retirement Study*. Washington, DC: The Urban Institute.

Kotlikoff, Laurence J. and Avia Spivak (1981). 'The Family as an Incomplete Annuities Market,' *Journal of Political Economy*, 89(April): 372–91.

—— and Lawrence H. Summers (1981). 'The Role of Intergenerational Transfers in Aggregate Capital Accumulation,' *Journal of Political Economy*, 89(4): 706–32.

Laitner, John and F. Thomas Juster (1996). 'New Evidence on Altruism: A Study of TIAA-CREF Retirees,' *American Economic Review*, 86(4): 893–908.

LIMRA International research (2006). 'Annuity Sales—4th Quarter 2006,' www.limra.com/pressroom/databank/.

Lopes, Paula and Alexander Michaelides (2007). 'Rare Events and Annuity Market Participation,' *Finance Research Letters*, 4(2): 82–91.

Milevsky, Moshe A. (2006). *The Calculus of Retirement Income*. New York: Cambridge University Press.

—— and Virginia R. Young (2007). 'The Timing of Annuitization: Investment Dominance and Mortality Risk,' *Insurance: Mathematics and Economics*, 40(1), January: 135–44.

—— and Vladyslav Kyrychenko (2008). 'Does a Variable Annuity Come with a License to Take on More Investment Risk?' this volume.

Milliman Consultants (2004). 'Long-Term Care Insurance—Combination Products. A Summary: April 2004,' www.milliman.com/expertise/life-financial/publications/rr/.

Mitchell, Olivia S., James Poterba, Mark Warshawsky, and Jeffrey Brown (1999). 'New Evidence on the Money's Worth of Individual Annuities,' *American Economic Review*, 89(5): 1299–318.

Murtaugh, Christopher M., Brenda C. Spillman, and Mark J. Warshawsky (2001). 'In Sickness and in Health: An Annuity Approach to Financing Long-term Care and Retirement Income,' *Journal of Risk and Insurance*, 68(2): 225–54.

National Alliance for Caregiving and AARP (2004). *Caregiving in the U.S.: Final Report*. caregiving.org/pubs/data.htm.

National Center for Health Statistics (2002). *Health, United States 2002: Chartbook on Trends in the Health of Americans*. Hyattsville, MD.

Norton, Edward and Courtney H. Van Houtven (2005). 'Intervivos Transfers and Exchange,' RAND Working paper. RAND Corporation.

Palumbo, Michael (1999). 'Uncertain Medical Expenses and Precautionary Saving Near the End Of the Life Cycle,' *Review of Economic Studies*, 66(2): 395–421.

Pauly, Mark V. (1990). 'The Rational Nonpurchase of Long-Term-Care Insurance,' *Journal of Political Economy*, 98(1): 153–68.

Sinclair, Sven and Kent Smetters (2004). 'Health Shocks and the Demand for Annuities,' CBO Technical Working Paper no. 2004–9. Washington, DC: Congressional Budget Office.

Spillman, Brenda C., Christopher M. Murtaugh, and Mark J. Warshawsky (2003). 'Policy Implications of an Annuity Approach to Integrating Long-term Care Financing and Retirement Income,' *Journal of Aging and Health*, 15(1): 45–73.

Stone, Robyn I. (2001). 'Providing Long-term Care Benefits in Cash: Moving to a Disability Model,' *Health Affairs*, 20(6): 96–108.

Turra, Cassio and Olivia Mitchell (2008). 'The Impact of Health Status and Out-of-Pocket Medical Expenditures on Annuity Valuation,' Chapter 10, this volume.

Walker, Lina (2004). 'Elderly Households and Housing Wealth: Do They Use It or Lose It?' Working paper, Michigan Retirement Research Center, University of Michigan.

Warshawsky, Mark J., Brenda C. Spillman, and Christopher M. Murtaugh (2002). 'Integrating Life Annuities and Long-term Care Insurance: Theory, Evidence, Practice and Policy,' in Z. Bodie, B. Hammond, and O. Mitchell (eds.), *Innovations in Retirement Financing*. Philadelphia, PA: University of Pennsylvania Press, pp. 198–221.

Yaari, Menahem E. (1965). 'Uncertain Lifetime, Life Insurance, and the Theory of the Consumer,' *Review of Economic Studies*, 32(2): 137–50.

Chapter 12

Asset Allocation within Variable Annuities: The Impact of Guarantees

Moshe A. Milevsky and Vladyslav Kyrychenko

Variable annuities (VAs) are close cousins of mutual funds, which bundle individual securities such as stocks and bonds into diversified units or trusts. Nevertheless, they are formally classified as insurance policies, since they are sold by insurance companies and contain insurance guarantees, in addition to being registered as securities. The most recent generation of variable annuity contracts has been financially engineered to provide a range of income guarantees meant to protect the policyholder against what the industry has coined the 'sequence of returns' risk. This refers to the chance that a retirement portfolio from which cash is being withdrawn suffers early losses. The common denominator of all these insurance riders is that they contain an implicit put option on financial markets plus some form of longevity insurance, akin to a pure life annuity. Of course, using the concept of put-call parity, they can also be viewed as call options to annuitize at a variable strike price. It is estimated that ~70 to 80 percent of VAs currently sold contain these living benefit riders, for a total of around $100 billion.

The promotional material for such products often claims that these guarantees should induce purchasers to take on more financial risk than they normally would without these guarantees. In fact, some of these products are referred to as a 'bond substitute' within a diversified portfolio, or even as a risk-free instrument. This chapter explores these new products using a unique database of policyholder behavior supplied by the Life Insurance Marketing Research Association (LIMRA). We show that VA policyholders are indeed adopting more aggressive allocations (i.e., higher equity exposures) when these riders are actually selected. We also examine the theoretical merits of this advice by deriving the optimal asset allocation—under a stylized model of these products—in the presence of these optional riders.[1]

In what follows, we review some of the relevant academic literature on the topic of portfolio choice over the life cycle. Next, we describe our data and provide summary results. The subsequent section provides an analytic model of portfolio choice in the presence of these guarantees, and a section offers conclusions and additional observations.

Background

As of early 2007, over US $1.2 trillion has been invested in VAs in the USA, with gross annual sales in the hundred billion dollar range; clearly it is a substantial market. VAs have long provided tax-sheltered growth and deferral; currently they also embed a number of put-like derivatives that provide guarantees on the account value. Like all insurance riders, and in contrast to standard exchange traded options, insurance companies charge for this downside protection by deducting an ongoing fraction of assets as opposed to an up-front fee. These unique features differentiate the pricing of this derivative security from the standard Black-Scholes approach where the option premiums are paid up front and in advance. (This will be important later when we examine optimal portfolio allocations.)

In what follows, we focus on a type of rider called the Guaranteed Minimum Income Benefit (GMIB). The mechanics of this option are explained analytically below, but for now it is important to know that the essence of a GMIB consists of a market put option that allows the holder of the VA to annuitize the account at a guaranteed rate—which then provides a guaranteed level of lifetime income.[2] At the point of purchase, the investor may select the GMIB; this rider gives the holder the ability to annuitize some minimally guaranteed amount at some contractually guaranteed rate. Thus, for example, if a $10,000 premium were placed into a variable annuity, the insurance company might guarantee that at least $15,000 worth of life-annuity income can be purchased in 10 years. The purchase price (or annuity factor) would be specified within the contract, for example $20 per dollar of lifetime income. Thus this contract would guarantee a life annuity of $15,000/$20 = $750 per year in the worst case scenario; if the market value of the (subaccounts within the) variable annuity were worth more than $15,000 in 10 years, the policyholder could annuitize the market value at *market* annuity rates.

A number of recent papers have extended the set of decisions included in the portfolio choice problem to highlight the interaction and the risks faced by the household, broadly defined.[3] The common denominator in these studies, and an oft-debated question, is how portfolio allocations to risky assets (stocks) should evolve with investors' age. Finance practitioners often recommend lowering the equity content of one's portfolio with increasing age. Much of this is at the heart of the life-cycle funds recently promoted by many mutual fund companies. A popular rule of thumb is to have the share of equities equal to 100 minus the investor's age.

By contrast, academic analysts have built on Merton's classical result (1969, 1971) that age should *not* matter in the absence of human capital considerations. Several authors who include human capital in their models by and large support the recommendation to decrease equity share in the portfolio with increasing age, although the generated profiles are not necessarily monotonic.[4] Other stylized facts have also emerged regarding the determinants of the optimal equity share in investors' portfolios with age. For instance, most document the importance of a declining age-equity share profile.[5] Others document a hump-shaped pattern, with a declining part starting at the ages of 50–60.[6]

Empirical Methods

In what follows, we use data containing VA policy purchase information on 812,367 individual variable annuity contracts collected by LIMRA. That organization gathered contract and product information from 10 member life-insurance firms which sold variable annuity policies during the period January 2000–June 2004; these policies had to be in force as of June 2004 and had to *offer* at least one guaranteed living benefit (GLB) rider at the time of purchase. This data-set has several advantages compared to commonly used financial micro-level survey information such as the Survey of Consumer Finances (SCF) and the Panel Study of Income Dynamics (PSID). First, LIMRA's data-set has a definite size advantage, as it provides information on more than 812,000 annuity contracts. In comparison, PSID follows only about 8,000 families while the SCF contacts some 4,000 households in its triennial surveys. Second, LIMRA's information comes directly from insurance firms' original contracts, so they are much more accurate than self-reported information from household surveys. Third, the LIMRA data provide much greater detail with respect to asset allocation choices (e.g., amounts invested in small-cap, medium-cap, large-cap, or international stock funds, investment grade or high-yield bond funds, and balanced funds). Finally, and most importantly, the LIMRA data are unique in providing information for asset allocation within variable annuities with and without GLB riders.

Of course, as Campbell (2006) points out, there is no perfect source of household financial data. To this end, the LIMRA data do not include comprehensive information about investors' personal characteristics and other investment accounts. What the LIMRA files do provide is some 60 variables about investor and contract characteristics including the investor's age, sex, and state of residence. We also have data on the investor's account value and how it is invested, the distribution intermediary channel, whether a GLB rider was selected, and the features of each type of GLB rider. Records were eliminated with missing age information and those records for which the values of different sub-accounts did not add up to the account value; this reduced our sample from 812,367 to 679,579 observations. We further limit our sample to those investors who (*a*) either selected no GLB rider; or (*b*) selected the GMIB only. We do this for two reasons. First, the GMIB is the closest equivalent to a life annuity with longevity insurance [compared to other GLB riders, such as the Guaranteed Minimum Withdrawal Benefit (GMWB) or Guaranteed Minimum Accumulation Benefit (GMAB)]. Second, the GMIB is by far the most popular GLB rider selected by individuals. Of all contacts we examined, where at least one GLB rider was selected, only a GMIB was selected 95 percent of the time. These exclusions produce a 'clean' data-set of 660,336 observations with either GMIB or no GLB riders selected.

Empirical Findings

Next, we describe the relationship between age and asset allocation for investors who selected GMIBs, compared to those who did not select any GLB. More specifically, we consider the percentage of the investor's VA account held in high and medium risk (HMR) assets, which we describe below as 'risky assets,' as a function of the investor's age. The following funds are included in the HMR category: large-cap, mid-cap, and small-cap stock funds, high-yield bond fund, balanced fund, specialty/sector fund, and international equity fund. Conversely low risk (LR) investments are those held in investment-grade bond funds, money-market funds, and fixed funds.

Next, we analyze the two companies referred to here as companies A and B with the highest number of annuity policies in our sample, 170,462 and 126,118 annuity contracts, respectively. These two companies combined represent 52 percent of VAs with selected GMIBs in the LIMRA sample. Figure 12-1 and Table 12-1 describe the percentages invested in HRM assets by age groups. In both cases, we present two age versus HMR results: one for investors who selected GMIB and another for those who selected no GLB rider. For company A, for example, investors who did not select any GLB rider have a declining percentage invested in HMR assets by age. The decline is almost monotonic, from 77 percent for the under-age 40 group, to 54 percent for the over-age 80 group. A very different profile emerges for investors who selected GMIB: here, the percentage invested in HMR assets declines with age much more slowly to age 71–75, and then it starts to rise. The GMIB group's exposure to HMR assets is much higher, being in the 80–86 percent range. We conclude that additional HMR (risk) exposure in the group of GMIB selectors in company A is between 11 and 31 percent.

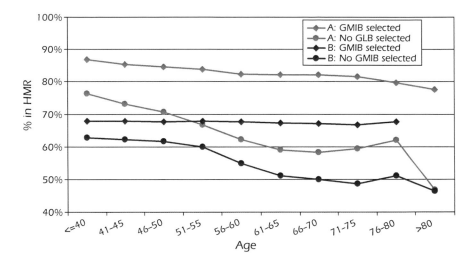

Figure 12-1. Allocation to risky assets, with and without GMIB option. *Source:* Authors' computations. *Note:* This figure displays the percent of the variable annuity sub-account within the policy sold by Companies A and B allocated to high and medium risk (HMR) asset classes, when the GMIB is selected and when no Guaranteed Living Benefit (GLB RIDER) is selected.

The impact of age on the HMR allocation graph is similar for company B. The allocation to risky assets for investors who selected a GMIB is substantially higher and again declines with age much more slowly than for investors not selecting a GLB rider. Interestingly, the total share of assets invested in HMR assets is significantly lower for company B than for A at all age groups. Furthermore, in company B, for investors who selected GMIB, this share is very stable regardless of age. These differences are probably attributable to the different investment choices available in each company, as well as to different asset allocation restrictions applied when a GMIB rider is selected. Additional HMR exposure in the group of GMIB selectors in company B is between 5 and 18 percent.

Finally, Figure 12-2 illustrates how the selection of HMR versus LR assets varies with the distribution channel. What we mean by distribution channel is the type of intermediary selling the variable annuity product to the customer. The patterns show stark differences in the HMR equity exposure, both with and without the selection of the GMIB, depending on whether the VA was purchased through a bank, an independent financial adviser, a wirehouse broker, or some other source. For example, in company A, policies with the highest allocation to risky assets, with or without a GMIB, were sold by financial planners. Policies sold through banks have the biggest

TABLE 12-1 Fraction of Variable Annuity Portfolio Held in High or Medium Risk (HMR) Assets

Investor Age	Company A			Company B		
	% in HMR		Additional HMR Exposure (%)	% in HMR		Additional HMR Exposure (%)
	GMIB only	No GLB RIDER		GMIB only	No GLB RIDER	
≤40	86.90	76.30	10.60	67.80	62.80	5.00
41–45	85.30	73.10	12.20	67.80	62.20	5.60
46–50	84.60	70.60	14.00	67.60	61.70	5.90
51–55	83.80	66.70	17.10	67.90	59.90	8.00
56–60	82.40	62.20	20.30	67.60	54.90	12.70
61–65	82.00	59.00	23.00	67.30	51.10	16.10
66–70	82.10	58.30	23.80	67.10	50.00	17.20
71–75	81.60	59.30	22.20	66.80	48.70	18.10
76–80	79.70	61.90	17.80	67.60	51.10	16.40
>80	77.50	46.70	30.80	N/A	46.40	N/A
Total no. of policies	104,377	66,085		89,949	36,169	

Source: Authors' computations, see text.

Notes: This table presents the percentage invested in high and medium risk (HMR) assets for Companies A and B, for 10 age groups in five year groupings. The first column for each company represents the percentage allocation to HMR by investors who selected a Guaranteed Minimum Income Benefit (GMIB); the second column represents allocation to HMR by those who did not select any guaranteed living benefit (GLB rider). The table shows that VA policyholders hold more HMR assets when they select a GMIB. For company A, this ranges from 10–30%; for company B this ranges from 5–16%. Note that in the case of company B, contracts were not issued above the age of 80. The HMR allocations are not directly comparable across companies due to different investment options.

difference between the percentages allocated to HMR for investors who selected GMIB compared to those who did not. In company B, the VAs with the highest HMR allocations (where no GLB rider was selected) were sold by stockbrokers, while the policies which included GMIBs were sold by financial planners. Here the largest gap in allocations to risky assets was in the policies sold by stockbrokers. Of course, this is not to say that any of the channels necessarily influence or cause the particular allocation differences, as this could arise from differences in the clientele. People who are more 'conservative' and hence likely to hold less HMR assets might be more likely to purchase the VA through a bank, and vice versa. In our view, the most likely explanation for the asset allocation distribution channel effect is likely to be the type of customer who uses these intermediaries, as opposed to the intermediaries themselves.

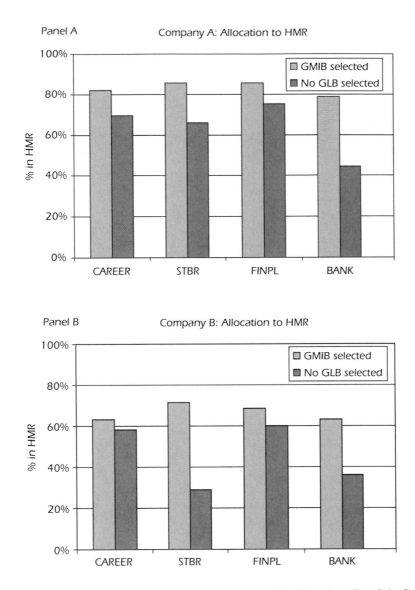

Figure 12-2. How distribution channel influences risky allocation. Panel A: Company A's allocation to high and medium risk (HMR) assets. Panel B: Company B's allocation to high and medium risk (HMR) assets. *Source*: Authors' computations. *Notes*: Funds regarded as high or medium risk include large-cap, mid-cap, and small-cap stock funds, high yield bond fund, balanced fund, specialty/sector fund, international equity fund. The rest of the fund classes available (including investment-grade bond fund, money-market fund, and fixed fund) are considered as low-risk assets. The HMR allocations are not directly comparable across companies due to different investment options. Variable annuities manufactured by Companies A and B can be purchased via several distribution channels including career insurance agents (CAREER), stockbrokers (STBR, including wirehouses), financial planners (FINPL), and banks. The two panels illustrate the impact of this distribution channel on the allocation to HMR assets, both with and without guarantees.

Multivariate Statistical Analysis

Next, we evaluate whether the relationship between age and HMR assets holdings observed in our previous tabulations is robust to controls for other variables. Accordingly, we employ a linear regression model where the dependent variable is the percentage invested in HMR assets. Control variables include the investor's age, as well as several others including age squared (AGE^2), to capture possible nonlinearities. We also control on the log of the investor's account value (LOGACC) as a proxy for investor's wealth; prior studies have reported that wealthier investors have more aggressive asset allocations. The investor's sex (MALE) is included as previous research has indicated that men tend to be more overconfident than women and so may invest proportionally more in risky assets. A qualitative variable (IRA) captures the tax status of the account. Since investments inside IRAs are tax sheltered, we might expect to see a higher share of fixed income assets in those accounts because interest income is taxed at a higher rate than dividends or capital gains on stocks. Of course, variable annuities are already tax-sheltered investments, so theoretically it should not make a difference in terms of the tax implications. Following our earlier discussion, we include a control for the distribution channel, or the intermediary by which the variable annuity contract was purchased. Four qualitative variables (CAREER, STBR, FINPL, and BANK) indicate, respectively, that the sale was made via an insurance agent, stockbroker, financial planner, or bank employee (the reference category is independent agent). These are included to allow for the possible impact and influence of the intermediary on the percentage of risky assets selected. Finally, we allow for company-specific controls by including seven company indicator variables for those firms that sold VA policies with GMIB riders (the omitted category is the three companies with the lowest number of VA contracts with GMIB.)

Linear regression results are presented for two subsamples: one includes only variable annuity contracts without any GLB rider (Model 1), and the second includes only those contracts where variable annuity holders selected a particular type of GLB rider, namely, the GMIB (Model 2). Table 12-2 summarizes findings. Most importantly, the negative coefficient on AGE indicates that the share invested in risky assets declines with age for both subsamples. Nevertheless, it declines much faster for those investors who did not select any GLB rider, as the AGE coefficient in Model 1 is three times larger (in absolute value) than in Model 2; their difference is highly significant based on t-test.[7] Moreover, AGE^2 coefficient is negative in Model 1 but positive in Model 2. This suggests that the share invested in risky assets is a concave function of age which declines faster at older ages for investors who do not select any GLB rider. For those who select GMIB

TABLE 12-2 Factors Associated with the Fraction of the VA Account Held in High or Medium Risk (HMR) Assets: Multivariate Regression Results

Variable	With GMIB		Without GLB RIDER	
	Estimate	t-value	Estimate	t-value
Intercept	0.913*	59.22	0.992*	131.92
LOGACC	−0.002*	−5.66	−0.018*	−30.42
MALE	0.012*	16.45	0.026*	18.24
AGE	−0.002*	−43.09	−0.004*	−76.1
AGE^2	1.8E–06*	5.57	−3.5E-06*	−8.02
IRA	−0.004*	−5.59	−0.010*	−6.37
CAREER	−0.039*	−8.8	0.076*	18.82
STBR	0.011*	2.6	0.0230*	7.27
FINPL	0.003	0.57	0.147*	31.75
BANK	−0.058*	−13.02	−0.143*	−34.42
C1	−0.133*	−9.26	−0.093*	−23.29
C2	0.038*	2.67	0.081*	21.68
C3	0.088*	6.14	0.201*	38.11
C7	0.029*	1.98	0.165*	44.29
C8	−0.049*	−3.33	−0.045*	−9.91
C9	−0.073*	−5.03	0.232*	48.5
C10	0.106*	7.38	0.206*	47.94
Adjusted R^2	0.154		0.159	
No. of observations	368,005		272,564	

Source: Authors' calculations. See text for variable definitions.

Notes: OLS regression estimates provided, where the dependent variable is the percentage invest in the HMR portfolio (see Table 12-1). The first regression is based on the subsample of variable annuity policies where no guaranteed living benefits (GLB rider) was selected; the sample pools data from seven firms. The second regression uses the subsample where longevity-put was selected; the pooled sample includes 10 companies (see text). We control for company differences using dummy variables representing the seven companies where many selected GMIBs. The omitted category is the other three companies.

* Significant at the 5% level.

products, however, the age decline is attenuated, and it even reverses at older ages. These results are generally in line with Figure 12-1.

Besides age, several other variables prove to be significant in explaining the percentage of an account invested in HMR assets in both models. We find that men do invest their VAs more aggressively than women, by holding more equity. VAs, which are part of a tax-sheltered (IRA) plan, have a lower share of risky assets and a higher proportion of low-risk bonds. This would be an intuitively pleasing result—that is, bonds are more likely to be placed in tax shelters—were it not for the fact that variable annuities are already tax sheltered. An unexpected finding is that account size (wealth level) is negatively associated with an allocation to HMR (risky) assets. The distribution channels variables lead one to conclude that, for investors who do not select a GLB rider, riskier portfolios result from having financial planners provide the product. For those who did select the GMIB, however, stockbrokers are those associated with relatively riskier asset allocations. In results not reported here, we also show that the company controls are statistically significant.

To explore further some of these empirical patterns, we next repeat the regression analysis for the two companies having the largest number of variable annuity policies. Results appear in Table 12-3, where we see that the age/equity patterns are similar to those in Table 12-2. That is, the share of risky assets declines with age much faster for investors who did not select a Guaranteed Living Benefit. Conversely, for investors who selected GMIB, the negative age effect is attenuated. Male investors generally allocate more to risky assets. In terms of account market value, however, the results are different depending on the company. In company A, the market value of the account is positively related to the share of risky assets, whereas in company B, the relationship is negative (similar to the result for the whole sample). Interestingly—and in contrast to the pooled results—in both companies the share invested in HMR is higher when the variable annuity is within tax-deferred account, but only when the GMIB is not selected. But when the GMIB is selected, the IRA status is associated with 'more bonds' and less HMR asset classes.

A Model of Portfolio Choice with a GMIB

Next, we construct a stylized model of portfolio choice in the presence of a GMIB option, so as to derive a measure for the amount of 'extra risk' a rational (utility-maximizing) investor would be willing to take when granted a GMIB option that protected him from downside risk. We do so by postulating a generic investor with W_0 of initial wealth initially optimally allocated α^* to risky assets, and $1 - \alpha^*$ to safe assets. At the outset, we assume that these allocations take place within a VA but one which lacks extra riders. The risky and safe assets correspond to the HMR and LR funds described in the earlier section. By selecting this particular allocation, assumed to be optimal, the investor has revealed his explicit risk preferences. We further assume constant relative risk aversion (CRRA) and lognormal asset returns, as per Merton (1969), the implied coefficient of relative risk-aversion γ will be equal to $(\mu - r)/\sigma^2$, where μ is the expected return, σ is the volatility and r is the risk-free rate of return. For example, an investor with a preexisting

TABLE 12-3 Factors Associated with the Fraction of the VA Account Held in High or Medium Risky (HMR) Assets: Multivariate Regression Results for Companies A and B Separately

Variable	Company A				Company B			
	With GMIB		Without GLB RIDER		With GMIB		Without GLB RIDER	
	Estimate	t-value	Estimate	t-value	Estimate	t-value	Estimate	t-value
Intercept	0.639*	83.56	0.514*	28.07	0.948*	111.09	0.985*	60.72
LOGACC	0.003*	5.12	0.005*	3.71	−0.007*	−10.24	−0.022*	−16.46
MALE	0.004*	2.76	0.004	1.15	0.020*	13.28	0.036*	12.18
AGE	−0.001*	−11.21	−0.003*	−20.62	−0.002*	−24.03	−0.005*	−37.13
AGE^2	1.7E-06*	2.79	−9.1E-06*	−8.7	3.8E-06*	5.69	−9.3E-06*	−10.1
IRA	−0.005*	−3.14	0.008*	2.1	−0.005*	−3.09	0.014*	4.14
CAREER	−0.002	−0.7	0.178*	22.99	0.027*	12.09	0.217*	56.23
STBR	0.078*	22.29	−0.059*	−6.94	0.069*	27.83	0.239*	58.29
FINPL	0.051*	18.67	0.236*	31.98	0.069*	27.84	0.310*	63.13
Adjusted R^2	0.017		0.121		0.018		0.1178	
No. of observations	89,947		36,165		103,348		65,855	

Source: Authors' computations. See text for variable definitions.

Notes: OLS regression estimates provided, where the dependent variable is the percentage invest in the HMR portfolio (see Table 12-1). The first regression for each company is based on the subsample of variable annuity policies where no guaranteed living benefits (GLB) were selected. The second regression is based on the subsample from the same company where longevity-put was selected. While some coefficient signs vary depending on the specific company studied, note that the age variable is always negative (with and without the GMIB) and the Male variable is positive (with and without the GMIB).

* Significant at the 5% level.

allocation of 50 percent HMR and 50 percent LR reveals a risk aversion of exactly four, when the expected return from the HMR investments is 9 percent, the volatility is 15 percent and the risk-free (LR) rate is 4.5 percent.

We then take this so-called $a^* \Rightarrow \gamma$ investor and evaluate how he might change his allocation to the HMR asset class, if he were to hypothetically be granted the annuity put option underlying the GMIB. More specifically, let a^{**} denote the new (presumably) optimal allocation to the HMR asset class when the GMIB is 'wrapped' around the investment account. Recall that the a^* is the original (optimal) allocation in the absence of this put option guarantee. The difference between a^{**} and a^*, which we define as ε, is the incremental allocation that is theoretically justifiable, based on the presence of the GMIB. We seek to investigate the behavior of this ε quantity as a function of the various underlying contractual parameters, such as the strike price of the embedded option, the preexisting allocation a^*, and other exogenous capital market parameter assumptions.

Recall the GMIB guarantees the ability to convert or annuitize (in the worst case scenario) the guaranteed amount $W_0 e^{\eta T}$ at a prespecified rate denoted by g_x, where η is a guaranteed investment return and T is the contract horizon. Alternatively, of course, the investor can annuitize the account value $\tilde{W}_T$ at the then-market rate denoted by $\bar{a}_x$. The quantity $\tilde{W}_T$ is obviously unknown in advance and depends on both the selected allocations of the investor and the random performance of underlying market sub-accounts. The subscript x on both annuity factors denotes the age at which the life annuity is priced or issued, for example, age 70 or 75.[8] Typical market values of $\bar{a}_x$ under the current interest rate environment might be \$10.2 at the age of $x = 70$, 8.44 at the age of $x = 75$ and 6.72 at the age of $x = 80$. This is the cost of \$1 of annual lifetime income, at the various purchase ages.

One can also think of g_x as the strike price of the GMIB option, although it is not really a put option to sell in the conventional sense, but more of an exchange rate between a guaranteed amount and a lifetime income. Either way the GMIB option pays off, or promises lifetime income in the amount:

$$I = \max\left[\frac{W_0 e^{\eta T}}{g_x}, \frac{\tilde{W}_T(a)}{a_x} \right] \tag{12-1}$$

The justification for this is as follows. If the underlying market and sub-accounts perform poorly (i.e., he earns less than η per annum during the T-year waiting period), the investor is guaranteed the ability to annuitize $W_0 e^{\eta T}$ at the guaranteed annuity factor rate of g_x. On the other hand, if the market value of the account $\tilde{W}_T(a)$ at time T is greater than the guaranteed amount $W_0 e^{\eta T}$, the investor can simply annuitize the (higher) account value, at the-then market annuity rates $\bar{a}_x$. In fact, he does not have to purchase this life annuity from the company that issued the GMIB at all. Instead, he could take his money anywhere and annuitize in the open market.

Note also that $\tilde{W}_T(a)$ is partially under the control of the investor and depends on the asset allocation vector a, which is to be determined. Another way to express this quantity is $\tilde{W}_T(a^* + \varepsilon)$, where a^* was the original allocation in the absence of the GMIB option. Finally, we multiply the guaranteed lifetime income denoted by I, by the then-market annuity factor $\bar{a}_x$ to convert this flow into a lump-sum value at the horizon time T. The objective is to locate an asset allocation vector a^{**}, or incremental allocation ε that maximizes expected utility of wealth:

$$U^{**} = \max_a E[U(I\bar{a}_x)] \tag{12-2}$$

The intuition is as follows. Imagine there is a liquid secondary market for guaranteed lifetime income. In theory, the annuitant could de-annuitize the guaranteed income I and obtain a lump sum in the amount of $I\bar{a}_x$. Thus, the true expected utility of wealth is as displayed in Equation (12-2). Indeed, if the option expires out-of-the-money and the market value of the lifetime income $\tilde{W}_T(a)/\bar{a}_x$ is greater than the guaranteed amount of lifetime income $W_0 e^{\eta T}/g_x$, the mark-to-market value is simply $\tilde{W}_T(a)$ itself. On the other hand, if the option expires in-the-money, the guaranteed lifetime income will kick in and provide income in the amount of $W_0 e^{\eta T}/g_x$ and the market value of this income stream will be: $\bar{a}_x W_0 e^{\eta T}/g_x$. The objective then is to find an asset allocation that maximizes the expected utility of this uniquely defined wealth.

Under the (new) optimal allocation, the expected return from the investment account will be $a^{**}\mu + (1 - a^{**})r - f$, where μ denotes the expected return from the HMR funds, r denotes the LR rate, and the new symbol f denotes the extra fee (a.k.a. mortality and expense charge) for the GMIB. The optimal allocation and the incremental justifiable risk allocations have been generated using a simulation approach, since an analytic approach is impossible and a numerical implementation is equally cumbersome. More specifically, our computational approach conducts simulations for which the GMIB annuity factors g_x are within the vicinity of market annuity factors $\bar{a}_x$, which can be viewed as a fair GMIB case. We also generated a few in which the GMIB annuity factors were set back relative to market-based annuity rates, so that: $g_x < \bar{a}_x$. For the majority of our simulations, we assumed that the guaranteed return η embedded within the GMIB was 6 percent per annum. Finally, we start with a 55-year-old investor who purchases a GMIB with a 15-year horizon. At the age of 70, he plans with 100 percent certainty to annuitize the account, either under the guarantee

Table 12-4 Optimal Allocations to GMIB Option

% in HMR Without GMIB a^*	Implied Risk Aversion γ	% in HMR with GMIB	CE with GMIB (%) $U^{-1}(U^{**})$	CE without GMIB (%) $U^{-1}(U^*)$
GMIB Annuity Factor $g_{70} = 15$				
30	6.67	100	230	140
40	5.00	100	250	17
50	4.00	100	260	210
GMIB Annuity Factor $g_{70} = 20$				
30	6.67	40–50	200	200
40	5.00	70–100	220	200
50	4.00	100	240	210
GMIB Annuity Factor $g_{70} = 25$				
30	6.67	35–40	200	200
4	5.00	50–60	210	210
50	4.00	70–100	230	220

Source: Authors' computations.

Note: This table illustrates the change in optimal asset allocation when a GMIB is offered on a VA account, as a function of the GMIB annuity factor. For example, an investor with a 40% allocation to risky equity (defined as HMR) reveals a coefficient of relative risk aversion of five. If this individual is offered a GMIB option at the price of $20 per dollar of lifetime income, he will change his allocation to something between 70% and 100% HMR because of the downside protection. This investor will also experience an increase in certainty equivalent (CE) utility from 200% of initial wealth to 220% of initial wealth. In other words this particular GMIB is welfare enhancing. The underlying parameters were calibrated to fit the historical risk and return parameters of the variable annuity sub-accounts.

(if the HMR asset earns less than 6 percent over the next 15 years) or under the market rates, generating lifetime income of I.

The results for the allocation a^{**}, which maximizes the CRRA utility function relative to the original allocations a^*, appear in Table 12-4. One striking feature is that the 'positivity' of the ε variable—the justification for additional risk exposure—depends on the strike price of the option. The strike price within a GMIB is not immediately obvious and unrelated to the contract's guaranteed investment return (η), which was in the vicinity of 6 percent for most of our examples. (Note that sometimes this is expressed with simple compounding, in which case the value must be converted to the true annualized return.) Our point here is more than just that the 'devil is in the details.' Rather, there can be remarkable heterogeneity between various GMIB contract provisions that all appear to offer a 6 percent guaranteed return.

In the course of extensive simulations to locate the optimal allocation, several interesting results were observed. First, in many instances, the optimal allocations are 'corner solutions'. What this means is that when the GMIB annuity factor is favorable to the policyholder, he tends to take on as much risk as allowed by the contract. In a sense, the policyholder has been granted a put option and he maximizes the personal value of this option by taking on as much risk as possible. This is consistent with the empirical evidence presented above (though it assumes full annuitization which we are unable to determine given our data). On the other hand, when the contractual provisions are less favorable, that is, with a higher parameter value of g_x, the optimal allocations in the presence of the GMIB are no longer corner solutions. In some cases, the additional risk exposure levels are only on the order of 5–10 percent.

Conclusion

Portfolio choice and optimal asset allocation over the life cycle are topics that continue to attract both academic and practical interest. This chapter examines how actual allocations to risky assets change when individuals are given 'downside protection' in the form of options to anuitize. Specifically, we assess asset allocation inside variable annuity products in which certain insurance riders are available that give investors the option to annuitize at some favorable rate. The data-set we use includes over half a million policyholder accounts, from age 40 to 80, and it permits us to observe their asset allocations, and whether certain riders were selected.

We show that individuals will invest more aggressively when they are granted this type of put option. Indeed, to anyone trained in the valuation and pricing of American-style derivative securities, this notion is straight-forward. However, what is less obvious is that these put options are not money-back guarantees but rather they are contingent on annuitization. In other words, the only way to exercise this put is to irreversibly annuitize the contract (at the strike price) in exchange for lifetime income. Thus, if there is some exogenous propensity to avoid annuitization despite its welfare-enhancing properties, it remains to be seen whether these put holders will in fact exercise their options if-and-when they expire in the money.

Our simple model of optimal asset allocation within a GMIB structure only scratches the surface of more accurate representations of the dynamic control problem. Future research should incorporate the American-style optionality of when to annuitize, as well as the stochasticity of interest rates and perhaps even the credit risk of the insurer, in the event the market collapses. Nevertheless, our result appears robust: more risk is acceptable provided the strike price is sufficiently near the money.

Acknowledgments

Both authors acknowledge funding from the IFID Centre and are especially grateful to LIMRA for providing access to their data. The authors also acknowledge helpful comments and discussions with Shlomo BenArtzi, Matthew Drinkwater, Huaxiong Huang, Thomas Salisbury, and Eric Sondergeld.

Notes

[1] This research sits squarely within the portfolio choice literature since we are investigating optimal asset allocations in the presence of various guarantees. We are aware, of course, that in some cases additional risky asset exposure might not be justified.

[2] The GMIB is closely related to the GMWB, which is not the focus of this analysis. The latter is yet another form of put option contained and selected within many variable annuities. Milevsky and Salisbury (2006) provide a separate analysis of GMWB-based products. Both GMIB and GMWB fall in the category of Guaranteed Living Benefits (GLB). A GLB rider is essentially an insurance rider which provides some sort of portfolio insurance for a VA policyholder, but only once the variable annuity is converted into income.

[3] Thus, for example, Goetzmann (1993), Yao and Zhang (2005) as well as Cocco (2005) focus on the role of the housing portfolio; Campbell and Cocco (2003) focus on optimal mortgage choices; Cairns, Blake, and Dowd (2006) examine portfolio choice in defined contribution pension plans, Sundaresan and Zapatero (1997) assess the role of DB pensions, while Dybvig and Liu (2004), and Bodie et al. (2004) model the impact of flexible retirement dates; Jagannathan and Kocherlakota (1996) and Viceira (2001) stress the impact of aging; Faig and Shum (2002) are motivated by the demand for illiquid assets; Koo (1998) as well as Hakansson (1969) and Davis and Willen (2000) model the role of labor income; Dammon, Spatt, and Zhang (2001) focus their attention on capital gains and income taxes; Heaton and Lucas (2000) focus on the role of background risk. Others go back to basics and extend portfolio choice models to include more sophisticated (and realistic) processes for investment returns, such as Chacko and Viceira (2005) or time-varying and mean-reverting risk premiums, such as Kim and Omberg (1996) or Detemple, Garcia, and Rindisbacher (2003).

[4] See, for instance, Bodie, Merton, and Samuelson (1992); Horneff et al. (2007); Jagannathan and Kocherlakota (1996); Cocco, Gomes, and Maenhout (2005); and Gomes and Michaelides (2005).

[5] See, for instance, Bodie and Crane (1997), VanDerhei et al. (1999), Agnew, Balduzzi, and Sunden (2003), and Curcuru et al. (2009).

[6] Examples of these would include Yoo (1994), Bertaut and Starr-McCluer (2001), and Faig and Shum (2006). It is important to remind the reader that Ameriks and Zeldes (2004) show that the age to equity share profile is sensitive to the model specification. In fact, any regression explaining portfolio choice with age can include only two of the possible three variables: age, time, and cohort. While Ameriks and

Zeldes (2004) find a hump-shaped relationship in a regression with age and time effects, they report an increasing allocation to stocks/equity with age in a regression with age and cohort effects. The majority of researchers, however, consider a cohort effect the least significant among the three and make the assumption that it is equal to zero.

[7] To assess whether regression results overall are different for GMIB selectors versus nonselectors, we combine the two subsamples into one pooled sample and cannot reject the hypothesis that the age differences are statistically significant.

[8] We refer the interested reader to Milevsky (2006) for a detailed explanation of the actuarial pricing underlying the annuity.

References

Agnew, Julie, Pierluigi Balduzzi, and Annika Sunden (2003). 'Portfolio Choice and Trading in a Large 401(k) Plan,' *American Economic Review*, 93(1): 193–215.

Ameriks, John and Stephen P. Zeldes (2004). 'How Do Household Portfolio Shares Vary with Age?' Working Paper, Columbia University.

Bertaut, Carol and Martha Starr-McCluer (2001). 'Household Portfolios in the United States,' in L. Guiso, M. Haliassos, and T. Jappelli (eds.), *Household Portfolios*. Cambridge, MA: MIT Press, pp. 181–218.

Bodie, Zvi and Dwight B. Crane (1997). 'Personal Investing: Advice, Theory, and Evidence,' *Financial Analysts Journal*, 53(6): 13–23.

—— Robert C. Merton, and William F. Samuelson (1992). 'Labor Supply Flexibility and Portfolio Choice in a Life Cycle Model,' *Journal of Economic Dynamics and Control*, 16: 427–49.

—— Jerome B. Detemple, Susanne Otruba, and Stephan Walter (2004). 'Optimal Consumption—Portfolio Choices and Retirement Planning,' *Journal of Economic Dynamics and Control*, 28(6): 1013–226.

Cairns, Andrew, David Blake, and Kevin Dowd (2006). 'Stochastic Lifestyling: Optimal Dynamic Asset Allocation for Defined-Contribution Pension Plans,' *Journal of Economic Dynamics and Control*, 30(5): 843–77.

Campbell, John Y. (2006). 'Household Finance,' *Journal of Finance*, 61(4): 1553–604.

—— and João F. Cocco (2003). 'Household Risk Management and Optimal Mortgage Choice,' *Quarterly Journal of Economics*, 118: 1149–94.

Chacko, G. and Luis M. Viceira (2005). 'Dynamic Consumption and Portfolio Choice with Stochastic Volatility in Incomplete Markets,' *Review of Financial Studies*, 18(4): 1369–402.

Cocco, João F. (2005). 'Portfolio Choice in the Presence of Housing,' *Review of Financial Studies*, 18(2): 535–67.

—— Francisco J. Gomes, and Pascal J. Maenhout (2005). 'Consumption and Portfolio Choice over the Life Cycle,' *Review of Financial Studies*, 18(2): 491–533.

Curcuru, Stephanie, John Heaton, Deborah Lucas, and Damien Moore (2009). 'Heterogeneity and Portfolio Choice: Theory and Evidence,' in Y. Ait-Sahalia and L. P. Hansen (eds.), *Handbook of Financial Econometrics*. Amsterdam: Elsevier Science, forthcoming.

Dammon, Robert M., Chester S. Spatt, and Harold H. Zhang (2001). 'Optimal Consumption and Investment with Capital Gains Taxes,' *Review of Financial Studies*, 14: 583–616.

Davis, Steven J. and Paul Willen (2000). 'Occupation-level income shocks and asset returns: their covariance and implications for portfolio choice,' NBER Working Paper no. 7905. Cambridge, MA: National Bureau of Economic Research.

Detemple, Jérôme B., René Garcia, and Marcel Rindisbacher (2003). 'A Monte Carlo Method for Optimal Portfolios,' *Journal of Finance*, 58(1): 401–46.

Dybvig, Phillip H. and Hong Liu (2004). 'Lifetime consumption and investment: retirement and constrained borrowing,' Working Paper, Washington University.

Faig, Miquel and Pauline M. Shum (2002). 'Portfolio Choice in the Presence of Personal Illiquid Projects,' *Journal of Finance*, 57: 303–28.

—— —— (2006). 'What Explains Household Stock Holdings,' *Journal of Banking and Finance*, 30(9): 2579–97.

Goetzmann, William N. (1993). 'The Single Family Home in the Investment Portfolio,' *Journal of Real Estate Finance and Economics*, 6: 201–22.

Gomes, Francisco and Alexander Michaelides (2005). 'Optimal Life-Cycle Asset Allocation: Understanding the Empirical Evidence,' *Journal of Finance*, 55(2): 869–904.

Hakansson, Nils H. (1969). 'Optimal Investment and Consumption Strategies Under Risk, an Uncertain Lifetime, and Insurance,' *International Economic Review*, 10(3): 443–66.

Heaton, John and Deborah Lucas (2000). 'Portfolio Choice in the Presence of Background Risk,' *The Economic Journal*, 110: 1–26.

Horneff, Wolfram, Raimond Maurer, Olivia S. Mitchell, and Ivica Dus (2007). 'Following the Rules: Integrating Asset Allocation and Annuitization in Retirement Portfolios,' *Insurance: Mathematics and Economics*, 42(1): 396–408.

Jagannathan, Ravi and Narayana R. Kocherlakota (1996). 'Why Should Older People Invest Less in Stocks than Younger People?' *Federal Reserve Bank of Minneapolis Quarterly Review*, 20: 11–23.

Kim, Tong Suk and Edward Omberg (1996). 'Dynamic Non-Myopic Portfolio Behavior,' *Review of Financial Studies*, 9: 141–61.

Koo, Hyeng Keun (1998). 'Consumption and Portfolio Selection with Labor Income: A Continuous Time Approach,' *Mathematical Finance*, 8(1): 49–65.

Merton, Robert C. (1969). 'Lifetime Portfolio Selection Under Uncertainty: The Continuous Time Case,' *Review of Economic Studies*, 51: 247–57.

—— (1971). 'Optimum Consumption and Portfolio Rules in a Continuous Time Model,' *Journal of Economic Theory*, 3: 373–413.

Milevsky, Moshe A. (2006). *The Calculus of Retirement Income: Financial Models for Pension Annuities and Life Insurance.* Cambridge: Cambridge University Press.

—— and Thomas S. Salisbury (2006). 'Financial Valuation of Guaranteed Minimum Withdrawal Benefits (GMWBs),' *Insurance: Mathematics and Economics*, 38: 21–38.

Sundaresan, Suresh M. and Fernando Zapatero (1997). 'Valuation, Asset Allocation and Incentive Retirements of Pension Plans,' *Review of Financial Studies*, 10(3): 631–60.

VanDerhei, Jack, Russell Galer, Carol Quick, and John Rea (1999). '401(k) Plan Asset Allocation, Account Balances, and Loan Activity,' EBRI Issue Brief no. 205.

Viceira, Luis (2001). 'Optimal Portfolio Choice for Long-Horizon Investors with Nontradable Labor Income,' *Journal of Finance*, 55: 1163–98.

Yao, Rui and Harold H. Zhang (2005). 'Optimal Consumption and Portfolio Choices with Risky Housing and Borrowing Constraints,' *Review of Financial Studies*, Spring(18): 197–239.

Yoo, Peter S. (1994). 'Age Dependent Portfolio Selection,' Federal Reserve Bank of St. Louis Working Paper no. 94-003A. St. Louis, MO: Federal Reserve.

Chapter 13

Tax Issues and Life Care Annuities

David Brazell, Jason Brown, and Mark Warshawsky

A life care annuity (LCA) is an integrated insurance product consisting of life annuity and long-term care insurance (LTCI) segments. It addresses inefficiencies in the separate private markets for its component parts—adverse selection, which increases the price of life annuities, and strict underwriting, which restricts the availability of LTCI. In this chapter, we argue that, by lowering prices and increasing availability, an LCA may be more attractive to retirees making critical choices in financing their lifetime retirement spending and insuring against the bankrupting contingency of severe disability. This attractiveness, in turn, may decrease pressures on government social insurance and welfare programs, such as Social Security and Medicaid, which are already underfinanced. This chapter first explains the present and future tax treatment of the LCA, both as an after-tax product and in a qualified retirement plan, and then turns to describe the product idea and its motivation in more detail.

Description of, and Motivation for, a Life Care Annuity

In return for the payment of one or more premium charges, an LCA product will pay a stream of fixed periodic income payments for the lifetime of the named annuitant, and, for a higher premium charge, any named co-annuitant survivor. These payments may be fixed in nominal terms, increasing, or inflation indexed. In addition, the LCA pays an extra stream ('pop-up') of fixed payments if the annuitant (and/or the co-annuitant) has severe cognitive impairment or is unable to perform without substantial human assistance at least two of the six recognized activities of daily living (ADLs), such as walking or eating. These are the same triggers used in LTCI policies that may be qualified under current tax law.

Because this pop-up segment of the LCA is intended to function as comprehensive LTCI, it is important that the level of the additional layer of payments to the disabled annuitant be sufficient to cover the extra expenses incurred for home health care or nursing home care, perhaps increasing with the degree of disability and therefore the costs of providing care. Over time, such costs of care have risen rapidly, often in excess of the rate of general inflation, and therefore inflation-indexing or automatic increases of the level of disability payments would seem particularly advantageous for these segments. That being said, it is difficult to set a standard level of payment for the LTCI portion, given substantial geographic variation in costs of care, as well as different personal preferences and means of payment for care (e.g., private vs shared room). Even more so, the appropriate or desired level of payments in the first or life-annuity segment of the LCA will vary considerably from household to household, reflecting preferences, means, and so on.

The premium (or premiums) charged for an LCA product would depend on many factors. Obviously, the number of insured, and whether there is a survivor benefit, would be influential. Risk factors such as the age(s) of the annuitant(s) at the start of the income payments also affect the price, but other observable risk factors may be prevented from being used by law or by marketing acceptance. Most significantly, of course, the premium of the LCA will reflect the level of income and disability payments being guaranteed and whether inflation indexing is to be applied to either or both segments. The premiums charged on newly issued contracts will change over time, inversely with movements in interest rates available in the financial markets on fixed-income investments used to underpin the LCA, as well as with changes in expected trends in mortality and disability experience.

The integration of two already widely available products, life annuities and LTCI, is intended to address inefficiencies in the separate markets for those products. Research by Friedman and Warshawsky (1990) and by Mitchell et al. (1999) has shown that the costs of immediate life annuities increase by as much as 10 percent because of adverse selection by mortality risk classes in voluntary choice situations (i.e., individuals with lower life expectancies avoid life-annuity purchase). Using simulation analyses using a life-cycle framework and reasonable estimates of risk aversion, this work also showed that a large improvement in utility could be achieved by the annuitization of assets at fair actuarial value in retirement. But this improvement in welfare is, at least in part, blocked by market inefficiencies. Especially for couples, deviation from fair value (i.e., loads arising from adverse selection and marketing costs) dissuades annuity purchases (Brown and Poterba 2000).

On the LTCI side, Murtaugh, Kemper, and Spillman (1995) show that insurance company underwriting practices prevent 25–33 percent of the retirement-age population (age 65–75) from purchasing individual LTCI policies because individuals in impaired health or unhealthy lifestyles cannot purchase LTCI. Brown and Finkelstein (2004a), using simulation analysis, predict a substantial willingness to pay for actuarially fair private LTCI coverage on top of Medicaid, by individuals in most income groups. So, here too, market inefficiencies compromise otherwise large welfare gains available from insurance markets. Many of these research findings about annuities and LTCI are confirmed by observations from the insurance industry, including high rejection rates on LTCI policy applications at older ages, and discussions among actuarial professionals of annuity pricing.

Nevertheless, enhancing the attractiveness of life-annuity and LTCI coverage is an important public policy issue. Employer's provision of retirement income support for workers has moved, for many, to the defined contribution (DC) plan form, where a life-annuity distribution is not required and indeed is not often even offered. Accordingly, the retiree must now search in the voluntary individual annuity market if he or she would like to purchase a life annuity at retirement. Even for workers covered by defined benefit (DB) pension plans, mandatory annuitization has become less common, and therefore the scope of adverse selection may have increased. Moreover, nearly all proposals for Social Security reform envision lower growth in scheduled retirement benefits, that is, life-annuity payments. Hence, the potential scope for the voluntary life-annuity market and the resulting need to improve its efficiency may be expected to get larger still.

In 2005, the US Congress tightened eligibility for the long-term care benefits of Medicaid because it was concerned with apparent abuses of the spend-down eligibility requirements as well as by the runaway program costs. Indeed, research by Brown and Finkelstein (2004*b*) demonstrates the substantial crowd-out effect of Medicaid on the desire for private LTCI coverage, even without considering possible efforts to 'game' the system. Hence, as Medicaid eligibility tightens, private LTCI coverage will become increasingly important for the lower ranges of the income and wealth distribution, and general concern about market inefficiencies will increase. Moreover, the conventionally proposed solutions by the insurance industry given the obvious problems of tight underwriting—sales of individual LTCI policies at young ages or employer provision of the benefit, where underwriting is a less significant factor—have not found wide favor in the marketplace. In addition, there is a natural focal point for the LCA in household life-cycle planning, namely, when that household is approaching or has just begun retirement and is considering the rest of its financial future in a serious way.

The idea of the LCA as a product that results in a more efficient market and better insurance product is an application of the economic insights of Rothschild and Stiglitz (1976). Specifically, it is a practical attempt to produce a self-sustaining pooling equilibrium that is superior to the separating equilibria currently in existence where insurance coverage is restricted and/or highly priced. The LCA works so as to blend the low-mortality risks of annuity buyers who would like cheaper life annuities with the high-disability (and -mortality) risks of those desiring, but currently denied access to, LTCI coverage, combining these population pools of risk classes. To the extent that there is a positive correlation between impaired health and mortality probability, an integrated insurance product that combines the life annuity and LTCI can draw disparate risk groups together in such a way that there is less adverse selection and less need for strict underwriting.

In their prior work, Murtaugh, Spillman, and Warshawsky (2001) proposed three hypotheses about the LCA:

1. The life expectancy of voluntary purchasers of an integrated product will be less than that of voluntary purchasers of life annuities;
2. With minimal medical underwriting, less severe than current underwriting for LTCI, the cost of the integrated product will be less than the sum of the cost of the two products sold separately (here minimal underwriting means that only those who would go immediately into claim status for LTCI benefits, e.g., nursing home residents would be rejected for the LCA or, alternatively, face coverage delays of, say, two to three years); and
3. The subpopulation eligible for, and likely to be attracted to, the integrated product will be larger than that eligible for, and attracted to, the two products issued separately.

The authors' empirical analysis suggested that only about 2 percent of the age 65+ population would be rejected by the lower underwriting standards, as opposed to 23 percent rejected by current underwriting criteria. The mean expected remaining life of the purchasers of the LCA at age 65 is 18 years, compared to 19.5 for current annuity purchasers. Hence, Murtaugh, Spillman, and Warshawsky (2001) provided support for their first and third hypotheses. They also calculated the premium at age 65 for a unisex individual for the simplest integrated product described above, and the authors reported that it would cost about 4 percent less than the two products sold separately. Finally, they also gave evidence for the assertion that a self-sustaining pooling equilibrium is likely. In particular, they showed that those who are rejected by current LTCI underwriting, but who would be eligible for the LCA, are made better off in simple value terms. That is, the ratio of actuarially fair premiums for the relevant risk groups (major illness, stroke, poor lifestyle) relative to those for the expanded purchase pool is above one for the LTCI coverage. The pooling property of this positive effect on value should be enhanced when the expected utility ('insurance') value of LTCI coverage is considered, to say nothing of the insurance value of having a life annuity.[1]

Possible Venues for the Life Care Annuity

Next, we explore two main forms of the LCA: an individual after-tax fixed annuity product, and a before-tax qualified retirement plan/individual retirement annuity. Home equity extraction through reverse LCA mortgages should also be considered eventually, as well as variable and gift annuities and other existing vehicles for distributing resources in retirement. The LCA might be a good distribution choice for personal retirement accounts in a reformed Social Security system.

LCAs as After-Tax Annuity Products

An LCA could be thought of as an individual immediate fixed annuity product; if purchased with after-tax income, this would be the most direct and straightforward application of their findings. As we explain below in more detail, the LCA could be offered as an immediate life annuity, with LTCI structured either as a single- or level-premium rider or as a contingent annuity. On the other hand, the market for immediate annuities is quite small at present. The after-tax deferred fixed annuity product which represents a much larger market could also be used as a venue for the LCA. In practice, the life-annuity distribution option under deferred annuity contracts is seldom used at present. Nonetheless, marketed deferred annuities contain the valuable right for the insured to get a life annuity at the better of the terms specified in the policy contract or as an immediate annuity available in the marketplace, and this right may be used increasingly in the future.[2] Moreover, inclusion of a deferred annuity product in the broad LCA concept framework could also result in the desirable outcome that LTCI coverage is provided even before any life-annuity distributions are made.

Of late, a few insurance companies have tentatively introduced product offerings that contain certain elements of the proposed product as either deferred or immediate annuities with LTCI riders. Reportedly, the relevant state insurance departments were mostly satisfied with the products, but federal tax issues with the combination product led to difficulties and ultimately caused these companies to stop issuance. Nevertheless, as is detailed below, an after-tax LCA will be more tax favored, beginning in 2010, owing to the passage of the PPA of 2006 (P.L. 109-280).

LCAs in Connection with Qualified Retirement Plans

An LCA could take various forms in a qualified retirement plan. One option would define it as the normal accruing benefit of a DB pension plan, with the LTCI segment denominated as some proportion of the final benefit. Thus for an average-wage full-career employee, the plan could be designed such that the level of disability-contingent benefits accrued would be sufficient to cover nearly all expected LTC needs. Another option would have the LCA added as an alternative choice to the DB pension plan's distribution options, just like various joint-and-survivor payout options are currently available at cost. In particular, if the plan sponsor would like to respond positively to a demand from participants for lump-sum distributions or already has a lump-sum distribution choice, but is concerned about the impact of adverse mortality selection on the cost of its annuity offering, providing the LCA could be an effective and responsible response. Moreover, provision through a retirement plan may be a more popular way for employers to offer LTCI coverage to workers than through group LTCI plans.

Similarly, if the sponsor of a DC plan offered a life-annuity distribution option, the LCA could be added to the menu of payout choices. Life-annuity options are currently somewhat rare in the DC context, but a few employers are offering their workers a service of rolling over DC account balances to pre-negotiated individual retirement annuities from one or a few insurance companies. Others offer their workers the option of rolling over DC account balances to the DB plans that, of course, pay out benefits as life annuities. And, indeed, insurers are increasingly viewing retirement plans, especially 401(k) plans, as fertile ground for new annuity products. More broadly, it is important to consider individual retirement accounts (IRAs) as a home for the LCA, which would open a very large market. Yet as is explained below, various regulations may pose significant hurdles to the LCA in qualified retirement plans, and its tax treatment under current law is unknown or unclear, and perhaps adverse.

Table 13-1 shows total assets in various types of retirement plans and annuities to give a sense of the relative magnitudes where the LCA could reside. It would be even more relevant here to report accrued DB plan liabilities rather than assets, but these are not readily available on a consistent basis for state and local government plans. For private DB plans, currently, assets are just about equal or slightly exceed accrued liabilities, according to estimates based on financial accounting information; for government plans, there are reports that liabilities are significantly higher than assets, especially if these pension liabilities were to be marked to the market.

Current Tax Treatment of Life Annuities and LTCI When Issued as Separate Contracts

Next, we turn to a discussion of tax treatment of different products underlying the LCA construct.

TABLE 13-1 Total Assets in Annuities and Pension and
Retirement Plans (as of 12/31/06)

	Assets (billion $)
Private DB plans[a]	2,308.0
Private DC plans[a]	4,060.0
IRA accounts[a]	4,232.0
Annuities[a]	1,624.0
Federal government DB plans[b]	918.8
Federal government DC plans[b]	223.5
State and local government DB plans[c]	2,776.0
State and local government DC plans[c]	240.0
Total assets	16,382.3

Sources: [a] Investment Company Institute (2007); [b] Investment
Company Institute (2007) and Thrift Savings Plan (2006) as
of 12/31/2006; [c] Investment Company Institute (2007), Public
Fund Survey (2007), and Watson Wyatt estimates.

After-tax Individual Life Annuity

Annuity payments from individual life annuities are treated partially as
taxable income and partially as an untaxed return of the policyholder's
cost, or 'investment in the contract'. In general, an annuity's investment in
the contract is recovered in equal increments over the annuitant's expected
remaining life, although the details differ for 'nonqualified' and 'qualified' annuities. Nonqualified annuities are those not paid from a qualified
employer plan or other qualified savings plan, such as an individual retirement account (Brown et al. 1999). The investment in the contract as of
the annuity start date is used to determine the annual annuity exclusion
amount.[3] It equals the sum of premiums or other consideration paid for
the contract before the annuity start date, less any refunded premiums, dividends, or other amounts that were received before that date but which were
not included in gross income. Premiums paid for additional coverages (say,
disability or double indemnity coverages) are excluded from investment in
the contract.

Under the general rule for taxing nonqualified annuities, one must compute the contract's 'expected return', or the total amount that annuitants
can expect to receive under the contract. For life annuities, it is obtained
by multiplying the annuity's initial periodic (annualized) payment by the
annuitant's life expectancy in years. The latter is determined using published unisex tables from the Internal Revenue Service (IRS).[4] Published
tables are also available for determining the expected return for temporary
life annuities (where the number of total payments is limited), for joint-
and-survivor annuities (where a periodic income is paid until the death of

one annuitant, and an equal or different amount is paid until the death of a second annuitant), and for joint life annuities (where payments are made only if both named annuitants remain alive). For cases not covered by the published tables, taxpayers must request a ruling from the IRS to determine the contract's expected return. Dividing investment in the contract by the contract's expected return yields the contract's 'exclusion percentage'. This percentage is multiplied by the first regular periodic payment, and the result is the tax-free-exclusion amount of each annuity payment. This exclusion amount remains the same for all years, even if the annual annuity payment changes.

Once investment in the contract is recovered through annual exclusion amounts, then the annuity payments are fully included in gross income. Any unrecovered investment in the contract remaining at the death of the last annuitant is allowed as a miscellaneous itemized deduction on the last return of the final decedent. This deduction is not subject to the usual floor on miscellaneous deductions [equal to 2 percent of adjusted gross income (AGI)], but it is allowed only for those (deceased) taxpayers that itemize their deductions on their final return.

For variable annuities, investment in the contract is simply divided by the number of expected payments to yield the tax-free-exclusion amount for each payment.[5] If the annual tax-free amount is more than the payments received for the year, then the excess may be divided by the expected number of remaining payments, and the result added to the previously determined exclusion amount.

Contract distributions that are not periodic annuity payments (including policy loan proceeds) are generally taxed in full if received after the annuity start date. If received before the annuity start date, distributions are generally taxable, but only to the extent that the contract's cash value (determined immediately before the amount is received) exceeds investment in the contract at that time (i.e., such distributions are taxed on an 'income-first' basis). Under certain circumstances, taxable distributions not received as an annuity payment are subject to an additional 10 percent tax.

Qualified Long-term Care Insurance Policy: Premiums and Benefits

A qualified LTCI policy enjoys certain tax benefits under current US law. To be qualified, the contract must meet certain conditions. Among these is the requirement that the only insurance protection provided under the contract is coverage of qualified long-term care services.[6] An exception to this restriction exists under current law for LTCI provided as a rider or as part of a life-insurance contract and, after 2009, for LTCI provided as a rider or as part of an annuity policy. In addition, the contract cannot provide a cash surrender value that can be borrowed, paid, assigned, or pledged as collateral for a loan. Premium refunds and policyholder dividends must be applied as a reduction in future premiums or as an increase in future benefits, except when paid as a refund on the death of the insured or upon complete surrender or cancellation of the contract. Any refund cannot exceed the aggregate premiums paid under the contract. A qualified long-term care contract must also meet certain consumer protection requirements specified in law.

A qualified LTCI policy may pay benefits on a per diem or other periodic basis without regard to the actual long-term care expenses incurred. However, such payments are subject to a per diem limitation. This limitation is set at $260 in 2007, and it is also indexed to the medical-care component of the Consumer Price Index (CPI). The aggregate of such LTCI benefits must be added to any periodic 'accelerated death' payments received (tax-free) by a chronically ill insured from life-insurance policies. Any excess of the aggregate payment over the per diem limit, calculated for the period of coverage, is treated as taxable income.

A qualified LTCI policy is treated as a health or accident insurance contract, and benefit payments are treated as amounts received for personal injuries and sickness, implying that such benefits are generally excludable from taxable income. Amounts received from qualified policies are treated as reimbursement for expenses actually incurred for medical care. Employer-provided coverage under a qualified LTCI contract is treated as an accident and health plan, so that employer-paid premiums are excludable from employee income. Nevertheless, LTCI cannot be offered as part of an employer cafeteria plan.

Qualified status also bestows tax benefits as regards premiums. Premiums paid on individual qualified policies, up to specified age-based, inflation-indexed limits, are treated as medical insurance premiums, and thus as potentially deductible medical-care expenses. The excess of medical-care expenses over 7.5 percent of an individual's AGI is deductible as a 'below-the-line' itemized deduction. Finally, premiums on qualified LTCI contracts may be paid from a health savings account (HSA) established in connection with a high-deductible health-insurance policy. Because HSA amounts are pretax amounts, such a use of HSA funds effectively allows a full exclusion of amounts used to pay qualified LTCI premiums.

Life Annuity and Long-term Care Insurance in a Qualified Retirement Plan

The life annuity is currently the required default form of distribution in qualified pension plans (i.e., DB and money purchase DC plans). There are various regulatory requirements that must be met for distributions in this form. Moreover, if a DC plan offers a life annuity as a distribution option, these requirements must also be met when a life annuity is chosen. A few of the requirements even extend to IRAs. Interpreted strictly, some of the requirements would likely prevent, or at least impair, the offering of an LCA in a qualified retirement plan or as an individual retirement annuity, and therefore legislative and/or regulatory adjustments may be needed to facilitate LCAs within such plans.

Minimum Distribution Requirements

Minimum distribution requirements have been established under section 401(a)(9) of the Internal Revenue Code (IRC) to ensure that retirement plans and IRAs serve their intended purpose to support income security in retirement, and not as tax avoidance schemes to accumulate assets on a favorable tax basis for wealth transfer to another generation. In general, taxable distributions from the plan or IRA must start at retirement or age $70^1/_2$, whichever is later, and be no less than a specified percentage of the account balance. If the distributions are in the form of a life annuity, then, according to the regulations, all annuity payments must be nonincreasing or increase only in accordance with one of six specifically allowed exceptions. For example, payments may increase in accordance with annual increases in the CPI, or they may increase to pay higher benefits resulting from a plan amendment.

These regulations do not contemplate distributions through an LCA, and hence that form or product would likely be disallowed under a strict reading of the regulation. That being said, the LCA does not appear to fall under the concerns that originally prompted the rules—the entire corpus of the account balance or accrued benefit is paid out over the lifetimes of the participant and spouse under the LCA, with nothing held back beyond any guaranteed periods chosen otherwise allowable under the regulation. Hence, it is possible that the LCA could be included as an allowable distribution form through an administrative process mentioned explicitly in the minimum distribution regulation. Under that process, the IRS Commissioner could provide more guidance on additional benefits that may be disregarded for individual accounts, or for other methods of increasing distributions from a pension plan. In the alternative, the regulation itself could be amended to make the necessary allowances.[7]

Sex Neutral Pricing of Life Annuities

As a result of Supreme Court decisions prohibiting the use of sex-specific mortality tables for group retirement benefits, pension plans and insurance companies issuing annuities to participants through employer-sponsored retirement plans must price life annuities using unisex mortality tables and determine benefits accordingly. This is in contrast to the general practice of insurance companies in the individual commercial market where life annuities (both on an after-tax basis and in IRAs) are priced on a sex-distinct basis. It should be noted, however, that current commercial practice in the individual market for LTCI is to make no distinction by sex in pricing, despite ample evidence that women, as a class, have a significantly higher incidence of longer LTCI claims (Murtaugh, Spillman, and Wershawsky 2001, Brown and Finkelstein 2004*a*). When offered as an employee benefit, LTCI clearly has to be priced on a unisex basis, by force of law, as would the LCA.

This legal requirement for unisex pricing could vitiate some of the reduction in adverse selection that is one of the goals of the LCA, as a unisex-priced product is more attractive to women than to men. That being said, the effect may be small, as most workers approaching retirement are married, and another legal requirement, explained immediately below, encourages the selection of joint-and-survivor annuities. Of course, the individual nonemployer market is not subject to the unisex rulings of the Supreme Court, and therefore is affected only indirectly, if at all, by those rulings.

Joint-and-Survivor Requirement

All tax-qualified pension plans provide that retirement benefits payable as a life annuity to an employee married to his or her current spouse for at least one year will be automatically paid in the form of a qualified joint-and-survivor annuity, unless the participant elects otherwise with the consent of the spouse. There are multiple provisions in law and regulation to ensure that surviving spouses receive more than a token stream of income from the annuity. DC plans must also follow these rules if they offer an annuity as a distribution option and the participant elects it. The rules do not apply, however, to IRAs and individual retirement annuities.

Again, these rules do not envision an LCA as a distribution option, and hence it is unclear if and how these requirements would be applied to the LCA. It is possible, but uncertain, that a regulatory interpretation would arise having the joint-and-survivor requirements applied just to the life-annuity segment of the integrated form, thereby leaving the plan participant in control of the choice whether the LTCI segment, as an ancillary benefit, was to just the participant or also for the spouse.[8] Alternatively, rules could be written to reflect a public policy desire so that a joint-and-survivor requirement similar to current law should apply to the LTCI segment as well.

Incidental Benefits

In recognition of their tax-advantaged status and to focus their design and activities on certain desired public policy goals, Treasury and the IRS, even before the passage of ERISA in 1974, limited employer-sponsored retirement plans to certain types of benefits. In general, medical benefits may only be provided if they are subordinate to the plan's retirement benefits and are paid from a separate account established for such benefits. Without language in existing laws and regulations specifically referring to LCAs, it is not immediately clear how the IRS would view the LCA as part of a qualified retirement plan. It is possible that it would regard the LTCI segment of the LCA as akin to disability benefits and therefore allowed as a customary pension benefit. Yet such benefits are usually considered for workers who retire because of a disability, not people who encounter a disability subsequent to retiring.

Alternatively, the IRS might take the view that the LTCI segment is a type of retiree health insurance, and hence, as long as it is 'incidental' to the retirement benefits, it would be permitted. In a pension plan, the LTCI segment would be allowed under the specific requirements of section 401(h) (e.g., a separate account, specified benefits), or in a profit-sharing plan (most section 401(k) plans are profit-sharing plans), it would apparently be more generically allowed. Also asset transfers under section 420 from an overfunded pension plan might be allowed to pay for the premiums for the LTCI segment of the LCA. A requirement for section 401(h) treatment of the LTCI segment of an annuity distribution form in a pension plan, however, would be inconsistent with an optional distribution mechanism— the most likely design to be embraced by plan sponsors.

The IRS could alternatively take the position that the LCA as part of a retirement plan was not envisioned by these regulations and hence it would need a more formal and well-defined clearance by a change in the incidental benefit regulation or legislation.

'Current Law' Taxation of the LCA in a Qualified Retirement Plan

On the bold assumption that the various regulatory challenges mentioned above (some of which are themselves related closely to tax treatment) facing the inclusion of the LCA in a qualified retirement plan or IRA were surmounted, what would be the likely current law tax treatment of the LCA premium and the life-annuity payments and LTCI benefits in that venue? To the extent that employer and employee contributions to the retirement plan or IRA were made on a pretax basis, then obviously all the payments from the life-annuity segment would be included in taxable income. What about the benefits from the LTCI segment? It is possible that the benefits could be treated exactly as an incidental disability benefit ('contingent annuity') from the plan and therefore included in taxable income, but not triggering a taxable distribution from the plan for the payment of a premium charge. Or benefits could be treated as a separate stand-alone qualified LTCI policy, where benefits are not included in taxable income, without triggering a distribution from the plan.

The allowance of 'health insurance' tax treatment outside of section 401(h) would require a bold interpretation by the IRS that, in the absence of a clear statement of law, the LTCI segment of the LCA in a retirement plan should receive 'all-in' tax treatment more favorable than that of a stand-alone qualified LTCI policy. It may be unlikely that the IRS, on its own, would allow a situation where the LTCI segment premiums would be essentially deductible (a full 'above-the-line' deduction) and benefits not included in taxable income. This would require the IRS to grant tax treatment superior to a qualified LTCI policy, under which premiums are rarely deductible, and then only subject to specified limits. The IRS would also note the provision in the PPA, mentioned below, that the favorable tax treatment of the LCA issued in an after-tax individual annuity is not available in employer plans and IRAs. On the other hand, employer payments for LTCI premiums in a group insurance plans or through HSAs and health reimbursement arrangements are not included in employee income and the IRS could find some comfort for favorable treatment there.

A different outcome would be one where the premiums for the LTCI segment would be considered to represent taxable distributions from the plan. In this case, the LTCI premiums might or might not be deductible from income (depending on the individual's income and tax situation and whether the LTCI policy was considered qualified) and benefits, as insurance would not be included in income.

The treatment of benefits is also unclear if the LTCI segment does not represent a qualified LTCI policy. The tax code is silent as to the treatment of benefits received from nonqualified LTCI contracts. It is possible that, as payments to retirees, they could be treated simply as taxable distributions from the plan. In this case, however, the amount of unreimbursed medical-care expenses would be higher, and the probability of deducting that larger amount would be fairly high for most people. For certain taxpayers, however, the loss of the standard deduction, a need to itemize deductions on their tax return, and the lack of a deduction equal to 7.5 percent of AGI are significant considerations. In addition, for some taxpayers, an increase in their gross income will increase the amount of Social Security benefits that are included in taxable income, and this distinction would become important, as we show below. In addition, if payments from the LTCI segment take the form of per diem or other periodic payments which are higher than the costs of qualified long-term services, then the question of the contract being qualified or not may be important; the excess payment amounts might be taxed if the policy were nonqualified, tax exempt if qualified and not too large.

As is illustrated below, this tax treatment would be inferior to the treatment provided under the PPA of 2006 to the LTCI segment of an after-tax, nonqualified, LCA issued after 2009. It is also inferior to an IRS position under which the LCA would be considered, not as an insurance policy, but as a contingent annuity. Finally, it would be inferior to the proposed policy that provided an 'above-the-line' deduction of LTCI premiums from gross income. The PPA provides an income tax exclusion for pension distributions that are used to pay for qualified health insurance premiums up to a maximum of $3,000 annually. This exclusion is available only to retired or disabled public safety officers but may be used for health insurance or LTCI. This is equivalent to an above-the-line deductibility of LTCI premiums, and, it is, by far, the most generous tax treatment currently available. It remains to be seen whether this limited PPA treatment will serve as a model in future legislation for the tax treatment of LTCI, whether as part of a LCA, or, otherwise, for a more widely defined set of retirees.

Tax Treatment of Life Annuities and LTCI When Combined in an After-Tax Product

Next, we turn to a discussion of tax treatment of different LTCI and annuity products when they are combined in an after-tax vehicle.

Life Care Annuity (Treatment through 2009)

Under current US law, combining an LTCI product with an annuity automatically causes the LTCI product to be nonqualified. It is clear that this denies an itemized medical-care deduction for any recognized LTCI premiums. However, a reasonable argument may be made for treating an LCA as a single (contingent) annuity contract. In this case, the cash premiums paid into the contract (whether funding the annuity portion or the LTCI portion) would constitute the annuity's investment in the contract, and thus would be excludable over the expected remaining life of the policyholder. In addition, under this single contract concept, there might not be any tax consequence associated with charges against annuity cash values for LTCI coverage. There is a question, however, as to whether the expected LTCI benefits should be taken into account in determining the contract's expected return. If added to the expected return, they would lower the annual exclusion amount; and recovery of investment in the contract could occur over a period of years in excess of the owner's expected remaining life. In the illustrations presented below, we have not included the contingent payments in the LCA's expected return.

A life-insurance contract combined with LTCI is treated as two separate policies under current law. This will also be true for a combined annuity-LTC contract after 2009 under the PPA. An inference might be made, therefore, that such treatment should apply to such combined policies under current law. In this case, it is possible that premiums, investment in the contract, and cash value of an LCA might have to be allocated between the annuity and long-term care portions.[9] Also, LTCI charges against the annuity's cash value would likely be viewed as taxable distributions from the contract.

It is unclear as to how benefits of a nonqualified LTCI contract are treated. While the tax code specifies that benefits from a qualified LTCI contract are to be treated 'as amounts received for personal injuries and sickness and shall be treated as reimbursement for expenses actually incurred for medical care,' the code is silent regarding the treatment of benefits from nonqualified long-term care contracts. Even less clear is the treatment of per diem payments from nonqualified LTCI. In the analysis below, we treat indemnity benefits generally as being bona fide insurance reimbursements for medical care, but are conspicuously silent regarding the legal status of per diem payments. Alternatively, we could have assumed that payments from nonqualified LTCI are treated simply as additions to gross income, potentially allowing greater itemized deductions for the costs of long-term care services. This view is adopted when analyzing the 'contingent annuity' below.

Life Care Annuity (Treatment after 2009)

The PPA altered the treatment of LTCI when combined with an annuity. In particular, it explicitly allows LTCI (whether qualified or not) to be offered by rider or as part of either a life-insurance contract or an annuity contract. In this case, the portion of the contract providing long-term care coverage is treated as a separate contract, but the law is silent as to whether this separate treatment requires an allocation of contract premiums or cash values.[10] The relevant provisions of the Act generally apply to contracts issued after 1996, but only with respect to taxable years beginning after 2009. Thus, although state regulators have the ultimate authority in approving insurance products, the PPA acknowledges that such a combined product can exist after 2009 without the LTCI portion losing its tax qualified status. This treatment, however, has not been extended to employer plans and other tax-exempt trusts, to IRAs or annuities, or to contracts purchased by an employer for the benefit of the employee or his or her spouse.

The PPA provides that any charges against the cash value of an annuity contract or life-insurance contract for coverage under a qualified LTCI contract will not be includable in taxable income. Such premium charges will not be treated as medical expenses for purposes of the itemized medical-care deduction, and the investment in the contract of the annuity or life-insurance policy will be reduced by the amount of the charge. The premium charge continues to be tax-exempt even if the investment in the contract is zero. Only under this circumstance will the provision provide an exclusion for the full amount of qualified long-term care premiums.

While clarifying the treatment of LTCI premiums that take the form of explicit charges against the cash value of the annuity or life-insurance contract, the PPA's language is less illuminating regarding the treatment of a policy that is not a rider with explicit charges, or of cases where the full cost of LTCI is not embedded in the specified rider charges. For LCAs, the more premium that one can allocate to the annuity's investment in the contract, the greater the tax savings will be.

Possible Structures of the Life Care Annuity and Illustrations of Tax Treatment

There are several different ways in which the LCA could be structured, and the particular format may influence its tax treatment.

LCA structures

One can imagine at least three different ways of integrating the LTCI policy with an annuity. One way is to set up the LCA as a life annuity with a single-premium LTCI policy rider. As such, an annuity is purchased, from which an immediate charge against it is made for the purchase of an LTCI policy. Subsequently, no more charges are made against the annuity for LTCI premiums. Another way of structuring the LCA is as a life annuity with an LTCI policy rider with an annual premium. As with the single-premium LTCI rider, charges are made against the annuity cash value to finance LTCI premiums, but the charges are made over the life of the policyholder. That the premium is not paid fully up front would presumably allow greater flexibility for either the policyholder or the insurer should future circumstances change. A final way of structuring the policy is as a contingent annuity, in which payments rise in the event of disability, but there is no explicit purchase of an LTCI rider. Such a policy would require an initial premium roughly comparable to that of a life annuity with a single-premium LTCI rider.

Illustrations

How the LCA is structured could play a large role in determining how it would be taxed. Furthermore, individual characteristics, particularly Social Security benefits, other sources of income, and health-care expenditures, also play a key role in determining how taxable income varies. A couple of simple illustrations bear this out.

In this exercise, two individuals are considering the purchase of the LCA whose LTC portion is organized in one of the three ways described in the prior section. The first way is as a level-premium LTCI rider, the second way is as a single-premium LTCI rider, the third way is as a contingent annuity that is treated as an annuity contract by the IRS. The issue of premium savings arising from purchasing an LTCI policy in conjunction with a life annuity is ignored here, as all policies can be assumed to be part of an LCA. Thus, we assume that the LCA pays nothing beyond what is required to finance LTCI premiums or benefits.

All three LTCI arrangements are assumed to be purchased by a single individual at age 65. They pay out $140/day, with 5 percent annual inflation compounding, in the event long-term care services are needed; these payouts are assumed to cover exactly the cost of qualified long-term care services. The expected present discounted value of the policy, in all cases, is $45,583. Thus, the single-premium LTCI policy and the LTCI portion of the contingent annuity will cost $45,583 up front, and the level-premium policy will cost $4,008 annually. In order to fund this level premium, the up-front cost of the LCA must be increased by $45,583, given the assumed mortality and morbidity assumptions.

Projected utilization is assumed to be a function of mortality. Each claim is expected to last for 760 days, spanning three years' time. Those who encounter disability are assumed to die at the end of the third year. Additionally, each individual is assumed to have $1,200 in unreimbursed medical expenses each year, not associated with qualified long-term care services. Each individual is assumed to purchase a life annuity at the same time that costs $136,300, which pays $12,000 annually. Other income is assumed constant over time, except for Social Security benefits, which are assumed to grow at 2 percent per year. Long-term care deductibility limits, which are $2,950 annually for 61- to 70-year-olds and $3,680 for 71-year-olds and older, are expected to increase at 4 percent per year. The discount rate is assumed to be 6 percent.

The first individual, characterized as having moderate income, is assumed to start with $12,000 in Social Security benefits and $7,000 in other taxable income. The second individual, characterized as being of high income, receives $75,000 annually in additional taxable income. For the high-income individual, the issue of taxable Social Security benefits is ignored, because this individual would be subject to the maximum tax rate for Social Security benefits in every year. As mentioned above, each individual also receives $12,000 (nonindexed) in individual annuity income.

This exercise estimates taxable income for the two individuals under the three different structures of LCA in three different regimes: before the implementation of the PPA, after implementation of PPA, and if, instead, LTCI premiums were subject to an above-the-line deduction. Over the past several session of Congress, above-the-line deductions for LTCI premiums have been proposed. This would allow all individuals to deduct LTCI premiums up to the annual cap regardless of whether they itemized their deductions or of whether their medical expenses exceeded 7.5 percent of AGI.

The tax impact is calculated relative to that where an immediate life-annuity policy and a qualified single-premium LTCI policy are purchased as separate contracts, under the (unrealistic) assumption that the aggregate pretax cost of the two separate policies equals the pretax cost of the LCA. Under this baseline, the moderate-income individual is able to deduct some medical expenses in the first year, because the sum of other medical expenses and tax deductible LTCI premiums in the first year exceeds 7.5 percent of AGI. The high-income individual cannot deduct any LTCI premiums. Table 13-2 shows the tax impact of the different scenarios relative to the baseline, with the tax impact measured as the differences in the actuarial present value of each individual's tax liabilities for the expected remaining lifetime.[11]

Under current law (pre-PPA), purchasing the LCA with a level-premium LTCI rider will increase taxable income relative to purchasing separate single-premium contracts. The annuity generates a return that is taxable,

TABLE 13-2 Net Effect on Taxable Income of Purchasing Lifetime Care Annuity Under Different Arrangements

Moderate Income	Level Premium ($) LTCI Policy	Single Premium ($) LTCI Policy	Contingent ($) Annuity
Before 2010	22,568	31,139	(17,657)
After 2009	(3,267)	(3,806)	(3,806)
w/ATL deduction	(23,590)	28,189	(17,657)
High Income			
Before 2010	15,878	15,878	(23,787)
After 2009	(8,571)	(8,286)	(8,286)
w/ATL deduction	(25,137)	12,928	(23,787)

Source: Authors' calculations.

Notes: LTCI policy refers to a long-term care insurance policy; ATL Deduction refers to an above-the-line deduction.

subject to the exclusion over time of the initial LCA premium, and the LTCI premiums are treated as a taxable distribution from the annuity, and thus includable as income.[12] For the moderate-income individual, the additional income paid out by the annuity increases the taxable Social Security benefits. The result is, in expectation, an increase in taxable income of $22,568 for the moderate-income individual, and an increase of $15,878 for the high-income individual.

The PPA will allow the exclusion of the distributions from the annuity cash value used to pay for the level-premium LTCI, a considerable tax benefit relative to current law. The corresponding reduction in the investment in the contract accelerates the exhaustion of that investment in the contract. For the moderate-income individual, this translates to a slight increase in the expected taxable Social Security benefits, and a slight reduction in other deductible medical expenses. Overall, the net impact is a reduction in taxable income of $3,267 for the moderate-income individual and a net reduction in taxable income of $8,571 for the high-income individual.

To model the effects of an above-the-line deduction for LTCI premiums, we imagine how above-the-line deductibility to LCAs before the implementation of PPA might have been granted. We posit that charges against annuities for the purposes of paying LTCI premiums would be fully taxable, but the premiums would be deductible above-the-line up to the annual cap on deductible LTCI premiums. The original investment in the annuity contract would be excluded over the expected remaining lifetime of the annuitant; but charges for LTCI premiums would not accelerate the exhaustion of that investment as under PPA. Consequently, an above-the-line deduction of LTCI premiums would further increase tax benefits conferred upon the level-premium LTCI policy. Deductibility of premiums above the line would reduce taxable income, increasing the amount of other deductible medical expenses for the moderate-income individual. And deductibility of premiums would not require an offsetting reduction in annuity basis, which would be excluded over the expected remaining lifetime of the individual. The net reduction in taxable income is substantial: for the moderate-income individual it is $23,590, and for the high-income individual, it is $25,137.

Single-premium policies, both before and after implementation of the PPA, receive similar tax treatment as level-premium policies. Before 2010, charges against the annuity for the single LTCI premium are included in taxable income. Because the charge is so large, for the moderate-income individual, Social Security benefits are taxable in the first year. For the high-income individual, the net effect on taxable income is identical for the single-premium LTCI policy and the level-premium LTCI policy. As with the level-premium policy, after 2010, the charge against the annuity for the LTCI policy is not taxable. There are some minor differences between LCAs with level-premium LTCI riders and those with single-premium LTCI riders as regards the timing of the exhaustion of investment in the contract which has minor ripple effects on deductibility of other medical expenses and taxable Social Security benefits. But the overall effect is to improve the tax treatment for the LCAs with single-premium LTCI riders relative to the baseline by roughly the same magnitude as LCAs with level-premium LTCI riders. However, extending an above-the-line deduction for LTCI premiums that supersede the relevant measures in the PPA causes the LCA to be treated much as it would under current law, with the exception of a one-year deduction of the capped limit on LTCI premium, currently $2,950 for a 65-year-old.

The contingent annuity, assuming it is viewed strictly as an annuity by the IRS, before 2010, would receive considerably more favorable tax treatment than the other two arrangements. Unlike with policies that require taxable charges to finance LTCI premiums, the entire premium is excludable as investment basis over the course of the remaining life of the annuitant. This exclusion lowers taxable Social Security benefits for the moderate-income individual in years without disability. If payouts are made, additional Social Security benefits become taxable for that individual. And the payouts raise taxable income considerably, but most of them are deductible because qualified medical expenses easily exceed 7.5 percent of AGI in those years. Projected taxable income falls by $17,657 for the moderate-income individual and $23,787 for the high-income individual. The PPA, however, uses broad language in defining insurance coverage as part of an annuity contract, raising the question of whether the IRS would allow a contingent annuity to be defined as strictly an annuity contract without an LTCI component. If the IRS requires this to be treated as two separate contracts, then the taxation of the product would likely be the same as for a life annuity with a single-premium LTCI rider, as shown in Table 13-2. Because we model the effects of allowing an above-the-line deduction for LTC insurance before implementation of PPA, we show that the tax treatment of the contingent annuity under above-the-line deductibility of insurance premiums would revert back to the pre-2010 treatment, before the product was assumed to have an LTCI component.

It would seem that the contingent annuity would offer more favorable tax treatment for anyone before the implementation of the PPA. Yet in the absence of clear guidance from the IRS, insurers may be fearful that such a product would not be granted the tax advantages detailed here. After the implementation of PPA, however, LCAs with traditional LTCI policy riders are clearly granted considerably more tax advantages than are currently available. Above-the-line deductibility would increase the tax advantages further for LCAs with level-premium LTCI policy riders.

Conclusions

Combining LTCI with an immediate life annuity into a single policy, the LCA, will result in a lower total price for the combined product less adverse selection in the individual annuity market, and greater availability of long-term care to more retired households, when compared to offering the two products separately. This chapter discusses two principal venues in which this product might be marketed: a qualified retirement plan, and an after-tax individual annuity. We explain both the tax and the regulatory treatment afforded to the product, highlighting the uncertainties that arise largely because of the different tax and regulatory treatments of stand-alone annuities and LTCI policies.

Looking ahead, we argue that the PPA will make the LCA a tax-preferred way of obtaining LTCI coverage, but that an above-the-line deduction of qualified LTCI premiums would provide an even greater tax preference. Such a preference was recently bestowed on distributions from qualified retirement plans of public safety officers used to purchase qualified LTCI.

Notes

[1] Moreover, sensitivity analysis demonstrated that the likely 'wood-work' effect on disability claims, as well as inflation indexing of the LTCI segment, increase value to those currently rejected by LTCI underwriting, and therefore further support the second maintained hypothesis that the integrated product will be cheaper and more desired, in a self-sustaining pooling equilibrium.

[2] The recently enacted PPA of 2006 expanded the tax-free exchange provisions contained in the IRC. After 2009, a policyholder will be able to exchange tax-free both a deferred annuity and a deferred annuity-LTCI integrated product for an immediate annuity-LTCI integrated product (or a stand-alone LTCI contract). However, the policyholder will not be able to exchange tax-free a stand-alone LTCI contract for an LCA.

[3] The annuity start date is generally the first day of the first period for which one receives an annuity payment under the contract (which may be earlier than the date of the first payment).

[4] In general, for contracts under which all contributions were made prior to June 30, 1986, the annuitant must use sex-based tables published by the IRS. However, for annuity payments received after that date, the annuitant can make a one-time election to use the unisex tables.

[5] This is similar to the simplified method used for taxing payments from qualified annuities, although different tables are used to determine the number of expected payments.

[6] Qualified long-term care services are necessary services (including personal care services) that are required by a chronically ill individual and are provided pursuant to a plan of care prescribed by a licensed health-care practitioner. A chronically ill individual is one that is generally unable to perform at least two out of six

listed ADL for a period of at least 90 days due to a loss of functional capacity, or one that requires substantial supervision due to severe cognitive impairment. To qualify as an itemized medical-care deduction, a qualified long-term care service cannot be performed by a spouse or other relative (unless such person is a licensed professional with respect to the service).

[7] The PPA of 2006 allows the combination of an annuity with an LTCI contract after 2009. It further states that the LTCI component will be treated as a separate contract, which seemingly would allow the minimum distribution rules to apply only to the life-annuity segment of a qualified plan LCA. However, the Act also states that a qualified employer plan or individual retirement account is not to be treated as an annuity contract for the purpose of the above separate contract rule, so that the impact of the Act on the issue at hand is somewhat unclear.

[8] This treatment would be similar to how the required minimum distribution rules treat a plan that also offers a disability pension—the disability benefit is considered separate from the retirement benefit. But the analogy may be stretched too far, as the IRS has taken the position that disability benefits cease once the participant attains the normal retirement age stated in the plan.

[9] Such allocations are not explicitly required under current law or the PPA. However, under an allocation regime, there would be an incentive to overstate the annuity's share of premiums, so as to maximize the amount of premiums that could be recovered through the annuity exclusion ratio.

[10] As under current law with respect to life-insurance combined products, 'portion' is defined as 'only the terms and benefits that are in addition to the terms and benefits under a life-insurance contract or annuity contract without regard to long-term care insurance coverage.'

[11] In these illustrations, the 'Before 2010' entries are computed on the basis that the PPA was not enacted. That is, under the PPA, the tax treatment of a contract issued after 1996 will change in 2010; we assume that it will not.

[12] We consider payouts for LTC services under the single-premium and level-premium riders as reimbursement for qualified LTC services, and thus excludable from taxable income. If the IRS considered the LTCI riders in either the single-premium or level-premium examples as components of an annuity, however, payouts from the LTC component would not be considered as reimbursements from an insurance policy, and the amount would be fully taxable. Nonetheless, LTC expenses would be deductible to the extent qualified medical expenses exceeded 7.5 percent of AGI, so the net tax impact would only be slightly higher than the amounts shown in the table.

References

Brown, Jeffrey R. and Amy N. Finkelstein (2004a). 'The Interaction of Public and Private Insurance: Medicaid and the Long-Term Care Insurance Market,' NBER Working Paper no. 10989, Cambridge, MA: National Bureau of Economic Research.

—— —— (2004b). 'Supply or Demand: Why is the Market for Long-Term Care Insurance So Small?' NBER Working Paper no. 10782, Cambridge, MA: National Bureau of Economic Research.

—— and James M. Poterba (2000). 'Joint Life Annuities and Annuity Demand by Married Couples,' *The Journal of Risk and Insurance*, 67(4): 527–53.

—— Olivia S. Mitchell, James Poterba, and Mark Warshawsky (1999). 'Taxing Retirement Income: Nonqualified Annuities and Distributions from Qualified Accounts,' *National Tax Journal*, 52(3): 563–91.

Friedman, Benjamin and Mark Warshawsky (1990). 'The Cost of Annuities: Implications for Saving Behavior and Bequests,' *Quarterly Journal of Economics*, 105(1): 135–54.

Investment Company Institute (2007). 'Appendix: Additional Data on the U.S. Retirement Market, 2006,' *Research Fundamentals*, 16(3A): 1–16.

Mitchell, Olivia S., James Poterba, Mark Warshawsky, and Jeffrey R. Brown (1999). 'New Evidence on the Money's Worth of Individual Annuities,' *American Economic Review*, 89(5): 1299–318.

Murtaugh, Christopher, Peter Kemper, and Brenda Spillman (1995).'Risky Business: Long-term Care Insurance Underwriting,' *Inquiry*, 32(3): 271–84.

—— Brenda Spillman, and Mark Warshawsky (2001). 'In Sickness and In Health: An Annuity Approach to Financing Long-term Care and Retirement Income,' *Journal of Risk and Insurance*, 68(2): 225–54.

Public Fund Survey (2007). 'Public Fund Survey,' National Association of State Retirement Administrators and the National Council on Teacher Retirement. www.publicfundsurvey.org/publicfundsurvey/index.htm.

Rothschild, Michael and Joseph Stiglitz (1976). 'Equilibrium in Competitive Insurance Markets: An Essay on the Economics of Imperfect Information,' *Quarterly Journal of Economics*, 90(4): 630–49.

Thrift Savings Plan (2006). 'The Official Thrift Savings Plan Homepage,' The Federal Retirement Thrift Investment Board. www.tsp.gov.

Index

Printed in the USA/Agawam, MA
February 8, 2011

556489.065